MW01623419

Japan's Sexual Gods

Brill's Japanese Studies Library

Edited by

Joshua Mostow (Managing Editor)
Caroline Rose
Kate Wildman Nakai

VOLUME 49

The titles published in this series are listed at *brill.com/bjsl*

Japan's Sexual Gods

Shrines, Roles and Rituals of Procreation and Protection

By

Stephen Turnbull

BRILL

LEIDEN | BOSTON

Cover illustration: A good example of a phallic shrine is the small *sai no kami* that is located within the precincts of the Jōman Shrine in Amarume (Yamagata Prefecture). It lies within a small grove of trees and houses votive phallic offerings. Two large phalluses stand beside the path as the epitome of the protecting god. (Photo by author)

Library of Congress Cataloging-in-Publication Data

Turnbull, Stephen R.
Japan's sexual gods : shrines, roles, and rituals of procreation and protection / by Stephen Turnbull.
pages cm. — (Brill's Japanese studies library, ISSN 0925-6512 ; volume 49)
Includes bibliographical references and index.
ISBN 978-90-04-28891-1 (hardback : alk. paper) — ISBN 978-90-04-29378-6 (e-book)
1. Japan—Religion. 2. Sex—Religious aspects. 3. Shrines—Japan. I. Title.

BL2203.T87 2015
299.5'6--dc23

2015011593

This publication has been typeset in the multilingual 'Brill' typeface. With over 5,100 characters covering Latin, IPA, Greek, and Cyrillic, this typeface is especially suitable for use in the humanities. For more information, please see www.brill.com/brill-typeface.

ISSN 0925-6512
ISBN 978-90-04-28891-1 (hardback)
ISBN 978-90-04-29378-6 (e-book)

This book is printed on acid-free paper.

Printed by Printforce, United Kingdom

For all the others in the Davies family of Llandybie

∵

Contents

Preface

It is the middle of March at the Tagata Shrine in central Japan, where the annual springtime festival is taking place. Thousands of people line the roadside in noisy and exuberant crowds drawn to the site more by the wide publicity and the prospect of titillation than by any overtly religious intent. They are there to see the procession from a sub-shrine to the main shrine of a huge wooden phallus, a votive offering to a goddess of fertility who will ensure a bumper harvest.

Meanwhile, cars stop at a service area in Akita Prefecture where the forecourt is dominated by the surprising sight of a wooden phallus almost as large as the one carried at the Tagata Shrine. It stands in a vertical position within a red-painted wooden enclosure at the entrance to a shopping arcade. One of a similar size lies on its side within a shrine in Miyazaki Prefecture, but that carved wooden phallus is not alone in its display. It shares the space with a representation of female genitalia, and is posed in front of it in a coital position. Many miles away inside the gate of a Buddhist temple in Tokyo stands a

FIGURE 1 *The 2014 version of the giant votive phallus of the Tagata Festival is carried along the processional route from the Shinmei Shrine to the Tagata Shrine as a communal offering to a female deity of fertility.*

small red wooden shrine. Its doors are not locked, and a glance inside reveals a small carved stone phallus standing about 15 cm high. There are two flower vases beside it, both holding short branches from a sacred tree. A few coins have been placed there as offerings. Finally, I am standing on a muddy river bank in Akita Prefecture. A local farmer has taken me there to see a small carved phallic stone that lies within a plain wooden shrine. He asks me not to disclose its precise location and explains that the object should really be in a museum. Nevertheless, the local people have looked after it here for many centuries because this is where it was found, and they will continue to do so.

What these five examples have in common is the presence of a phallus: the physical representation of the male sexual organ. Yet each location is different in the identity of the god therein enshrined and in the role and purpose of the phallic symbol that is the site's defining object. At the Tagata Shrine the huge phallus is offered to the goddess whose startlingly lifelike modern statue is the only feminine image in what appears to be a very male-dominated symbolic environment. The prominent phallus in Akita seems to be almost as large as the Tagata one but its purpose is entirely different. This is not an offering that will be carried in a parade. Instead it stays in a fixed place as a fierce protective god of the highways. The masculine and feminine pairing in Miyazaki express other sentiments. They stand for the harmony between the male and female principles without which nothing can be created. By contrast, the much smaller Tokyo phallus acts as the body of the powerful sexual deity Konsei Daimyōjin and is therefore an object of worship. The Akita riverbank phallus is different again, because this venerable object is a stone bar carved during the prehistoric Jōmon Period. Owing to its shape certain sacred properties of a sexual nature were assigned to it when it was discovered many centuries later, its original purpose being long forgotten.

Of the examples cited here only the giant phallus of the Tagata Shrine is in any sense well-known, its striking form providing a popular and somewhat misleading visual impression of Japanese sexual beliefs. The briefest internet search will reveal scores of photographs and video clips of the event where it is so conspicuously paraded, but even though most websites correctly stress that the Tagata phallus is not the object of adoration but an offering to a deity of fertility, the popular belief persists that the Tagata Shrine's 'penis festival' (as it is sometimes called) is a remnant or even the sole survivor of an ancient cult of sex worship. In this work I intend to look beyond the popular image of the Tagata Shrine and many other similar but less well-known places to investigate the identities of the sexual gods they enshrine, the reality of their iconography and the religious practices that currently sustain them.

The mapping, study and interpretation of these places have involved a true journey of discovery. Because so many accounts of the subject, both academic and popular, refer to the destruction, suppression and sanitisation of sexual imagery in Japan during the later Tokugawa and Meiji Periods I concluded some time ago that there were probably no more than thirty sexual shrines left in Japan. Yet this is not the case. Instead of two dozen the number of shrines and temples and wayside images that involve the display of a sexual symbol is at least two thousand. They are found from Okinawa to Hokkaidō and range from elaborate buildings to ones that are tiny and well-concealed. Some are valued as local cultural properties; in other places they appear to be something of an embarrassment. In Jūmonji (Akita Prefecture) for example, a certain shrine containing sexual imagery has been omitted from an official map of local religious sites, and its location was apparently unknown to the staff of the town's public library less than one kilometre away.

During the course of this study I have visited over five hundred examples of sexual shrines, temples, festivals and images, and throughout the entire project local wishes have been respected in relation to the security of sensitive or vulnerable sites. I have therefore exercised considerable discretion over which ones to photograph or to identify on the maps according to their precise locations. The reader may therefore rest assured that none of the places named or illustrated in this work is likely to be harmed in any way by visitors.

I would not have been able to write this book without the help and cooperation of many people, and I would particularly like to thank my colleagues at Akita International University, Mark Williams, Yuko Sawata, Eriko Fujita, Maiko Nishida and Darren Ashmore for their constant support. Others have conducted interviews or made fieldwork visits to shrines or festivals on my behalf. In that context I thank Ellen Usui, Tomoko Yamene, David Ranzini and above all Michael Gakuran who also accompanied me on five memorable trips. In 2012 I had the pleasure of accompanying Masuta Kimiyasu from the Aomori Folk Museum on fieldwork visits to the phallic shrines of Aomori Prefecture. Hamish Todd and Christopher Barnes facilitated my study of the original manuscript of Richard Cocks' diary. I would also like to thank Eileen Brayshaw and Ikuko Williams for their acute observations during visits in their company, Paul Norbury for his constant encouragement, Dr James McHugh of the University of Southern California for his advice concerning the depiction of Indian gods in Japan and Kyle Barghout for sharing with me his study of the Tsubaki Grand Shrine of America. Many other distinguished scholars, most of whom could have done a far better job than I have in writing this book, were also willing to share their insights into the topic. I must mention in particular John Breen, Ian Reader, Joy Hendry, Gaynor Sekimori, Ellis Tinios, Andrew Gerstle, Nicole Coolidge Rousmaniere and Andrew Cobbing. The directors of the Utsunomiya Seishin no Yakata, the Taga Shrine Museum of Uwajima and the Izu Gokurakuen provided very valuable information about their collections, supplying important source materials and giving promising leads, while successive chief priests of many shrines and temples have made we welcome and have patiently endured my questions concerning their festivals over the course of several visits. I thank in particular Mr Kuroda of the Nagomi Town Board of Education and Mr Fujimura who cares for the Sotsuda Shrine in Akita. The Great Britain-Sasakawa Foundation provided funding to help cover the cost of my visits to some important shrine festivals in 2008. The illustrations used here are all my own work except for six which are gratefully acknowledged in the captions.

Above all my thanks are due to the many local people who took me into their confidence and directed me to these places, of which the most amusing instance was the man in Utsunomiya who explained that I was actually standing in front of the tiny shrine that I had completely failed to see. Others took me to the remotest sites by car or on foot, in one case lending me a pair of wellington boots, and then acted patiently as guides, sharing with me their own understanding of the places that their communities have preserved, protected and hallowed for so long.

Stephen Turnbull

FIGURE 2 *A phallic rock in the courtyard of the Ōmiya Shrine in Oguni (Yamagata Prefecture).*

List of Illustrations

List of Maps

The locations given are only approximations.

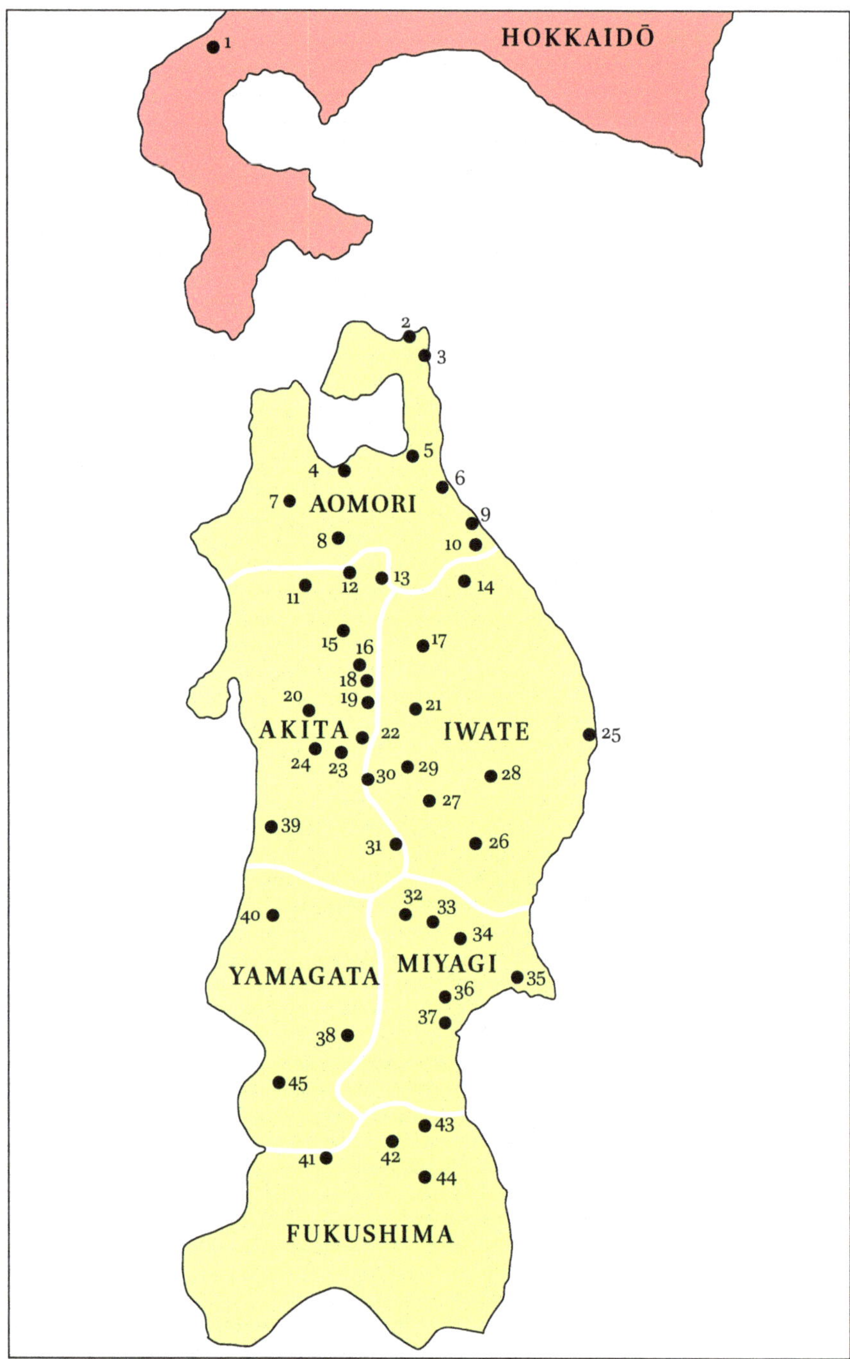

MAP 1 *Principal sexual shrines, related events or groups of sites in Hokkaidō and Tōhoku.*

Key to Map 1

1. Kamishimo Daimyōjin
2. Ōhata Konsei Daimyōjin
3. Kamitaya Konsei Daimyōjin
4. Awashima Shrine, Aomori
5. Kumano Shrine Konsei Daimyōjin
6. Misawa Onsen Konsei Daimyōjin
7. Fujimi Hotel Konsei Daimyōjin
8. Atago Shrine, Ikarigaseki
9. Suwa Shrine, Hachinohe
10. Jūni Yama no kami Shrine
11. Kogake Dōsojin
12. Yamada Dōsojin
13. Matsunoki Konsei Daimyōjin
14. Konsei Ōkami Shrine
15. Animatagi Yama no kami Shrine
16. Momobora Waterfall
17. Makibori Shrine
18. Hachimantai—former Konsei Festival
19. Kandekko Festival
20. Karamatsu Shrine, Sakai
21. Chiwaki Shrine, Morioka
22. Anchō Waterfall
23. Sotsuda Konsei Daimyōjin
24. Kakunodate shrines (various)
25. Miyako Konsei Daimyōjin
26. Senmaya In'yōseki
27. Hanamaki Konsei Daimyōjin
28. Tōno shrines (various)
29. Ōsawa Onsen
30. Ōmori Konsei Daimyōjin
31. Kashima-sama (various locations)
32. Nakayamasuku Konsei Daimyōjin
33. Araogawa Shrine
34. Ōzaki Dōsojin
35. Ishinomaki shrines (various)
36. Kano Hachiman Shrine
37. Kasajima Dōsojin
38. Yonezawa Yama no kami Shrine
39. Kisakata Sai no kami
40. Jōman Shrine, Amarume
41. Ashinomaki Onsen Dōsojin
42. Onnagata Shrine
43. Yama no Kami Shrine
44. Takashiba Deco Yashiki Craft Village
45. Ōmiya Shrine, Oguni

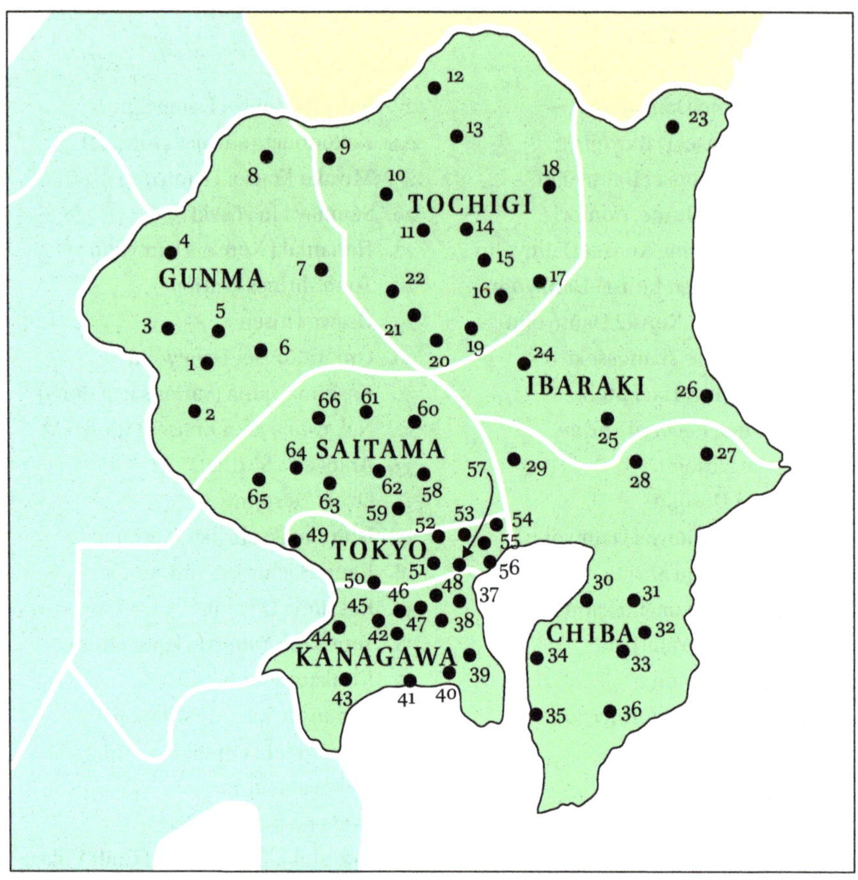

MAP 2 *Principal sexual shrines, related events or groups of sites in the Kantō.*

Key to Map 2

1. Nakamuroda Dōsojin
2. Annaka Dōsojin
3. Ochiai Dōsojin
4. Sawatari Shrine
5. Chinpōkan Sex Museum
6. Kinmara Yakushi
7. Tarō Shrine
8. Shirane Konsei Daimyōjin
9. Konsei Pass Konsei Daimyōjin
10. Nikkō shrines
11. Noguchi Yakushi-dō
12. Onade Ishi
13. Kinugawa Hihōden and Ryūō Festival
14. Ishinadamachi Konsei Daimyōjin
15. Seishin no Yakata Sex Museum
16. Nakatamatsuri Dōsojin
17. Hiraide Shrine
18. Gozen Iwa
19. Ashikaga Bannaji
20. Orihime Shrine
21. Mizushi Shrine
22. Itakura Shrine
23. Mifune Shrine
24. Chinzan Inari Shrine Dōkyō-sama
25. Kashima Shrine Dōkyō-sama
26. Kashima Jingū
27. Katori Shrine
28. Ōwashi Shrine Konsei Daimyōjin
29. Koroku Shrine Festival
30. Fudō-dō (Benten)
31. Enmyō-In (Fukurokuju)
32. Ennyoji (Jurōjin)
33. Enchōji Sekibō
34. Enkyōji (Ebisu)
35. Fudō-In (Hotei)
36. Mishima Shrine
37. Kanamara Festival, Kanayama Shrine
38. Tsurumi Shrine
39. Gumyōji, Yokohama
40. Tsurugaoka Hachiman Shrine
41. Hōan-dō, Enoshima
42. Kowada Dōsojin
43. Hadano Dōsojin
44. Kabuto Onsen Dōsojin
45. Kokagezan Sai no kami
46. Yasaka Shrine Aoyama Dōsojin
47. Matsudake-In
48. Okagami Shrine Konsei Daimyōjin
49. Okutama Himeseki
50. Konsei Inari Shrine, Hachiōji
51. Hanazono Shrine, Shinjuku
52. Ikebukuro Ta no kami
53. Honmyō-In Konsei Daimyōjin
54. Matsuchiyama Shōten
55. Asukabashi Inari Shrine
56. Eikenji Konsei Wagō Inari Shrine
57. Ueno Park shrines
58. O-Hijiri-sama
59. Honsenji Sekibō
60. Mitsugi Shrine
61. Fusegi Festival
62. Shirohige Shrine Konsei Daimyōjin
63. Koma Shrine
64. Tokuunji Jizō
65. Kobansawa Konsei Daimyōjin
66. Kodakara Yakushi-dō

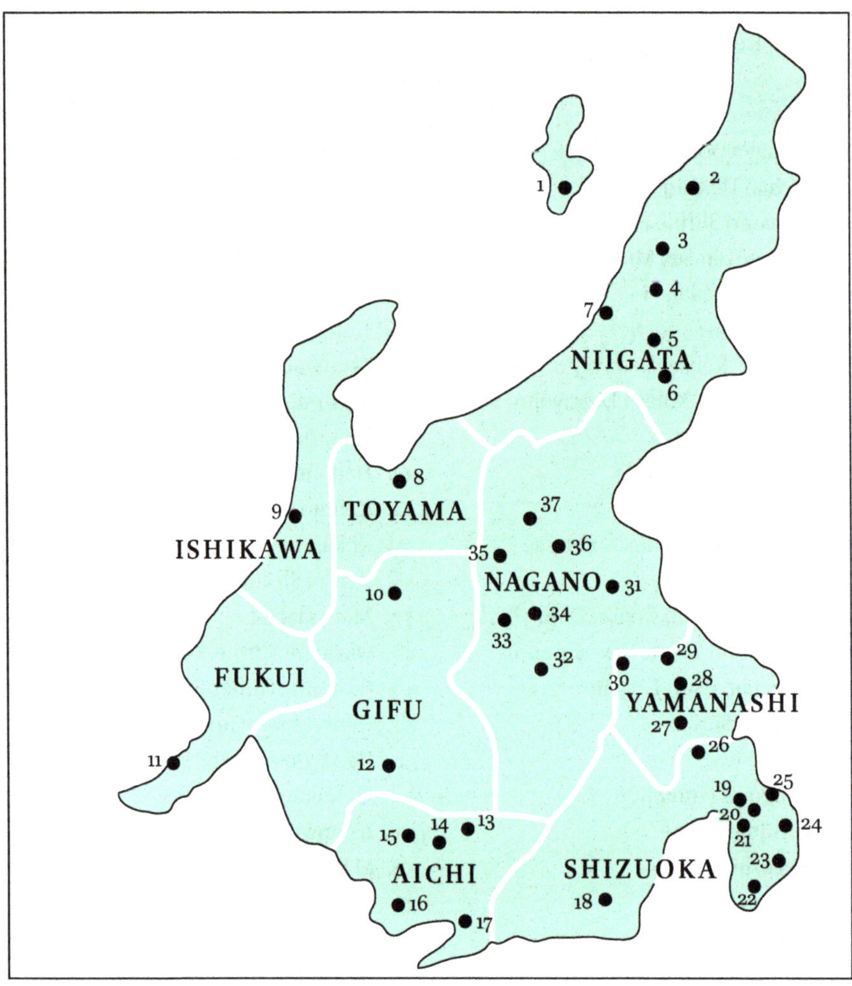

MAP 3 *Principal sexual shrines, related events or groups of sites in Central Japan.*

Key to Map 3

1. Tsuburosashi dance
2. Shōki-sama villages
3. Chombo Jizō
4. Hodare Shrine and Festival
5. Uonuma Festival
6. Shineri Benten Tataki Jizō Festival
7. Suwa Shrine's Raseki Shrine
8. Fūchū Sekibō Festival
9. Kenrokuen Garden, Kanazawa
10. Hida Kokubunji, Takayama
11. Hassaku Festival
12. Kasamatsu Konsei Daimyōjin
13. Tagata and Ōagata Shrines
14. Tōganji, Nagoya
15. Dōso Konsei Daimyōjin, Nagoya
16. Tenteko Festival
17. Daihiden, Gamagori
18. Saifukuji, Kakegawa
19. Yokoze Hachiman Shrine
20. Usu-sama Myōō-dō
21. Izu Gokurakuen
22. Ryōsenji and Chōrakuji, Shimoda
23. Dontsuku Festival
24. Shiritsumi Festival
25. Atami Hihōkan
26. Otainai Onsen
27. Sengen Shrine, Kōfu
28. Myōtogi Shrine and Hime no Miya
29. Ishizumi Dōsojin
30. Dōsojin (various sites)
31. Kitasawa Sekibō
32. Hime Seki-sama Dōsojin, Chino
33. Matsumoto City Dōsojin
34. Utsukushigahara Onsen and Tokuunji
35. Azumino City Dōsojin
36. Danseki Shrine
37. Okitsu Shrine

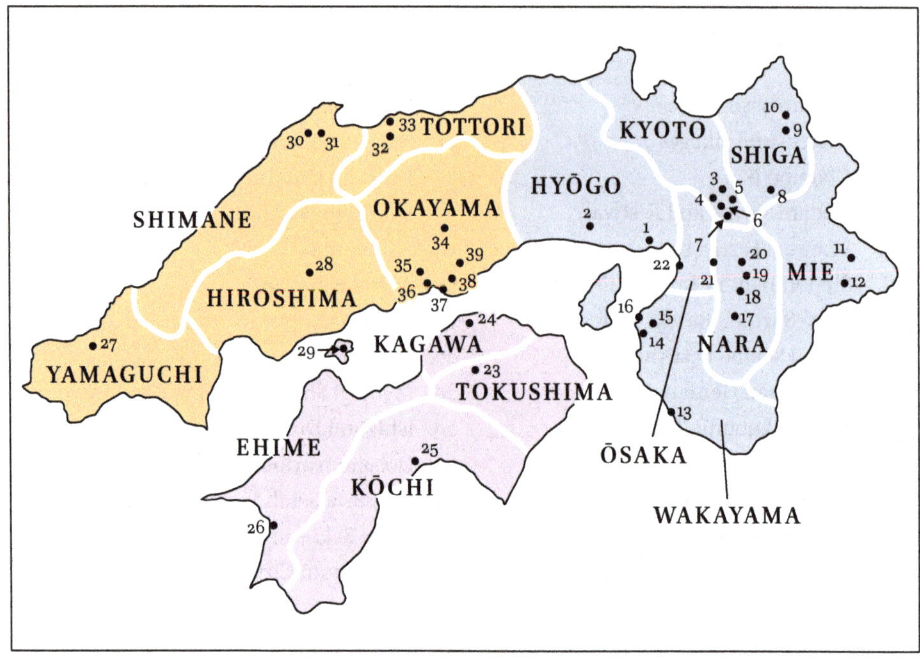

MAP 4 *Principal sexual shrines, related events or groups of sites in Western Honshū and Shikoku.*

Key to Map 4

1. Ōmononushi Shrine
2. Raseki Shrine
3. Kamigamo Shrine
4. Yōtoku-In, Daitokuji
5. Yasaka Kōshin-dō
6. Mishima Shrine, Tōfukuji
7. Fushimi Inari Taisha
8. Tsuchiyama Yama no kami
9. Taga Taisha
10. Chikuma Shrine
11. Sarutahiko Shrine, Ise
12. Saida Yama no kami
13. Kanki Shrine, Shirahama
14. Shinmei Shrine, Wakayama
15. Wakamiya Hachiman Shrine
16. Awashima Shrine, Wakayama
17. Asuka Niimasu Shrine
18. Kagami Shrine, Nara
19. Mizutani Shrine, Nara
20. Sangatsu-dō, Nara
21. Ikoma Hōzanji
22. Takatsu Shrine, Ōsaka
23. Ohana Daigongen
24. Ritsurin Garden, Takamatsu
25. Asamine Shrine
26. Taga Shrine and Sex Museum
27. Mara Kannon, Tawarayama Onsen
28. Omara-sama, Mukabaki
29. Anaba Shrine, Ōmishima
30. Yaegaki Shrine, Matsue
31. Yomotsu Hirasaka
32. Sai no kami-san (various)
33. Kinone Shrine
34. Akaiwa Konsei Daimyōjin
35. Karube Shrine
36. Aoe Shrine
37. Hikozaki Tenjin Shrine
38. Korakuen Garden
39. Ontokuji, Okayama

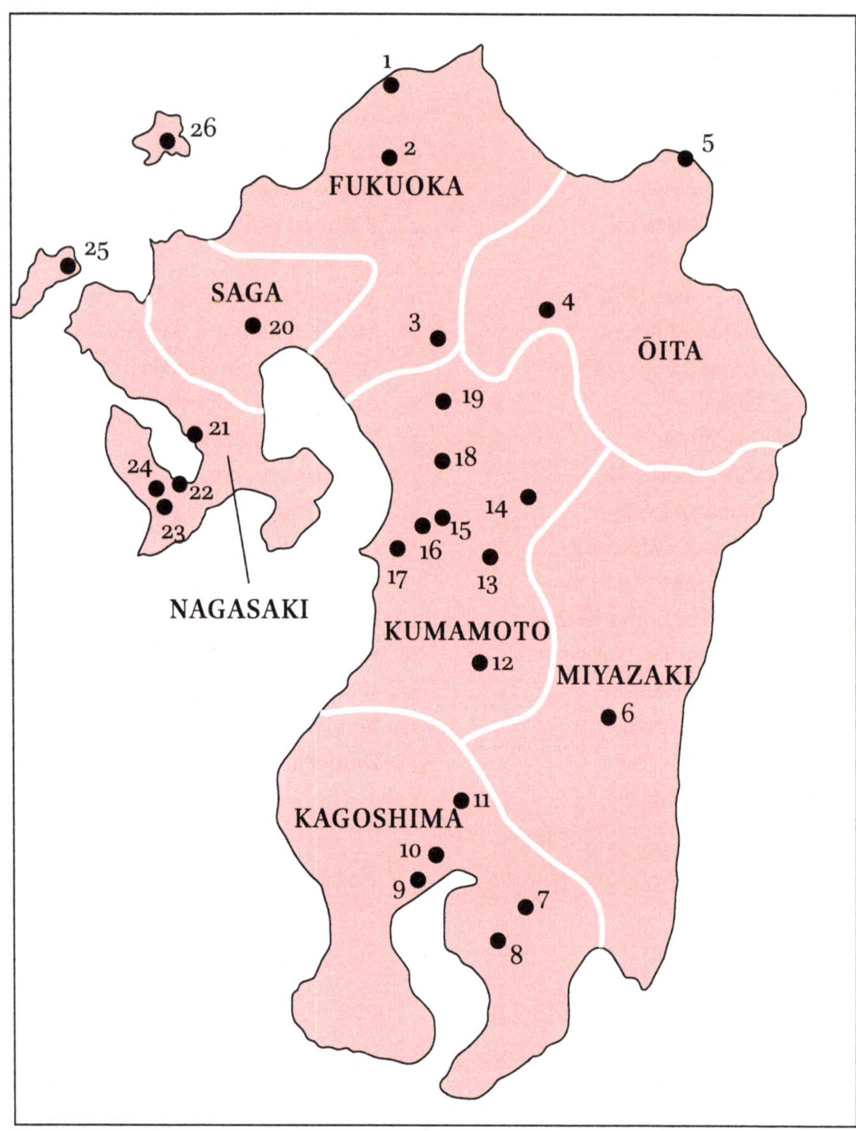

MAP 5 *Principal sexual shrines, related events or groups of sites in Kyūshū.*

Key to Map 5

1. Onitsuka Mara Kannon
2. Mizuki Mara Kannon
3. Reiganji
4. Hita Sai no kami
5. Imi Betsugu
6. In'yōseki Shrine
7. Magai Ta no kami
8. Nozato Ta no kami
9. Iriki Ta no kami
10. Tōsō Dōsojin
11. Shugi-En Ta no kami
12. Shibatate Hime Shrine
13. Kai Shrine, Kumamoto
14. Yuge shrines, Dōkyō-sama
15. Inari Shrine, Kumamoto
16. Kitaoka Shrine
17. Awashima Shrine
18. Konoha
19. Shichirōjin
20. Takeo-Ureshino Onsen
21. Saya no Gozen
22. Shōkakuji
23. Matsumori Tenmangu
24. Suwa Shrine
25. Midorigaoka Shrine
26. Sai no kami, Gonoura

CHAPTER 1

Sexual Beliefs in Japanese Religion

This book is a study of Japan's *seishin* 性神 (sexual gods), the deities associated with certain present-day shrines and temples that lie at the interface between organised religion and folk beliefs. The behaviours associated with them provide a unique and valuable insight into Japanese religion, not only into the system known as Shintō 神道 ('the way of the gods') but other traditions too. The sexual gods' locations have their own histories, their own ritual cycles and their own local traditions of festivity and worship. They also share activities common to all Japanese shrines that involve personal intercession, the making of offerings and the acquisition of talismanic souvenirs. What distinguishes them is the presence on site of objects representing male and female genitalia, features that are not merely incidental but crucial elements in the reason why the religious establishment is there in the first place.[1]

The link between and a sexual god and a certain place may be indicated by no more than some form of image standing beside a road or a field. These objects are valued because of the protection they offer against evil or epidemics and the assurance of agricultural fertility that they may also provide. The larger sites involve increasingly elaborate buildings where the enshrined gods address a form of fertility that is more specifically human, adding to prayers for bountiful harvests the conception of children, safe childbirth, easy delivery, cures for sexually transmitted diseases or the desire to find a partner. In many cases several small votive phalluses are also to be found there. Most of these will have been donated by worshippers seeking divine assistance to bring about conception. The petitioner will either present one when praying for help or borrow a phallus from the existing display to take home. In the latter case, when the baby arrives the loan phallus is returned to the shrine along with a similar emblem as a gift of thanks.

1 The presence of a sexual object has provided the overall working definition as to which religious establishments should be included in this study and which should be excluded from it, but this has not been without its difficulties. For example, the Hachiman Shrine in Tōno (Iwate Prefecture) contains a phallic portable shrine. Yet this does not mean that Hachiman is regarded as a sexual god. The shrine is merely a convenient location where the object is kept for use in a local festival. Nevertheless, the phallus is not locked away in a store room but can openly be seen and attracts devotional attention in its own right.

 DOI 10.1163/9789004293786_002

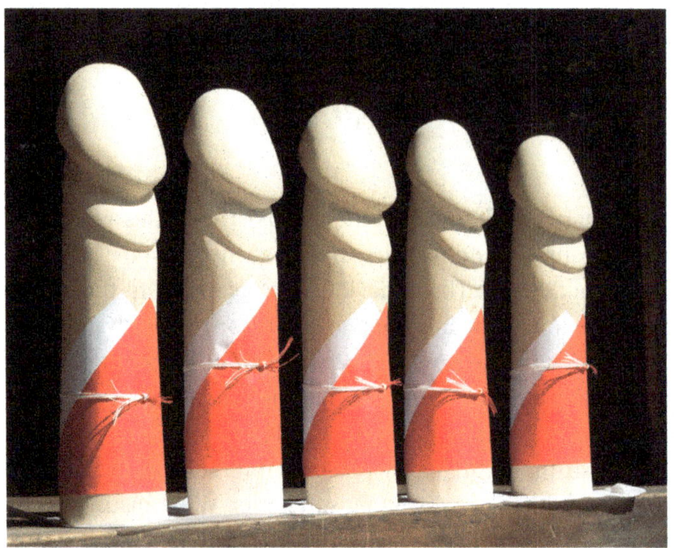

FIGURE 3 *Small carved wooden phalluses at the Shinmei Shrine, from where the Tagata Festival departs on even-numbered years.*

FIGURE 4 *A phallic stone relief carving standing beside a field boundary at the rear of the Dōsojin Yashiro in Takasai (Ibaraki Prefecture).*

The one thing that all of these places have in common is that they have been known to, valued and preserved by their local communities over the course of many years. Edmund Buckley, the pioneer of the subject in the English language, wrote in 1895, 'Though I found no one in Europe or America aware of the presence of phallicism in Japan, I never found an old resident in Japan ignorant of it'.[2] The latter situation has continued into the present century, although the knowledge of phallicism is now spread more by the mass media than by word of mouth or enduring local tradition. Certain historical trends may also be identified that have influenced the way the sexual gods are presented in their shrines today. These arise from the attacks on phallic beliefs launched by Tokugawa Period moralisers, then by the effect of the edicts of the Meiji Restoration that separated Shintō from Buddhism while embracing Western concepts of modernity and propriety, and more recently by what can only be described as a revival of phallicism.

FIGURE 5 *A good example of a phallic shrine is the small* sai no kami *that is located within the precincts of the Jōman Shrine in Amarume (Yamagata Prefecture). It lies within a small grove of trees and houses votive phallic offerings. Two large phalluses stand beside the path as the epitome of the protecting god.*

2 Buckley, Edmund 1895. *Phallicism in Japan* (Chicago), p. 9.

The Naming of Parts

Phallicism is the word most commonly employed anywhere in the world for religious beliefs and rituals that involve the phallus.[3] However, as the following pages will show, the Japanese context requires a more inclusive expression because female needs are frequently addressed through female sexual symbolism. At the Kanayama Shrine 金山神社 in Kawasaki (Kanagawa Prefecture) for example, its prominent iron phallus is surrounded by votive pictures bearing the feminine sexual image of a peach. Many other shrines include representations of the phallus's harmonious cooperation with the female principle, while in some an image of female genitalia stands confidently and ritually alone, self-sufficient in its power to grant petitions.

FIGURE 6 *At the Kanayama Shrine in Kawasaki (Kanagawa Prefecture) a* kana mara *(iron phallus) is surrounded by* ema *(painted prayer boards), many of which bear the ktenic image of a womb-like peach, out of which the child Momotarō is emerging.*

3 An example is provided by Stone, Lee Alexander 1927. 'The Story of Phallicism' in Stone, Lee Alexander and Starr, Frederick *The Story of Phallicism with other essays on related subjects by eminent authorities: Volume 1* (Chicago).

In the majority of Japan's sexual-related shrines it is nevertheless the male symbol that catches the eye, and it is no doubt for this reason that in early works on the subject, which were often lacking in first-hand observation, the associated corpus of rituals and beliefs was rendered into English as 'Japanese Phallicism' even though female imagery was involved. This may have happened simply because the image of the phallus was more easily recognisable, but it may also illustrate an out-dated attitude that regarded the male role as both dominant and more important. For example, although Buckley's innovative work of 1895 stressed the importance of the male/female balance it was nevertheless entitled *Phallicism in Japan*.

Japanese scholars have tended to prefer a more inclusive expression. Deguchi Yonekichi used the expression *seishokki sūhai* 生殖器崇拝 (genital worship) as a translation for the title of Buckley's work in 1919 and then used it again for his own book on the subject in 1920, while Satō Tetsurō preferred the term *seiki shinkō* 性器信仰 (sexual beliefs) for the title of his 1995 book.[4] Other writers such as Kokonoe Kyōji prefer to begin with the expression *seishin* (sexual gods) and then discuss the beliefs and worship associated with them.[5] Similarly, Nishioka Hideo entitled his important book *Nihon Seishin-shi* (A history of Japan's sexual gods), but when he re-published it in 1961 he translated the title into English as 'A History of Phallicism in Japan' even though he gave appropriate weight to female symbolism.[6]

In this work the neutral term 'sexual beliefs' will be preferred to phallicism except where the context demands the latter. The word penis will also be confined to situations where the actual male physiological organ is implied, using phallus (from the Greek *φαλλός* with a plural of either phalluses or phalli) only to indicate a representation of the penis. Such a representation may be intentional, whether or not some concealment or disguise is in operation, or it may simply be an attribution placed on to a natural or artificially created object by outside observers. The latter case implies an act of judgement on behalf of the viewer, so the expression 'phallic symbol' would be more appropriate in those situations. Thus a tall stone lantern or a distinctively shaped natural rock formation may be seen by some as a phallic symbol and by others as not, whereas a carved wooden phallus cannot be seen as anything other than a phallic symbol. Similarly, the word vulva will be confined to the actual female

4 Deguchi, Yonekichi (trans.) 1919. *Nihon ni okeru seishokki sūhai* (Tokyo); Deguchi, Yonekichi. 1920. *Nihon seishokki sūhai ryakusetsu* (Tokyo); Satō, Tetsurō 1995. *Seiki shinkō no keifu* (Tokyo).

5 Kokonoe, Kyōji 1976. *Seishin* (Tokyo).

6 Nishioka, Hideo 1961. *Nihon Seishin shi* (*History of Phallicism in Japan*) (Tokyo).

external genitalia. Yoni is often used in English for a representation of the vulva or vagina, but as this is the Sanskrit-derived female equivalent of the male lingam,[7] for linguistic consistency this book will employ the somewhat archaic word kteis (from the Greek *κτεἰσ*, plural ktenes) for a representation of female genitalia with ktenic being the adjectival expression.

Phallus and kteis will therefore be used to translate a number of different words for the sexual organs and for representations of them, a distinction that is not made quite so precisely in Japanese. In the literature on sexual beliefs the most common word for genitalia is *seishokki* 生殖器 or, for the male and female expressed separately, *dankon* 男根 and *join* 女陰. Thus Nishioka brackets *dankon sūhai* 男根崇拝 (penis/phallus worship) with *join sūhai* 女陰崇拝 (vulva/kteis worship).[8] Otherwise a phallus found within a shrine may be described simply as a *dansei shinboru* 男性シンボル 'male symbol'. In the first written mention of a phallic symbol in Japan (in the *Kogoshūi* of 807) it is simply said to have the shape of a *dankei* 男茎 (penis or phallus).[9] *Mara* 魔羅 (more commonly written phonetically as まら or マラ) comes from the Sanskrit word *māra* and also means penis or phallus. It may be used in the names of shrines where the deity is acting in a sexual role such as the Mara Kannon shrine in Yamaguchi Prefecture, but is also encountered in the names given to certain enshrined phalluses such as *omara-sama* オマラサマ ('honourable lord phallus') and *kana mara* かなまら (metal, iron or gold phallus) where the reference is to the material from which the object is made.[10]

Aims and Methodology of the Present Work

The overall aim of this book is to provide an introduction to Japanese sexual beliefs through a study of the nature of the sexual gods, the places where they

7 Lingam, written as *ringa* リンガ may be encountered in Japan where the worshipped deity is the Hindu god Śiva.

8 Nishioka 1961, pp. 82–133; Masuta, Hideko (ed.) 1993. *Onmyōdō no hon* (Tokyo), p. 161.

9 Katō, Genchi and Hoshino, Hikoshirō (trans.) 1926, p. 48. *The Kogoshūi: Gleanings from Ancient Stories* (Tokyo). For the original text see http://miko.org/~uraki/kuon/furu/text/kogosyuui/syuui01.htm (Accessed 15 October 2014).

10 The object in question may also be labelled 'penis-shaped', as used by Nishioka to describe a votive phallus in a shrine (1961a, p. 239), and by Satō to describe the phallic spout on an earthenware vessel (1995, p. 14). Other phalluses are described as a *mokusei dankon* 木製男根 'wooden penis' or *sekisei dankon* 石製男根 'stone penis'. For examples see Kokonoe 1976, p. 132 and Masuta 2012, p. 42. Similarly Satō describes a prehistoric carved kteis simply as being 'a stone in the shape of female genitalia' (1995, p. 16).

are worshipped and the religious behaviours that associate them with procreation and protection. It will explore in particular their place within modern Japanese society, the dynamic nature of the practices related to them and any continuity with ancient beliefs that may be inferred from them. I have no doubt that all these topics require greater analysis than present space affords and that many more issues need to be examined, so I trust that this work will provide a useful starting point for scholars from other disciplines to develop their own research in this important and fascinating field.

The present study is based on three levels of investigation. The first consists of systematic personal observations of current practices in 521 different locations. This figure includes the most important sexual shrines, temples and images in every Japanese prefecture except Okinawa, and represents about one in four of all the places listed in the published literature up to March 2015 and some sites that have never been recorded anywhere beyond their immediate locations.[11] The fieldwork has involved wherever possible a contribution from those who have care of the shrines or are participants in their related rituals. The second level of study is the augmentation and enhancement of these observations by written accounts of shrines, rituals and events produced during the past hundred years or so. That exercise has provided clarification on several points of detail and has revealed many changes and innovations. The third level has involved an attempt to relate these modern and recent historical practices to what may have existed in ancient times, as revealed by archaeological discoveries and early written accounts.

The specific objectives of this work include first of all an attempt to estimate the numbers and types of sexual shrines in Japan today and to give some idea of the prevalence of ktenic imagery within them compared to the more prominent phalluses. The origins of these objects and the functions they perform will also be studied, and the question will be addressed of whether the phalluses and ktenes are symbols of deities or of the sexual organs themselves, a situation that would imply 'sex worship' in a literal sense. These issues will be tackled first by examining the identities and natures of the sexual gods in a systematic way through a meaningful categorisation. This will also be done for the symbols that represent them and the functions those symbols perform in relation to the balance between human and agricultural fertility.

---

11 Okinawa does not appear to add much of interest to the present study, although two sites have been identified by Kokonoe as being sexual-related. One concerns the attribution of a ktenic shape to certain tombs, the other is a phallic stalactite within a popular tourist cave. See Kokonoe 1981, pp. 289–290.

FIGURE 7 *This small erotic wooden carving in the collection of the Ryōsenji in Shimoda (Shizuoka Prefecture) is of a phallus dressed in a Shinto priest's robe.*

Another important objective is to make some assessment of the level of continuity that exists between older practices and those seen today. There is certainly a dynamic nature to modern practices because some contemporary behaviours associated with sexual shrines, particularly activities relating to festivals, often seem to be influenced more by present-day social attitudes, trends and concerns than by any notions derived from traditional religion. Sexual-related festivals can also be shown to have experienced more change than any other aspect of Japanese sexual beliefs, and it will be demonstrated that certain popular festivals have originated only within the past thirty years. This means that a researcher must exercise great care in drawing conclusions about past practices from what is seen today, a point that also applies to the exuberant sexual displays seen in some shrines and the choice of design for modern wayside images. These phenomena may indicate a return to a time before the repression of the Tokugawa and Meiji eras, or they may simply reflect modern attitudes towards sex and its visual depiction.

The issue of continuity, particularly in terms of any links that can be made with ancient practices, is closely related to the question of the relationship between sexual beliefs and Shintō. Are they an integral part of a supposedly ancient Shintō belief system (a controversial topic in its own right), as is implied by the reference to some very important sexual gods in the Shintō creation myths, or do they represent a more recent addition to it? Alternatively, do certain practices suggest that the sexual gods represent a religious tradition that pre-dates Shintō, or is it simply the case that innovation and transformation have always been present?

Modern sexual-related beliefs are derived from several recent historical contexts, one of which is the effect caused by the periodic repression of them. The sexual gods clearly survived, but what were the strategies that their believers employed? Related to this topic is the oft-repeated claim that in spite of these sporadic acts of repression there has always been a greater acceptance of sexual display within Japanese society than in the West. A further consideration is prompted by the respect with which the sexual shrines are treated and maintained today. This is something they have in common with other concrete

FIGURE 8 *This small phallic shrine stands outside the Hikozaki Tenjin Shrine in Okayama.*

manifestations of Japanese religious beliefs, and the absence of vandalism and graffiti from isolated sites is something often remarked upon by Western visitors. The sexual shrines are clearly cared for as valuable local cultural assets, but does this also imply that the beliefs lying behind them are still as vigorous as ever and that secularisation has not taken hold? The answer to this question requires evidence of their continued use and an appreciation of the relationship between these beliefs and present-day concerns such as the sexual behaviour of young people and Japan's declining birthrate.

The Characteristics of Japan's Sexual Gods

The phallic and ktenic symbols found within certain Japanese shrines and temples, beside roads or in the middle of fields are associated with a number of named deities who make themselves known to the human world and interact with it through these objects in terms of the forms the symbols take and the functions they perform, and I propose that each dimension is open to a simple and practical categorisation. Beginning with the forms the objects take, they comprise a wide range of natural or created images which may be classified as follows:

1. Ancient created objects such as the prehistoric *sekibō* (stone rods or bars) which may or may not have had a phallic role in antiquity but have had that attribution attached to them because of their shape and their mysterious origins.
2. 'Modern' created objects from wood, stone, metal or pottery where the phallic or ktenic shape is deliberately intended and which are then used either as permanent symbols in a shrine or as votive objects to be borrowed or presented.
3. Natural formations of stone or peculiarly shaped trees where the shape of a phallus or a kteis is suggested.

I also propose that the objects may be further categorised under three additional headings according to the functions they perform:

1. The devotional function, whereby the object provides a symbolic focus for worship, prayer and veneration including acting specifically as a *goshintai* (the body of the enshrined god). This is essentially a representative role and will tend to be exercised by a central and often solitary image.

2. The votive function, whereby the object is a gift-offering to a god to ensure agricultural fertility or the fulfilment of a wide range of sexual-related human desires, of which the most important is the successful achievement of conception. This role will be exercised by numerous smaller images placed in the vicinity of the *goshintai* or by one large phallus carried during a festival.
3. The protective function, whereby the object has been set up to guard the area against unwanted influences such as evil or pestilence, thereby aiding fertility either directly or indirectly. This role may be exercised outside the shrine area, for example at a crossroads or beside a field.

The identities of the gods who are represented by these sexual objects and have others offered to them are rarely difficult to determine because their names are usually displayed on an accompanying notice board at the shrine, although there is often a certain vagueness over their precise nature that is a well-known characteristic of Japanese religious belief. There is also usually a narrative that explains the relationship between the god and the specific locality that led to the shrine being founded. These stories may locate the shrine's origins in ancient history or relate a comparatively modern incident of death or discovery across a wide range of religious traditions, hence the use here of the general term 'god' or 'deity' rather than just *kami* 神, the word used for a deity in Shintō. This terminology also acknowledges a considerable merging between different traditions to create over time a system that may, with some justification, be referred to as 'Japanese Religion'. The resulting mix may not be a unified whole but it is a system that can initially be approached in practical terms as an entity. This is particularly true in terms of the willingness of its adherents to participate in what Westerners would regard as conflicting belief systems, so that Shintō and Buddhism meet alongside Confucianism, Daoism and folk religion and their followers are happy to join in rituals and events that derive from different traditions. Thus in one area of north-east Tokyo prayers for conception may be offered at a tiny shrine to the phallic *kami* Konsei Daimyōjin, whose shrine lies next to a shrine to Inari, a *kami* associated with the fertility of the rice crop. Both of them are however located within the courtyard of a temple of the Nichiren Sect of Buddhism. Japan's sexual gods therefore cover a wide area of religious belief, and their identities may be usefully categorised as follows:

1. A god brought to Japan from the East Asian continent along with some sexual association.
2. A Japanese *kami* who has some ancient mythological association with sexual matters.

FIGURE 9 *No better illustration of the mingling of Japanese religious traditions can be found than this juxtaposition whereby the shrine on the left to the phallic deity Konsei Daimyōjin stands next to a shrine to Inari within the precincts of the Honmyōji, a temple of the Nichiren sect of Buddhism in Tokyo.*

3. A human being deified after death as a *kami* who has some association with sexual matters that have been discovered and then developed.
4. A *kami* who is unique to a particular shrine or locality and may be anonymous.
5. A *kami* derived solely from an abstraction of the male sexual organ.

The first category is mainly encountered within the Buddhist pantheon, while all the others are regarded as Japanese *kami*, the numinous inhabitants of Shintō shrines. Much of this book, therefore, will be concerned with *kami* and, as Daniel Holtom writes, 'No other word in the entire Japanese vocabulary has a richer or more varied content and no other has presented greater difficulties to the philologists than the word *kami*'.[12] This expression is fundamental to understanding Japanese religious beliefs, but to define it has taxed the minds of scholars for centuries. Even the classic definition of *kami* posed by Motoori Norinaga (1730–1801) as 'the deities of heaven and earth that appear in the

12 Holtom, Daniel 1993. 'The Meaning of Kami' in Reader, Ian et al. *Japanese Religions Past and Present* (Folkestone), p. 77.

ancient records and also the spirits of the shrines where they are worshipped', which goes on to list examples drawn from the animate and the inanimate, the awesome and the mysterious, begins very modestly with the words, 'I do not yet understand the meaning of *kami*.'[13] The modern scholar might well add to Norinaga's frustration the observation that the role and significance of certain *kami* may have changed throughout history even if the name remains the same, while different interpretations may also be placed upon the same named *kami* in different parts of Japan. But even if Norinaga did not understand *kami* the great scholar would have appreciated that even though they were mysterious and in so many ways unspeakably 'other', that same mystery and vagueness of identity added to their holiness rather than detracting from it. It is no doubt for this reason that the Japanese have long been content to worship, entreat and serve that which is not fully understood. Definition may therefore be difficult but it is still possible for an outside researcher to classify the *kami* and their associated rituals, although this too is no easy task, as acknowledged by Herbert Plutschow in his study of *matsuri* (shrine festivals) where he tackles the problems posed by the nature of *kami* and the additional complexity provided by Shintō-Buddhist syncretism.[14]

The second category identifies a sexual role for some of the best-known *kami* in Shintō. These are 'the deities of heaven and earth that appear in the ancient records' in Motoori Norinaga's definition such as the creator pair Izanagi and Izanami. The third category comprises those who were once human beings. All *kami* have a capricious side and need to be treated appropriately, but these once-human gods present a more acute problem because of the circumstances of their lives or deaths. Some present a special case of the treatment that has to be given to people who have experienced injustice or died a tragic death. Misfortune may attend the locality where the incident occurred and be attributed to the unhappy spirit who needs to be placated through the process of enshrinement.[15] Examples of once-human *kami* who now respond to sexual needs include the lascivious priest Dōkyō who loved an empress and the tragic Shibatate Hime, a victim of incest and murder.

The fourth category of highly localised and often anonymous sexual *kami* reflects the differences between some *kami* and others concerning the number of shrines and the extensiveness of their traditions. Unlike those who bear

---

13 Tsunoda, Ryūsaku; De Bary, Wm. Theodore; Keene, Donald (eds.) 1958. *Sources of Japanese Tradition Volume 1* (New York), p. 21.

14 Plutschow, Herbert with O'Neill, P.G. 1996. *Matsuri: The Festivals of Japan* (Richmond).

15 For a full account of Japan's most famous historical examples see Yamada, Yūji 2014. *Onryō to wa nanki ka* (Tokyo).

FIGURE 10 *The Shibatate Hime Shrine enshrines a deified victim of incest and murder. Local villagers erected the shrine to comfort her spirit, and the place is responsive to female health needs. Note the very large phallus set up outside it and the votive offerings inside.*

names for which there is a considerable written mythology and a widespread worship tradition, some are known only within their immediate locality. One example is Kawashimo Daimyōjin 川下大明神 who is enshrined in the simple Kawashimo Shrine in the Chihase area of Shimamaki on the coast of Hokkaidō. Phalluses are offered to Kawashimo Daimyōjin but no further information is provided about him within his modest dwelling.[16] A *kami* may also be identified in some way with a tree or rock whose strange shape indicates its presence and its powers. One example is the sacred tree trunk that constitutes the Kinone Shrine 木ノ根神社 (literally 'the tree root shrine') in Tottori Prefecture. It lies at the foot of a hill on which stands a shrine to Hachiman, and its foundation legend tells of a mother whose son was unable to produce children. She was told by Hachiman to visit this tree where the phallic-shaped root

16 From a personal observation made on 24 June 2013 and Kokonoe, Kyōji 1981. *Nippon no Seishin*, (Tokyo), p. 32.

FIGURE 11 *Phallic votive offerings stand inside the shrine to Kawashimo Daimyōjin in Shimamaki on the coast of Hokkaidō.*

indicated the presence of a *kami* with sexual powers. Her prayers achieved the desired result and afterwards the tree became a focus for similar intercessions.[17]

The localised nature of the Kinone Shrine's *kami* contrasts markedly with the religious tradition of the powerful phallic deity Konsei Daimyōjin, a *kami* so important that an entire chapter will be devoted to discovering the true identity of the only god to fit into the fifth category of a *kami* devoted to and derived solely from the male sexual organ. The discussion of Konsei Daimyōjin

17 From a personal observations made on 7 June 2013 and 1 March 2014. See also Yato, Sadahiko 2004. *Sai no kami to ryū—kodai ga wakaru ken* (Tokyo), pp. 29–30.

will also explore the widely held notion that Japanese phallicism involves the actual worship of the genital organs rather than of the gods they represent.

As their foundation legends make clear, the sexual gods are enshrined in particular locations for some historical reason such as the fortuitous presence of a sacred object or because of an event that took place there. This ensures that every shrine is closely tied to a locality and a community, and such a link may be noted particularly in the case of a small shrine that lacks both a priest and any formal shrine organisation. In most instances its upkeep is maintained on a casual but caring basis by its local neighbours assisted by the income derived from donations and offerings. One excellent example of a long-established local continuity is revealed by comparing old photographs with the present appearance of one small shrine that can be reliably dated to at least the early Tokugawa Period. It is in Urawa (Saitama Prefecture) and houses a phallus known variously as Mara kami-sama 魔羅神様 or O-Hijiri-sama お聖さま. Katō Genchi depicted it in his article of 1924 and Nishioka Hideo shows it unchanged in 1961.[18] The open fields have now been replaced by an urban landscape and a busy road as part of Saitama City, but the rebuilt shrine building and its gateway still stand within their individual plot of land, and inside is the same ancient stone phallus and the same two votive pictures.[19]

Just like other *kami* the sexual gods are regarded as responding to human needs, and because many of these needs are closely connected to human health these benevolent sexual deities may be regarded as a particular sub-set

---

18 Katō Genchi 1924. 'A Study of the Development of Religious Ideas Among the Japanese People as Illustrated by Japanese Phallicism' *Transactions of the Asiatic Society of Japan* (Supplement to the Second Series, Volume I, p. 9 & Plate 12; Nishioka 1961, Plate XXXVII and from a personal observation made on 3 July 2013.

19 This description of O-Hijiri-sama provides a useful opportunity for a brief look at the vocabulary of Shintō shrines. The general expression for a shrine is *jinja* 神社 or, depending upon the identity and status of the *kami* enshrined there, it may be called a *miya* 宮 or a *jingū* 神宮. When the name of the *kami* includes the first character of *jinja* the duplication of the first character is avoided and the second character is read as *yashiro*, e.g the Sai no kami Yashiro 幸の神社 in Kyoto. In the example given here O-Hijiri-sama is the only enshrined *kami* on site. In other places the sexual deity may be confined to a small shrine of its own within the grounds of a place dedicated to another *kami* enshrined within a *honden* 本殿 (main hall), which may be combined in some way with a *haiden* 拝殿 (worship hall) that stands in front of it to accommodate worshippers. Sexual *kami* may also be found enshrined in very small shrines less than 1 metre in height known as *hokora* 祠 that may be made from either stone or wood. Others are represented only by images standing in the open air. A shrine is normally approached through a *torii* 鳥居, the characteristic open gateway shaped like the Greek letter '*pi*'.

FIGURE 12 *The phallus called O-Hijiri-sama in Urawa (Saitama Prefecture) with its votive* ema.

of a wider category of *kami* who 'exercise a medical role', to use the terminology adopted by Emiko Ohnuki-Tierney in her book *Illness and Culture in Contemporary Japan*. Not only are particular *kami* involved in health and healing, they actually specialise in certain conditions or disorders as the *kami* of the ears, the eyes, the limbs and even specific diseases.[20] The sexual gods are therefore Japan's great divine specialists in matters relating to procreation and fertility, although the precise mechanism by which a petitioner's prayers are granted troubles believers no more than their vague understanding of the

20 Ohnuki-Tierney, Emiko 1984. *Illness and Culture in Contemporary Japan* (Cambridge), pp. 613–164.

kami's true nature. That question has been left to anthropologists, who have addressed it in the specific context of the relationship between the sexual gods and fertility. Nelly Naumann wrote simply of the *kami* 'accepting an erotic gift' and responding to it in an appropriately benevolent manner.[21] Itō Kenkichi examined the topic more closely and related beliefs in agricultural fertility to ancient practices whereby a farmer and his wife had sexual intercourse in a field while the seed was being sown in order to enhance the field's bounty. 'A belief in phallicism implies a belief in the magic resulting in fertility,' he writes. 'Therefore, though the organs are powerful, their conjunction is even more so. Copulation becomes a ritual that ensures a good crop'.[22] This is the notion of 'sympathetic magic' whereby 'like produces like'.[23] Even though ritual acts of copulation are no longer performed in Japan, the carved images of phalluses and human coitus placed beside fields and the simulation of intercourse in dance or drama at shrine festivals may be regarded as influencing agricultural fertility in this same sympathetic manner.

Previous Work on Japan's Sexual Gods

It was suggested earlier that the presence of ktenic imagery in some shrines means that the terms 'phallic shrine' and 'phallic worship' are often used inappropriately, and this is not just a recent observation. In 1895 Buckley criticised that which 'faultily neglects to duly express the duality of the cult', and the view has been repeated quite recently in the narrower context of Inari worship.[24] The work in question is Karen A. Smyers' *The Fox and the Jewel: Shared and Private Meanings in Contemporary Inari Worship*.[25] One section of this well-researched and thoughtful book is devoted to the phallic imagery

21 Naumann, Nelly 2000. *Japanese Prehistory: The Material and Spiritual Culture of the Jomon Period* (Wiesbaden), pp. 79–80.

22 Itō Kenkichi with Richie, Donald 1967. *The Erotic Gods: Phallicism in Japan* (Tokyo), p. 101.

23 Strictly speaking this is imitative magic, one of the two forms of sympathetic magic formulated by Sir James Frazer in *The Golden Bough*, and one of the few elements of that much-criticised work to have passed the test of time. Imitative magic assumes a causal relationship between things that were similar. The other form, contagious magic, requires that two things have to have been in contact at some time. For a good modern discussion of the concept see Stein-Frankle, Rebecca L. and Stein, Philip L. 2005. *The Anthropology of Religion, Magic and Witchcraft* (Boston), pp. 143–146.

24 Buckley 1895, p. 27.

25 Smyers, Karen A. 1999. *The Fox and the Jewel: Shared and Private Meanings in Contemporary Inari Worship* (Honolulu).

associated with the ubiquitous fox of Inari. I shall return to the details of this topic later, but for now certain comments by Smyers deserve our attention. In her book she discusses and criticises an early article entitled 'Inari, its Origins, Development and Nature' which was written by D.C. Buchanan and published by the Asiatic Society of Japan in their *Transactions* in 1935.[26] Smyers makes two points about Buchanan's work that have application beyond Inari and are of relevance to the present study. First, she observes that Buchanan 'uses the term "phallic" when he sometimes means sexual, genital, or even vaginal'. Second, referring to Buchanan's identification of phallic symbolism in Inari worship, Smyers writes:

> ... he goes overboard in describing all the phallic objects used in religious ways in Japan. In addition to the fox tails and keys held in the foxes' mouths, which may reasonably be seen as phallic, he describes boulders on the mountain, stone lanterns, the Shintō fire drill, and Ainu *imao* worship sticks as phallic.'[27]

Smyers concludes the above paragraph with the memorable sentence, 'Sometimes a cylindrical object is just a cylindrical object', and it was with this timely warning ringing in my ears that I began a fresh literature search on the subject.[28]

The first article to be examined was the work by Buchanan. Far from dismissing his efforts Smyers is in fact quite generous towards him, describing the work as 'valuable as a starting point' yet, 'reflecting much about the scholarly concerns of the day'.[29] The latter point, that any discussion of Japanese sexual beliefs is always tinged with contemporary attitudes towards sexuality, was to be reinforced when I studied earlier English language descriptions and discerned a certain Victorian prudery. This is best illustrated by the publication in 1883 of an important historical source that contains what is certainly the first English-language mention of a Japanese sexual shrine. The original reference dates from 1617 and may be found in the diary of Richard Cocks, Head of the East India Company's factory (i.e. trading post) on the island of Hirado (Nagasaki Prefecture). In a passage easy to miss within his entry for

26 Buchanan D.C. 1935. 'Inari, its Origins, Development and Nature' *Transactions of the Asiatic Society of Japan* 2nd Series XII, pp. 1–191.

27 Smyers 1999, p. 134.

28 Smyers 1999, p. 134.

29 Smyers, 1999, p. 233 n. 28.

26 February 1617, Cocks describes how his colleague William Nealson came across an interesting shrine:

> Mr. Nealson going a-walking, perchance found an altar of the ancient god Priapus (or the lecherous god) ... as well women that are with child, to have speedy deliverance, as also them which are barren, to be fruitful ...[30]

From the mention of the name Priapus (a phallic deity from the classical world) I concluded that William Nealson must have come across a shrine with some overt phallic imagery, but I was intrigued by the presence in this passage (unique in the whole of Cocks' diary) of the three dots indicating omissions. The fact that Cocks is by no means a prude in his descriptions of Japanese customs led me to suspect that some form of censorship of the original had taken place at the hands of the editor from the Hakluyt Society when the diary was published in 1883. This was confirmed by examining the uncensored 1979 edition of the diary published by the Historiographical Institute of Tokyo and the original manuscript in the British Library, where a restoration of the missing passages makes the whole entry read as follows:

> Mr. Nealson going a-walking, perchance found an altar of the ancient god Priapus (or the lecherous god) with a great tool, whereunto women go on pilgrimage carrying wooden pricks with them like unto a man's member, the which they first put into their nature (or member) and after offer it up to the god, as well women that are with child, to have speedy deliverance, as also them which are barren, to be fruitful. One of which pricks he brought away with him, & showed it to me, & learned by them which dwelled by to what use they were ordained, which was as above said.[31]

Cocks finishes the passage with a description of a place in France known to him where similar practices were carried out. No indication is given in the diary of the name of the shrine or its location, but it is almost certain to be the Midorigaoka Shrine 緑岡神社 located on a hill not far from the suspension

30 Cocks, Richard 1883. *Diary of Richard Cocks; Cape Merchant in the English Factory in Japan 1615–1622 with correspondence* (Hakluyt Society, London), Volume I p. 238. I have modernised the original Jacobean spelling for the convenience of the reader whose first language is not English.

31 Cocks, Richard 1979. *Diary of Richard Cocks 1615–1622 Volume II January 1 1617–January 14, 1619* (Historiographical Institute, Tokyo 1979), pp. 34–35. Here I acknowledge the help received from Hamish Todd and Christopher Barnes.

FIGURE 13 *These phallic offerings are at the rear of the Midorigaoka Shrine (Hirado, Nagasaki Prefecture). This was the first sexual-related shrine to be described in the English language.*

bridge that now links Hirado to the mainland of Kyūshū. It enshrines a deity called Omuta-sama お牟田様 and still includes a considerable phallic element.[32]

A reticence similar to that displayed by the Hakluyt Society's editor may also be discerned twelve years later in the preface to the first English-language study of Japanese sexual beliefs, the classic monograph *Phallicism in Japan* published in 1895 by Edmund Buckley. Warning his readers that this academic work, which was his dissertation for a PhD at the University of Chicago, contained 'detail and frankness in the treatment of phallicism which would be inadmissible in work deemed for the general public', Buckley suggests that, 'Should any general reader happen upon this article and find it unduly stimulating [to] his lower sensibility, he ... will do better in passing the article to fitter hands'. In a later passage Buckley adds a further warning that, '[as] soon as one begins to study phallicism he goes crazy', a point of view with which I am in considerable sympathy.[33]

32 Nishioka 1961, pp. 278–279 and from a personal observation made on 5 April 2012.

33 Buckley 1895, pp. 4 & 7.

Although the work is short and somewhat constrained by fear of offending his readers Buckley provides a concise, accurate and useful account that has been very influential, and at the time of its publication nothing comparable had ever been published even in Japan. Much of the thesis was based on Buckley's own observations within Japanese shrines, which makes his achievement all the greater. It was known to W.G. Aston (1841–1911) who mentions Buckley's work in a footnote to his translation of the *Nihongi* before relating how he had witnessed at first hand the continuing vigour of the traditions Buckley had described:

> Travelling from Utsunomiya to Nikko in 1871, I found the road lined at intervals with groups of phalli, connected, no doubt, with the worship of the Sacred Mountain Nan-tai (male form) which was visited every summer by hundreds of pilgrims of the male sex, access to females being at that time rigorously prohibited.[34]

Aston was one of a small handful of English-speaking travellers who gave similar descriptions of phallic shrines. Lafcadio Hearn visited the sexual tree of Tottori's Kinone Shrine in 1891 and described it as follows in 1894 in *Glimpses of Unfamiliar Japan*:

> Near a sleepy little village called Kanii-ichi I make a brief halt in order to visit a famous sacred tree. It is in a grove close to the public highway, but upon a low hill … One pushes out three huge roots of a very singular shape; and the ends of these have been wrapped about with long white papers bearing written prayers, and with offerings of seaweed. The shape of these roots, rather than any tradition, would seem to have made the tree sacred in popular belief: it is the object of a special cult; and a little torii has been erected before it, bearing a votive annunciation of the most artless and curious kind … The worship of the tree, or at least of the Kami supposed to dwell therein, is one rare survival of a phallic cult probably common to most primitive races, and formerly widespread in Japan. Indeed it was suppressed by the Government scarcely more than a generation ago.[35]

---

34 Aston, W.G. 1972. *Nihongi: Chronicles of Japan from the Earliest Times to A.D. 697* (Volume I and II) (Reprint) (Rutland Vt.), pp. 11–12.

35 Hearn, Lafcadio 1894a. *Glimpses of Unfamiliar Japan Volume II* (London), p. 110.

FIGURE 14 *The huge phallus at the Taga Shrine in Uwajima, which also contains Japan's largest sex museum.*

In contrast to Hearn's understanding and appreciation of the reasons behind phallic displays in shrines his contemporary W.E. Griffis was simply shocked by them. In *The Religions of Japan* of 1895 Griffis revealed his approval of the Meiji government's clampdown:

> Into the details of the former display and carriage of these now obscene symbols in the popular celebrations; of the behaviour of even respectable citizens during the excitement and frenzy of the festivals; of their presence in wayside shrines; of the philosophy, hideousness or pathos of the subject, we cannot here enter.[36]

A few years after Buckley the German scholar Friedrich Krauss wrote *Japanisches Geschlechtsleben; Abhandlungen und Erhebungen über das Geschlechtsleben des Japanischen Volkes.* In this important book of 1907 Krauss succeeded in portraying through words and pictures the frank essence of Japanese sexual life and the behaviours associated with it such as prostitution, homosexuality and

36 Griffis, W.E. 1895. *The Religions of Japan: From the dawn of history to the era of Meiji* (New York), p. 29.

erotic art. It may have shocked some of his audience, but Krauss was expressing an opinion shared by other contemporary writers who believed they had discovered the sex life of the Japanese people. It was a view driven by nostalgia for a time that supposedly had once existed in the world when sexual matters were joyful and free of hypocrisy, but at the same time it acted as a critique of the authors' own societies. Thus Krauss contrasted the liberated sexual life of the Japanese with Western double-standards, an attitude he summed up as outside observers looking at Japan through Western glasses and seeing moral degeneracy where in reality there was just an uncomplicated and unrestricted love of life.[37]

Krauss has comparatively little to say about Japan's sexual shrines, so the European-language successor to Buckley's work was to be an article published by the Asiatic Society of Japan in 1924. Entitled 'A Study of the Development of Religious Ideas Among the Japanese People as Illustrated by Japanese Phallicism', it is by Katō Genchi, who acknowledges a certain debt to Buckley but goes on to produce a very valuable account of his own that has stood the test of time and is still widely quoted. Katō provides very useful material relating to important shrines that can still be identified and the names of their enshrined *kami*, although his presentation of them is somewhat haphazard and unsystematic. In the context of describing important places he identifies both the agricultural and the human aspects of fertility, and within the latter topic the guardian deities of marriage and protectors against sexual diseases, together with patrons of infertile women and even the guardian *kami* of prostitutes, demonstrating clearly that sexual shrines cover a wide area of religious belief.[38]

Three years after Katō's article appeared Japan received a brief and largely anecdotal mention among the wide collection of snippets relating to ancient and modern phallic cults contained in Lee Alexander Stone's highly polemical *The Story of Phallicism*. This was the first reference to Japan in a general work on sexual beliefs.[39] Thirty years then went by until 1959 when a serious

37 Krauss, Friedrich S. 1907. *Japanisches Geschlechtsleben. Abhandlungen und Erhebungen über das Geschlechtsleben des Japanischen Volkes. Folkloristische Studien von Friedrich S. Krauss und Tamio Satow. Bearbeitet von Hermann Ihm. Neu hrg. von G. Prunner.* (New edition 1931), p. 10.

38 Katō 1924, p. 7.

39 Stone, 1927, pp. 110–111. An important book of 1889 about phallicism made no mention of Japan. That work is Jennings, Hargrave 1889. *Phallism: A description of the worship of lingam-yoni in various parts of the world, and in different ages, with an account of ancient & modern crosses particularly of the Cruz Ansata (or handled cross) and other symbols connected with the mysteries of sex worship.* (London).

academic article in English about the Tagata Shrine and its festival was published in the journal *Acta Tropica*.[40] It was not until 1967 that the first full-length book in English was published on the subject of Japanese phallicism. This was *The Erotic Gods: Phallicism in Japan* by Itō Kenkichi and Donald Richie. This remarkable book, which is essentially a translated and expanded version of Itō's 1965 book *Robō no Seizō*, has been the standard work on the subject for a Western audience for over forty years.[41] It is rich in its detail and its illustrations, with page after page of interesting photographs of sexual-related folk art objects and images. The descriptions of shrine festivals, often written using the past tense, provide confirmation of how many have been revived or even invented since the time of the book's publication. Unfortunately the English text sometimes does not do justice to the illustrations, being limited in its analysis of the material, lacking in fieldwork, without any references and sometimes prone to unscholarly comments.[42]

Michael Czaja's 1974 *Gods of Myth and Stone: Phallicism in Japanese folk religion* has long been the only other English-language book on the topic. It is somewhat disappointing by comparison to the Itō and Richie work because he never seems to come to grips with the broader aspects of his subject, concentrating instead on *dōsojin*, the images placed at the sides of roads and next to fields. His analysis of them is limited but the wealth of description and interpretation of the symbolism that lies in the details carved into them is excellent. Czaja's book also provides the most accessible photographic collection of *dōsojin*.[43] Also of some use is the MA thesis of Ellen Quejada entitled *Phallic Worship in Japan: Celebrating the Phallus*, a project that makes the reader want to know much more than is contained within its limited scope. She includes translations of source material that are useful as leads, but the work as a whole is prone to errors.[44] Unfortunately, in terms of the English language, these are all the publications that exist apart from monographs and articles that include sexual beliefs somewhere in their deliberations. The works by Nelly Naumann

---

40 Numazawa, Kiichi 1959. 'The Fertility Festival at Tagata Shintō Shrine' *Acta Tropica* XVI, pp. 193–217.

41 Itō, Kenkichi 1965. *Robō no Seizō* (Tokyo).

42 The statement on page 101 that, 'not only are they [the Japanese] sexually slow, but the male organ is not noteworthy for its size or potency' is one example.

43 Czaja, Michael 1974. *Gods of Myth and Stone: Phallicism in Japanese folk religion* (New York).

44 Quejada, Ellen 1998. *Phallic Worship in Japan: Celebrating the Phallus* (Unpublished MA Thesis, University of Toronto).

on the spiritual aspects of prehistoric Japan are particularly relevant here.[45] Other excellent academic articles on related subjects will be cited as they appear, such as Carmen Blacker on the mountain goddess,[46] James H. Sanford on the Tachikawa-ryū,[47] John Nelson's excellent work on the sexual symbolism at Kyoto's Kamigamo Shrine[48] and various chapters in the catalogue that accompanied the British Museum's exhibition of *shunga* in 2013.[49]

Japanese Sources for the Sexual Gods

Turning now to Japanese sources, because the renowned folklorist Yanagita Kunio made little reference to sexual shrines, Japanese scholarship on the topic effectively begins with Deguchi Yonekichi, who published a translation of Buckley in 1919 and added his own book on phallicism in 1920.[50] In 1927 Saitō Shōzō published *Hentai sūhai shi*, a book that provides many interesting old photographs similar to Katō's.[51] Of more modern works, Gōrai Shigeru's *Ishi no shūkyō* includes a chapter on *dōsojin*.[52] Meshida Taitei's *Ishigami sekibutsu shinkō no kenkyū* discusses a variety of sexual gods, while Ashida Eiichi's *Dōso no kamigami* contains a fine collection of photographs of *dōsojin*.[53]

---

45 Naumann, Nelly 1963. '"Yama no Kami": die japanische Berggottheit (Teil I: Grundvorstellungen)' *Asian Folklore Studies* 22, pp. 133–366; Naumann, Nelly 1964. '"Yama no Kami": die japanische Berggottheit. (Teil II: Zusätzliche Vorstellungen)' *Asian Folklore Studies* 23, pp. 48–199; Naumann, Nelly. 2000.

46 Blacker, Carmen 1996. 'The Mistress of Animals in Japan: Yamanokami' in Billington, Sandra and Green, Miranda (eds.) *The Concept of the* Goddess (London) pp. 178–185.

47 Sanford, James H. 1991. 'The Abominable Tachikawa Skull Ritual' *Monumenta Nipponica* 46, pp. 1–20.

48 Nelson, John 1993. 'Of flowers and Phalli: Sexual Symbolism at Kamigamo Shrine' *Japanese Religions* 18 (1993) pp. 2–14, incorporated into Nelson, John 2000 *Enduring Identities: the guise of Shintō in contemporary Japan* (Honolulu).

49 These are contained in the lavish catalogue, referenced as Clark, Timothy; Gerstle, C. Andrew; Ishigami, Aki and Yano, Akiko (eds.) 2013. *Shunga: Sex and Pleasure in Japanese Art* (London). A special edition of the journal *Japan Review* was also published. This is Gerstle, C. Andrew and Clark, Timothy (eds.) 2013. *Shunga: Sex and Humor in Japanese Art and Literature* (*Japan Review Special Issue*) *Volume 26* (Kyoto).

50 Deguchi 1919 & 1920.

51 Saitō, Shōzō 1922. *Hentai Sūhai shi:* (*Hentai jūni shi Volume* 9) (Tokyo).

52 Gōrai, Shigeru 2007. *Ishi no shūkyō* (Tokyo), pp. 141–178.

53 Meshida, Taitei 1962. *Ishigami sekibutsu shinkō no kenkyū* (Tokyo); Ashida, Eiichi 1963. *Dōso no kamigami* (Tokyo).

FIGURE 15 *A phallic rock protruding from the ground at the Shinmei Shrine in Wakayama City.*

Otherwise, publications within the past half century are dominated by the name of Nishioka Hideo, whose important book of 1950 *Nihon ni okeru seishin no shiteki kenkyū* was revised over several editions with changes to the title and the addition of English subtitles to the photographs, culminating in a smaller format work in 1961 known as *Zusetsu Sei no kamigami.* The version entitled *Nihon Seishin-shi* of 1961 will be the Nishioka work cited most frequently here. Nishioka's books are very valuable, particularly as he lists many of the shrines and their deities in an extensive gazetteer of 642 places and 39 related festivals derived from early published literature. These brief descriptions were usually enough to allow the sites to be located for the purpose of observation. He also writes about the etymology of the names given to the associated *kami*, which is one of the book's great strengths. However, Nishioka's work did not include fieldwork and because his descriptions of the shrines are drawn from literature rather than personal observation certain errors of transcription and reporting have crept in.

Nishioka is cited frequently in Abe Michiyoshi's 1963 gazetteer of Kyūshū's sexual shrines called *Kyūshū sei sūhai shiryō.*[54] Itō Kenkichi's *Robō no Seizō* of

54 Abe, Michiyoshi 1963. *Kyūshū sei sūhai shiryō* (Ōita).

1965 complements Nishioka's book by including good black and white photographs of *dōsojin* together with folk art erotica.[55] Much more ambitious and useful are the three reference books covering the whole of Japan produced by the film actor and phallic enthusiast Kokonoe Kyōji. Kokonoe's books contain detailed physical descriptions, brief but good historical analysis and some examination of the underlying philosophy. The first, simply entitled *Seishin* is a beautifully bound and lavishly illustrated guide to a wide selection of sexual shrines, many of which are not listed in Nishioka's books. This very rare and expensive work put on to the market in 1976 colour photographs and descriptions of key shrines and their festivals that were available nowhere else. *Seishin* is so vividly illustrated that it has allowed direct visual comparison with present-day observations of the same places, and it remains the best pictorial account of sexual shrines that exists.[56] Fortunately, in view of the book's rarity, in the same year Kokonoe also published *Furusato no Seishin*, which is essentially a pocket-sized version of *Seishin* designed to be used as a guidebook as it is arranged by prefecture with line drawings instead of photographs.[57] This was followed in 1981 by *Nippon no Seishin*, a revised edition of the earlier guide where some shrines had been omitted and replaced by others in a total list of 211 sites. It includes photographs and a few colour plates and is the handiest guide to use for modern exploration even though administrative developments have led to some place names changing over the past forty years.[58]

More recent works add a welcome analytic rigour to Kokonoe's outstanding descriptive and illustrative skills. Hashimoto Mineo's *Sei no kami* of 1976 places Japanese sexual beliefs in the wider context of practices to be found elsewhere in the world, as does Ōta Saburō in *Sei sūhai* (1986).[59] Two other distinguished authors provide valuable analyses of the phenomenon from very different perspectives. The first is Miyata Noboru who, in contrast to Yanagita, embraced sexuality as an element within folklore and folk beliefs. In a number of publications he discusses the relationship between human reproduction and agricultural fertility, and in a chapter in *Onna no reiryoku to ie no kami* of 1983 he examines the changing role of the phallus between hunter/gatherer and agricultural societies.[60]

55 Itō, Kenkichi 1965. *Robō no Seizō* (Tokyo).

56 Kokonoe, Kyōji 1976. *Seishin* (Tokyo).

57 Kokonoe, Kyōji 1976a *Furusato no Seishin* (Tokyo).

58 Kokonoe, Kyōji 1981. *Nippon no Seishin* (Tokyo).

59 Hashimoto Mineo 1976. *Sei no kami* (Tokyo); Ōta Saburō 1976. *Sei Sūhai* (Tokyo).

60 Miyata, Noboru 1983. *Onna no reiryoku to ie no kami* (Tokyo). The chapter originated as an article entitled 'Sei shinkō oboegaki' in Chiba, Tokuji (ed.) 1980. *Nihon Minzoku Fūdoron* (Tokyo), pp. 307–319.

The second is Satō Tetsurō, whose excellent *Seiki shinkō no keifu* is an academic work based on observation that neatly complements Nishioka. The first half provides a thorough account of the sexual gods and their origins while the latter part concentrates on the shrines of Akita Prefecture, where Satō begins with descriptions of the places left by the Late-Tokugawa Period traveller Sugae Masumi. Satō analyses the old material and then describes the shrines as they are today, and his detailed study of the places and their associated rituals is the best that is currently available.[61] Otherwise short descriptions of sexual shrines may be found in broader accounts of local folk customs such as those listed and illustrated in *Tōhoku no minkan shinkō* by Miyura Teiji et al.[62] Even some apparently trivial popular publications can provide valuable leads for a researcher to follow. The imaginatively titled *I ♡ Hihōkan* (I 'love' sex museums) published in 2009 turns out to include an excellent and up-to-date illustrated pocket guide to Japan's most important sexual shrines, some of which are not included in either Nishioka's or Kokonoe's books.[63]

Japanese scholars of a younger generation are now taking a renewed interest in this aspect of their culture and are providing rich material at local levels. Yato Sadahiko's *Sai no kami to ryū—kodai ga wakaru ken* tackles the wider issues around sexual gods, and much of his material is concerned with little-known shrines in Shimane and Tottori Prefectures, most of which are not mentioned by Nishioka.[64] Yato's later work *Shichi fukujin to Shōtensan: minkan shinkō no rekishi* provides a thorough account of the worship of the seven gods of good luck and of Shōten (Kangiten).[65] Masuta Kimiyasu of the Aomori Prefectural Folk Museum is currently mapping and analysing the sexual shrines in Aomori and in 2006 he edited a book that was based on excellent fieldwork done by local high school students under his supervision into the folk beliefs of the area. It contains a chapter on sexual shrines.[66] Masuta's 2012 article 'Aomori-ken ni okeru seishokuki sūhai shiryō' is a systematic and fully referenced academic work that lists all the sexual shrines in the prefecture which he had located up to the date of writing, while his article of 2013 examines the presence of phalluses within shrines to Tenjin.[67] Finally, Kitahara Jirōta's 2014 book

61 Satō Tetsurō 1995. *Seiki shinkō no keifu* (Tokyo).

62 Miyura Teiji, Ishii Takeshi, Igari Bunji, Eguchi Bunshirō, Misaki Kazuo, Igarashi Yūsaku (eds.) 1973. *Tōhoku no minkan Shinkō.* (Tokyo).

63 Shui, Ryūji 2009. I ♡ Hihōkan (Tokyo).

64 Yato, Sadahiko 2004. *Sai no kami to ryū—kodai ga wakaru ken* (Tokyo).

65 Yato, Sadahiko 2005. *Shichi fukujin to Shōtensan: minkan shinkō no rekishi* (Tokyo).

66 Masuta Kimiyasu (ed.) 2006. *Tsugaru no shinkō: fushiki fushiki* (Aomori).

67 Masuta, Kimiyasu 2012. 'Aomori-ken ni okeru seishokuki sūhai shiryō' *Aomori Kenritsu Kyōdokan Kenkyū Kiyō* 36, pp. 37–54. Masuta, Kimiyasu 2013. 'Tenjin-sama to Tenma-sama—Tenmangū dankon-gata' *Aomori Kenritsu Kyōdokan Kenkyū Kiyō* 37, pp. 63–72.

indicates a possibly phallic nature for the *inau* (worship sticks) among the Ainu of Hokkaidō and Sakhalin.[68] All this bodes well for the future of research into Japan's sexual gods.

Not surprisingly, the modern growth of the internet has provided some very useful leads relating to the identification, location and description of previously little-known sites. Many of the larger sexual shrines now have their own websites, and visitors regularly upload video clips of sexual-related festivals on to *YouTube*. These simple movies record processions, rituals and drama from events such as the Tagata Festival and several less famous ones. They therefore provide genuinely valuable research material, enabling one to observe at second-hand some obscure but important events held in remote places and to note any changes made from year to year in the better-known examples.[69]

A few years ago a group of Japanese enthusiasts began a website under the banner of the *Nihon Seishin Kenkyūshō* (Japanese Sexual Gods Research Institute) where information about sexual shrines could be pooled, but unfortunately this ambitious project is now defunct with no new postings having been made since 2006. The simple list that was created by this date contained the names and locations of 1,215 sites including 33 museum collections and 44 festivals. Nearly all of Nishioka's and Kokonoe's places were listed and there was also some attempt at classification.[70] Another website entitled *Seishin Hakubutsukan* (Museum of Sexual Gods) attempted to link a similar but shorter list to pages containing more details about individual sites, but this again has received no updating since 2010.[71] An active professional website is devoted to the sexual shrines of Miyagi Prefecture under the auspices of the Prefectural Museum in Sendai. This detailed survey has had the effect of indicating that the total number of sexual shrines in Japan may be much greater than is supposed, because the 29 places identified for Miyagi on the defunct 2006 website has now risen to 214.[72]

---

68 Kitahara, Jirōta. 2014. *Ainu no saigu inau no kenkyū* (Sapporo).

69 I have uploaded on to YouTube all the videos I made in conjunction with the research for this book. They are identified individually in these footnotes and may be accessed more generally by an internet search. Each title begins with the words 'Japan's Sexual Gods:'

70 http://homepage2.nifty.com/japanpi/ (accessed 6 June 2012). This site was partially inaccessible by May 2013.

71 http://members3.jcom.home.ne.jp/seihaku/ (accessed 6 June 2012).

72 http://www11.atpages.jp/ruisho/index.htm (accessed 19 April 2013).

By the end of 2014 the books by Nishioka and Kokonoe, the articles by Masuta and the various websites had yielded a list of about 2,000 sites worthy of investigation, and in several cases visits to selected venues have revealed the existence of others. As is indicated by the maps of principal sites included in this work, there appears to be a greater concentration of sexual-related shrines and images in the northern half of Japan compared to the southern part. This could suggest a genuine cultural difference, although it is likely that there has been a considerable amount of under-reporting of southern and western Japanese sites because the informants for the two defunct websites seem to have concentrated their earlier efforts on northern Japan.

Finally, in terms of the objects contained in the shrines, much useful information about their nature and history may be gathered from examples of them kept in museum collections. Some of these places are small local folk museums, while others are larger establishments completely given over to the topic of sex such as the Seishin no Yakata 性神の館 (Utsunomiya City, Tochigi Prefecture) and the Chinpōkan 珍宝館 near Takasaki (Gunma Prefecture).[73] Places like these are highly commercialised, but they still provide much valuable research material including reproductions of phallic *goshintai* from remote or otherwise inaccessible shrines. The rich collection of objects in the Taga Shrine Sex Museum in Uwajima (Ehime Prefecture) for example, is sensationalised in all popular guidebooks about Japan but has a serious purpose that is somewhat overwhelmed by the supposedly 50,000 items it owns. The display cases are packed and there are so many pictures that some are even pasted on the ceiling.[74]

In conclusion, as well as indicating where obscure sexual shrines are to be found, the older published research shows the broad nature of the topic and demonstrates the ways in which change has taken place. More recent scholarly contributions involve a greater depth of analysis for selected areas, while internet sources and popular publications have greatly expanded the list of locations and suggest at the very least that there is still much more to be discovered.

73 Visits were made to these places on 27 April 2012 and 11 March 2014 respectively and thanks are due to the proprietors for allowing me to take and publish unlimited photographs of their collections.

74 Visits were made to the museum on 21 January 2003 and 16 February 2011.

FIGURE 16 *Aizu-Wakamatsu (Fukushima Prefecture) has a local form of phallic symbol that consists of two testicles made from balls of straw attached to a wooden phallus.*

Structure of the Present Work

The structure of this book is designed to provide a framework that is understandable to the general reader as well as to a specialist in Japanese religious studies. Chapter 2 continues this introduction to the subject by examining the historical context and recognising the difficulty of tracing back developments in Japan any further than the seventeenth century. The core of each subsequent chapter is the description and illustration of the sexual shrines as they exist today, which are placed in context and analysed using previously published material relating to them or to their types. So Chapter 3 discusses the possible significance of the sexual elements presented by the *dogū* (clay figurines) and *sekibō* from the prehistoric Jōmon Period. The use of *sekibō* as phallic symbols in present-day shrines provides an introduction to the ways in which the *kami* are believed to enter the human world. Chapter 4 introduces Yama no kami, the mountain deity, who is probably the first *kami* to be named in connection with sexuality. Chapter 5 presents important *kami* whose written mythology relates directly to many important sexual shrines and who are presented in the *Kojiki* and the *Nihongi*, the defining compilations that are closely related to the development of the imperial system. Chapter 6 introduces more sexual *kami* in the context of the current worship activities to be found in their shrines. Chapter 7 then looks specifically at female sexual *kami* and the much neglected topic of ktenic imagery in Japanese religion.

Chapter 8 tackles the male-dominated imagery that is crucial to the devotional role of the shrines to Konsei Daimyōjin, the powerful sexual *kami* who appears to provide the only true example of actual phallic worship. Chapter 9 then widens the scope to take in places dedicated to the deities who have their origins on the East Asian mainland, while Chapter 10 studies in detail the important protective function that is exercised most visibly by the wayside gods. Chapter 11 provides a critical examination of the sexual shrines' festivals, the means by which these places are best known to the outside world but one that is open to commercialisation and exploitation. Finally, the shrines' continued vitality in an increasingly urban and secular environment is summarised in Chapter 12 in the form of some tentative conclusions.

To sum up, through the observation and analysis of Japan's present-day sexual shrines this book will show how one particular nation's religious tradition has tackled humanity's greatest challenge: its own survival. That, in all its mystery, provides the underlying context of the need for both human and agricultural fertility, a goal that was always threatened by hazards such as crop failures, the need to find a mate and the safe delivery of a wanted child. Anxiety is present throughout all these processes, both in this supposedly sophisticated modern age and at a time when causes of failure were not understood and the onset of disaster was believed to be avoidable only through the practice of religious behaviour for which the protective and procreative phallus was to become such an important symbol.

CHAPTER 2

Encountering the Sexual in Japanese Culture

The present-day beliefs and behaviours associated with Japan's sexual gods do not exist in isolation. They are expressed in a number of different contexts, and the first that will be explored is the popular impression that in spite of periodic repression there has long been a ready acceptance of sexual display within Japanese society.[1] A consideration of this topic sheds important light on the sexual gods and their related beliefs as they stand today, but it also gives important pointers towards how they may have been expressed in the past.

The acceptance of frank sexual display within the modern Japanese religious environment contrasts so markedly with conventional Western attitudes that when a foreign tourist catches sight of a phallus in a Japanese shrine the experience may well provoke feelings of surprise and even shock. This was indeed my own reaction during my first visit to Japan in 1970 when I purchased a 1965 edition of the popular history journal *Rekishi Dokuhon* in a second-hand bookshop. The magazine included an article with photographs published at the time of that year's annual festivals at the Tagata and Ōagata Shrines in Aichi Prefecture. The prominent portable wooden phallus at the Tagata Shrine was startling enough, but even more remarkable to an outsider was the banner carried during the Ōagata Festival (and now omitted from the event) that depicted starkly drawn female genitalia.[2]

My reaction was probably not an untypical one forty-five years ago, although the gap between Japanese and Western attitudes has since narrowed considerably, as was indicated by the public reaction to two recent ground-breaking exhibitions in the United Kingdom. The first revealed the extent of sexual imagery that had existed in the Western world in antiquity. Entitled *Roman Sexuality: Images, Myths and Meanings*, it was mounted at Brading Roman Villa on the Isle of Wight in 2014 and consisted of over fifty items from the British Museum that had once been firmly locked away from public gaze. Its display of erotic lamps, drinking cups and figurines proved so popular that its stay at

1 Smith, Henry D. II. 1996. 'Overcoming the Modern History of Edo "Shunga"' in Jones, Sumie (ed.) *Imaging/Reading Eros: Proceedings for the conference, Sexuality and Edo Culture, 1750–1850 Indiana University, Bloomington August 17–20, 1995* (Bloomington), p. 27.

2 Anonymous 1965. 'Kagerō ni kudaru sei no kamigami.' *Rekishi Dokuhon* (May 1965) pp. 184–189.

 | DOI 10.1163/9789004293786_003

FIGURE 17 *A banner once carried during the Ōagata Festival including a depiction of female genitalia. Here it is illustrated in an edition of* Rekishi Dokuhon *from 1965. (Photograph by courtesy of* Rekishi Dokuhon).

Brading had to be extended by two months.[3] As a recently published study has shown, to the ancient Romans the phallus was both procreative and protective, and instead of recoiling from its image Roman citizens felt it was their duty to display this powerful emblem in situations of worship and at sites where danger lurked.[4]

A similar attitude has long persisted in much of East Asia, for which this present study of Japan is but a small instance of a widely recognised historical phenomenon. But the phallus has also been a symbol of pleasure, an aspect demonstrated to a new and highly appreciative Western audience by another recent exhibition. Entitled *Shunga: Sex and Pleasure in Japanese Art*, it ran at the British Museum from October 2013 to January 2014 and complemented the Roman exhibition with its extensive display of Japanese *shunga* 春画 (erotic prints and books, literally 'springtime paintings').[5] The British newspapers treated the revelations with a mixture of surprise and wry amusement, but most visitors, no doubt, took the erotic exuberance in their stride and may well have found the items a little quaint compared to what is now so readily available on the internet.[6]

The Roman exhibition, with its sexual depiction of ancient gods and goddesses, contained many more references to religious belief than did the *shunga* exhibition, where the pleasurable human side of the medium predominated. Nevertheless, taken together the two events provided a vivid reminder that in Western European culture the inclusion of a phallus or kteis in any discussion of religion has been a rare event for many centuries. This is exemplified by Hegel who, when analysing the Ancient Egyptian myth of Isis and Osiris in the light of the concept of the death of God, omitted any discussion of one particularly striking feature of the original tale that involved a phallus.[7] It is related as follows by Plutarch, who tells in his *Moralia* how Osiris, whom the Ancient Greeks identified with Dionysius, is put to death by his rival Typhon by being persuaded to lie down in a beautiful wooden chest. The lid is hammered down and sealed and the chest is thrown into the sea. Hearing that Isis is search-

3 http://www.bradingromanvilla.org.uk/ (Accessed 25 May 2014).

4 Clarke, John R. 2014. 'Sexuality and Visual Representation' in Hubbard, Thomas K. (ed.) *A Companion to Greek and Roman Sexualities* (Oxford), p. 254.

5 *Shunga* is a comparatively modern word derived from Chinese and used almost universally now to describe Japan's explicit sexual illustrations.

6 *The Sun* reviewed the exhibition under the headline 'Shunga Bunga' and the *Daily Mail* ran a cartoon with the caption, 'Apparently men think about Japanese art nineteen times a day'.

7 Hegel, Georg Wilhelm Friedrich 1987 *Lectures on the Philosophy of Religion. Vol 2 Determinate Religion* (edited by Hodgson, Peter C.; translated by Brown, R.F.; Hodgson, P.C. and Stewart T.M. (Berkeley), p. 626.

FIGURE 18 *There is a ready acceptance of phallic imagery throughout much of East and Southeast Asia, as shown by this phallic shrine in Bangkok.*

ing for the chest, Typhon retrieves it and dismembers Osiris's body into fourteen parts, which he scatters far afield. Isis, however, manages to recover all of Osiris's body except for one item:

> Of the parts of Osiris's body the only one which Isis could not find was the male member, for the reason that this had been at once tossed into the river and the lepidotus, the sea bream, and the pike had fed upon it.

Isis, however, hits on a solution, and 'made a replica of the member to take its place, and consecrated the phallus, in honour of which the Egyptians even at the present day celebrate a festival'.[8] A procession involving the carrying of phallic symbols played a part in these festivities, and the tradition was carried over by the Ancient Greeks in their celebrations of Dionysius. Herodotus accepts it so much as a matter of fact that he is moved to describe a development in the tradition among the Egyptians as follows:

> ... they have invented another contrivance, namely figures of about a cubit in height worked by strings, which women carry about the villages,

8 Page, T.E. et al. (translated and edited) 1927. *Plutarch's* Moralia (London), pp. 46–47.

> with the privy member made to move and not much less in size than the rest of the body; and a flute goes before and they follow singing the praise of Dionysius. As to the reason why this figure has this member larger than is natural and moves it, though it moves no other part of the body, about this there is a sacred story told.[9]

Herodotus' account impressed Voltaire, who contrasted the contemporary moralising attitudes he saw around him with that of the Ancient World. 'Our ideas of propriety lead us to suppose that a ceremony which appears to us infamous could only be invented by licentiousness', writes Voltaire, who genuinely believed that such practices originated in an age of innocence, so that '... profligacy may have crept in in the lapse of time, but the original institution was always innocent and free from it'.[10]

The point of mentioning Voltaire and Hegel in this discussion is that for source material dealing with phallicism Herodotus and Plutarch were almost all they would have had to hand, because little else was written about the subject in European languages until the eighteenth-century rediscovery of Pompeii and Herculaneum. This confirmed the existence of erotica in the ancient world, ranging from the lamps and cups showing love-making displayed at Brading to wall-paintings of the well-endowed god Priapus.[11] Such was the interest in the discoveries that copies were produced to add to the genuine articles uncovered, and in 1819 a 'Secret Cabinet' was established at the Museum of Naples to accommodate the collections, a practice copied by the British Museum in 1865.[12] Some writers may also have had an acquaintance with the phallic traditions of India and erotic statues from Tibet or Nepal. Others may have seen the exhibitionist figures carved into the fabric of some

---

9 Macaulay, G.C. (translated) 1904. *The* History *of Herodotus* (London), p. 139.

10 As translated in Stone 1927, pp. 136–137.

11 For the famous Warren cup that features scenes of homosexual love see Williams, Dyfri 2006. *The Warren Cup* (London).

12 As illustrated, for example, in Famin, Stanislas Marie César 1871. *The Royal Museum at Naples, being some account of the erotic paintings, bronzes and statues contained in that famous 'Cabinet Secret' by Colonel Fanin* (London). Available at http://www.sacred-texts.com/sex/rmn/rmn00.htm (accessed 11 February 2013), pp. 20–21. The stories included references to rituals of defloration using statues of Priapus where he was shown with a permanently erect penis. This led to prints like *The Sacrifice to Priapus* by the Italian printmaker known as the Master of the Die (1530–1560) being censored by having Priapus' genitalia completely excised, thus resulting in the loss of most of its significance.

medieval churches.[13] Yet so thoroughly suppressed was the topic that when the noted antiquarian Richard Payne Knight examined the subject in 1786 and received a violently hostile reaction he took it upon himself to withdraw his own book from sale.[14]

Shrines and *shunga* in Tokugawa Japan

How different things were in Japan in 1786! This was the mid-point of the Tokugawa Period when, in a similar manner to Ancient Rome, the phalluses and ktenes in *shunga* were employed erotically, humorously and satirically. By this time they were also firmly established within sexual shrines, some of which were already centuries old, although genuine continuity with the past is often difficult to assess. It is known that sometime around the year 800 ink-drawn graffiti including phalluses and a kteis were painted on to the middle pedestal of a Buddhist statue in the Tōshōdaiji at Nara, although when a further pedestal was added the graffiti were concealed from view.[15] This unique incident probably indicates a mischievous act rather than any devotional intent, and the pleasure motive in erotic art is certainly easier to trace back within Japanese history than is religious sexual display. Erotic painted scrolls were produced throughout the Medieval Period and the enthusiasm for the genre reached its heights in the vibrant metropolis from which the Tokugawa Period took its alternative name. In the city of Edo there was an 'intense interest in

13 They are known as Sheela-na-Gigs and have received scholarly attention since 1840. Most are female figures but some include phallic symbolism. An interesting example is in All Saints' Church in Ilkley, West Yorkshire. One of its three magnificent ancient stone crosses once sported a small phallic symbol that has since worn away completely. It is however indicated on a drawing from early in the twentieth century that is displayed next to the crosses. For contrasting views of the figures' significance see Weir, Anthony & Jerman, James 1986. *Images of Lust: Sexual Carvings on Medieval Churches* (London) and Freitag, Barbara A. 2004. *Sheela-na-gigs: Unravelling an Enigma* (London).

14 Knight, Richard Payne 1786. *A Discourse on the Worship of Priapus and its Connection with the Mystic Theology of the Ancients* (London), p. vii.

15 Yano, Akiko 2013. 'Shunga Paintings before the 'Floating World' in Clark, Timothy; Gerstle, C. Andrew; Ishigami, Aki and Yano, Akiko (eds.) *Shunga: Sex and Pleasure in Japanese Art* (London), p. 63.

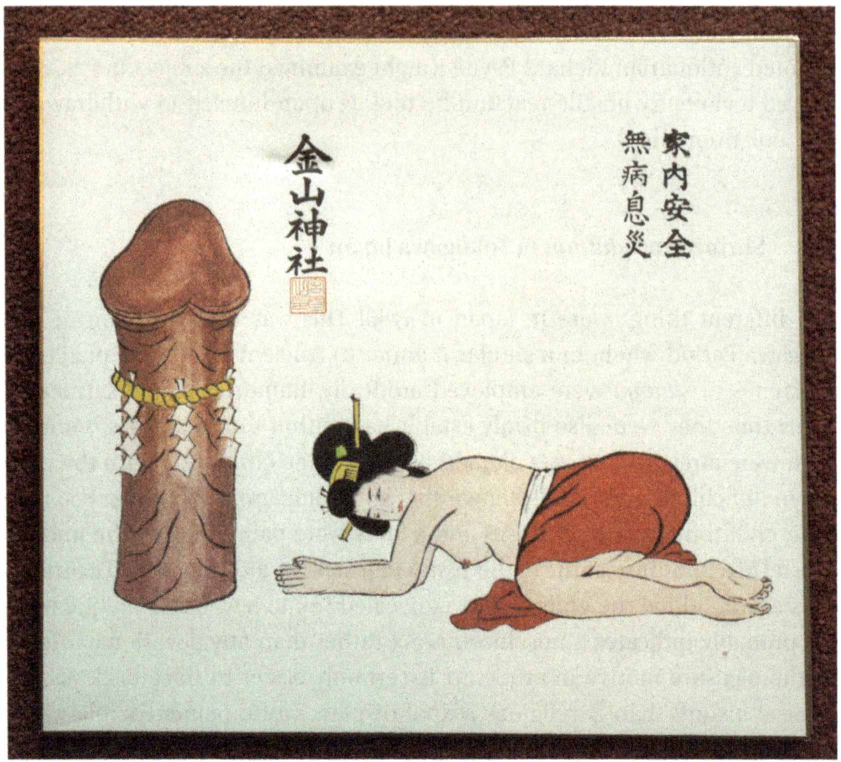

FIGURE 19 *This modern votive painting from the Kanayama Shrine in Kawasaki showing a woman bowing to a large phallus was probably inspired by erotic* shunga *prints.*

eroticism apparent in every facet of the city's culture'.[16] The prominent phalluses depicted in Edo's *shunga* complemented the sight of them in the sexual shrines, so that throughout Japan the male sexual organ could be seen in every possible guise.[17]

To a very large extent the devotional phalluses and ktenes in the present-day shrines that form the theme of this book and the erotic depictions on *shunga* must be treated as two separate topics, but they both exist within a common

16 Hayakawa, Monta 1996. 'Shunga and Mitate: Suzuki Harunobu's *Eight Modern Views of the Interior* (Fūryū Zashiki Hakkei)' in Jones, Sumie (ed.) *Imaging/Reading Eros: Proceedings for the conference, Sexuality and Edo Culture, 1750–1850 Indiana University, Bloomington August 17–20, 1995* (Bloomington), p. 128.

17 The exception was any Japanese version of the ancient Egyptian mechanical member that so impressed Herodotus, a creation that would have provided but a minor challenge to the skilful makers of *karakuri ningyō* (mechanical dolls)!

historical environment that has usually accepted unambiguous sexual display as a valid way of expressing these two very different human concerns. There are also some occasional and revealing overlaps, as shown by two illustrations in the catalogue to the British Museum exhibition. The first is a parody of one of the most solemn scenes in Buddhist belief: the *Parinirvana*, or Death of the Buddha.[18] The conventional version is hung in Japanese temples on the fifteenth day of the second month to commemorate that profoundly spiritually event, yet here we have the Buddha depicted as a phallus.[19] Behind the reclining figure stand female mourners holding sex toys rather than ritual implements and with ktenic faces. In front are figures in attitudes of sorrow with the upper part of their bodies depicted as phalluses. If a Western artist had produced a comparable image in a Christian context an accusation of blasphemy would have been a likely outcome, yet in the caption to the illustration we are merely reminded that, 'In the popular culture of the Edo Period, such personifications or objectifications of the phallus and the vulva were on one hand profane and bawdy, but on the other, they also retained elements of sacred awe'.[20] The second picture, this time a book illustration, includes a seated figure of the Buddha Shakyamuni in an otherwise erotic display, where the caption notes that, 'In Edo Period culture apparently nothing was inviolable'.[21]

Other examples exist where the sexual gods discussed in this book became the models for erotic compositions and their priests became the butt of satirical sexual jokes.[22] An alternative name for *shunga*, after all, was *warai-e* 笑い絵 (laughter pictures). Itō and Richie provide examples of statuettes where the goddess Kannon is presented in a suggestively sexual way. In one she is holding a ktenic flower and exposing her vulva, and on a statue of Benten kept in the museum of the Taga Shrine in Uwajima the artist has taken great delight in depicting her vulva in fine detail.[23] On another carving she is being penetrated from behind, so there was clearly no notional religious boundary to inhibit or restrain an artist.[24] This was in complete contrast to the ban on the depic-

18 Clark, Timothy; Gerstle, C. Andrew; Ishigami, Aki and Yano, Akiko (*eds.*) 2013. *Shunga: Sex and Pleasure in Japanese Art* (London), p. 369. A similar painting appears in Kenkichi and 1967, p. 178. The example illustrated here is from the collection of the Chinpōkan in Shibukawa City (Gunma Prefecture).

19 Zwalf, W. (ed.) 1985. *Buddhism: Art and Faith* (London), p. 261.

20 Clark et al. 2013, p. 368.

21 Clark et al. 2013, p. 372.

22 For examples see Clark et al. 2013, pp. 85 & 90.

23 Kenkichi and Richie 1967, p. 178 and from a personal observation made on 16 February 2011.

24 Kenkichi and Richie 1967, pp. 186–187.

FIGURE 20 *A phallic variation on the theme of the* Death of the Buddha *on display in the Chinpōkan. The Buddha is depicted as a phallus while the male and female mourners are shown in a sexual guise. The painting reminds us that during the Tokugawa Period there were no taboos over the use of religious subjects in erotic art.*

tion of political figures, but even sex-obsessed Edo recognised a dividing line when it came to the question of where items derived from religion could be displayed. The phallic Buddha images would not be hung in any Buddhist temple; they were produced for private collectors. It is also interesting to see some of the famous sacred phalluses and ktenes described later in this work being depicted in an erotic publication of 1776 called *Katakiuchi insenroku* (Tales of Lusty Revenge) by Terasawa Masatsugu. On the right hand page are interpretations of the sexual organs of Dōkyō-sama and Empress Kōken and on the left there is the important sexual *kami* Konsei Daimyōjin and the naturally ktenic rock in Tochigi Prefecture called the Gozen Iwa.[25]

Such pictures were produced for amusement or titillation, but some of the votive and protective functions associated with shrine phalluses could be carried over into the urban environment of samurai barracks, merchants'

25 Suzuki, Kenzō 2013. 'Popular Cults of Sex Organs in Japan: Guardian Deities, Auspicious Objects and Votive Paintings' in Clark, Timothy; Gerstle, C. Andrew; Ishigami, Aki and Yano, Akiko (eds.) *Shunga: Sex and Pleasure in Japanese Art* (London), p. 365.

FIGURE 21 *In 1776 an erotic book called* Katakiuchi insenroku (*Tales of Lusty Revenge*) *by Terasawa Masatsugu featured this spread of sacred phalluses and ktenes. (Photograph by courtesy of the Ebi collection* ARC *Database, Ritsumeikan University, Kyoto, Ebi 0877).*

homes and city brothels through the medium of *shunga*.[26] The protective role of the phallus was to be mirrored through beliefs in *shunga* guarding a home or storehouse against fire, a very real danger in the city of Edo and a constant obsession among its population. Women of the pleasure quarters would also carry lucky *shunga* in their purses so that they were never without money, and towards the end of the Tokugawa Period the custom developed of offering phalluses and other sexual items as votive *engimono* 縁起物 (auspicious objects) at New Year to ensure commercial prosperity and the safety of premises.[27] They would be placed upon an *engidana* 縁起棚, a smaller version of the conventional *kamidana* 神棚 (household god-shelf) located nearer

26 For excellent accounts of this world see Lindsey, William 2007. *Fertility and Pleasure: Ritual and Sexual Values in Tokugawa Japan* (Honolulu) and Stanley, Amy 2012. *Selling Women: Prostitution, Markets, and the Household in Early Modern Japan* (Berkeley).

27 Smith 1996, p. 28.

FIGURE 22 A kamidana (*god-shelf hanging just below the ceiling line at the Takashiba Deco Yashiki in Kōriyama (Fukushima Prefecture) shows the inclusion of sexual objects. There is a mask of Otafuku and several phalluses to ensure the safety of the premises and commercial prosperity.*

the ceiling. An illustration of one holding a phallus appears in the 1827 book *Wakamidori* by the artist Utagawa Kuninao.[28]

In the samurai quarters of Edo the under-employed and bored warriors kept *shunga* in their armour boxes and may have regarded them as talismans. One contemporary wrote, 'In boxes where armour is kept, a *shunga* should be placed. Then before the warrior goes out to battle he should look at this and so go out with a smile on his face'.[29] Some writers went so far as to claim that samurai during the age of war had regarded them as amulets for victory and even marched into battle with an erotic picture concealed in their helmets. Others disputed this notion, arguing that to gaze upon an erotic image before combat

28 Suzuki 2013, p. 366. Similar practices still exist as shown by the accompanying illustration. On 7 November 2012 I was taken to see a small iron phallus that was still displayed on the same *kamidana* of a private house in Aomori Prefecture.

29 Waley, Arthur 1931. 'Magical use of phallic representations, its late survival in China and Japan' *Bulletin of the Museum of Far-Eastern Antiquities, Stockholm* 3, p. 62.

FIGURE 23 *A phallus placed on the* kamidana, *from the 1827 book* Wakamidori *by the artist Utagawa Kuninao. (Photograph by courtesy of the Art Research Center, Ritsumeikan University (Hayashi Yoshikazu collection) Kyoto, hayBKE2-0008).*

was not likely to steel a warrior's nerve and could have the opposite effect.[30] A different role is also included in Arthur Waley's translation of the above document. 'When I was a lad I looked into the book-boxes at a house where I was visiting and found that in each there was inserted a Spring Painting. When I asked the reason I was told it was a counter-charm against [the bad influences caused by possessing] many books'.[31]

The most important religious belief associated with a phallus, that of assisting conception, was not transferred to the urban environment through the medium of *shunga*. *Shunga* were for sexual pleasure, not procreation. The latter aim might be helped if *shunga* increased the owner's libido but they are hardly likely to have possessed any spiritual dimension in that regard, so carved votive phalluses would retain their undisputed roles in such intercession.

Japanese Sexual Beliefs from the Tokugawa Period to the Present Day

Written records allow us to trace many of today's sexual shrines back to the early Tokugawa Period and for some even beyond it although, compared to the familiarity with *shunga* in urban centres, most of the shrines existed then in a state of highly localised rural obscurity. Some were to be sketched and described by a handful of travellers such as Sugae Masumi (1754–1829) who journeyed through Tōhoku and Hokkaidō. These accounts often provide the only proof of the shrines' existence at the time.

One observant traveller was the famous poet Matsuo Bashō. On his 'Narrow Road to the Deep North' Bashō visited the ancient Kasajima Dōsojin Yashiro 笠島道祖神社 on the outskirts of the town of Natori in Miyagi Prefecture. Bashō's visit allowed him to honour a fellow poet, because the *Gempei Seisuiki* of the thirteenth century relates how an aristocratic official and poet called Fujiwara Sanetaka was sent from Kyoto to distant Mutsu Province and found that his journey took him past this shrine. Sanetaka was told by the local people that he should dismount from his horse and pay his respects to its *kami*, the daughter of the great Sarutahiko. She was worshipped in the area because of her power over fertility, but Sanetaka refused to honour her although the reasons for his disrespect are not recorded. There may have been an overt sexual

30 Smith, Henry D. II 1996, p. 28; Yamamoto Yukari 'Traditional Uses of *Shunga*' in Clark, Timothy; Gerstle, C. Andrew; Ishigami, Aki and Yano, Akiko (eds.) *Shunga: Sex and Pleasure in Japanese Art* (London, 2013), pp. 298–299.

31 Waley 1931, p. 62.

FIGURE 24 *A sketch of a phallic shrine in Akita Prefecture made by the Edo Period traveller Sugae Masumi (Sugae Masumi Memorial Hall, Akita Prefectural Museum).*

FIGURE 25 *The courtier poet called Fujiwara Sanetaka refused to dismount from his horse in front of the* torii *of the Kasajima Shrine and pay his respects to its sexual* kami. *His horse threw him and he was killed. The site was later visited by Matsuo Bashō.*

display at the shrine, or Sanetaka may just have been expressing a Kyoto grandee's contempt for the simple beliefs of the rough country people. His refusal provoked horror among the bystanders, at which the horse took matters into its own hands (as it were) and threw him. Sanetaka was killed in the fall and is buried nearby.[32] When Bashō visited the Kasajima Shrine he sought out Sanetaka's grave and composed a *haiku* that makes use of the name *kasa* (rain hat) and the rainy weather he experienced.[33]

During the final century of the Tokugawa Period a certain degree of philosophical support for sexual beliefs began to emerge from scholars of *kokugaku*

32 The story is related in several sources including Katō 1924, pp. 20–21; Miyata 1983, p. 107 and Satō 1995, pp. 56–57.

33 For the original poem and an English translation see Britton, Dorothy 1980. *A Haiku Journey: Bashō's Narrow Road to a Far Province* (Tokyo) pp. 46 & 99–100. The Kasajima Shrine now enshrines Sarutahiko and his wife Ame no Uzume. There were once many phallic votive offerings on show but all but ten were destroyed by fire during World War II. The survivors are shown in Kokonoe 1981, p. 51.

国学 (national learning). *Kokugaku* regarded Buddhism and Confucianism as alien imports that threatened the native *kami* of Japan, a viewpoint that was to have an important influence on the founding fathers of the Meiji regime. One prominent member was Hirata Atsutane (1776–1843), whom the Tokugawa regime silenced for the last few years of his life.[34] Atsutane's devotion to Shintō included a passion for phallic worship, and at cherry blossom time the Hirata family performed religious rituals in honour of a phallic deity which 'was neither natural nor artificial, so that it was of supernatural origin, i.e. a deity of stone'.[35] So attached was Atsutane to his favourite phallic symbol that it was sought after his death by a group of his followers who were building a shrine to honour him.[36] The opponents of *kokugaku* within the Tokugawa hierarchy took a different view of phallicism. As Confucians they conventionally regarded sexual excess with disdain.[37] *Shunga* therefore suffered periodic bans, and in 1841 Mizuno Tadakuni (1794–1851) introduced the Tempō Reforms which included 'prohibiting all exhibitions of immoral character and the use of decorations and other devices of a questionable taste', so that many sexual images in shrines or beside roads were destroyed or concealed.[38]

In 1868 the long rule of the *shōgun* was replaced by that of the restored imperial power, but the Meiji Restoration did not result in a revival of phallicism. Instead the new government took steps to re-draw the religious map of the nation through the process of *shinbutsu bunri* 神仏分離 (the separation of *kami* and Buddhas), thereby reversing the cooperative situation of *shinbutsu shūgō* 神仏習合 that had existed happily over many centuries. Newly re-defined Shintō shrines were purged of long-standing Buddhist influences, sometimes at the cost of great physical destruction involving the burning of buildings and the smashing or selling of Buddhist statues. The result was a great number of distinct establishments that would support the fledgling state through a complex structure of patriotic teachings, designated shrines and dedicated priests. No longer could *kami* exist within a Buddhist framework. Instead they were seen exclusively as native gods of Japan.

---

34 Kitagawa, Joseph M. 1987. *On Understanding Japanese Religion* (Princeton), pp. 165–166.

35 See Katō 1924, p. 11 & 45.

36 Walthall, Anne 1998. *The Weak Body of a Useless Woman: Matsuo Taseko and the Meiji Restoration* (Chicago), p. 118.

37 McClelland, Mark 2012. *Love, Sex and Democracy in Japan during the American Occupation* (New York), p. 16.

38 Katō 1924, p. 20.

Some imperial enthusiasts may have yearned to eradicate Buddhism completely.[39] It was too firmly rooted in the national consciousness for that to happen, but as long as Buddhism recognised the superiority of the *kami* it could be a bulwark to the state, not a threat to it. At a practical level the first edict of 9 April 1868 required any priests who served a combined institution to abandon their Buddhist positions and await re-appointment as priests of the new shrines. The 'battle lines of sacred legitimisation', as Sarah Thal puts it, were now drawn.[40] Two weeks late a second edict forbade the display of Buddhist images in a shrine or the use of Buddhist titles for *kami*.[41] Through the implementation of these processes the priests ensured their survival and prosperity in a new world that both required and demanded their loyalty and co-operation. Out of this grew the shrines, the rituals and the *kami* of Shintō as we see them today and the existence of totally separate Buddhist temples. Thus did the Meiji reformers replicate their absolute political authority in the form of an absolute religious authority.[42]

The overall process with regard to the two axes of Buddhism and Shintō is well-recognised, but less known is the process that took place within Shintō itself. Local shrines to obscure and ancient *kami* associated only with their immediate neighbourhoods were forced to change their names and even their enshrined deities in a purge of something that was as old and every bit as Japanese as the emperor-centred nationalistic Shintō that was now being so enthusiastically promulgated. The result was that far from achieving the respectability once envisaged by the *kokugaku* scholars, the sexual shrines

---

39 Collcutt, Martin 1986. 'Buddhism: The Threat of Eradication' in Jansen, Marius B. and Rozman, Gilbert *Japan in Transition: From Tokugawa to Meiji* (Princeton), pp. 143–167.

40 Thal, Sarah 2005. *Rearranging the Landscape of the Gods: The Politics of a Pilgrimage Site in Japan, 1573–1912*. (Chicago), pp. 130–131.

41 Collcutt 1986, p. 152.

42 Thal 2005, pp. 130–131. Certain rituals were also banned, with magical diviners and mountain ascetics being eliminated in favour of a purified and rarefied Shintō. In many cases this was a clumsy and insensitive process that, in the words of Gaynor Sekimori, 'did not reflect even the practices of local communities, let alone the contemporary religious matrix of *kami*-buddha combination'. See Sekimori, Gaynor 2005. 'Paper Fowl and Wooden Fish: The Separation of Kami and Buddha Worship in Haguro Shugendō, 1869–1875' Japanese Journal of Religious Studies 32, p. 197. Even if they felt it was nonsense the guardians of shrines were of course required to comply, and within the space of a few years priests who had the care of sacred places ranging from small wayside shrines to large and important institutions totally transformed the sites for which they had responsibility to withdraw them from the alien pantheon of *bodhisattvas*, avatars and guardians of heaven that was now so unacceptable.

suffered as badly as any others with the removal of supposed Buddhist influence and in some cases their re-dedication to *kami* who were believed to be more acceptable. In an edict of 1873 for Akita Prefecture the veneration of a wide range of folk-religious objects including the protective straw figures called Shōki Daimyōjin were scornfully likened to holding memorial services for broken eggs.[43] In some cases the sexual shrines fared worse than the others because they had to suffer a further layer of condemnation from Meiji reformers to whom the worship of phallic symbols was neither appropriate nor in any way modern. Nor too did it tally with the morality espoused by the Western powers that the Meiji government sought to emulate and whose goodwill they wished to retain. *Shunga* were treated in a similar way and under the Meiji regime erotic publications were seized because they 'corrupt public behaviours'.[44]

All this was highly ironic in view of the enthusiasm for phallicism once expressed by the *kokugaku* scholars, yet in spite of the Meiji repression sexual beliefs survived into the twentieth century. Some Japanese would probably have agreed with Krauss's nostalgic idea that phallicism was the echo of a time of sexual innocence, because such attitudes struck a chord among those who thought that sexual beliefs represented the positive nature of native Shintō compared to the negative nature of alien Buddhism. The exuberance of Shintō was happily contrasted with the supposed dourness of the Buddhist world view, so that the ancient Japanese could be seen as an optimistic and life-affirming people. The existence of sexual shrines and the openness of their display was evidence of a national personality trait, a positive element within the 'Japanese-ness' that they prized so highly.

The sexual shrines therefore stayed much as they had been while Japan modernised around them. Some of their physical representation may have been destroyed during World War II, although the extent of the damage is difficult to determine. It is known that the Kanayama Shrine in Kawasaki was razed to the ground during an air raid and fire took almost all the phallic symbols from the Kasajima Shrine.[45] By contrast, the Allied Occupation does not seem to have affected the sexual shrines in any way. Sex was a very important issue at the time, but unlike the Western pioneers of the Meiji Period the occupying troops do not appear to have made any acquaintance with Japan's religious traditions of sexuality, and lively phallic festivals hardly suited the tenor

---

43 Satō 1995, p. 204.

44 Ishigami 2013, p. 280.

45 Kokonoe 1981, pp. 124–126 & 51.

of the age.[46] There was something of a revival of domestic interest during the 1950s when writers on sexuality like Takahashi Tetsu rediscovered Japan's ancient traditions of sexual knowledge from art and folk practices, and as Japan's economic boom developed the restoration of its visual display began.[47] Shrines were repaired and long dormant sexual-related shrine festivals were revived, resulting in the present-day environment within which this study was conducted.

At the same time a new phenomenon was born that would make its own contribution to the context of the acceptability of sexual display. This was the world of Japan's *hihōkan* 秘宝館. The word means 'hidden treasure hall' but is usually translated as 'sex museum', although this is somewhat misleading because the more extreme examples lie at the far end of the spectrum from serious museums of ethnography or even the Taga Shrine's vast collection of erotica. They were characterised by kitsch architecture (the Yumoto Onsen *hihōkan* was designed to look like a Japanese castle), garish colours and a fading tackiness, and are best described as indoor adult sexual theme parks. A typical *hihōkan* included life-sized mechanical tableaux engaging in sexual activity for the amusement and titillation of visitors. Over the years these have involved characters from Japanese history and worldwide popular culture. Marilyn Monroe appeared at three locations. The large central hall of Takeo-Ureshino's *hihōkan* in Saga Prefecture once featured a full-scale animated Roman orgy with lights, water features and music that started automatically when a visitor descended the stairs, and the use of Japanese deities in these set-pieces makes the phallic *Death of the Buddha* look almost respectable.[48] In the Atami Hihōkan mechanical sexual performances by Kannon (who holds a large phallus) and Ebisu (who squirts water from his erect member) are triggered by pressing a button. A pornographic film theatre, photographic displays of sexual shrines and straightforward sex education materials are also usually included. *Hihōkan* may also contain items such as *ema*, *shunga* and ancient sexual aids together with full-sized copies of famous shrine phalluses. They can therefore be very useful for research into sexual beliefs, but the overall emphasis is on entertainment rather than education.

The first *hihōkan* opened in Ise in 1972 and included live shows of horses copulating (a feature mercifully never repeated anywhere else) whereby a stallion

---

46 For excellent accounts of sexual relations at the time see Kovner, Sarah 2012. *Occupying Power: Sex Workers and Servicemen in Postwar Japan* (Stanford) and McClelland 2012.

47 McClelland 2012, p. 180.

48 The topic has been given scholarly coverage in Myōki, Shinobu 2014. Hihōkan to iu Bunka Sōchi (Tokyo).

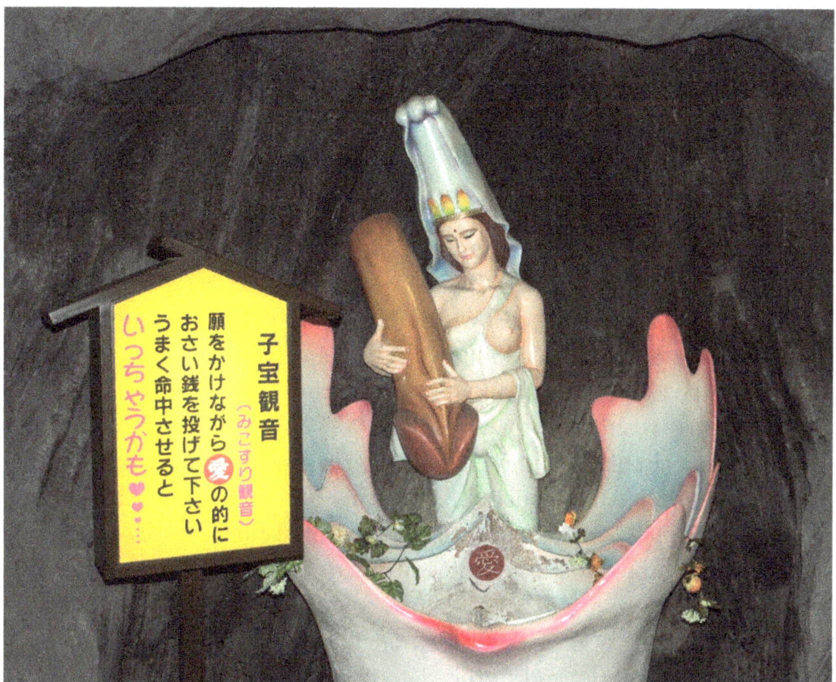

FIGURE 26 *In the Atami Hihōkan there is a plastic statue of Kodakara Kannon who is scantily clad and holding a phallus. Visitors are invited to throw a coin into the lotus in which she stands. With that gesture they will find love.*

was encouraged to mount a tethered mare to the accompaniment of a live commentary.[49] In 1981 Kokonoe included descriptions of eleven *hihōkan* in his guide book, and it might have been expected that in an age when uncensored *shunga* can easily be bought and phallic festivals proliferate the *hihōkan* would be flourishing, but instead they have gone into a rapid decline. Ise was shut in 2007 and the ones at Numazu, Beppu, Yumoto, Numata, Shōdojima, Isawa and Sapporo had all closed their doors by 2013. Takeo-Ureshino Hihōkan sold off all its contents at auction in April 2014 and Kinugawa Hihōden closed in December 2014 for economic reasons. Only the Atami Hihōkan now remains.[50] In all other cases the *hihōkan* have become casualties of Japan's economic decline in just the same way that the economic boom led to their creation and

---

49 From the illustrated souvenir guidebook to the Ise Hihōkan: Funahashi, Kurando 2006. *Ganso Kokusai Hihōkan: Kōshiki Gaidobukku.* (Nagoya), p. 16.

50 The numbers attending the Takeo-Ureshino Hihōkan went down from 45,575 in 1994 to 6,020 in 2013 (Myōki 2014, p. 27). Photographs of the closed *hihōkan* may be found in Shui 2009.

proliferation during the 1970s. Visitors who choose to spend their vacations in hot spring resorts that are themselves in decline are dissuaded from entering the *hihōkan* because of the high admission charges and the obvious signs of neglect shown by peeling paintwork and the growth of weeds. Yet there is another reason for their passing. The *hihōkan* were the *shunga* of the late twentieth century. They were high-tech, colourful and daring, and most importantly in a time when magazine photographs and reproductions of *shunga* were highly and rigorously censored, the *hihōkan* allowed access to an otherwise unattainable world of erotica. Now through the spread of the internet all is freely available at the click of a mouse. This is the new world within which the *hihōkan* have become a quaint and decaying curiosity, an antiquarian exhibit worthy of display within their own premises.

Yet in spite of all this apparent liberalisation some old taboos have not quite disappeared from Japanese society. It was mentioned in the preface to this book that Jūmonji's sexual shrine has been omitted from the town's map of religious establishments. Also, as Ishigami noted in the catalogue to the British Museum's exhibition, even though books containing uncensored reproductions of *shunga* may now be purchased openly, 'including *shunga* in exhibitions is still problematic, and to this date in Japan there has never been an exhibition principally devoted to *shunga* in a public museum or art gallery'.[51] The position is however expected to change in Autumn 2015, when an exhibition of *shunga* based on the one at the British Museum will be mounted at the Eisei Bunko Museum in Tokyo. This will draw to a close the intriguing situation that the exhibition that opened so many eyes in the United Kingdom could not be mounted in a museum in Tokyo, even though certain shrines and temples in the same city had for centuries contained frank sexual images on open display.

---

51 Ishigami 2013, p. 288.

CHAPTER 3

The Phallus in the 'Age of the Gods'

In the year 1623 a diarist noted the finding in northern Japan of an ancient clay figurine. To him and to his contemporaries who discovered similar examples the object was a relic from the 'Age of the Gods', the mysterious time that the accepted mythology placed between the creation of the Japanese islands and the founding of the imperial system. As to the identity of those who created the figure, its location at the northern extremity of Honshū would probably have suggested to him that it was made by the Emishi, the legendary aboriginal occupants of Japan who were regarded as the ancestors of the Ainu.[1] Many thousands of these *dogū* 土偶 (ceramic figurines) have now been found. In terms of dating the seventeenth-century scholars were broadly correct in concluding that they were made long before the creation of the written records that provided the yardstick of official mythology around which they had based their idea of an age of the gods. The *dogū* are now known to date from the Neolithic Jōmon Period (c. 14,500–300 BC). Some depict female figures with breasts, genitalia and swollen abdomens that probably indicate pregnancy, while a few are simple phallic or ktenic symbols.

Pottery appeared in Japan a little over 12,000 years ago and marks the transition from the Palaeolithic Period to the Neolithic, so that Japan's 'Old Stone Age' has sometimes been referred to as the Pre-Ceramic Period.[2] The ensuing ceramic-making Jōmon Period takes its name from the *jōmon* 縄文 or markings made with cords on the surfaces of the fine quality pottery with which the Jōmon people engaged extensively in trade. As the Jōmon pottery tradition is the oldest in world history, to have chosen that feature as the name for the era was very appropriate.[3]

In contrast to the farmers of the subsequent Yayoi Period (c. 300 BC–AD 300), who came to Japan from the East Asian continent with skills of rice cultivation and metal working, the Jōmon people are regarded as forming a simpler hunter-gatherer culture, although there is some evidence for plant and tree cultivation.[4] The absence of farming therefore means that the Jōmon Period

1 Kaner, Simon (*ed.*) 2009. *The Power of Dogū: Ceramic Figures from Ancient Japan* (London), p. 24.

2 Imamura, Keiji 1996. *Prehistoric Japan: New perspectives on insular East Asia* (London), p. 9.

3 Kaner 2009, p. 9.

4 Imamura 1996, p. 13.

 | DOI 10.1163/9789004293786_004

FIGURE 27 *A 'goggle-eyed'* dogū *dating from the Final Jōmon Period (1000–300 BC). Although its body is somewhat out of proportion it seems to possess female sexual characteristics with modest breasts and external genitalia. The large eyes may represent Siberian snow-goggles designed to protect the wearer from snow-blindness. This figure was excavated from the Teshiromori site in Morioka City and was exhibited at Akita Prefectural Museum during 2012.*

cannot be regarded as Neolithic in the conventional sense, yet it was a society that showed a remarkable sophistication in the production of ceramics and stone implements within large scale and well-ordered settlements. There is much evidence to suggest that the Jōmon environment was a rich one of abundant food resources, so that 'nowhere else did human beings manage to support such apparently high population densities prior to the advent of farming'.[5] The change from the pre-ceramic Palaeolithic Period to the Jōmon Period was therefore a technological one characterised by the introduction of pottery, while the change to the Yayoi Period would be an economic one based on the creation of wet-rice paddy fields, leaving behind a rich tradition of ceramics. The production of *dogū* flourished from the Middle Jōmon Period onwards (about 2500 BC) to create a wide range of styles and concepts that now tantalise experts about the possible meaning expressed by about 18,000 surviving examples. The fine detail of their sometimes exaggerated and sometimes very realistic facial features, build, clothing and personal adornment has led to wide speculation among archaeologists over the intentions behind their creation, a puzzle made greater by the fact that some *dogū* were intentionally broken and the fragments relocated over a wide area.

Many *dogū* are of female figures. Some may indicate pregnancy (including one with a clay ball within a representative womb), while others apparently show the act of giving birth, all of which has led to the suggestion that they were intended as symbols of deities of safe delivery.[6] They may even be impressions of a Japanese version of an 'earth mother' or 'mother goddess', an idea that has been heavily debated. The richness of the supportive natural environment around them may also have produced within this settled and stable society a feeling that there was a need for harmony with whatever power produced the fruit and the game. That this relationship could be precarious may also have been suggested by times of temporary shortage, and this may have led to the symbolic representation of benevolent deities in the *dogū* and through the rituals of systematic destruction. Otherwise the breaking of *dogū* could indicate the act of sending off a spirit to some other world. In the absence of any written accounts all these suggestions have to involve in some way a comparison being made with later practices, and Naumann neatly sums up the methodological problem in two concise paragraphs:

5 Kaner 2009, p. 15.

6 Kaner 2009, p. 35.

> The small, realistic phallic clay objects closely resemble similar wooden objects found to this day as votive gifts for certain deities such as Dōsojin, the phallic deity of the roads…
>
> Is it justified to view the phallic clay objects of the Jōmon Period in the light of the recent use of wooden ones? There might have been still other practices, but since none can be proved we must be content to point to the *possibility* that they served as offerings, either accompanying prayers for help in special cases or as an erotic gift to a deity craving it.[7]

One therefore notes that two pottery vessels in Akita Prefectural Museum have spouts of phallic appearance and another even has a scrotum depicted beneath the phallus.[8] These items confirm that there was a contemporary acceptance of phallic display, even if the motivation behind creating them is unknown. Similar considerations apply to an illustration in Nishioka's book that shows a ceramic object made in the overall shape of the letter 'T'. From the side the longer arm is of phallic appearance; on looking from underneath the broad cross piece may be interpreted as the shape of a kteis.[9] This item is remarkably similar to certain objects made from carved stone known as *sekkan* 石冠 (stone crowns). Two are illustrated by Habu. Both may be phallic in one arm but the ktenic element is not discernible from the drawings.[10] Another *sekkan* is on permanent display at Akita Prefectural Museum and shows both characteristics more clearly. Kidder provides drawings of three other phallic-looking examples together with the observation that one excavated 'stone hat or crown' was found placed on the forehead of the remains of a dead body.[11]

Most *sekkan* are more phallic than ktenic in their constituent parts, and only one unquestionably ktenic stone carving appears to have survived. This is the unique representation of female genitalia that was found in 1966 at the Sanjūgari site in Higashi-Yuri (Akita Prefecture). The overall size of the stone, which is a finely detailed carved kteis, is 10.3 cm long by 7.1 cm wide. Satō suggests that through it the people of Sanjūgari were expressing a hope that a woman was strong and sturdy enough for the process of giving birth.[12]

---

7 Naumann 2000, pp. 79–80.

8 The first is from a personal observation made on 29 October 2012. The second is illustrated in Satō 1995, pp. 14–15.

9 Nishioka 1961, Plate VII.

10 Habu, Junko 2004. *Ancient Jomon of Japan* (Cambridge), pp. 150, 157, 158.

11 Kidder, J.E. 1966. *Japan before Buddhism* (Revised Edition) (London) pp. 77–78.

12 Satō 1995, pp. 14–16 and from personal observation at Akita Prefectural Museum on 29 October 2012.

FIGURE 28 *This carved stone object is known as a* sekkan (*stone crown*). *From the side the longer arm is of phallic appearance and on looking from underneath the broad cross piece may be interpreted as the shape of a kteis. This example dates from the Final Jōmon Period* (*1000–300* BC) *and was excavated in Akita City. It is on permanent display at Akita Prefectural Museum.*

Similar considerations may also apply to the *dogū*, and the sexual characteristics of some cannot be ignored. The fine 27 cm tall standing *dogū* known as the 'Tanabatake Venus' from Nagano Prefecture has protruding breasts and a swollen belly, while another *dogū* made with outstretched arms excavated at Ubagasawa in Nagano Prefecture bears a detailed depiction of female genitalia.[13] Yet many figures lack this fine detail, so even though they may involve the depiction of female organs they do not necessarily draw our attention to them in isolation; it is the intention behind the creation of the whole figure that should be considered.[14]

One of those intentions could simply be a personal desire on the part of carvers or potters to express some personal feelings through their craft. Naumann illustrates two clay plaques bearing the imprints of a child's hand and foot. About a dozen examples are known, and some have a hole at one end so that

13 Kaner 2009, p. 101.

14 A consideration explored more fully in Naumann 2000, p. 96.

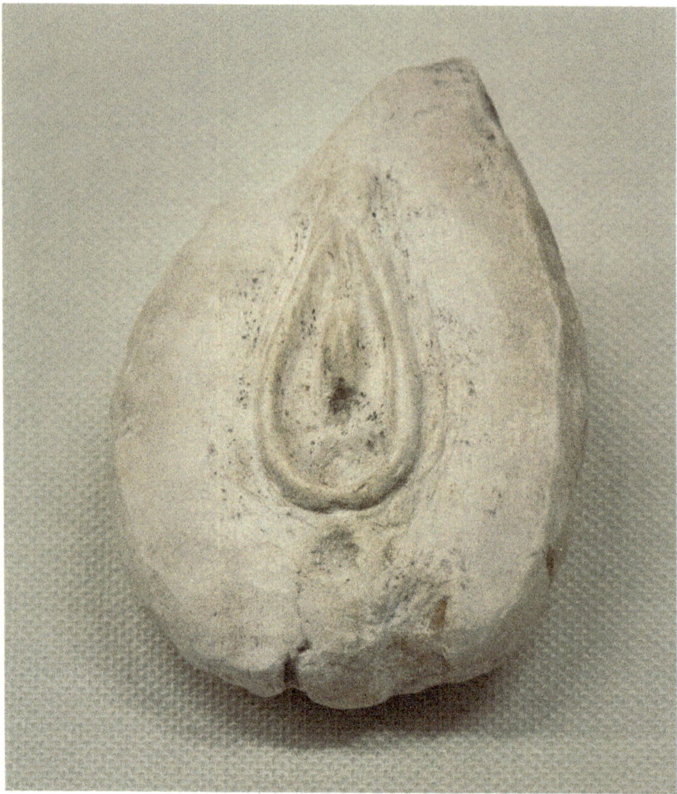

FIGURE 29 *This unique kteis carved from stone during the Jōmon Period was found in 1966 at the Sanjūgari site. The finely detailed carved kteis is 10.3 cm long by 7.1 cm wide. (Akita Prefectural Museum).*

a cord could be threaded through to make a pendant. Naumann states that, 'the meaning … escapes us', but surely they indicate no more or no less than a touching attempt by the maker to preserve the likeness of a much-loved child? Just like the apparently meaningless engraved nutshells illustrated later by Naumann, perhaps the Sanjūgari kteis, in the words she uses to explain these otherwise puzzling decorative items, 'shows Jōmon man from a playful side'.[15] Following this line of reasoning the Sanjūgari kteis could be Japan's oldest surviving object to indicate eroticism and nothing more: a prehistoric *shunga*.

15 Naumann 2000, pp. 48 & 62. I thank Nicole Coolidge Rousmaniere for also drawing my attention to an additional explanation for the child's footprint: that it represents the child having survived the crucial and hazardous first months of life.

The *Sekibō* of the Jōmon Period

Dōgu make up one of two types of apparently sexual prehistoric objects found in Japan. The others are the *sekibō* 石棒, the phallic-shaped 'stone rods' or 'stone bars' that were also made during the Jōmon Period. They vary in size from hand-held items to heavy carved stones over two metres in length. Many have prominent heads reminiscent of the glans of the penis, and uses for them have been suggested that include digging sticks and symbols of authority. At this point Smyer's comment, 'Sometimes a cylindrical object is just a cylindrical object', may well be recalled and applied to the *sekibō* were it not for a wealth of archaeological opinion that accepts a phallic role for these most phallus-like of ancient artefacts. The purpose that lay behind the carving of them can of course only be inferred, but more importantly for this present work, unlike the *dogū* many of the ancient *sekibō* that were subsequently unearthed over a period of many centuries went on to acquire an indisputable sexual function. This came about when they were installed as the central feature in certain phallic shrines that still exist today. The most phallic styles of *sekibō* discovered in this way may well have been interpreted by their finders as very special gifts from a powerful sexual *kami*.

Sekibō have survived in large enough numbers to allow some form of classification to be made and certain common conclusions to be drawn. For example, Inamura concluded that, 'the religion of the Jōmon period seems to have been based around sexual themes', and even sceptics recognise the strength of certain evidence.[16] Kitagawa acknowledged that such finds had 'led others to conclude that there must have been belief in phallicism', while Naumann accepted that, 'this [phallic] interpretation cannot easily be pushed aside'.[17] Many *sekibō* are indeed very phallic in appearance, and Kidder decided that a *sekibō* would be 'too consistently phallic in nature to have had its beginnings only as a small pestle for pulverising wild grain and nuts, and the long ones, that may reach 5 feet in length, are impractically heavy for normal use'.[18] Habu sees an important male/female divide between them and the *dogū*:

> While clay and stone figures are generally considered as representations of females, scholars suggest that stone rods (*sekibō*) represent male sexuality. Because the shape is reminiscent of male genitals, many scholars believe that, just like clay figurines, stone rods are essentially a symbol of

16 Imamura 1996, p. 97.

17 Kitagawa 1963, p. 32; Naumann 2000, pp. 79–80.

18 Kidder 1966, p. 56.

FIGURE 30 *The tip of a* sekibō *from the Middle to Late Jōmon Period on display in the Yokoze History and Folk Museum in Yokoze (Chichibu City, Saitama Prefecture). This example has the 'glans' at one end only, making it look very phallic.*

> fertility. Others ... suggest that stone rods are specifically related to hunting rituals conducted exclusively by men.[19]

Most of the excavated *sekibō* are associated with the characteristic individual Jōmon pit dwellings. Many have been examined in Nagano Prefecture where the Yatsugatake archaeological site once provided a rich environment for the Jōmon people. Included in this area was the Tanabatake settlement (the site where the 'Venus' was discovered), which consisted of clusters of dwellings made by excavating a pit and putting a thatched roof over it on wooden supports. Most of these pit dwellings had fireplaces often surrounded by stones from the river bed and containing one small standing stone of a phallic shape.[20] Stone circles are also known, of which the most famous example is at Ōyu in Akita Prefecture. The Nonakadō Circle's arrangement with one large standing

19 Habu 2004, p. 151.

20 Kaner 2009, pp. 37–38.

stone of vaguely phallic shape and four stones at the cardinal points has been compared to a sundial.[21]

Other *sekibō*, by contrast, are finely carved and have been polished to precise cross sections. The larger category, measuring between 5 and 20 cm in diameter and sometimes more than one metre in length, are associated with the Middle and Later Jōmon sites, while the smaller ones are associated with Late and Final Jōmon sites. They often possess a distinctive rounded end that adds considerably to their phallic appearance, although sometimes this shape appears at each end which makes the object look much less phallic. Habu also notes two variations on the overall shape of the smaller *sekibō* that depend upon the shape of the cross section. Flatter stone rods with a more oval cross section are referred to as *sekken* 石剣 or stone swords, while those of a curved triangular and knife-like cross section are called *sekitō* 石刀 (single-edged stone swords).[22]

Twenty-eight *sekibō* were recovered from the Sankōjindaira site in Akita Prefecture alone.[23] *Sekibō* have also been found within the burial complexes in Hokkaidō that have a circular embankment, which has led to the suggestion that these were the graves of shamans.[24] *Sekibō* were clearly much in demand among the Jōmon people, as shown by the discovery of a production site for them at the Kinsei Jinja site in Gifu Prefecture. The presence of 800 finished and unfinished *sekibō* there suggests that the ease of working led the site to be used for a form of mass-production of these items.[25] Although he did not have access to modern archaeological discoveries, Nishioka discusses at some length the number and shape of *sekibō* both in the form of the shaft itself and in that of the head and provides drawings of fourteen different shapes of *sekibō* and forty-four different styles of head. He concludes that there was some connection between their phallic shape and the ceremonial occasions on which they were used. They were perhaps also weapons and signs of authority, but Nishioka firmly believed that they were somehow related to the idea of fertility.[26]

21 Satō 1995, p. 14; Naumann 2000, p. 37.
22 Habu 2004, pp. 151–153.
23 Kaner 2009, p. 36.
24 Habu 2004, pp. 187–189.
25 Habu 2004, p. 235.
26 Nishioka 1961, pp. 87–88.

FIGURE 31 *This large* sekibō *is known as Oshakuji-sama and is associated with prayers for conception. It sits within the courtyard of the Honsenji in Saitama City.*

The Discovery of *Sekibō* and the Attribution of Phallicism

Even if all the speculation by archaeologists is wrong and the *sekibō* were not phallic symbols at all and were only ever used as tools or signs of authority, the important point about them in connection with the present work is not how they may have been used in the Jōmon Period but how they have been used subsequently as phallic symbols, a development that never happened with any *dogū*. They appear in this role today as *goshintai* in shrines or as highly prized loan phalluses, although this does not imply any continuity with what may have happened in prehistoric times. This aspect of their history can only be traced back as far as their discovery, when the adoption of a new role for these ancient artefacts came about simply because an association was made between their phallic shape and contemporary beliefs relating to phallic symbolism. So, for example, a *sekibō* might be unearthed during the excavation of a drainage ditch or some other building project, and one such instance is noted by Masuta. The find, recorded by the antiquarian Hirao Rosen for the Tempō Era (1830–44), was of a 'strange stone' of a phallic shape inside an earthenware pot that had been dug out of a ditch.[27]

27 Masuta 2006, p. 144.

It is sometimes difficult to reach a decision based on observation alone as to whether a particular enshrined phallus is an ancient carved *sekibō* or a stone that nature alone has rendered into its final shape. Local tradition based upon its provenance is often the only reliable guide, but it is important to note that an identification of what one might loosely call a phallus from heaven has been placed upon both types of stones. This is because any attribution as a heavenly gift with a divine nature is closely linked to wider beliefs concerning the means of a *kami*'s arrival in the world of humans. Simply put, *kami* can travel from 'there' to 'here' across the invisible barrier that divides their world from ours. *Kami* may come of their own free will, bursting unexpectedly into our realm, or they may be summoned by some human intervention and then persuaded to stay and make the human sphere their abode. For this to happen there must be some defined object that is either natural or man-made which the *kami* might then possess or in some other mysterious way occupy so that through it communication may be achieved. Such a thing bears the ancient name of *yorishiro* 依代, which Grapard compares to a 'support' or even a 'landing site', a useful metaphor if employed with caution.[28] The *yorishiro* may be a large natural object such as a curiously shaped rock at the foot of a mountain where a *kami*, many of whom were believed to dwell in mountains, might be persuaded to rest after a dramatic descent. Otherwise Blacker draws our attention to objects such as a branch held in a shaman's hands, thus conjuring up a delicate and persuasive image of a *kami* descending like a bird to settle peacefully and contentedly on an outstretched human finger.[29]

During the early stages of the development of beliefs in *kami* their arrival in the world of humans was seen as the start of a temporary visit, with the *kami* remaining only as long as its presence was required for the performance of the ritual for which it had been summoned. In time this gave way to the notion that the *kami* could be found a lasting home, so the temporary *yorishiro* became the more permanent *goshintai* 御神体 or more simply *shintai* 神体, the (honourable) 'body of the god'. This object provided a location within the world of mankind for the *kami*, or, in some interpretations, the *kami*'s *mitama* 御霊 or spirit, a distinction examined by Aston:

> It is clearly not the Sun-Goddess herself who lives in Ise. Her true place is in Heaven; but she is present in some way on earth, as is proved by

---

28 Grapard, Allan G. 1982. 'Flying mountains and walkers of emptiness: toward a definition of sacred space in Japanese religions' *History of Religions* 21, p. 197.

29 Blacker, Carmen 1975. *The Catalpa Bow: A Study of Shamanistic Practices in Japan* (London), p. 38.

FIGURE 32 *It is sometimes difficult to tell whether a phallus is a carved* sekibō *or a naturally occurring stone. Local tradition is often the only guide, as shown by this example, the phallic stone identified locally as a* sekibō *and known as the Tōsō Dōsojin. It is located at the Hoshoku Shrine in the Tōsō district of Kagoshima City.*

> her answering the prayers which are addressed to her at her shrine. The explanation which is ultimately forthcoming is that it is the *Mitama*, or spirit of the Goddess which resides there. We have here a foreshadowing of the doctrine of the omnipresence of deity.[30]

Aston also quotes from Shintō scholars who strove to understand the distinction. Motoori Norinaga wrote of, 'the thing, be it a mirror or aught else, to which the divine spirit attaches itself', while Hirata Atsutane envisaged that the deity was like a fire that could be communicated to a lamp or to firewood while the original fire remained the same.[31] In the present context this *kami/mitama* distinction is less important than the result of the process, because the

30 Aston, W.G. 1974. *Shintō the Way of the Gods* (Reprint) (New York), p. 27.

31 Aston 1974, pp. 32 & 34.

entry of a *kami* can take the phallic object far beyond any simple representative role to the achievement of a divine nature. When this is accomplished the object and the *kami* are indistinguishable in their ability to provide benefits in response to intercession, a notion that will be discussed more fully later in the context of the worship of Konsei Daimyōjin.

Some *goshintai* are man-made objects kept securely hidden deep in the safest recesses of the shrine, wrapped up for centuries so that their identity has become lost even to their closest guardians. Others are natural objects such as an ancient gnarled tree or a small stone that nature has fashioned into an appearance that proclaims something holy about them. Blacker notes that long and thin objects were popular choices for *yorishiro* and *goshintai*, a role that would be fulfilled perfectly by the discovery of a phallic-shaped *sekibō*.[32] The appropriate response would then be to enshrine it as the *goshintai* of the deity that it was or somehow represented. This devotional role is still being played by some *sekibō* to this day, but it is important to note that there is no uniformity or inevitability as to how they were and are used. Those that did not find their way into museums have clearly received special treatment and protection among the local communities where they were found, but this does not necessarily mean that they are all venerated in any clearly understood sense. A mere note in a book or on a website indicating that a *sekibō* is to be found in a Buddhist temple, a Shintō shrine or even just the open air gives little indication as to how the object is actually preserved, displayed or regarded. Even Japan's largest, the Kitasawa Sekibō 北沢石棒 in Saku (Nagano Prefecture) stands alone on a path between some rice fields at the place where it was found and no shrine protects it.[33]

Some *sekibō* do play a clear role as phallic symbols and have been installed as such in Buddhist temples and Shintō shrines, and their presence in the former suggests that the forceful separation of the two traditions that occurred during the Meiji Restoration was not total.[34] Two are preserved in temples located quite close to each other on the Bosō peninsula of Chiba Prefecture. One is at the Enchōji and stands within a stone *hokora*. The other at the Ennyoji occupies a position to the rear of the main temple hall. It is simpler than its neighbour and may be missing its head, but here it acts as the *goshintai* of Konsei Daimyōjin and thus receives a degree of veneration not found in examples that have not received that attribution.[35] A similar association with

32 Blacker 1975, p. 38.

33 From a personal observation made on 15 November 2012.

34 Satō 1995, p. 171.

35 From a personal observation made on 17 November 2012.

FIGURE 33 *Japan's largest* sekibō *is the Kitasawa Sekibō located near Haguroshita (Nagano Prefecture). It is 2.3 metres tall and was recorded as early as the year 1622.*

Konsei Daimyōjin is made for a *sekibō* in Kakunodate (Akita Prefecture) that stands in a small wooden shrine within a Buddhist graveyard. Satō suggests that as the graveyard belongs to the neighbouring Buddhist temple the Konsei Daimyōjin may have been an object of worship prior to the separation process of the Meiji Restoration.[36] In Kanagawa Prefecture an ancient *sekibō* acts in a protective role at a crossroads in Shimokuzawa in Sagamihara City. It has been

36 From a personal observation made on 22 April 2012.

FIGURE 34 *The* sekibō *at the Enchōji on the Bosō peninsula of Chiba Prefecture stands in the open air within a three-sided stone enclosure built to protect its one metre-tall body.*

set firmly into a large supporting stone but a cage has been erected around it to keep this wayside guardian from being damaged by passing traffic.[37]

As for larger-sized *sekibō*, the Fuji Sengen (or Asama) Shrine 富士浅間神社 dedicated to the goddess of Mount Fuji near Kotobuki (Yamanashi Prefecture) has in its precincts a small shrine for conception containing a large

37 From a personal observation made on 12 March 2014.

FIGURE 35 *This* sekibō *acts in a protective role at a crossroads in Sagamihara City (Kanagawa Prefecture) but has had to be protected from the traffic by a cage.*

sekibō lying on its side, half-concealed by a red cloth.[38] A further example is a large and heavy *sekibō* that provides one of several interesting phallic displays at the historic Makibori Shrine 巻堀神社 in Iwate. It lies on its side with its tip resting above a ktenic stone bowl within the shrine grounds.[39] A *sekibō* may also be the explanation for the curious *kaname ishi* 要石 at the Kashima Jingū 鹿島神宮 in Ibaraki Prefecture. This stone protrudes from the ground and is

38 From a personal observation made on 12 November 2012.

39 From a personal observation made on 3 November 2012.

FIGURE 36 *The Mishima Shrine* sekibō *on the Bosō Peninsula of Chiba Prefecture has four votive wooden phalluses placed in front of it.*

FIGURE 37 *The* sekibō *at the Itakura Shrine near Ashikaga in Tochigi Prefecture lies at an angle, supported by two concrete pillars at 45 degrees and pointing towards a ktenic rock. Nishioka includes a photograph of it from the mid-twentieth century which shows that it was then standing upright by being wedged into what looks like rough concrete. A sign relates that the* sekibō *is 1.57 metres long and provides for family needs and match-making.*

said to be the end of a long stone that a *kami* used to pin down the head of the mythical giant catfish that causes earthquakes.[40]

Sekibō in Life and Death

A more intimate use of *sekibō* is to be found in Aomori Prefecture in a localised development of the religious tradition of Awashima-sama 淡島様 (also Awashima Daimyōjin 淡島大明神 or Awaji Myōjin 淡路明神), the name given to a deity said in some accounts to be a child of Izanagi and Izanami, whose efficacy for women's ailments was promulgated during the seventeenth century by itinerant priests:

> … carrying a small altar enshrining Awaji Myōjin from which pieces of coloured cloth were hung. As these priests walked around a village, they proclaimed in loud singing voices the healing power of this deity for "the illnesses of women below the belt".[41]

Gerald Groemer describes the object carried by the priests in words that make it sound more phallic as a 'staff with reddish-purple paper strips topped off by a miniature shrine'.[42] A unique feature in Aomori is the use of *sekibō* dressed in tiny kimono. They are known as *hōseki* 抱石 (embracing stones) and are found in an Awashima Shrine in Aomori City. In 1685 the then priest discovered in the mountains a number of phallic stones and brought them back to the shrine where a tradition of belief in their efficacy developed. Their reputation grew and they were formerly placed on show at festivals. The stones are believed to ensure an easy delivery but are also used by a woman who is concerned about her fertility. She may simply pray to the *kami* that they represent, but there is also an old tradition whereby the woman will place one of these dressed stones within her clothing, and if the 'stone baby' starts to sweat that is taken as an indication that she is capable of having children. Nowadays about ten wrapped *hōseki* may be seen in a small compartment. One was unwrapped for my inspection and certainly looked like a *sekibō*, although it could just

40 Kokonoe 1981, p. 79.

41 Ohnuki-Tierney 1984, p. 163.

42 Groemer, Gerald 1999. 'The Arts of the Gannin' *Asian Folklore Studies* 58, p. 285.

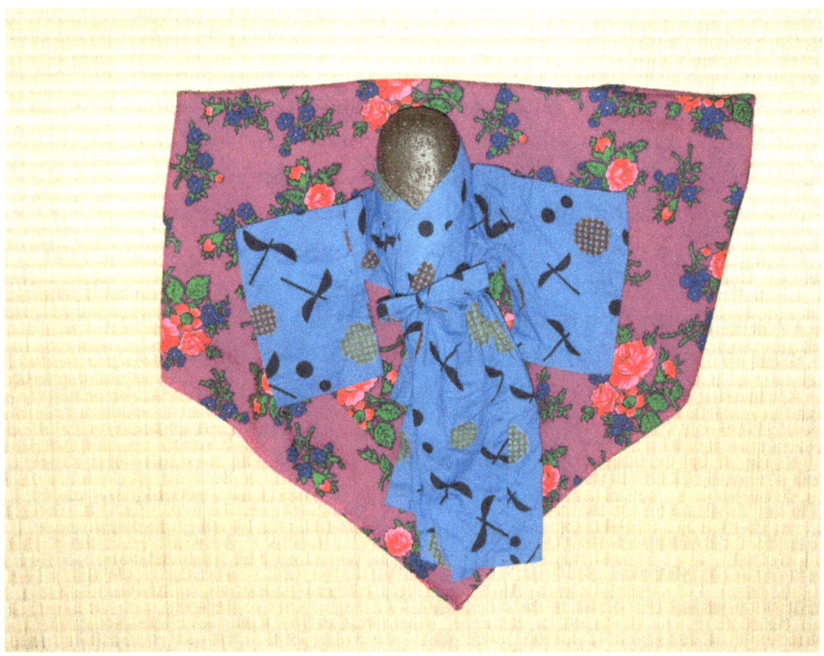

FIGURE 38 *In the Awashima Shrine in Aomori are* sekibō *that are known as* hōseki (*embracing stones*). *They are believed to ensure an easy delivery but are also used by a woman who is concerned about her fertility. She will place one of these dressed stones within her clothing, and if the 'stone baby' starts to sweat that is taken as an indication that she is capable of having children.*

have been a stone of a natural phallic shape. A framed photograph on the wall depicts some satisfied mothers.[43]

An object that sounds very similar to a *hōseki* provides a possible explanation for one of the most enigmatic stories to appear in the folk tales collected in Tōno (Iwate Prefecture) during the first half of the twentieth century. It appears in *Tōno Monogatari Shūi*, the appendix of 299 stories added in 1935 by Sasaki Kizen to Yanagita Kunio's classic *Tōno Monogatari*, the anthology of folk legends originally told to him by Sasaki. The item in question is the *sekibō* that now forms the *goshintai* of the Komagata Shrine 駒形神社 in Ayaori Town.

43 From an interview conducted with the caretaker of the shrine on 5 November 2012 and Masuta 2006, pp. 174–175. Two other shrines in Aomori Prefecture contain *hōseki*. The first, a small sub-shrine on private land in Namioka Town contains two wrapped-up *sekibō*. The second is a shrine in Hachinohe, where two *hōseki* are on display along with a number of other sexual-related items including phalluses.

The building is kept locked and the object cannot be seen, but a photograph of it appears in the illustrated guidebook *Tōno Monogatari Sekai*. It is known as Okoma-sama 御駒様 and is a *sekibō* with a small head and a broad elongated body, making it look somewhat like a baseball bat, although it is impossible to gauge the scale of it from the picture.[44] Perhaps surprisingly, this enshrined *sekibō* is only mentioned in passing in the puzzling foundation legend for the shrine related by Sasaki as Tale 15 of his collection. Noting only that an *ishigami* 石神 (stone god) 'of male appearance' known as Okoma-sama is venerated at the shrine, he goes on to say that at the time of seed-transplantation many years ago the young women working in the fields were approached by a traveller who was passing by. He bore upon his back a mysterious expressionless child with no eyes or nose, covered in a red cloth. The traveller stayed at the place where the Komagata Shrine now stands. It was built there when he died.[45]

In Japanese folk religion the image of the stranger is often an ambiguous one. The outsider who arrives and enters a community can be seen as good or evil, but the visitor to the Tōno village brought only benefits to the community through the special powers he possessed.[46] When the strange visitor died a shrine may well have been built to console his spirit, but an additional local tradition, recorded on the notice board in front of the shrine, makes a link between the two parts of Sasaki's story by relating the belief that the *goshintai* of the shrine was a thing he left behind.[47] Thus the visit of a mysterious stranger provides the explanation for the presence in the shrine of the phallic *sekibō*. It was the 'strange expressionless child carried on his back', a description that makes the enshrined *sekibō* sound like a *hōseki*. A possible explanation of the story could therefore be that the traveller was an itinerant priest who was carrying with him a *sekibō* with certain powers. One of the girls received it from him for some reason related to her child-bearing needs. The traveller made his home there and when he died the local people raised the shrine to him and installed the miraculous *sekibō* as the *goshintai*.

Miyata Noboru, however, envisages a very different explanation whereby the mysterious child with no ears or eyes is a euphemism for the traveller's

---

44 Ishii Masumi 2010. *Tōno Monogatari Sekai* (Tokyo), p. 79.

45 Yanagita Kunio 1955. *Shinpon Tōno Monogatari fu Tōno Monogatari Shūi* (Tokyo), p. 86.

46 See Yoshida, Teigo 1981. 'The Stranger as God: The Place of the Outsider in Japanese Folk Religion' *Ethnology* 20, pp. 87–99. The point is also summarised in Yoshida, Teigo 2007. 'Strangers and pilgrimage in village Japan' in Rodríguez del Alisal, Maria, Ackermann, Peter and Martinez, Dolores P. (eds.) *Pilgrimages and Spiritual Quests in* Japan (London), p. 48.

47 From a personal observation made on 2 November 2012.

kyokon 巨根 (abnormal penis), an organ so massive that he was incapable of normal sexual intercourse and therefore unable to find a mate. In his retelling of the Tōno story Miyata states that the village girls take pity on the traveller and build a hut where he can live, where they take turns consoling him. Having known kindness only in this village, the man returns the favour after his death by becoming a preventative *kami* for women's illnesses.[48] Humorous stories of men who possess abnormally large penises predate the depiction of huge genitalia in erotic prints.[49] The interpretation also fits in with Miyata's other ideas concerning the efficacy of the phallus, but it does not explain the presence of the phallic-shaped *sekibō* inside the shrine. He may of course be quoting a more authentic version of the story which was subsequently sanitised for publication, but nowhere does he make this clear. The word *kyokon* is repeated in Ishii's description of the *sekibō* in the guide to Tōno, but again there are unfortunately no references given that would enable one to trace back this version of the story any further.[50]

A very revealing account of another ancient *sekibō* and the widely differing attitudes these objects might provoke is related as Tale 16 of the same continuation volume of *Tōno Monogatari* where Sasaki tells of a particular stone god that caused problems in the village of Tsuchibuchi. The object was a *sekibō* that stood in the middle of a farmer's field. It was believed to heal women's illnesses, but the farmer was determined to get rid of it. We are not told why; was it perhaps just a reaction again visits by worshippers who trampled his crops? Yet when the farmer began to dig round it he discovered human bones. Fearing a curse, he prudently left the *sekibō* undisturbed. Sasaki concludes the story by telling of two other places in the Tōno area where, according to his informants, *sekibō* were known to mark the sites of graves, although none can now be identified.[51] One interesting feature of this story is the difference in attitude towards the *sekibō* as displayed by the local women who sought its help and the farmer who attributed no respect towards the *sekibō* until it was revealed as a grave marker. It was fear of the spiritual power of the dead, not the *sekibō* itself, which led to it being left undisturbed.

48 Miyata 1983, pp. 108–109.

49 Schalow, Paul G. 1996. 'Response to the Panel: "The Rhythm and Play of Flesh and Words" in Jones, Sumie (ed.) *Imaging/Reading Eros: Proceedings for the conference, Sexuality and Edo Culture, 1750–1850 Indiana University, Bloomington August 17–20, 1995* (Bloomington), p. 141.

50 Miyata 1983, pp. 108–109; Ishii 2010, pp. 79 & 110.

51 Yanagita 1955, p. 87.

The presence of *sekibō* at grave sites is by no means uncommon and the rich finds of *sekibō* that were associated with graveyards led Satō towards his theory that they were originally placed on the liminal boundary between the world of the living and the world of the dead to protect the living from the spirits of the dead.[52] *Sekibō* have therefore continued to provoke feelings of awe and reverence throughout history, whatever might subsequently be done with them. They are still being unearthed in the twenty-first century, and to judge by the homepage of the local newspaper of Fuchū (Toyama Prefecture) they still provoke the same feelings of respect and an unqualified association with phallicism. In 2002 a *sekibō*, minus its head but measuring 56 cm in length and with a weight of 22 kilograms was excavated in the village of Dōjima. During early 2010 discussions were held about creating a 'Sekibō Festival' to pray for a good harvest and family harmony. The centrepiece of the festivities, a large-sized wooden replica of the discovered *sekibō* that was 1.2 m in length and weighed 15 kg, was created and plans drawn up whereby it might be carried in an event that would bring benefits to the local economy.[53] The scheme was agreed and the first Sekibō *matsuri* was held in October 2010.[54]

It may therefore be concluded that whatever might have been their significance to the Jōmon people, *sekibō* have for many centuries been adopted for use in shrines that involve sexual beliefs. They were accorded special reverence because of their phallic shape and their mysterious origins, and it may have been believed that no human hand had ever fashioned them. They could therefore become the ideal *goshintai* for a sexual *kami*, and thus the vehicle for the manifestation of that *kami*'s influence on human needs. Yet there was no inevitability about this, and although the respect they have received seems universal throughout Japan, to extend their treatment beyond mere respect to an association with religious belief and ritual would appear to be governed entirely by local sentiment.

---

52 Satō 1995, pp. 11 & 79.

53 http://www.toyama.hokkoku.co.jp/subpage/T20100209203.htm (Accessed 12 October 2012).

54 http://www.toyama.hokkoku.co.jp/subpage/TH20110213411.htm (Accessed 12 October 2012).

CHAPTER 4

Phallic Beliefs and Mountain Deities

In a remote location beside the narrow forest road that snakes around Mount Miyuki to the east of Fukushima City stands a large wooden phallus. It appears to be alone, but a brief examination of the site reveals another phallus, this one worn and decayed, standing on slightly higher ground a few metres away. A path is discernible between them that continues upwards into the dense undergrowth, where a climb of about ten minutes along the overgrown track reveals a possible answer as to why the phalluses are there, because to the side of the path beside a fallen tree stands a small stone shrine to Yama no kami 山の神 the deity of the mountains, whose name is engraved upon a large boulder.

There are many other shrines to mountain goddesses (or mountain gods, because both genders are involved in the narrative) in Japan today, and certain

FIGURE 39 *On one side of Mount Miyuki near Fukushima City is an overgrown path marked by two wooden phalluses. The track leads uphill past a shrine to Yama no kami, the deity of the mountains.*

 | DOI 10.1163/9789004293786_005

aspects of the tradition may reveal something as old as the devotional practices inferred from the existence of *dogū* and *sekibō*. There may even be a direct connection between Yama no kami and *sekibō* through the practice of hunting, because Habu's discussion of these items notes the suggestion made by other archaeologists that *sekibō* might be specifically related to hunting rituals conducted exclusively by men.[1] Like these concrete items, Yama no kami belief is likely to be a survivor from a pre-agricultural age, and a unique phallic element of the cult recorded as late as the twentieth century adds a further dimension to the topic of Japan's sexual gods.

Nelly Naumann believed that Yama no kami worship constituted a 'very old layer within the whole [of] Japanese folklore', and, in the oldest layer of all, the mountain deities were considered to be female and were 'moody, jealous and lewd'.[2] Naumann tells us little more about these jealous goddesses, who represent what Carmen Blacker describes as an 'older, feminine form' of the more common type of Yama no kami now to be found among agricultural communities. The earlier version was the goddess of those whose livelihoods required them to go into the mountains to hunt or to gather wood, a concept that may be contrasted with the later development of the divinity who descends from the mountain in spring to become the rice-field god and returns to the mountain in autumn.[3] The differentiation by type probably reflects a differentiation by time, with the hunters' deity being gradually replaced by a god that served the needs of agriculturalists as farming spread with the Yayoi Period while hunting declined as the primary means of survival.

As will be discussed below, there is evidence of a blending between the two traditions as time goes by, but among modern hunting communities some unique beliefs surrounding 'their' goddess may still be identified. This older female type of mountain deity never leaves the mountain and is therefore only approached both physically and ritually by hunters, charcoal burners and woodcutters. Of the three the hunters are the most important group to consider because their role involved taking life within her domain. A rich tradition of ritual therefore developed that was based around the need to obtain permission from the goddess to carry out the hunter's craft. Yama no kami was therefore paradoxically at one and the same time the protector of animals and the bringer of good luck to their hunters, a contradiction explained by myths that

1 Habu 2004, p. 151.

2 Naumann 1963, p. 342; Naumann 2000, p. 79.

3 Blacker, Carmen 1996. 'The Mistress of Animals in Japan: Yamanokami' in Billington, Sandra and Green, Miranda (eds.) *The Concept of the* Goddess (London) p. 184. See also Sasaki, Kome 1971. *Inasaku izen* (Tokyo), pp. 243–250.

told of the hunters' ancestors rendering help to the mountain goddess in times past and being granted this privilege in return. In spite of this her permission still had to be sought on a regular basis and was only granted if the hunters met certain criteria and displayed certain behaviours before, during and after an expedition, of which the most important elements were male exclusivity and ritual purity.[4]

Belief in Yama no kami in this earlier form survives today among the *matagi* マタギ, the hunting communities of Tōhoku. The *matagi* were once shunned as people who lived on the fringes of civilised society, a status that derived partly from the ancient Buddhist prohibition against eating the meat of four-footed creatures. At one time no one from a farming community would intermarry with them, and even today during their hunts a further level of segregation takes place when the exclusively male hunting group moves away from its own community to live in the mountains in small huts. While on the mountain the mountain goddess will protect them as she also protects the animals, and there are certain very complex conditions to be fulfilled if the hunter

FIGURE 40 *The interior of the Yama no kami Shrine in Animatagi (Akita Prefecture), showing a statuette of the goddess who was at one and the same time the protector of the animals and the giver of permission for the hunters to operate on her mountain.*

4 Naumann 1963, p. 342.

wishes to receive a blessing and not her curse. Certain words are prohibited from being uttered on the mountain and others are required in their place, creating thereby a hunters' language. The hunt itself must also be conducted according to very strict rules. No pregnant bear must be killed; the dead animal must be laid out for dismembering in a precise manner and prayers of thanks offered to Yama no kami both before and afterwards.

The hunters' Yama no kami is unquestionably female, but she does not always appear as a woman to those lucky or unlucky enough to meet her, because she may choose to reveal herself as an imperious version of the prey she protects such as a mysterious pure white deer or even as a dragon. When she takes her true form she may be young and beautiful, only to transform herself in the twinkling of an eye into Yamauba 山姥, an old hag with a mouth that splits open from ear to ear, a character responsible for many legends and folk tales.[5]

The mountain goddess is also very demanding. The hunters will go to enormous lengths to bring her the gift of a certain fish called *okoze* オコゼ (the

FIGURE 41 *This undated photograph in the Animatagi Folk Museum shows a group identified as the last traditional* matagi *hunters in Japan. They are from Niigata Prefecture and are posed with their kill.*

5 Murakami, Kenji and Mizuki, Shigeru 2005. *Nihon Yōkai Daijiten* (Tokyo), pp. 335–336.

stonefish, *Synanceia verrucosa*). It is an ugly creature and may have been chosen for the role to provide a contrast to the beauty of Yama no kami, but the most important beliefs about her preferences lie in her relationship to women, because Yama no kami is violently jealous of other women and none of the female sex may trespass on her mountain. No item belonging to a woman such as a towel may be taken along by a hunter, and newly married men are discouraged from participating.[6] Prior to setting off on a hunt a man must avoid contact with a menstruating woman and men must abstain from hunting for a week after their wives have given birth.[7]

Judging by her jealous character and these associated rituals the hunters' mountain goddess comes across as the product of a very male-dominated society, and nowhere is this more vividly suggested than by certain elements in the hunters' traditional behaviour, because Yama no kami traditionally delights in the sight of a penis. However, unlike all the other examples of phallicism described in this book, the hunters' rituals once involved the display by a novice hunter of his sexual organ rather than any symbolic representation of it. The sight was regarded as bringing her much pleasure. She was then even more willing to protect and grant the wishes of the young men who had otherwise fulfilled all her ritual requirements.

Descriptions of penis-exposure rituals are provided by Miyata Noboru (who draws on the research of Chiba Tokuji) and Wakamori Tarō.[8] Miyata writes about the *matagi* of Akita Prefecture. On the night when the bear hunt was to begin, the young *matagi* who were gathered in their mountain hut would open their garments to expose their penises, to which they tied embers from the fire using hemp cords. Despite the fire and the smoke the young men would roast their members until the veins swelled up abnormally. At a command from the leader the ordeal would cease.[9] This is very similar to a ritual noted by Wakamori for Niigata, although he makes no association with Yama no kami:

---

6 Blacker 1996, p. 181.

7 Earhart, H. Byron 1970. *A Religious Study of the Mount Hagurō Sect of Shugendō: An Example of Japanese Mountain* Religion (Tokyo), p. 14.

8 Miyata 1983, pp. 110–111; Wakamori, Tarō 1963. 'Initiation Rites and Young Men's Associations' in Dorson, Richard M. (ed.) *Studies in Japanese Folklore* (Bloomington) p. 295. Miyata's work is not based on first-hand observation but draws from work by Chiba which Miyata acknowledges, citing in particular a publication dated 1975 (Miyata 1980). Chiba and Wakamori are probably referring to observations made at the latest in the early 1960s.

9 Miyata 1983, p. 111.

> And in Miomote village in Niigata-ken, the test was an extraordinary one: A half-burned end of firewood or charcoal was hung from the penis as a simultaneous examination of the initiate's manly endurance and sexual virility.[10]

Miyata is probably describing this very ritual when he writes also that in the mountains that now lie within the administrative area of Shibata City in Niigata Prefecture an initiation ritual was held for the young hunters who were gathered in the mountain hut for the first time. On their third day there the novice *matagi* would tie an ember using hemp cords to their exposed penises and pass beneath a *torii*. Through this ritual the young *matagi* became the disciples of the Yama no kami.[11] Miyata then discusses the ideas that lay behind these dramatic and painful acts. The exposure of the penis was first of all an initiation rite that signified the approval of the mountain goddess for a novice hunter to enjoy his share of the spoils, but it was also a device that firmly emphasised the exclusion of women both from the hunt itself and from the mountain goddess's fiercely protected domain. There was also an element of bravado, of showing the young hunter's courage in facing up her strict rules on the mountain.[12] Yet underlying these human aspirations was the belief that because she was a jealous and lascivious woman the mountain goddess enjoyed the sight of a penis, and that by her delight at seeing one she would be willing to protect the hunters and grant their desires.[13]

It is highly unlikely that such a ritual is performed nowadays, a conclusion I base on a report from the unpublished fieldwork of David Ranzini, who interviewed 'Mr S', a member of the *matagi* community of Akita Prefecture in 2013. In personal correspondence with the author Ranzini writes:

> I asked him about rituals in general and he revealed that his father, who taught him to hunt, deliberately chose not to reveal any of the secret rituals he knew, for reasons Mr. S wasn't willing to speculate on. He also told me that since he had researched *matagi* himself since then he'd heard about the phallic rituals, but had never participated, and felt certain that his father's generation wasn't practising them, passing them on, or even mentioning them to their children when he began as a hunter in 1961.[14]

---

10 Wakamori 1963, p. 295.
11 Miyata 1983, pp. 110–111.
12 Miyata 1983, pp. 113–114.
13 Naumann 2000, p. 79.
14 From personal correspondence of 21 July 2013.

Other folk beliefs exist that indicate that the sight of a penis can have a similarly positive effect on the behaviour of *kami* who enjoy such a spectacle. Naumann notes that there is an erotic element in the rituals of woodcutters, who share some of the behaviours of the hunters, but she gives no examples.[15] Miyata adds penis-exposure rituals among fishermen, who are of course hunters,[16] and this is also discussed briefly by Masuta Kimiyasu in his compendium of folk beliefs in Aomori Prefecture. He states that the young fishermen ritually exposed themselves on the high seas, a rite that had nothing to do with the reproductive role of the male member and everything to do with male energy and bravado.[17] In their 1967 book Itō and Richie claimed that in the former Province of Bingo (modern Hiroshima Prefecture) there was a belief that if Kōjin-sama, the deity of the kitchen, made the rice-pot boil too vigorously, he could be quieted by the man of the house showing him his exposed organ. They also mention a festival once performed in Takatsuki, possibly for the goddess Benten, where the men carrying the *kami*'s palanquin exposed themselves for her delight.[18] A *kami* that brought rain might also receive similar treatment. Miyata writes that at times of drought in a certain village in Okayama Prefecture when conventional prayers to the local *kami* had failed to bring rain, males of the village from old people to children would strip naked and smear their faces with white face powder. In this state of anonymity they would visit the *kami* and dance, flourishing their exposed penises.[19]

Mountain Deities and Farming Communities

Miyata Noboru identifies another consequence of the mountain goddess's delight as being an increase in her fecundity. For the hunters this would be shown by plentiful spoils, but the reference to fecundity, Miyata believes, shows a shift towards the image of Yama no kami that is more associated with agricultural communities than hunters. In the *matagi*'s unique form of phallicism the sight of a penis had an effect on the attitude and behaviour of the mountain goddess, but any symbolism involving the act of sexual intercourse was conspicuous by its absence. It is only with the coming of agriculture in the

15 Naumann 1963, p. 343.
16 Miyata 1983, pp. 100–101.
17 Masuta 2006, pp. 140–142.
18 Itō and Richie 1967, p. 107.
19 Miyata 1983, p. 110.

Yayoi Period that the tradition changes in response to the different needs of farming people.

With this change an association was made between the human sexual reproductive force and the productivity of the fields. Itō suggests that ritualised copulation was once carried out, but Miyata stresses instead the notion of the harmonious balance of the male and female principles. In the case of Yama no kami the symbolism changes from the brief and brave exposure of the penis prior to a few days of hunting to the permanent display of a sexual symbol beside the location of the longer-term process of growing food. These objects, which may include depictions of human coitus, would enhance the field's fertility by sympathetic magic. The mountain deity is now not merely the imperious ruler of the domain. He or she is also the benevolent provider of water that flows generously in the streams that pour down to irrigate the fields, the protector of water sources and the provider of rain, and there has been an interesting development whereby the god is no longer confined to the mountain. In a beautiful expression that acknowledges the reality of the seasons we encounter the notion of the deity coming down from the mountains in the spring to become the rice field god. She then returns in autumn to become the mountain deity once again.[20]

Although maleness is possible, the overwhelming imagery presented by the farmers' Yama no kami is still female, and one manifestation of her is held in common by both hunters and farmers. This is the naming of the mountain goddess as Jūni-sama 十二様 'Honourable Lady Twelve'. In the case of the hunters' Yama no kami twelve is her mystical and private number and is so jealously guarded that the hunting party must never consist of exactly twelve people. Her festival day on the twelfth day of the twelfth month is so ritually precious that her hatred for other women reaches its peak on that date, and at one time women in the *matagi* communities would not venture out of doors on that day.[21] Yet there is a gentler association, because once a year she gives birth to twelve children who symbolise the twelve months of the year, and the connection with birth makes her also into a goddess of easy delivery. If a woman was having a difficult labour her husband would lead a horse towards the mountain to receive the goddess and a special symbol would then be hung by the woman's bedside. Often this was a rice spoon acting as a phallic symbol.[22]

---

20 Miyata 1983, pp. 109–110; Hori, Ichiro 1966. 'Mountains and their importance for the idea of the other world in Japanese folk religion' *History of Religions* 6, pp. 7–8.

21 Blacker 1996, p. 181.

22 Hori 1966, p. 17.

FIGURE 42 *In a shrine near Hachinohe the mountain goddess is named as Jūni-sama (Honourable Lady Twelve). She gives birth to twelve children who symbolise the twelve months of the year.*

Another feature held in common with the hunters' rituals was the offering of fish, which further indicates a merging of the two traditions.[23]

The modern image of Yama no kami is therefore predominantly that of a benevolent earth mother, yet in spite of the gift of fertility through her annual transformation the later mountain deity may still be feared as much as the original hunting goddess. Like all *kami* she still needs to be kept in a positive frame of mind through the offering of gifts. Neglect may lead to disaster, a belief reflected in the use of the term Yama no kami as a 'half-disrespectful, half-joking term' for one's wife. 'Behind this popular usage', writes Earhart, 'is a clue to the *yama no kami*'s power of sexuality and fertility'.[24] Some of the special fear of Yama no kami is explained because the notion of her as a shape shifter has persisted from the earlier hunting environment where she could transform herself into something terrifying. Several folk tales relate how people

23 Earhart 1970, p. 12.

24 Earhart 1970, p. 13. See also Miyata 1983, p. 100.

have encountered Yama no kami and been cursed rather than blessed by her, and the area around Tōno is a particularly rich environment for this. In Tale 89 of *Tōno Monogatari* Yanagita Kunio describes a surprise meeting with a Yama no kami at the hill in Tsujibuchi on which stands the Atago Shrine 愛宕神社. In Morse's translation:

> The face looking at the youth was bright red, had radiant eyes, and indeed contained an expression of surprise. The youth knew it had to be the mountain *kami*, and he ran off to Kashiwazaki without ever looking back.[25]

In a footnote Yanagita notes that there are many stones bearing the inscription 'Yama no kami' in the Tōno area. They mark the places where people have either met a Yama no kami or have received a curse from one. No less than four still stand below the Atago Shrine.[26] Another mountain *kami* with a red

FIGURE 43 *These stones at the foot of the hill on which stands the Atago Shrine in Tōno bear the inscription* yama no kami *and record encounters with the mountain goddess, meetings that can be either positive or terrifying.*

25 Morse, Ronald A. (trans.) 2008. *The Legends of Tono (100th Anniversary Edition) by Yanagita Kunio* (Plymouth), p. 52; The original tale is in Yanagita 1955, pp. 53–54.

26 From a personal observation made on 2 November 2012; See also Ishii 2010, p. 9.

face appears in Tale 107, while Tale 108 tells of people being possessed by Yama no kami and performing divination.[27] Tōno also illustrates how localised the Yama no kami are. Tale 2, which reflects the notion of jealousy expressed by the mountain dwellers' Yama no kami, relates how a *kami* came to the area with her three daughters:

> Before going to sleep the mother *kami* told her daughters that she would give the best mountain to the one who had the finest dream ... Each of the three young female *kami* took up residence on her own mountain, and even now they rule over these mountains. Women in Tōno are told, even today, not to climb these mountains lest they arouse the jealousy of these *kami*.[28]

Phallic Symbolism in Yama no kami Shrines

Shrines to Yama no kami may be found all over Japan and it is likely that the vast majority of them represent the farmers' type.[29] One that is without question still associated with a hunting community lies in Animatagi (Akita Prefecture), the village that has developed into a centre for the study of Akita's *matagi* traditions. The shrine stands across the road from the rather touristy complex that the place has become, and contains a stone statuette of female appearance that represents the deity. No phalluses are to be seen, which is in keeping with the *matagi* tradition that it is the sight of a penis that she enjoys, not a representation of one.[30] Similar carved figures may be found elsewhere. A white banner bearing the inscription 'Jūni yama no kami' and the date of its painting, the goddess's festival day of 12 December 1981, hangs inside one shrine near Hachinohe. Next to the flag is a small modern wooden statuette depicting the mountain goddess as a young woman, but there are no phallic symbols. The Yama no kami shrine on a hillside below the modern Fukushima to Yonezawa road has a small wooden statue that shows a deity of indeterminate gender. In the Isonokami Shrine 石上神社 in Tōno there is a statue of Yama no kami as a goddess, but the deity is otherwise depicted within the same general area as a fierce-looking male god.[31]

27 Morse 2008, p. 63.
28 Morse 2008, p. 12.
29 Sasaki 1971, pp. 243–246.
30 From a personal observation made on 8 August 2008.
31 Ishii 2010, p. 46.

FIGURE 44 *The interior of the Yama no Kami Shrine beside the road from Fukushima to Yonezawa showing offerings and a small statuette that may be of the deity.*

FIGURE 45 *In the Isonokami Shrine in Tōno the deity of the mountains is shown as unmistakably female.*

There is no phallic display in any of these examples, but phalluses may be found elsewhere. Sadly, what must have been one of the most interesting examples of a phallic Yama no kami shrine has recently been changed out of all recognition owing to the building of a new road and the felling of the beech tree that once provided the *kami*'s *goshintai*. This use of a tree reflects a tradition associating Yama no kami and woodcutters in that she was believed to dwell in certain trees which should not be cut down.[32] The shrine, now totally rebuilt, lies beside the new road that heads up from the village of Nagate to the east of Yonezawa City in Yamagata Prefecture. Its original appearance is described by Kokonoe as lying deep within a wild area and enshrining a female Yama no kami to whom no women paid any visits, and the devotion offered to her shows a merging of the two types into one. Storms on the mountain were regarded as evidence of her anger, but she was pleased when men worshipped her. In front of the beech tree was a small *hokora* that acted as a receptacle for offerings of stone and wooden phalluses. The goddess was regarded as descending in spring and ascending in autumn, and to add to her benefits to the rice field she was also believed to bestow safe delivery, relief from sexual illnesses and a successful match. Two other large phalluses once stood like sentries on either side, but none is visible now.[33]

Phalluses are however still to be found at a few Yama no kami shrines elsewhere in Japan. Naumann states that in Hachinoe, where the Yama no kami could be both male and female, a ktenic object would be presented to the male variety of the god, although I have found no examples of this.[34] In various districts of Shiga and Nara Prefectures there is a tradition of making phallic and ktenic objects from small bifurcated tree branches for use in Yama no kami worship events. For the male a stick with three branches is selected and the central branch is carved into a rudimentary phallus. In some areas cute faces are added to the main trunks. The couples are placed together in a situation of copulation as part of the rituals.[35] Kitahara illustrates similar

32 Naumann 1963, p. 343.

33 Kokonoe 1976, p. 147 and from a personal observation made on 1 November 2012.

34 Naumann 1963, p. 224.

35 For the Kōka area of Shiga see Kokonoe 1981, p. 215. There is a permanent exhibition about this type of local Yama no kami worship at the Rittō City History and Folk Museum in Shiga Prefecture. Between January and March 2015 a temporary exhibition on the same theme was held at the Nara Prefectural Folk Museum. (From personal observations made on 3 & 17 February 2015). See also Rittō City History and Folk Museum 2001. *Kikaku ten Matsuri, matsuri, sairei*, (Rittō, Shiga Prefecture), pp. 21–32.

examples from Nagano and compares them to the small wooden protective gods produced by the Ainu.[36]

Large phalluses are found at two present-day Yama no kami shrines. The important Yaegaki Shrine 八重垣神社 in Matsue (Shimane Prefecture) has a Yama no kami shrine that was rebuilt in 2004. Several wooden phalluses lie in a bucket underneath it and a very prominent large phallus quickly catches one's attention. The main complex enshrines the *kami* Susano-o and the maiden whom he rescued from the eight-headed serpent in the well-known story. It has acquired a reputation for matters associated with marriage.[37] A popular tradition invites worshippers to float a five-yen coin on a special sheet of paper (purchased from the shrine) in the pond to the rear of the precincts. The length of time it stays afloat indicates how long one must wait to acquire a partner.

Lafcadio Hearn described the Yaegaki Shrine at some length in *Glimpses of Unfamiliar Japan*, beginning with words, 'Unto Yaegaki-jinja, which is in the village of Sakusa in the Land of Izumo, all youths and maidens go who are in love, and who can make the pilgrimage'.[38] Hearn did not mention the phallic Yama no kami shrine, an omission simply explained by the statement on the shrine's notice board that it was moved to the Yaegaki Shrine 'during the Meiji Period', from which one may assume that this happened after Hearn's visit. The phallic shrine is also not featured in the Yaegaki Shrine's glossy brochure, even though sexual-related beliefs are stressed in the pamphlet and the shrine itself is very visible. This apparent coyness probably reflects a desire on the part of the shrine committee not to distract worshippers from focussing on its principle *kami*.[39]

Much less visited is the Yama no kami Shrine in Saida (Mie Prefecture). Its small wooden *hokora* stands just in front of the apex of a cleft formed by an overhanging and progressively narrower cliff face above a river. It contains a small phallus, but of greater interest is the offering of a large wooden phallus about 180 cm long that is made in December every year. This is placed at an angle of forty-five degrees at the start of a flight of rough steps. The previous year's phallus is then removed and added to the line of progressively decaying phalluses that snake up towards the focal point. Twenty-nine were so arranged by 2013.[40]

36 Kitahara 2014, p. 266.

37 Aston 1972, pp. 55–56.

38 Hearn, Lafcadio 1894a. *Glimpses of Unfamiliar Japan Volume I* (London), p. 294.

39 From a personal observation made on 06 June 2013. For a photograph of the shrine before the rebuilding see Kokonoe 1976, p. 148.

40 From a personal observation made on 14 June 2013.

FIGURE 46 *This shrine to Yama no kami is located within the precincts of the Yaegaki Shrine in Matsue City.*

To summarise this chapter, the worship tradition of Yama no kami presents an interesting example of continuity and change within Japanese sexual beliefs. Although much has to be inferred from comparatively modern practices

FIGURE 47 *Phallic votive offerings are placed in this receptacle located underneath the shrine to Yama no kami at the Yaegaki Shrine.*

FIGURE 48 *The Yama no kami Shrine in Saida (Mie Prefecture), showing the current year's offerings placed at the apex of the cliff that shelters the shrine to the right. Previous years' offerings can be seen along the path.*

it would appear that the Yama no kami cult began at a time prior to written records to honour a fierce mountain goddess whose favour the hunters had to solicit and who took pleasure in the sight of the male sexual organ. With the coming of agriculture the emphasis changed to her benevolence as the provider of water, although the fear of her never quite went away. Her transformation at spring and autumn expresses the passing of the seasons, and her new role reflects the principle of sexual harmony, which in a few places has involved the use of phallic symbolism.

CHAPTER 5

Sexual Symbolism and Shintō Mythology

To modern eyes the *sekibō* of the Jōmon Period appear to be phallic symbols, although the intentions that lay behind that shape can only be inferred. Within a few centuries, however, the first unquestionably phallic object in Japanese history can be positively identified. It is found on a *haniwa* はにわ, an example of the clay figures placed within the large earthen tombs called *kofun* 古墳 from the third century onwards. The ancestors of the present imperial line were buried in these *kofun* and an important characteristic of the grave goods found within them was the presence of *haniwa*, which may have had a protective role after death. One excavated in Gunma Prefecture is of a male figure with an erect penis, so for the first time in Japanese history an apparent phallic symbol may be firmly identified as a representation of the male sexual organ by virtue of it being attached to a body. Yet just like the supposedly phallic *sekibō* there are no written records for this unique figure, so once again the overall intention behind its creation and any specific relationship that it may have had to religious beliefs can only be surmised.

The first written records from which sexual beliefs may be inferred date from the early eighth century. In the year 710, inspired by the example presented by contemporary Chinese civilisation, the dominant Yamato line established Japan's first permanent capital city at Nara, and among other significant developments the rulers ordered the compilation of two great collections of mythology: the *Kojiki* 古事記 and the *Nihongi* 日本記. The former, which was written in Japanese, was finished in 712 and recounts in lively style the creation myths of the Japanese people, their history, customs and religious practices. The *Nihongi* appeared eight years later in Chinese and contains additional material that shows considerable influence from Chinese thought, some of which was intended as a corrective to the *Kojiki*. These works performed an important political function by providing the justification for the existence of the ruling imperial family and the governance of Japan through the emperors. Yet they also represented a reaction to a religious upheaval, because Buddhism, introduced to Japan only a century earlier, had been established as a State religion alongside the indigenous traditions. This event sparked a re-assessment of what had gone before: a belief system that was still respected and treasured and would later be given the appellation of Shintō as a means of distinguishing it from the imported tradition.

 | DOI 10.1163/9789004293786_006

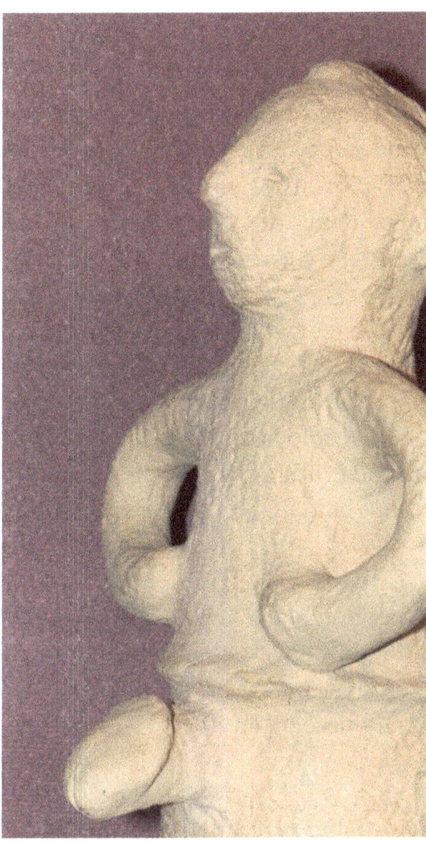

FIGURE 49
From the third century AD *onwards the ancestors of the present imperial line were buried in large mound tombs called* kofun. *One important characteristic of the grave goods found within* kofun *was the presence of* haniwa (*clay figures*). *One excavated in Gunma Prefecture is of a male figure showing an erect penis. This is a copy of it in the Atami Hihōkan.*

A huge contribution was made to Shintō by the *Kojiki* and *Nihongi*, where we encounter for the first time written accounts of the greatest *kami* of all. Their mythology often has a pronounced sexual flavour, and the *kami* described there are enshrined as sexual gods in certain places today on the basis of these stories, although the characters and the themes they represent were by no means newly created when the myths were written down. As Naumann puts it, 'archaic thoughts of worldwide distribution like those present in the said myths were not newly invented ... they might reach back for millennia'.[1] There is therefore the possibility, at the very least, that the stories about them may go back beyond the *Kojiki* and the *Nihongi* to provide a link to ancient sexual beliefs similar to those inferred from the existence of *sekibō* and the religious traditions of Yama no kami.

1 Naumann 2000, p. 81.

The Mythology of Izanagi and Izanami

The *Kojiki* begins with the creation of the universe and the heavenly deities, who simply come into being. They are followed by a male and female pair of deities called Izanagi no Mikoto 伊奘諾尊 ('the male deity who invites') and Izanami no Mikoto 伊奘冉尊 ('the female deity who invites'). Izanagi and Izanami first create the islands of Japan and the gods who are to become the ancestors of the imperial house for whom the *Kojiki* was compiled and whose ruling position was thereby justified. Yet Izanagi and Izanami do not merely generate from nothing. Instead their means of creation is of a very human kind, and a thinly disguised sexual metaphor appears early on in the story when they are commanded by the heavenly deities to 'solidify' the unformed land that had up till then had been like 'floating oil and drifting like a jellyfish'.[2] For this purpose they are given use of the *ame no nuboko* 天之瓊矛 (the jewelled spear of heaven) and:

> [They] stood on the Heavenly Floating Bridge and lowering the jewelled spear, stirred with it. They stirred the brine with a churning-churning sound, and when they lifted up the spear again, the brine dripping down from the tip of the spear piled up and became an island. This was the island Onogoro.[3]

The account of the island's creation in the *Nihongi* is practically identical, and in a long accompanying footnote to the floating bridge scene Aston makes clear his identification of the jewel spear as a phallic symbol.[4] Katō agrees with him and quotes in support the Tokugawa Period scholar Satō Nobuhiro (1767–1850):

> The Ame no Nuboko, or 'Heavenly-Jewel Spear', which the Ancestral Deities in Heaven bestowed upon Izanagi and Izanami had the shape of a phallus, so that the divine couple got a suggestion through it and were overjoyed in their nuptial union, begetting different gods successively ... Without a male and a female principle nothing on earth can be born and grow ... So it is quite natural and reasonable, thanks to the unseen protection of the August Producing Divinity, that all sentient beings are sexually connected ...'[5]

2 Philippi, Donald L. 1969. *Kojiki* (Princeton), p. 47.

3 Philippi 1969, p. 49.

4 Aston 1972, pp. 11–12.

5 Katō 1924, pp. 8–9.

The island of Onogoro, created from the congealed or solidified brine, then becomes the base for further acts of creation, and again these are not acts of spontaneous generation because Izanagi has sexual intercourse with Izanami and she gives birth. The description of their 'first sexual act' (in Satō's words)[6] is in fact so explicit that the prudent Buckley felt he could only present it to the readers of *Phallicism in Japan* in a Latin translation:[7]

> At this time [Izanagi no Mikoto] asked his spouse Izanami no Mikoto, saying: 'How is your body formed?'
>
> She replied saying, 'My body, formed though it be formed, has one place which is formed insufficiently'.
>
> Then Izanagi no Mikoto said, 'My body, formed though it be formed, has one place which is formed to excess. Therefore I would like to take that place in my body which is formed to excess and insert it into that place in your body which is formed insufficiently, and [thus] give birth to the land'.[8]

After walking ritually around a central pillar, identified by some scholars as another phallic symbol, the two deities copulate and Izanami gives birth, first to islands and then to deities.[9] The story then takes a sad and dramatic turn, because their first-born is deformed and finally Izanami dies giving birth to the fire god. While enduring the agonies of dying Izanami vomits and out of the vomit grow Kanayama Hiko and his sister Kanayama Hime, two *kami* whom we will encounter later in a sexual context. Izanami is then taken to the underworld. Wishing to meet her again, Izanagi makes the perilous journey, but the sight of her in a state of decomposition leads him to flee in terror, pursued by numerous horrors. To make good his escape Izanagi places various objects in the path of his pursuers, all of which were to find later expression in the form of the *sai no kami* or blocking gods. He first drops his staff which was to become the protective *kami* Kunado 久那斗. He then pulls peaches off a tree:

> ... he took three peaches which were there and waiting for [his pursuers] attacked [them with the peaches]. They all turned and fled. Then Izanagi no Mikoto said to the peaches; 'Just as you have saved me, when, in the

6 Satō 1995, p. 17.
7 Buckley 1895, p. 23.
8 Philippi 1969, p. 50.
9 Philippi 1969, p. 398.

> Central Land of the Reed Plains, any of the race of mortal men fall into painful strain and suffer in anguish, then do you save them also.'[10]

The demons may have been thwarted but then his dead and terrifying wife comes in pursuit of him. Izanagi realises that distraction will not be enough for her so he pulls over a boulder, described as one requiring a thousand men to move it, and closes off the passageway. Naumann sees the blocking as a magical act, but Philippi believes that Izanagi's rock is used to block physically the passage of Izanami, rather than doing so in any supernatural sense.[11] This boulder will become the most powerful of the blocking deities and would later take the form of a rock placed at the boundary between this world and the next, or simply at the crossroads outside a village that represented the point of departure from the inhabited area. Protective images of a phallic nature are commonly traced back to this primeval item.

FIGURE 50 *The Yomotsu Hirasaka in Shimane Prefecture is supposed to be the site of the entrance to the underworld, and indeed the sight of this enormous boulder, associated with the one Izanagi set in place to prevent evil spirits from pursuing him, provides a suitable atmosphere. The mythical boulder is regarded as the precursor of the blocking deities.*

---

10 Philippi 1969, p. 65.

11 Naumann 2000, p. 81; Philippi 1969, p. 65.

The Descent of the Gods

Izanagi and Izanami thus provide Japanese mythology with its first sexual couple, and shortly afterwards they are joined by the female *kami* Ame no Uzume no Mikoto 天鈿女命 and the male Sarutahiko 猿田彦.[12] Ame no Uzume is the first to be introduced. There is some disagreement over the derivation of her name and suggestions have been made that the 'uzu' derives from *usu* 臼 (mortar) so that she is symbolically the female counterpart to the phallic-shaped pestle that enters the mortar in a manner reminiscent of sexual intercourse.[13]

Ame no Uzume is first encountered when she performs a vital role in the creation myths. In a well-known account Amaterasu, the female *kami* of the sun, is terrified by the violent behaviour of her brother Susano-o and takes refuge in a cave, thereby plunging the world into darkness. The other deities try desperately to persuade her to come out. Their tactics include the making of gifts by the blacksmith *kami* Amatsumara who has at times been identified as a phallic *kami* when *mara* in his name is written using the characters 麻羅.[14] Ame no Uzume plays a crucial part in gaining Amaterasu's attention. As Aston notes with profound understatement, the *Kojiki* version 'gives other details of the conduct of this Goddess which the *Nihongi* draws a veil over'.[15] She 'became divinely possessed, exposing her breasts, and pushed her skirt-band down to her genitals'.[16] There is no indecent exposure in the *Nihongi*. Instead Ame no Uzume holds a spear which may be a phallic symbol.[17] Amaterasu is curious at the uproar she can hear outside, at which Ame no Uzume tells her that a deity superior to Amaterasu has joined them. Unable to resist taking a peek at the new arrival, Amaterasu looks out, not realising she is gazing into a mirror and seeing her own face reflected. While she is thus distracted another *kami* seizes her and pulls her out, thus restoring light to the world.[18] The narrative then takes an important turn because up to this point the gods have been confined to heaven. They are now to descend and possess the earth, and

12 Satō 1995, pp. 20–25.

13 Philippi 1969, p. 460. A similar imagery regarding the pestle and mortar in other cultural traditions is discussed in Stone 1927, pp. 57–58.

14 Philippi believes that it is a later addition derived from 'priestly cant of the late Nara and Heian Periods' (1969, pp. 82 and 454).

15 Aston 1972, p. 45.

16 Philippi 1969, p. 84.

17 Aston 1972, p. 44; Satō 1995, pp. 21–22.

18 Philippi 1969, p. 85.

Amaterasu commands her 'August Grandchild' Prince Ninigi to take the lead in this momentous task, but there is a problem:

> When he was about to descend one, who had been sent in advance to clear the way, returned and said:—'There is one God who dwells at the eight cross-roads of Heaven, the length of whose nose is seven hands, the length of whose back is more than seven fathoms. Moreover a light shines from his mouth and from his posteriors. His eye-balls are like an eight-hand mirror and have a ruddy glow like the Akakaguchi'.[19]

This frightening deity of earthly origin is Sarutahiko. He stands for the old gods whom the new gods wish to supplant or, in the words of Philippi, a 'priestly figure of the earthly deities performing a magic rite to keep the heavenly deities out'.[20] Sarutahiko is also the divine guardian of the crossroads, a living barrier as formidable as Izanagi's boulder. He is so terrible in his appearance that none of the deities dares confront him, but if Sarutahiko cannot be faced down at least he might be seduced. This task is given to Ame no Uzume because she is assured by her fellow gods that, 'Thou art superior to others in the power of thy looks'.[21] She therefore attracts Sarutahiko's attention in a similar manner to that she adopted for Amaterasu by baring her breasts and pushing the band of her garment below her navel. She squares up to him with a mocking laugh, at which the terrible Sarutahiko explains meekly that his intentions towards Prince Ninigi are peaceful because he has come to be an escort for him, a task in which he invites Ame no Uzume to participate. She returns to heaven to report the event and accepts just this commission from Prince Ninigi, who descends as planned and is escorted through the land by her and Sarutahiko:

> Now the August Grandchild commanded Ame no Uzume no Mikoto, saying:—'Let the name of the Deity whom thou didst discover be made thy title'. Thereupon he conferred on her the designation of Sarume no Kimi.[22]

Nishioka sees Ame no Uzume as an archetype of the female shaman, and a footnote in Philippi's translation of the *Kojiki* version of the story suggests that Ame no Uzume's role in confronting Sarutahiko equates to that of a female

19 Aston 1972, p. 77.
20 Philippi 1969, p. 138.
21 Aston 1972, p. 77.
22 Aston 1972, pp. 76–78.

FIGURE 51 *The encounter between Sarutahiko and Ame no Uzume whereby the descending gods from heaven were reconciled with the earthly gods is re-enacted in a mechanical tableau at the Kinugawa Hihōden.*

shaman performing a counter-rite to Sarutahiko's actions similar to that performed by the ancient female shamans supposedly sent ahead of an army to use their ritual powers against an enemy.[23] Yet whatever additional interpretation may be placed upon this story Sarutahiko and Ame no Uzume are henceforth joined forever in a mystical marriage with a common purpose. The old gods of earth are not displaced. Instead they are happily absorbed through the union of this couple from the two realms. Confrontation is replaced by cooperation as the old earth deities of the Jōmon Period join the gods brought with the farmers of Yayoi.

The earth now has its own fertile couple who beget children just as Izanagi and Izanami once did, and the two of them continue to represent the themes of protection and procreation in numerous shrines throughout Japan to this day. Sarutahiko and Ame no Uzume are also a well-travelled pair of *kami* and are the enshrined deities of the Tsubaki Grand Shrine of America in Granite Falls, Washington, an hour's drive from Seattle. In the shrine's brochure they are described as a 'wedded couple' with Sarutahiko being the 'primal earth

23 Nishioka 1961, pp. 116–117; Philippi 1969, p. 138.

kami of guidance, positiveness and protection' and Ame no Uzume acting as the *kami* of 'arts and entertainment, harmony, mediation and joy'.[24]

The Creator *kami* as Sexual Gods

Even though the stories of the two divine couples include sexual behaviour there is no overt sexual imagery in either the *Kojiki* or the *Nihongi*. The jewelled spear is usually identified as a phallic symbol and the great boulder as a precursor to the phallic blocking deities, but it is not until the compilation of the *Kogoshūi* 古語拾遺 in 807 that an actual phallic symbol is mentioned in a written account. This work is by Imbe Hironari and was written as a way

FIGURE 52 *At the Tsubaki Grand Shrine of America near Seattle the* ema *bears a painting of Sarutahiko, the primeval earthly deity who was to acquire an important role in both procreation and protection.*

---

24 From the brochure of the Tsubaki Grand Shrine of America, 17720, Crooked Mile Rd, Granite Falls, WA 98252, kindly supplied by Kyle Barghout.

of proclaiming his family's pre-eminence over their rivals concerning matters of imperial religious functions. The phallic symbol is intended to appease a wrathful god:

> On one occasion in the Divine Age, when cultivating rice in a paddy field, Ōtokonushi-no-Kami served his men with beef, while the son of the Rice-God Mitoshi-no-Kami, when visiting that field, spat in disgust upon the dainty offered to him, and returning home, reported the matter to his father. Then Mitoshi-no-Kami in wrath sent a number of noxious insects, or locusts, to Ōtokonushi-no-Kami's paddy field to kill the young rice-plants and in consequence the leafless rice-plants appeared like *shino* or short bamboo grass.

Divination is carried out, which reveals that Mitoshi no Kami will be appeased by the offering of a wild white boar, a white horse and white domestic fowls. Mitoshi no Kami is indeed placated by these offerings and gives instructions to the farmers as to how the locusts can now be driven away. He ends his advice by saying, 'if, nevertheless, they will not retreat, place some beef at the mouth of the ditch in the field together with a phallic symbol'. It is explained in parentheses that the phallic symbol is 'to appease the divine wrath'.[25] With this reference we have the first mention of a phallus performing one of the three functions identified for the phalluses seen today in shrines to Japan's sexual gods, suggesting that by the early ninth century the use of a phallus in a votive role was already an accepted ritual practice.[26]

These stories in the *Kojiki*, the *Nihongi* and the *Kogoshūi* may represent an ancient tradition of sexual beliefs that predate Shintō, but all that can be said for certain is that sometime in Japanese history the behaviour of the *kami* described in their narratives was interpreted in a way that supported beliefs in the mysterious power of sexual symbolism over procreation and protection. The situation has continued to the present day. For example, Izanagi and Izanami are sometimes associated with large naturally occurring outcrops of rock that have phallic and ktenic shapes, although any manufactured sexual symbolism of them tends to be suggested rather than explicit, probably owing to their close association with the imperial line. So instead of a phallic symbol at the Taga Great Shrine 多賀大社 (Shiga Prefecture) the *ema* on which prayers for needs relating to human reproduction and family matters are written take the vaguely phallic shape of a rice spoon with an image suggestive of

25 Katō and Hoshino 1926, p. 48.
26 Katō 1924, p. 5.

a kteis.[27] Exceptions to this general principle can be found, but such objects tend to have their origins in popular erotica rather than religious devotion. One from the thirteenth century is on show in the Ryōsenji Treasure Museum in Shimoda (Shizuoka Prefecture) and consists of statuettes of the pair on top of a rock that is made from a number of protruding phalluses. The face of Izanagi is a phallus and the face of Izanami is a kteis.[28] On rare occasions such depictions have been placed in shrines. For example, the artist Hokusai once produced an erotic drawing of the two *kami* in a phallic and ktenic guise. The drawing was used as the design for a large-sized votive *ema* now displayed at the shrine to the female sexual *kami* Ohana Daigongen お花大権現 at Eguchi (Tokushima Prefecture).[29] A similar reticence is shown at most establishments

FIGURE 53 *At the Taga Great Shrine in Shiga Prefecture, where Izanagi and Izanami are enshrined, the* ema *on which prayers for needs relating to human reproduction and family matters may be written takes the vaguely phallic shape of a rice spoon, with a tiny image impressed upon it that also suggests a kteis.*

---

27 From a personal observation made on 3 May 2012.

28 From a personal observation made on 11 November 2012.

29 From a personal observation made on 11 June 2013.

FIGURE 54 *In this votive painting at the Ohana Daigongen the design showing Izanagi and Izanami with phallic and ktenic faces has been taken from an original concept by the* ukiyo-e *artist Hokusai.*

dedicated to Sarutahiko and Ame no Uzume, and nothing at all sexual may be encountered at Japan's most important Sarutahiko Shrine in Ise (Mie Prefecture) unless one counts the paper *gohei* 御幣 beside the ritually important rice field.[30] In another possible exception the Shinmei Shrine 新明神社 in Wakayama City has a large vertical sliver of rock in its grounds. The stone bears Sarutahiko's name and may suggest an abstract phallus.[31]

Sexual imagery for Sarutahiko and Ame no Uzume is nowadays most noticeable when they are acting as protectors of the wayside.[32] This is best appreciated in Hita (Ōita Prefecture) where there is a local tradition of using *in'yōseki* 陰陽石 (paired phallic and ktenic stones) to represent the couple in their protective role. One prominent pair stands just inside the *torii* of Hita's Yasaka Shrine. Another is at a crossroads and a third consists of a long phallic stone and a perfectly spherical ktenic stone.[33] Other shrines to the couple include

30 From a personal observation made on 14 June 2013. According to Hashimoto primitive Shintō derives from sex worship and the shape of the *gohei* after it has been cut and folded from a paper rectangle is a phallus (1976, Plate 1).

31 From a personal observation made on 1 May 2012.

32 From a personal observation made on 1 May 2012.

33 From personal observations made on 4 June 2013.

FIGURE 55 *A* gohei *at the Sarutahiko Shrine in Ise. After it has been cut and folded from a rectangle, it might be seen as having the appearance of a phallus.*

the Sai Shrine 賽神社 at Gonoura on the island of Iki (Nagasaki Prefecture), where a huge wooden phallus acts as a protective *sai no kami*.[34]

The earliest recorded tradition of Sarutahiko and Ame no Uzume acting as guardian *kami* refers to the Sai no kami Yashiro 幸の神社 in Kyoto. This is the ancient 'Izumo Road Shrine', although the main thoroughfare of Imadegawa Street (the old Izumo Road) has shifted a little way to the south in modern times. It is Japan's oldest recorded guardian shrine and was written about as early as 672. A century later it grew in importance because it was in the perfect position to provide protection from evil for the imperial palace when the capital was transferred from Nara to Heian-kyō (modern Kyoto) in 794. Ancient beliefs in geomancy stated that the northeastern quarter was the direction from which evil was most likely to emanate, and this little protective shrine fortunately lay in that precise orientation to the new imperial palace. Sarutahiko heads the list of its nine enshrined *kami* who provide a wide range of benefits including the acquisition of a marriage partner, but protection is his key role here and is given an explicitly phallic representation at the rear of the *honden* by a phallic rock.[35]

34 From a personal observation made on 13 October 2005.

35 Kokonoe 1981, p. 216 and from a personal observation made on 02 April 2012.

FIGURE 56 *Inside the Yasaka Shrine in Hita two stones representing Sarutahiko and Ame no Uzume make up a protective pair.*

FIGURE 57 *In Hita Sarutahiko continues to perform his role as guardian of the crossroads in the guise of a phallic stone that bear his name.*

FIGURE 58 *At the ancient 'Izumo Road Shrine' in Kyoto, the protective Sai no kami Yashiro, Sarutahiko is represented in his guardian role by this phallic rock.*

It is very likely that other shrines to Sarutahiko were once much more strongly phallic than they are today. This may be concluded from Katō's account of him, because Sarutahiko's cult became a target for moral reformers throughout Japanese history. An early example is the story in *Konjaku Monogatari* about a monk's prayers convincing Sarutahiko that he should transform himself into something more suitable. During the early Tokugawa Period, in a reaction against what he regarded as the degeneracy of sexual-related beliefs and practices, the Confucian scholar Yamazaki Ansai (1619–1682) criticised the sexual frankness he saw in Sarutahiko and provided his own re-interpretation of the god's role with respect to Prince Ninigi. To Anzai the guidance provided by Sarutahiko was not a physical protection on the road warding off evil spirits but guidance of a serious moral nature for which the development of phallic-related beliefs was entirely inappropriate and offensive. In this he agreed with his contemporary Hayashi Razan (1583–1657), who denounced all phallic religious behaviour as 'a nasty false belief injurious to public morality'.[36]

Some repression of Sarutahiko's shrines often followed statements such as these, but he and his wife always survived, albeit in a different guise, because

36 Katō 1924, pp. 19–20.

at some time in history these two sexual gods with important imperial connections were transformed into anonymised archetypal male and female characters. They are still to be found like this today, and their sexual associations are much less inhibited in this 'undercover' form. Sarutahiko is customarily presented as a male character wearing the red mask otherwise associated with *tengu* 天狗 (mountain goblins). It has a prominent nose which can easily act as a phallic symbol and sometimes there is the addition of a ktenic mouth.[37] He is often found leading festival processions in a *tengu* mask but it will not usually be phallic on such occasions.

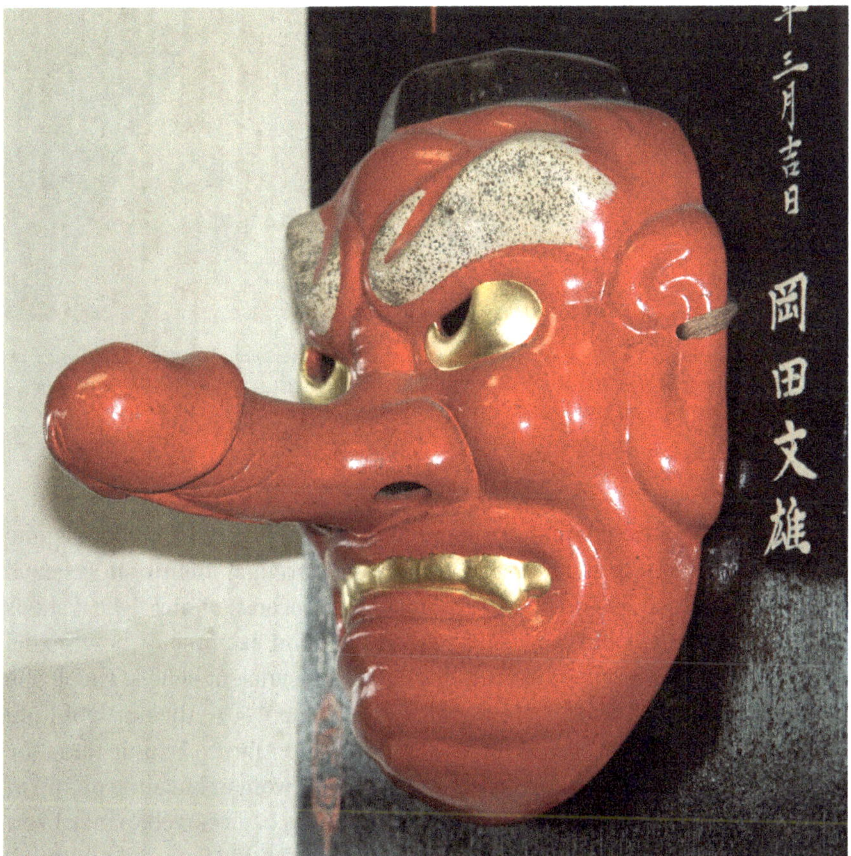

FIGURE 59 *This* tengu *mask with a phallic nose is on sale in the souvenir shop of the museum attached to the Kanki Shrine in Shirahama.*

37 Satō 1995, p. 24.

FIGURE 60 *Sarutahiko is often encountered leading festival processions wearing the red mask of a* tengu*. Here he takes part in the Nabe kamuri* matsuri *of the Chikuma Shrine in Maibara (Shiga Prefecture).*

Ame no Uzume's transformation was more thorough, although there is one modern shrine where she is depicted under her original identity in a sexual manner. This place will be discussed briefly, not because of any light it sheds on ancient practices but because it provides a good example of how sexual symbolism can reflect modern attitudes rather than ancient beliefs. The shrine in question is the Myōtogi Hime no Miya 夫婦木姫の宮 to the north of Kōfu (Yamanashi Prefecture). It was founded in 1980, and Ame no Uzume takes the unique form of a carved wooden statue of a naked woman kneeling on top of the trunk of a long-dead tree, inside which a root has been carved to look like a phallus. Behind her are a large number of *ema* of a phallic shape and a painting that shows her performing the ribald dance for Amaterasu. The statue, however, says more about modern tastes than ancient practices and has much to do with the shrine's location, because about one kilometre away is the Myōtogi Shrine, of which the Hime no Miya is a sub-shrine. The main Myōtogi Shrine is an ancient foundation, and its central feature is an enormous hollow tree trunk. Like the Kinone Shrine in Tottori the tree has a huge phallic protrusion, and when the tree died in 1959 its trunk was moved to the shrine. The atmosphere at the Myōtogi Shrine is very serious and it is one of only a few shrines studied in the course of this research where photography is not allowed. By contrast, the Hime no Miya lies within a busy tourist complex, and Ame no Uzume is only one of a large number of sexual images on show or on sale at the brash and lively shrine. As her depiction there is so unusual the probable explanation for it is the commercialisation of a site that is deliberately intended to draw the casual visitor away from the more devotional main institution.[38]

In all other modern locations Ame no Uzume is encountered only in a transformed state where she is identified as the inspiration for the jolly female character called Otafuku お多福. Her instantly recognisable face is found on shrine amulets, shop displays and numerous advertisements, but Otafuku has few shrines in her own name. Instead she appears more frequently, in Casals' well-chosen words, as 'the deity of rollicking fun, venerated by those who like a good cup and a wench on the knee, plenty of laughter and a carefree life'.[39] She is also known as Okame お亀 meaning 'a plain woman'. Her face is round and thus lends itself to caricature of a sexual nature when her nose and pursed lips become a kteis. Small pottery bells based on Otafuku's distended ktenic face may be obtained at several shrines.[40] A pairing-up of her and Sarutahiko appears at the annual Ryūō *matsuri* 竜王祭り in Tochigi Prefecture, where the two *mikoshi* paraded from neighbouring shrines carry masks depicting phallic and ktenic distortions of Sarutahiko and Ame no Uzume as Otafuku and a *tengu*.[41]

Characters derived from Sarutahiko and Ame no Uzume also feature in dramatic performances at festivals as a symbolic couple through whose copulation the fertility of local fields is assured, and one sequence forms a small section of the recently revived drama at the festival of Yokohama's Tsurumi Shrine

38 From a personal observation made on 13 November 2012 and Kokonoe 1981, pp. 144–145.

39 Casal, U.A. 1950. 'Ramblings in Chinese and Japanese Lore: O-Tafuku' *Ethnos* 1, p. 34.

40 From a personal observation made on 9 April 1992. She can also be seen with different male companions. Hyottoko 火男 sometimes appears alongside her in a pairing used popularly as dolls. His character has one bad eye and a pursed mouth through which he blows the embers of a fire.

41 Kokonoe 1976, pp. 14–15.

FIGURE 61 *Ame no Uzume is depicted in a unique manner at the modern Meotogi Hime no Miya. The choice of design has probably been influenced more by present-day ideas of sexual display rather than traditional religious belief.*

鶴見神社.[42] A longer and more sexually explicit performance forms part of the Onta *matsuri* おん田祭り at the Asuka Niimasu Shrine 飛鳥坐神社

42 From a personal observation made on 29 April 2012. The full script and the story behind the re-creation are presented by the Tsurumi ta matsuri hōzon kai in *Tsurumi no ta matsuri fukattsu shiryō* (Yokohama, 2007) and in a booklet specific to the current year such as *Tsurumi no ta matsuri*.

FIGURE 62 *During the Ryūō Matsuri in Tochigi Prefecture the two* mikoshi *paraded from neighbouring shrines carry masks depicting sexual distortions of the faces of Sarutahiko and Ame no Uzume. On this painted screen of the procession (on display in the Kinugawa Hihōden) Ame no Uzume's nose and pursed lips have become a kteis.*

in Nara Prefecture. The festival is stated by Itō and Richie as having died out before 1953, but it had clearly been revived by 1976 at the latest as it appears in Kokonoe's first book.[43] I observed it in its entirety in 2011.[44]

The Onta *matsuri* drama is believed to enhance the fertility of the rice fields that surround the hill on which the Niimasu Shrine is built. Before the performance begins two men, one wearing Sarutahiko's *tengu* mask and the other an *okina* 翁 mask of an old man with a beard, take it in turns to mingle with the festive crowds and beat people on the buttocks to ward off evil. For this purpose they use a pole of green bamboo, and the smacking may be heavy or light dependent upon the stated preference of the victim or the whim of the

43 Itō and Richie 1976, pp. 16–17.

44 From a personal observation made on 6 February 2011. For my videos of the performance see https://www.youtube.com/watch?v=MHonwh-N1_s; https://www.youtube.com/watch?v=VTZfpEQJBR4 and https://www.youtube.com/watch?v=zZiZ6xb9pyY&feature=youtu.be. See also Kononoe 1976, pp. 16–17.

perpetrator. The dramatic performance is given on a small stage opposite the main shrine, and while various dignitaries take their places the *tengu* and *okina* amuse the crowd by brandishing their bamboo sticks in a mock-threatening manner. The play consists of two acts. The first is a straightforward and largely serious theatrical presentation similar to ones performed in other shrines that mimic the successive processes of the agricultural cycle.[45] A third actor plays a draught animal. The threesome sit at the rear of the stage and calm descends while a Shintō priest makes offerings and intones prayers. Soon afterwards the drama begins. The *okina* digs and the ox pulls the *tengu*'s plough round the stage. The *okina* then hoes and a seed drill is pulled. Young rice plants are symbolically laid on the stage by the priest to be thrown into the crowd by the three actors. A young female shrine attendant then dances.

There is then a considerable change in the tone of the proceedings as the symbolic fertilisation changes from agricultural to human in a way that is both

FIGURE 63 *The* tengu *character in the drama of the Onta Matsuri at the Asuka Nümasu Shrine (Nara Prefecture) begins the proceedings by mingling with the crowds and hitting people with a bamboo stick.*

45 Plutschow and O'Neill, 1996, pp. 154–155 and 169.

ribald and boisterous. The *okina* begins the performance by interacting with the audience in what appears to be jealousy, waving his phallic bamboo pole. The reason for his envy is soon revealed, because the *tengu* now has a prospective bride wearing an Okame mask. There is a certain amount of sexual violence when the *tengu* beats her on the buttocks with his cane, although she

FIGURE 64 *On stage the* tengu *anticipates his marriage by waving his phallus at the crowd.*

later repeats it on him. Their wedding ceremony is conducted by the Niimasu Shrine's priest, to whom they present offerings of two cups of cooked rice. The *tengu* then prepares for the consummation of the marriage. He manipulates a lacquered bamboo pole at groin level as a phallic symbol, waving it to the audience and to the priest, and then invites his wife to join him on a straw mat. As their wedding night gets under way the *okina* pretends to shield the coupling from the audience using his outstretched jacket. Finally he decides to join in, so while Okame lies with her legs apart, straddled by the *tengu*, he approaches the *tengu* from behind and mounts him in turn. The threesome finishes with Okame cleaning herself up with handfuls of paper tissues. These tissues are then shredded and thrown into the crowd as talismans for conception to add the assurance of human fertility to the agricultural fertility that will be brought about by sympathetic magic from the simulated sexual act.

To summarise this chapter, one unique phallic object from the Kofun Period is followed centuries later by two important written works where the creator gods are depicted engaging in various forms of sexual behaviour, although

FIGURE 65 *The* tengu *straddles the figure of Otafuku and through their intercourse the fertility of the fields is assured.*

there is no overt sexual imagery in these narratives. Yet within a further hundred years that imagery has appeared, suggesting that by the year 800 the use of phallic symbolism is well-established. From that time onwards phallic and ktenic symbolism are firmly associated with the two most important pairs of *kami*, although political considerations meant either that the imagery was highly abstract or the gods themselves were transformed into archetypal characters. These are the forms in which the great creator *kami* are encountered in sexual shrines today.

CHAPTER 6

'Erotic Gifts': The Votive Role of Sexual Objects

Shintō provides a rich symbolic environment where the worshipper interacts with the *kami* in the two-way process of asking for help and then giving thanks when the desire is granted. Since the time of the myth of Mitoshi no Kami the phallus has been the symbol of choice for matters involving fertility, with the object becoming 'an erotic gift to a deity craving it'.[1] The vast majority of phalluses seen in today's shrines are performing this votive function, and when agricultural fertility is the goal a large phallus is presented to the *kami* during a festival. The desire for human fertility is usually expressed on a more personal and individual scale, and over the years many thousands of phalluses have been donated to gods as requests for help with match-making, marital harmony, the cure or avoidance of sexually transmitted diseases, successful conception and the safe delivery and nurture of children. Rarer votive intentions exist, including one legendary instance of the samurai general Minamoto Yoshitsune (1154–1189) praying for victory to a phallic symbol at the Ōmononushi Shrine in Amagasaki (Hyōgo Prefecture) before pursuing the Taira family along the Inland Sea.[2]

The achievement of conception has always been the most important request associated with these most sexual of objects, and this was probably the intention lying behind the behaviour witnessed in 1864 by a Victorian traveller to Japan called Dr Sinclair Coghill:

> The male symbol was the only object of veneration, apparently; in various sizes, some quite colossal, more or less faithfully modelled from nature, it held the sole place of honour on the altars in the principle hall and subsidiary chapels of the temple. Before each, the fair devotees might be seen fervently addressing their petitions and laying upright on the altar, already thickly studded with similar oblations, a votive phallus, whether of plain or wrought cut wood from the surrounding grove or of other more elaborately prepared materials.[3]

---

1 Naumann 2000, pp. 79–80.

2 No items of a phallic nature are now present at the rebuilt shrine (from a personal observation made on 24 October 2012). This is probably why was omitted from the 1981 version of Kokonoe's guidebook. It may be found only in his first handbook (Kokonoe 1976a).

3 Stone 1927, pp. 110–111.

 | DOI 10.1163/9789004293786_007

In 1895 Buckley stated that at one place known to him, 'a phallus is offered to produce (depending upon the intention) a husband or a son, and a kteis if the intention is to acquire a wife or a daughter,' but there is no evidence of this taking place nowadays.[4] In addition to the offering of phalluses, loan phalluses may be taken away from shrines on a temporary basis to be prayed to in the home, and the most efficacious examples are borrowed time and time again. The phalluses at the Ōhata Konsei Daimyōjin in Aomori Prefecture are borrowed overnight.[5] In most other places the objects are retained until conception occurs and the shrine's collection is then augmented by a further gift.

The phalluses donated to a shrine are usually arranged neatly on shelves around the *goshintai*, but because old phalluses are not thrown away the accumulated numbers can be quite staggering, although it is only at the most remote shrines where they now appear to be stored indefinitely. At the Akaiwa Konsei Shrine in Okayama the tightly packed piles of old phallic symbols fade into the darkness of the separate building set aside to preserve them, and at another shrine in Chiba Prefecture large piles of dusty phalluses are stacked in cardboard boxes.[6] The process is slightly different at the very popular Mara Kannon near Tawarayama Onsen (Yamaguchi Prefecture) where the custom is to purchase a ceramic phallus and write one's intentions on it with a felt-tip pen. They are then placed at the shrine. There were about 300 donated specimens visible within the *honden* in March 2014, but thousands more were packed into an adjacent shrine that acted as a repository. It was almost full and many more were arranged neatly on the ground outside.[7]

The Nagomi Shichirōjin as a Case Study

In order to observe how the pattern of borrowing and donating phalluses might operate, one shrine was monitored over a period of six years through five visits to the site.[8] The place chosen was the shrine known simply as the Shichirōjin 七郎神. It lies in Nagomi, a rural district of northern Kumamoto Prefecture. Its *kami* was once Sanaga Shichirōemon, a priest of the Aso Shrine who went to the area about 800 years ago to teach agricultural technology to the villagers.

4 Buckley 1895, p. 28.

5 From a photograph of the sign displayed at http://www11.atpages.jp/ruisho/myweb3_04444.htm.

6 From a personal observation made on 8 July 2013.

7 From a personal observation made on 4 March 2014.

8 The visits were made on 2 June 2010, 10 February 2011, 11 April 2012, 30 May 2013 and 8 February 2015. For a video tour see https://www.youtube.com/watch?v=S6tZprsT-p8.

FIGURE 66 *At the Konsei Daimyōjin Shrine at Akaiwa (Okayama Prefecture) row upon row of old donated votive phalluses lie packed together in a building set aside to house them.*

FIGURE 67 *A few of the thousands of donated phalluses at the Mara Kannon shrine in Tawarayama Onsen (Yamaguchi Prefecture). The phalluses are ceramic and have the petitioners' names written on them with felt pen.*

Now deified, he is a *kami* of fertility, successful conception, safe delivery and marital harmony, and there are written records from 1813 onwards linking his shrine to such concerns. The Shichirōjin is one of eight shrines in the Nagomi area that specialise in the health of different bodily parts and are unique for being found as a cluster. The others enshrine the *kami* of general vitality, eyes, teeth, ears, warts, the stomach and limbs. Within the last few years the local council have begun publicising them as a feature of interest using directional signs and information boards.[9]

The tiny sexual shrine, which has neither office buildings nor formal structure, lies within a small attractive mountain gorge beside a stream that runs beneath the modern road to join the Wani River about twenty metres further on. It is accessed by means of stone steps beneath a *torii*. A small footbridge crosses the stream where, on a raised area in a compact space lies a rich collection of sexual imagery with much evidence of active involvement. There are four main areas of interest:

FIGURE 68 *This photograph provides a panoramic shot of the Shichirōjin in Nagomi (Kumamoto Prefecture). On the extreme left the* in'yōseki *rocks are just visible. Carved wooden phalluses have been presented as votive offerings along with the local tradition of using white and red flags.*

9 They are illustrated and described in a multilingual tourist booklet produced by Nagomi Town Office.

(i) The paired boulders that make up an *in'yōseki*
(ii) a roofed wooden shrine with only a rear wall
(iii) a roofed wooden shrine open on one side
(iv) a small stone *hokora* next to a tree

The *in'yōseki* lie to the rear of the gorge and consist of two large boulders of similar size and are not of any great sexual appearance. In front of the phallic stone stands a vertical iron phallus cemented into the ground that acts as the equivalent of the hanging bell to be found in conventional Shintō shrines. Next to it a hammer hangs from a chain, and judging by the dent in the top of the phallus the worshippers strike it with some force. A notice invites the visitor to hit it three times: 'once for your life, once for your desires and once for your joy'.

The open-sided building was always immaculately maintained over the six-year period and continued to house three items of interest. At the rear is a huge wooden phallus lying on its side in front of a red and white striped curtain. In front is a pairing in a coital position involving a plain wooden phallus and a kteis made from a tree trunk. In front of the second shrine stands another pair. The phallus is an elaborate symbol carved from a tree, where the bifurcated trunk becomes legs and a curving branch has been carved to represent a phallus from which a bell hangs. The kteis is another bifurcated trunk. This place provides the main centre for intercessions, which are of two kinds. The first is the donation of phallic symbols by worshippers whose prayers have been answered. Several are on show and are of different sizes and complexity, but the main type of votive offering at the Shichirōjin is the presentation of small cloth flags. Traditionally they are white for men and red for women, although this rule is no longer kept rigorously. On them are written the petitioner's name, address and age, and none of these little banners seems to stay for more than one year. The examples seen in 2011 and 2012 contained only basic personal information, but in 2010 one white flag bore a message of thanks written in French on behalf of a couple who clearly had French names. Dated July 2009, it thanked the *kami* for granting their petition of 2005 and then enabling them to return with their child, whose name was given on the banner and who was the result of their prayers to Shichirōjin. In 2015 one flag thanked the *kami* for a safe delivery. Prayers are also offered for matters other than conception, such as relief from back pain.

Next to the wooden shrine is a small stone *hokora* that is overgrown with moss. Beside it are many votive phalluses, and one or two others lie against the trunk of the living tree next to it, from where the steps are taken to exit the gorge. A glance backwards shows how meticulously everything is kept, and the overall impression given by the Shichirōjin is that it represents an active

FIGURE 69 *Instead of the usual shrine bell at the Shichirōjin worshippers are invited to strike this iron phallus 'once for your life, once for your desires and once for your joy'.*

tradition that is still cherished as much for its religious efficacy as for being the site of an intangible local folk belief that is worth preserving for its own sake. There is also a note of humour at the site, because across the narrow country road is a small rest area with a toilet and a hand-washing bowl. The

FIGURE 70 *Two phallic offerings presented to the Shichirōjin and photographed in 2013.*

water outlet is of a design chosen to reflect the nature of the shrine's objects of devotion, and I have it on no less authority than the Chairman of the Nagomi Town Board of Education that it was added simply as a joke.[10]

Sexual Symbolism on *ema* and *ofuda*

The employment of coloured flags at the Shichirōjin is one example of the use of votive symbols other than phalluses at sexual shrines, and they may also be augmented or even replaced by erotica, intimate items of clothing, written comments in a visitors' book or the more conventional *ema* 絵馬. These are the small wooden boards upon which petitioners write their individual intentions. They are then hung from a frame to implore the favour of the god. *Ema* are often inscribed with a desire to find a partner or to ask to help with a relationship, but these intentions are not confined to the *ema* on sale at explicitly sexual establishments. At the Orihime Shrine 織姫神社 in Ashikaga (Tochigi Prefecture) its popular *ema* for successful match-making bear an innocuous

10 From an interview conducted at the shrine with Mr Kuroda of Nagomi Town Board of Education on 30 May 2013. See my video of the fountain at http://youtu.be/Vro5Gip3EF8.

FIGURE 71 *The humorous phallic water outlet beside the Shichirōjin reflects the serious sexual ambience inside it.*

heart.[11] Other designs may be more suggestive. At the Kitaoka Shrine 北岡神社 in Kumamoto the *ema* for success in love shows a vaguely phallic cupid's arrow hitting its target. *Ema* are normally purchased at the shrine, although at some sexual shrines there is a tradition of displaying professionally commissioned *ema* painted by leading artists and also of allowing 'do it yourself' *ema*. The designs produced for these places may display very stark sexual content, and in Saitō Shōzō's *Hentai Sūhai shi* of 1927 there appear two photographs of *ema* from the Danseki Shrine 男石神社 in Ueda (Nagano Prefecture). Each shows a very realistically painted kteis.[12] In some cases erotic designs have been inspired by or are copies of *shunga* and a remarkable collection by contemporary artists is on show inside the Ema-dō of the Konsei Daimyōjin Shrine at

11 From a personal observation made on 20 October 2012.

12 Saitō, 1927, frontispiece plate. A personal observation made on 18 April 2012 confirmed that no *ema* like these can now be seen.

FIGURE 72 *This somewhat phallic 'cupid's arrow' is on the* ema *of the Kitaoka Shrine in Kumamoto.*

Shirane (Gunma Prefecture).[13] The pictures contain graphic sexual detail and in almost any other context would be regarded as pornographic.

Ema are supposed to be left behind at a shrine. Visitors take home instead talismanic souvenirs in two traditional forms: *omamori* お守り (small brocade bags) and *ofuda* お札 printed paper slips). Both the Ōwashi Shrine 大鷲神社 in Ajiki (Chiba Prefecture) and the In'yōseki Shrine 陰陽石神社 (Miyazaki Prefecture) provide their worshippers with a very subtle sexual *ofuda*. When folded vertically in a precise concertina fashion its picture of a goddess and a dragon becomes an erect penis heading for a vulva. Nowadays traditional *ofuda* and *omamori* are often replaced by items such as phallic *sake* bottles and jars, ash-trays, key-rings and plastic novelties. They include tiny wooden boxes or clam shells that slide apart to allow a phallus to pop up.

Sometimes the sexual symbolism in a shrine and its souvenirs take a more abstract form. This is particularly so in the case of the enigmatic *kami* Inari 稲荷. Some authorities suggest that Inari is a primeval *kami* from the *Kojiki*, the food goddess known as Oganomitama no Ōkami. He is certainly very closely associated with fertility, in particular that of the rice crop, but his procreative

13 Suzuki 2013, pp. 366–367.

FIGURE 73 *It is the tradition at the Konsei Daimyōjin Shrine within the precincts of the Shirane Fish Farm in Gunma Prefecture to paint one's own* ema. *The frankly sexual motifs chosen reflect those adopted by professional artists whose work is on display inside the building.*

functions have also been carried over into the human sphere.[14] Shrines to Inari, of which many thousand exist, frequently constitute a sub-shrine of another shrine or temple, where they often stand out because of the vermilion colour of their woodwork. Yet even if the shrine is not painted bright red the pair of foxes standing guard at the entrance provide instant identification. Their tails can act as phallic symbols, and depending on how they have been carved, moulded or painted the phallic nature is either stressed or played down.

Inari's foxes also act as symbols of human fertility through the construction of 'fox-holes' for them. These are described by Smyers and consist of small round openings in a large irregular natural rock that are regarded as womb-like enclosures for the spirit fox. Expectant mothers would go there to pray for easy delivery.[15] An Inari Shrine in Shinjuku (Tokyo) features a rock for

---

14 Buchanan 1935; Smyers 1999.

15 Smyers 1999, p. 132.

FIGURE 74 *The paper* ofuda *from the Ōwashi Shrine at Ajiki* (*Chiba Prefecture*).

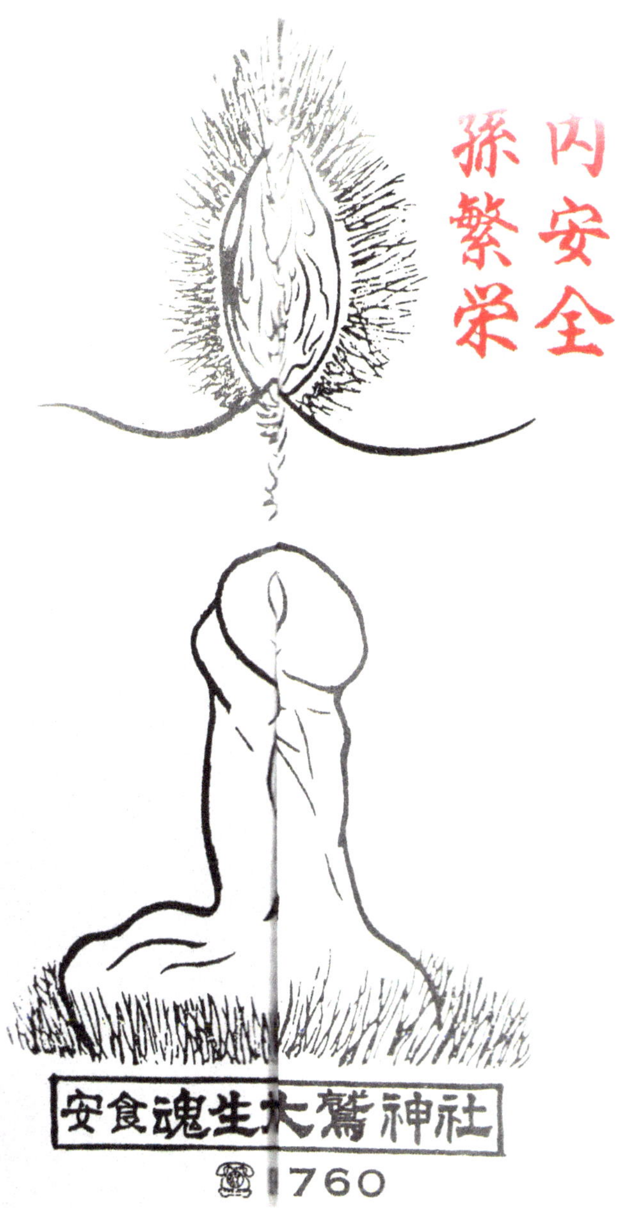

FIGURE 75 *The same* ofuda *after it has been folded in a precise fashion.*

FIGURE 76 *Hodare* sake*, brewed specially for the Hodare Festival, is on sale in phallic bottles. The 'glans' is a removable cup.*

FIGURE 77 *Two mementoes from the Kanayama Shrine in Kawasaki are shown here. On the left is a box from which a phallus pops up on lifting the lid. On the right is a phallus made from linked metal sections that achieves erection when the chain is tightened.*

FIGURE 78 *The fox of Inari, whose tail is often used as a phallic symbol. This example is at the Fushimi Inari Shrine in Kyoto.*

FIGURE 79 *One of the 'fox-holes' at the Fushimi Inari Shrine in Kyoto.*

fox-holes on top of which several stone foxes crawl, and among them is a small stone phallus complete with a pair of testicles. Among his other roles Inari became the guardian of prostitutes, so phallic imagery is not to be unexpected in this area of Tokyo, and a far more prominent phallic symbol hangs in a horizontal position from the eaves of this shrine just above the spot where most worshippers stand.

Another animal used in sexual symbolism is the monkey, who is personified as Sannō Daigongen 山王大権現, the messenger and *gongen* 権現 (avatar) of Sannō the mountain king, the original *kami* of the Hiyoshi Shrine on Mount Hiei near Kyoto. A shrine to Sannō Daigongen stands inside the Wakamiya Hachiman Shrine in the Nakanoshima area of Wakayama City where the approach to the *honden* is flanked by statues of a male and a female monkey. The female is cradling a baby monkey as the patroness of harmonious marriage and safe childbirth, and on sale are little red-faced pottery monkeys holding a peach of a distinctive ktenic shape. They are believed to ensure easy delivery and as well as being taken home are placed inside the shrine on a series of shelves.[16]

Monkey images also abound at Sannō Gongen's Mitsugi Shrine 三ツ木神社 in Kōnosu City (Saitama Prefecture). Beside the *torii* is a venerable old tree

16 From a personal observation made on 1 May 2012.

FIGURE 80 *A fox and its hole which also contains a phallic symbol at the Sakaki Inari Shrine in the Asukabashi district of Tokyo.*

with a ktenic slit in its trunk, inside which is a small relief carving of a monkey showing somewhat indistinct genitalia.[17] To the side of the offertory box is a small statue of a mother monkey with hands clasped in prayer. Both it and an

17 Nishioka's book has a photograph of the statuette which confirms it to be of a female monkey with genitals displayed (1961, Plate XLIV & p. 234).

FIGURE 81 *The fox hole of the Inari Shrine inside the Hanazono Shrine in Shinjuku, showing the stone foxes clustering round the small shrine and the solitary phallic symbol on the extreme right.*

FIGURE 82 *This large phallus hangs under the roof of the Inari Shrine within the precincts of the Hanazono Shrine in Shinjuku.*

FIGURE 83 *A female monkey cradling a baby at the shrine to Sannō Daigongen within the grounds of the Hachiman Shrine in the Nakanoshima area of Wakayama City.*

FIGURE 84 *The votive pottery monkeys holding a peach in the shrine to Sannō Daigongen at the Hachiman Shrine in Wakayama City.*

adjacent baby monkey are coated in vivid orange ochre applied by worshippers. This theme of prayers for fertility is echoed in a shrine to the side of the courtyard, where a locked wooden lattice houses thousands of small donated pottery monkeys. One or two others rubbed with ochre stand outside, and the lattice itself is covered with babies' bibs presented in thanks.

The sexual prowess of the male monkey finds expression in the cheerful pottery figures known as *konohazaru* 木葉猿 (Konoha monkeys) from the town of Konoha in Kumamoto Prefecture. The classic depiction is of a solitary *konohazaru* who is seated and cradling in his hands what is referred to euphemistically as his 'giant mushroom'. A leaflet handed out by the craft studio where they are now made reads as follows:

> Konohazaru originated from the following legend. In 723 AD (Yoro 7) about 1300 years ago, a fugitive from Nara was leading a solitary life in the village called Konoha. In a dream an old man appeared and told him to build another shrine here and to make Shintō ritualistic implements using red clay in Konoha. When he finished this work and threw away the rest of the clay, these bits of clay miraculously turned into monkeys. It is believed these monkeys can prevent disasters, disease, create the concord of husband and wife, and ensure fertility. Many people in this district love them as their guardian spirits. The monkeys are made by hand

FIGURE 85 *The mother and baby monkeys at Sannō Gongen's Mitsugi Shrine in Konosu City (Saitama Prefecture) are coated in vivid orange ochre applied by worshippers.*

FIGURE 86 *Another area of the Mitsugi Shrine where more ochre-covered monkeys stand guard over donated babies' bibs. Behind the wooden lattice are thousands of small votive monkeys.*

> without using a mould and they are very simple and traditional pretty without glaze.

At some sexual shrines their erotic souvenirs are left among the shrine's displays by visitors as if they were *ema*, and further erotic items brought in from outside may also be added. A craft shop called the Ōzaki Monzendō in Takamatsu (Kagawa Prefecture) once produced some unique and simple erotic folk art objects that often found their way into shrines. They were pottery phalluses called *kinmara* 金魔羅 and *ginmara* 銀魔羅 (gold and silver penis) respectively with a variation as statuettes of women cradling them.[18] The Konoha monkeys are another popular choice for donation and may be spotted inside several shrines, while among the votive phalluses at the Ohana Daigongen there is a crude ceramic statuette of Otafuku with a removable nose that conceals a kteis.

On rare occasions some very unexpected items appear. The Sai Shrine at Gonoura displays *shunga* and a pair of imitation plastic breasts.[19] These items

18 Nishioka 1961, Plate XLVII; Kokonoe 1981, p. 255.

19 From a personal observation made on 13 October 2005.

FIGURE 87 *A* konohazaru *monkey from Konoha (Kumamoto Prefecture) cradling his 'giant mushroom'.*

FIGURE 88 *A* kappa *at the Shibatate Hime Shrine adds a note of erotic humour.*

may have been donated as votive offerings but are far more likely to be there simply to add to the sexual ambience of the place. In this they play a similar role to the collections of naturally shaped phallic stones that are often placed in a shrine's courtyard and occasional attempts at phallic topiary. These things add a not unwelcome touch of humour, as was noted above at the Shichirōjin.

The Use of Phalluses and *ema* for Sexual Vows and Promises

The presence of an *ema* on a shrine's frame does not always mean that the worshipper is asking for something. It may also mean that something is being promised such as a vow to give up smoking, and certain establishments provide *ema* dedicated specifically to sexual-related vows and promises. At the Ikoma Hōzanji 宝山寺 (Nara Prefecture) *ema* are sold that depict the written character for heart held within an iron lock to signify the worshipper's resolve to perform whatever may be written on the reverse.[20] In 1938 Holtom published

20 From a personal observation made on 23 October 1993.

FIGURE 89 *A woman holding a* kinmara, *a folk art object made in Takamatsu (Kagawa Prefecture) and on display at the* sex museum *at the Deco Yashiki Artists' Village near Kōriyama.*

FIGURE 90 *An Okame mask at the Ohana Daigongen. The nose is removable to disclose a kteis.*

FIGURE 91 *Phallic stones collected and displayed in the courtyard of the Ohana Daigongen.*

FIGURE 92 *Carefully shaped phallic topiary at the Yamazaki Konsei Daimyōjin in Tōno.*

FIGURE 93 *The* ema *from the Ikoma Hōzanji showing the character for heart held within a lock. It signifies the resolve to make a vow, and some of the intentions written on them are of a sexual nature.*

the results of an interesting study carried out at the Hōzanji to discover the nature of the vows that people made in the words written on the back of the *ema*. Many were of a sexual nature, such as promising to give up sexual relations with anyone other than the person to whom the petitioner was married. Here are a few of Holtom's readings:

> A woman of twenty-nine, born in the year of the horse, vows to sever relations with men for the rest of her life, with the exception of her present man, forty years of age. Accompanied by a prayer for health and long life, for prosperity in shelter and sustenance, and for success in the vow. Date September 29 1934
>
> A man of thirty, born in the year of the goat, abstains from women for two years. Undated
>
> A man of forty pledges to abstain from women and *sake* for a period of three years beginning May 29 1929
>
> A man of forty pledges to abstain from tea-house dissipation and amorous excess for a period of three years, beginning April 20 1932.[21]

When the research exercise was repeated during the 1980s it was found that the Ikoma Hōzanji still attracted a large number of pledges but that the number concerned with sexual abstention and infidelity was much smaller, standing at about two per cent of the total. This probably reflects changing attitudes towards sexual relationships.[22] Vows to suspend sexual relations are also noted by Itō and Richie for the Gumyōji in Yokohama, although I failed to find an example of the *ema* illustrated in their book that shows a bifurcated radish pierced by a needle as a promise of sexual sacrifice.[23] They also mention the use of staves, swords and other punishing instruments in such depictions.[24] This may again reflect changed attitudes towards adultery and sexual fidelity.

Sexual infidelity is however still a serious concern at the remarkable pair of shrines known as the Yuge Jingū 弓削神宮 and the Yuge Hōō Jinja 弓削法皇神社 in Kumamoto Prefecture. These places are associated with the pretentious and lascivious priest Yuge no Dōkyō 弓削の道鏡 (700–772). Dōkyō was a favourite of the Empress Kōken who reigned between 749 and 759. He is credited with curing the Empress's illnesses and grew to exert a considerable influence over her that has been compared to that exercised by Rasputin in

21 Holtom. Daniel C. 1938. 'Japanese Votive Pictures (The Ikoma ema)' *Monumenta Nipponica* 1, p. 162.
22 Reader, Ian 1991. *Religion in Contemporary Japan* (London), p. 180.
23 Itō and Richie 1967, p. 205 and a personal observation made on 29 April 2012.
24 Itō and Richie 1967, p. 202.

FIGURE 94 *The Yuge Hōō Shrine in Kumamoto enshrines the sexual* kami *Dōkyō-sama, in life the lover of an empress and renowned for his abnormally large penis.*

the Russian Imperial Court. Dōkyō was ambitious and ruthless with his rivals, and even developed imperial aspirations of his own. After allegedly faking an oracle from the Usa Hachiman Shrine he received the title of Hōō that was normally reserved for an ex-emperor. This made more enemies for him, and on the death of the Empress he was demoted and exiled to a lowly post at a temple in Shimotsuke Province (modern Tochigi Prefecture), but died on the way.[25] Following his death Dōkyō was deified as Dōkyō-sama, an act of devotion that bore some relation to a belief that he possessed an abnormally large penis. During the Edo Period a tortoiseshell sex toy designed to be worn over the penis to increase female satisfaction was known as 'Dōkyō's armour and helmet'.[26] Dōkyō's large member also made him the subject of popular ribald *haiku*. A literal yet still poetic translation of one poem reads:

> When Dōkyō knelt to take his ease
> It looked as though he had three knees.

---

25 Bender, Ross 1979. 'The Hachiman Cult and the Dōkyō Incident' *Monumenta Nipponica* 34, pp. 125–126.

26 Clark et al. 2013, pp. 316–317.

Another poem implies that Dōkyō's sexual attributes made him 'too wide for the Floating World'.[27] Dōkyō-sama is still a popular *kami* and a website run by a Dōkyō enthusiast lists seventy-eight places associated either with him or Empress Kōken.[28] For example, at the rear of the Kashima Shrine in Kasumigaura (Ibaraki Prefecture) are four phalluses known collectively as Dōkyō-sama beside an engraved stone that states that the shrine is good for conception.[29] Another Dōkyō-sama shrine stands behind the Chinzan Inari Shrine 椿山稲荷神社 in Takehara (Ibaraki Prefecture). It has several phallic symbols beneath it. This shrine is related to the story of Dōkyō's exile because the local people had offered him a dwelling there. He died before he could accept their offer, so was enshrined there instead as a sexual *kami* to whom one might pray for easy delivery.[30]

FIGURE 95 *Behind the Kashima Shrine in Kasumigaura in Ibaraki Prefecture there is a collection of phalluses known as Dōkyō-sama.*

27 Miyata 1983, p. 108. The Floating World (*ukiyo*) is the name given to the pleasure-seeking urban milieu of Tokugawa Japan. *Ukiyo-e* (woodblock prints) of which *shunga* was but one genre, provide many famous illustrations of the time and its mores.

28 http://www18.ocn.ne.jp/~doukyou/shiryou/yukarinoti/yukari.html (Accessed 11 August 2013).

29 From a personal observation made on 6 July 2013.

30 Kokonoe 1981, p. 78 and from a personal observation made on 6 July 2013. A shrine to Empress Kōken lies within walking distance.

Kumamoto's two shrines are the most important places to enshrine Dōkyō-sama and relate to a different and more positive version of the story of his exile, because on the banks of the Shirakawa he fell in love at first sight with a beautiful local woman called Fujiko Hime. He rejected his former life, married her and by all accounts lived happily ever after, having given up all his extra-marital philandering. Fujiko Hime is the female *kami* enshrined at the Yuge Jingū while Dōkyō is enshrined at the Yuge Hōō Jinja on the opposite bank. A local legend relates that every night the two lovers still meet for a secret tryst in the middle of the river.

Because of Dōkyō's rejection of adultery the Kumamoto shrines are uniquely associated with matters of infidelity in addition to the usual list of benefits including bumper harvests, peace within families and the gift of children. Both shrines have on show numerous phalluses of different sizes for these conventional intentions, but in order to prevent adultery and unfaithfulness a unique form of painful sexual imagery is employed whereby the petitioner will hammer nails into flat boards or into wooden phalluses. The former are for use by women seeking to control a male partner. The phalluses are for a male seeking to control a woman. The nails driven into the boards are arranged in a ktenic shape and the intention is then written beside the pattern. In 2012 one among the many on show bore the simple words 'that my husband will not commit adultery', while another requested 'that my husband will abandon his relationship'. Visibly more dramatic are the wooden phalluses into which a man will hammer up to fifty nails arranged in rows around the object's length to prevent his partner from being unfaithful. The result is then dedicated to Dōkyō-sama and in 2012 one freshly prepared example lay in a tray awaiting the priest's prayerful attentions. Older ones are piled up within an open-sided shrine at the side of the *honden*, and there appear to be many more female petitions against male adultery than male against female.[31]

In conclusion, the vast majority of phallic symbols encountered in today's sexual shrines are there as votive offerings. An eclectic mix of phalluses, *ema* and other objects are employed to invoke the favours of a number of powerful sexual gods, to make promises to them or to give thanks. The row upon row of donated phalluses may surprise the Western visitor, but they stand within a dignified and reverent atmosphere. Yet the tone is far from sombre because frivolous touches add a lighter note in an environment that is intensely human.

31 From personal observations made on 10 April 2012 and during a return visit on 8 February 2015 following a partial restoration of the Yuge Jingū.

FIGURE 96 *A freshly prepared nailed phallus at the Yuge Jingū awaiting the blessing of a priest. Women do the same in a ktenic shape on to* ema.

FIGURE 97 *Old donated objects at the Yuge Jingū in Kumamoto designed to prevent partners from being unfaithful.*

CHAPTER 7

Ktenic Imagery in Japan's Sexual Shrines

Although the expression 'phallic shrine' provides a suitable working description for most present-day Japanese sexual-related religious establishments a number also contain ktenic imagery, and in these places female needs may be more readily addressed. Most ktenic symbols are paired with a phallus to symbolise a named pair of male and female *kami* or as an expression of harmony between the male and the female principles, but in other cases the image stands alone as the focus of devotion to a single powerful female *kami*.

FIGURE 98 *The ktenic Onnagata Stone stands beside a road to the east of Fukushima City in a small wooden shrine where it receives prayers for relief from female illnesses.*

 | DOI 10.1163/9789004293786_008

A very rough estimate of the proportion of places that involve ktenic imagery may be made by using the broad classifications on the defunct website of the *Nihon Seishin Kenkyūshō*, where each place was marked with the type of image contained there. Out of the total of 1,215 entries added by 2006, 405 places were stated as displaying a phallic symbol with the implication that no other type of image was present. A further 119 places displayed some form of kteis either alone or paired with a phallus as *in'yōseki*. There were also 100 *dōsojin* on the list, but unfortunately a further 438 were listed only as 'other'. First-hand observation of some of these has shown them to include various combinations of naturally occurring or artificially created phallic and ktenic symbols, so it may be that at the very least one out of every ten places contains some form of ktenic image.[1] Although this is a very approximate calculation it is sufficient to call into question the casual attribution of the word phallicism to the totality of Japan's sexual-related belief system.

Ktenes in shrines carry out the same three functions that were identified earlier for the phallus in that they act as a focus for devotion, protection and intercession, although there are considerable differences in how these roles are exercised. First, only a few ktenic images act in a protective manner and this is always carried out in conjunction with a phallus. The votive function is also quite rare, and the most common observation is of phalluses being offered to the ktenic representation of the female *kami*. Third, unlike most phallic symbols ktenic images tend to be things of natural occurrence rather than created objects, and the most common type is a stone or boulder in which a crack or fissure facilitates a ktenic appearance. In most cases the rock's natural shape is regarded as sufficient for its symbolic role. Some extra carving appears to have been applied to others and sometimes also the area representing the vulva is painted red. An early visitor to Japan called Adam Scott sketched one example in his diary on 4 October 1864 together with the following caption:

> Close outside the Royal Joss house or temple of Kamakura, formerly a residence of the Emperors of Japan, there is a natural stone representing the female vulva, about five and a half feet in length. It is a volcanic water worn stone lying in the open air on the grass railed in by a strong post and rail wooden fence.

1 http://homepage2.nifty.com/japanpi/ (accessed 6 June 2012).

In a later entry for 21 February 1865 he describes their enhancement:

> Stones in representation of the female organ, similar to that at Kamakura, but not so large, are found in various locations in Japan, occasionally by the wayside. For this purpose natural stones are selected such as seem accidentally to bear some resemblance to this part of a woman, but the vulva itself is increased in similitude by artificial means.[2]

At the Ōwashi Shrine today a living tree provides natural female imagery because of a long vertical slit in its trunk.[3] In the Tōganji 桃巌寺 at Nagoya a *coco de mer* from the Seychelles, a natural item of ktenic appearance, is displayed alongside phalluses carved from wood.[4] There is also a tradition of recognising a ktenic shape in seashells, and Bernard Karlgren mentions a species of cowry shell called *koyasu gai* 子安貝 (easy delivery shell) which Japanese women once held in their hands at confinement to ensure a safe and easy delivery.[5] Abalone shells play an unusual role as ktenic offerings to a phallus and kteis at the Raseki Shrine 裸石神社, a sub-shrine of the Kande Shrine 神出神社 in Hyōgo Prefecture.[6]

Several shrines use the image of a peach to represent female genitalia, a topic to which Nishioka devotes an interesting analysis because *momo* (peach) is a homonym for the loins. The symbolism must have come to Japan from the continent, as shown by twenty-three citations provided by Nishioka from Chinese literature.[7] Mementoes in the shape of peaches may be purchased at the very female-orientated Awashima Shrine in Uto (Kumamoto Prefecture), and the iron phallus of the Kanayama Shrine in Kawasaki is framed by numerous hanging *ema* bearing these female images. Some of them show the child Momotarō (the 'peach boy' of the fairy story) emerging from the peach as from the womb. Momotarō's speciality was the subjugation of demons, a special power possessed by peaches ever since Izanagi made use of them to distract his pursuers. They also act as a charm against epidemics and lightning, which

---

2 The ktenic stone of Kamakura has been identified in the grounds of the Tsurugaoka Hachiman Shrine. The original diary pages are illustrated in Kinoshita, Naoyuki 2012. 'Kaettekita kokan wakashū' *Geijutsu Shinchō* 63, 11 (November) p. 96.

3 From a personal observation made on 19 April 2012.

4 From a personal observation made on 22 October 2012.

5 Karlgren, Bernhard 1930. 'Some fecundity symbols in Ancient China' *Bulletin of the Museum of Far-Eastern Antiquities, Stockholm* 3, p. 35.

6 From a personal observation made on 12 June 2013.

7 Nishioka 1961, pp. 119–122 & 126–127.

FIGURE 99 *This tree in the grounds of the Ōwashi Shrine is ktenic by virtue of the long slit in its trunk and bears the name of the 'great child-begetting tree'.*

FIGURE 100 *At the Raseki Shrine, a sub-shrine of the Kande Shrine in Hyōgo Prefecture, it is the custom to offer ktenic abalone shells to the enshrined kteis and phallus.*

FIGURE 101 *The peach is an ancient female symbol that can also act as a charm against lightning. Here a ktenic peach performs that function on the gateway of the Yōtoku-In within the Daitokuji complex in Kyoto.*

would explain the presence of peaches as roof ornaments. Some of these have a sexual element whereby part of the peach is protruding in a suggestive manner. There are prominent examples on the gateway of the temple called the Yōtoku-In 養徳院 within the Daitokuji complex in Kyoto.[8]

A watermelon represents the womb on the *ema* of the Mishima Shrine near the Tōfukuji in Kyoto where a picture of three eels escaping from it presents an analogy with giving birth to a baby as easily as to a slippery eel. Another *ema* at the Mishima Shrine showing two intertwined eels suggests happy marriage, conception and a large family, the latter being symbolised by the eel's numerous offspring.[9] Female symbolism of a very different kind is found at Otainai Onsen 御胎内温泉 near Gotemba (Shizuoka Prefecture). When Mount Fuji erupted in 1707 its lava created a 68-metre long cave that is now regarded as a sacred place representing the womb. Expectant mothers go there to pray for easy childbirth and safe delivery. They are not required to enter the low, wet

8 A personal observation made on 1 May 2012 showed that the similar examples illustrated by Nishioka in Wakayama City have been replaced during rebuilding (1961, p. 127).

9 From a personal observation made on 3 April 2012.

FIGURE 102 *At the Mishima Shrine in Kyoto an* ema *shows three eels escaping from what looks like a melon, an analogy with giving birth to a baby.*

FIGURE 103 *The* ema *of the Karube Shrine in Okayama represent petitions to the* kami *Amaterasu and Kodakara Kannon for matters such as relief from breast cancer.*

passages, but the map printed on the shrine leaflet shows it as a cross-section of the female reproductive system.[10] As an alternative to ktenic imagery the *honden* of the Karube Shrine 軽部神社 in Okayama Prefecture is filled with *ema* depicting breasts on which are written petitions for the healing of breast cancer and other related matters.[11]

Female Sexual *kami* and their Shrines

The most common form of ktenic image within a shrine is a natural rock that provides the *goshintai* for a named female *kami*, some of whom are to be found within the *Kojiki* and *Nihongi*. One was created when Izanami was dying and vomited. Out of her vomit grew the female *kami* Kanayama Hime who, along with her brother Kanayama Hiko, may be encountered at several Kanayama shrines.[12] Awashima-sama, the deity of women's ailments, is also said in some accounts to be the daughter of Izanami. The Sengen (or Asama) 浅間 shrines that are centred on Mount Fuji are dedicated to the notable female deity Konohana Sakuya Hime no Mikoto 木花之開耶姫尊 who is one of the most important *kami* with direct links to women's health needs. She was the wife of Prince Ninigi and in one single night became pregnant and gave birth to three children while engulfed in flames. In some versions she died in the fire, so that her short life is likened to the brief beauty of the cherry blossom of which she is the *kami* along with being the *kami* of Mount Fuji. She is also venerated as Koyasu-sama 子安様 the *kami* of easy childbirth, although in this respect her cult was largely supplanted by that of Kannon.

In Miyagi Prefecture there are several shrines where Konohana Sakuya Hime no Mikoto receives phallic offerings. The Araogawa Shrine 荒雄川神社 beside the road towards Naruko Onsen at Kaminomiya houses a small sub-shrine in which stands a statuette of her cradling a baby.[13] Konohana Sakuya Hime's most striking imagery is however to be found at the Asamine Shrine 朝峰神社 at Nera (Kōchi Prefecture). Her shrine stands in front of a tall cliff accessible by means of a short but steep flight of stone steps leading up to a large triangular cleft in the rock about six metres tall that is framed by bamboo. It resembles a kteis and provides Konohana Sakuya Hime's *goshintai*. Some water had collected in the cave when I visited the site in 2011. I was told by the shrine's priest

---

10 From a personal observation made on 30 April 2012.

11 From a personal observation made on 22 October 2012.

12 Philippi 1969, pp. 57 & 489.

13 From a personal observation made on 18 June 2013.

FIGURE 104 *Konohana Sakuya Hime was the wife of Prince Ninigi and in one single night became pregnant and gave birth to three children while engulfed in flames. She is the* kami *of cherry blossoms, Mount Fuji and easy childbirth. This painting of her is from a votive scroll presented to the Yama Jinja in Kogota (Miyagi Prefecture) where she is enshrined.*

FIGURE 105 *At the Yama Jinja in Ishinomaki (Miyagi Prefecture) a phallus provides a votive offering for Konohana Sakuya Hime, whose picture hangs on the wall.*

that there is in fact a natural spring that was once used for brewing the finest local *sake*, and indeed the list of recommended prayer intentions on the notice board adds *sake* brewing and water supply to conception and easy delivery. The *kami* is depicted in a modern bas-relief inside the shrine. She is shown reclining on a couch, cradling beneath her a peach. A single anonymous large phallus stands in front of her shrine.[14]

Another female *kami* mentioned in the *Nihongi* is the semi-mythical empress Jingō Kōgō who led an invasion of Korea. She was pregnant at the time with the future Emperor Ōjin (deified as Hachiman) and did not want the impending birth to delay her campaign. She therefore 'took a stone which she inserted into her loins'.[15] The account continues to say that the stone was afterwards venerated. Jingō Kōgō responds to female health needs and is venerated at the distinguished and very beautiful Karamatsu Shrine 唐松神社 in Sakai (Akita Prefecture) which attracts attention from all over Japan. Offerings of thanks are made in the form of vaguely phallic-shaped stuffed cloths with large bells attached. Hundreds hang from the walls inside the *honden*, and

14 From a personal observation made on 20 February 2011.

15 Aston 1972, p. 229.

FIGURE 106 *At the Asamine Shrine in Nera (Kōchi Prefecture) a large ktenic cave acts as the* goshintai *for the* kami *Konohana Sakuya Hime. Because of its natural spring water the list of recommended prayer intentions adds* sake *brewing and water supply to conception and easy delivery.*

some reflect the gift of a child by being made from swatches depicting popular cartoon characters. The shrine also contains three important sexual rocks that are placed more discretely round the back of an adjacent building. On the right is a stone of ktenic appearance. On left is a stone that consists of natural sedimentary rock enclosing a basalt core like a womb holding an unborn child, while in between them is a perfectly egg-shaped natural boulder like a testicle that shines from having been rubbed so often.[16]

Reference was made earlier to the category of sexual gods whose origins are to be found in human beings deified after their deaths and associated with sexual matters. Of the twelve identified in the course of this study eight were women and three of them died tragic deaths. The first, Shibatate Hime, was the victim of an incestuous relationship. She is enshrined at the Shibatate Hime Shrine 柴立姫神社 in Ashikita (Kumamoto Prefecture). The shrine's founding legend tells of an aristocratic father and daughter who were on a journey and

16 Satō 1995, pp. 133 & 135 and from personal observations made on 22 April 2012 and 22 February 2014.

FIGURE 107 *The vaguely phallic stuffed cloths with large bells attached that are the votive offerings at the Karamatsu Shrine in Sakai (Akita Prefecture).*

FIGURE 108 *The three sexual stones located behind the Karamatsu Shrine. On the right is a stone of vaguely ktenic appearance. On left is a stone that consists of natural sedimentary rock enclosing a basalt core like a womb holding an unborn child, while in between them is a perfectly egg-shaped natural boulder like a testicle that shines from having been rubbed so often.*

FIGURE 109 *The interior of the Shibatate Hime Shrine showing a statuette of the girl and the phalluses that are presented and borrowed.*

stopped to rest. There they crossed the line of acceptable behaviour. The father killed the girl in remorse and buried her under a tree. Local villagers erected the shrine to comfort her spirit, and the place is responsive to female health needs. There is a small statue of the girl inside surrounded by votive phallic symbols. On one phallus are written eleven names of people who have benefitted from its powers.[17]

Another tragic woman became the *kami* Mizuha no Me no Mikoto 水波女尊 after dying by drowning in a river in Ashikaga (Tochigi Prefecture). Following this terrible incident great misfortune attended the area and was attributed to her unhappy spirit, so she was enshrined as a *kami* of water to whom prayers were also offered for women's needs. Her shrine, the Mizushi Shrine 水使神社, provides a wealth of phallic and ktenic imagery and Nishioka devotes an entire section of his book to the place.[18] A depiction of the

17 From a personal observation made on 12 April 2012.

18 Nishioka 1961, pp. 284–290. The personal observations were made on 24 April 2012 and at the autumn *matsuri* of 21 October 2012.

FIGURE 110 *The Mizushi Shrine in Ashikaga enshrines the tragic Mizuha no Me no Mikoto. Here is an* ema *with a modern painting of her, flanked by a more traditional design. The other* ema *are of a nursing mother and one unique to the shrine which is of a woman's lower body in a dress. There are also various items of women's clothing and a traditional* omamori *consisting of a cloth bag.*

kami holding a rice tub in her left hand and a rice scoop in her right is found at the shrine in the form of a statuette and may be bought as an *ofuda*, while the aerial roots of a tree in the precincts look like dangling phalluses.

Another interesting feature of the Mizushi Shrine is the offering to the *kami* of items of women's clothing and babies' bibs, which are tied to a frame behind the rails at the front of the sanctuary. The clothing consists mainly of bonnets but included two brassieres in 2012, and in 2005 the practice prompted an article in the popular newspaper *Tokyo Sports* (東ソポ *To-spo*). It described how, 'With her beautiful large G-cup breasts *To-Spo*'s stunning sex festival gal Aika Jun visits the "panty shrine", takes off her sexy panties and presents them as a lively offering!'. The feature continues:

> 'Fantastic!' says the wide-eyed Aika Jun as she throws a coin into the offertory box and promptly begins a lively disrobing. Placing her hands up inside her miniskirt she continues to undress. Her sexy orange thong

FIGURE 111 *The curious collection of 'aerial phalluses' at the Mizushi Shrine that are formed by the aerial roots of a tree that grows beside the steps.*

> is revealed. She finishes undressing and ties the still-warm panties to the balustrade. On successfully concluding the lively offering, she clasps her hands and approaches the shrine.

Needless to say, undressing in front of the shrine is not the normal practice for worshippers, but Miss Jun is depicted in two accompanying photographs removing and presenting the garments she is presently wearing. Yet Aika Jun reveals that she is fully aware of the benefits associated with her lively offering

FIGURE 112 *This picture shows the transformation of the Mizushi Shrine for its* matsuri. *The doors are now open and the donated clothing has been moved round to the side to make way for a number of phallic and ktenic items. The offertory box now stands at the foot of the steps and the shrine is framed by a blue curtain.*

to the shrine. They involve 'progeny, prosperity, women's illnesses and for men enhanced vigour and so on', and the suitably moved Aika Jun says that what she prayed for was 'protection against sexual disease and women's illnesses'.[19]

The Mizushi Shrine's phallic and ktenic symbols are normally kept in a storehouse and are placed on show only during the two festival days each year. There is no portable shrine and no procession on these occasions, but the shrine's doors are opened and the sexual objects are arranged as symbolic votive offerings. One iron phallus stands within the ablutions fountain and receives its own libations from visitors. The doors of the Ema-dō (*ema* hall) are also open to display some unique *ema* that show the clothed lower half of a female body crowned by the image of the sun. During the morning a small bonfire is held to burn old *ofuda* and *ema*, but this is the only moment of real drama, and the only loud noise in 2012 was supplied by a *karaoke* session.

The third example of a woman who died a tragic death is the *kami* of the Ohana Daigongen in Eguchi. The 24 year-old Ohana is said in some accounts to be a daughter of the Hachisuka family and in others a courtesan who was strangled to death by a jealous rival within the women's quarters of the lord's

19 Jun, Aika 2005. 'T-bakku nama hōnō' *Tokyo Sport* (*Tōpo*) 21 June, p. 15.

FIGURE 113 *The interior of the Ohana Daigongen shows its wonderfully eclectic contents that include statues of gods, donated phalluses, various erotica and photographs of babies who have been born following prayers to the* kami.

castle. Her unhappy spirit was then held responsible for a series of mysterious deaths, and one night she appeared at the lord's bedside pleading to be deified. A splendid shrine was created for her within the castle and when the Hachisuka family were transferred to Shikoku in 1614 Ohana went with them. She was moved again in 1913 to the shrine's present location within the grounds of a Shingon temple. The main shrine building houses numerous votive phalluses presented to Ohana, whose image appears on the *ema*. The central images are a naturally occurring *in'yōseki* flanked by statues of Ohana Daigongen and Benten. Around them are grouped wooden phalluses and ktenes, paintings and some amusing erotic creations with moving parts.[20]

No personal tragedy appears to be associated with the Midorigaoka Shrine on Hirado Island, the place once described by Richard Cocks. It enshrines a deity called Omuta-sama or Omuda-san, in some accounts identified as the licentious daughter of the local lord, in others as a mysterious visitor from across the sea. Her *goshintai* is an object that is locked away but numerous

20 From a personal observation made on 11 June 2013, the pamphlet supplied by the shrine and Kokonoe 1981, p. 258.

FIGURE 114 *A priest demonstrates the operation of a hinged wooden phallus, one of a large number of donated objects kept in a separate shrine building at the Ohana Daigongen.*

phalluses are offered to her. They stand in the open air at the rear of the shrine and were illustrated earlier.[21]

At other ktenic shrines the sacred emphasis arises not from a link to a named human or mythological character but from the existence of a natural outcrop of rock of a ktenic appearance. In *Phallicism in Japan* Buckley maintained that any naturally occurring sexual symbol was prized more highly than manufactured ones, 'and being found in nature could hardly be taken for ought else than the veritable organ of the god', a belief illustrated by the attributions made following the discovery of some *sekibō*.[22] Enshrined ktenes draw a similar power from their natural occurrence, and an excellent example is provided by the large solitary rock face called the Gozen Iwa 御前岩 that lies among a dense growth of trees across a river to the east of Utsunomiya (Tochigi Prefecture). This 15 metre high cliff is of a remarkably ktenic appearance as indicated in particular by a 1.5 metre long vertical slit with foliage adding a believable touch of pubic hair. On the opposite bank is a small box for offerings that acts as a focus for prayers, which, as the notice board relates, include

21 Nishioka 1961, pp. 278–279.

22 Buckley 1895, p. 26.

FIGURE 115 *The Gozen Iwa in Tochigi Prefecture is a 15 metre high cliff of a remarkably ktenic appearance as indicated in particular by a 1.5 metre long vertical slit.*

conception, easy delivery and women's illnesses. The sign explains that there was once also a phallic rock but many years ago it collapsed during a flood, leaving behind Japan's most striking example of natural ktenic imagery.[23]

Although of a much smaller size, the protruding edge of a small ktenic rocky outcrop to the west of Tokyo possesses an even closer resemblance to female genitalia. It is at Okutama, a village just inside the border where the Tokyo metropolitan district ends and the mountain pass into Yamanashi Prefecture begins. After a very steep climb of about fifteen minutes through the forest a simple wooden shrine is revealed, inside which is a natural kteis known as Hime Seki Kannon 姫石観音 whose *kami* will answer prayers for easy delivery and also for rain. On entering the shrine the stone appears to be a solitary boulder that has been placed there. It is only on examining the site from outside that it is revealed to be part of a rocky outcrop embraced by the trunk of a tree round which the shrine was cleverly constructed to protect it in 1962. Phallic symbols are offered to this prominent ktenic object.[24]

23 From a personal observation made on 27 April 2012 and Kokonoe 1981, p. 75.

24 Kokonoe 1976, pp. 54–55 and from a personal observation made on 15 November 2012.

FIGURE 116 *At the village of Okutama at the western edge of Tokyo there is a ktenic rock known as Hime Seki Kannon who will answer prayers for easy delivery and also for rain. A phallus has been presented to this natural phenomenon.*

FIGURE 117 *The view from the rear of the Hime Seki Kannon shows that it is a rocky outcrop around which a shrine has been built and not a boulder brought from somewhere else to the site.*

FIGURE 118 *The ktenic waterfall known as the Anchō Taki near Lake Tazawa (Akita Prefecture).*

An impression of female genitalia may also be discerned in the natural shape of waterfalls, for which Akita Prefecture provides two examples. The Momobora no Taki 桃洞の滝 lies deep in the mountains south of Ōdate and under certain conditions has the appearance of open labia.[25] A more accessible one is the Anchō Taki アンチョウ滝 near Lake Tazawa, where the water emerges from a ktenic rock formation. Beside it sits a little *hokora* that is quite sufficient for devotional use to its unnamed *kami*, but across the stream is a prominent wooden phallus identified as Konsei Daimyōjin. Unlike the above examples this physically separated representation of the powerful phallic deity is probably not an offering to the female *kami* of the waterfall but is likely to be an attempt to balance the ktenic ambience with a phallic symbol.[26]

Far more numerous than these natural images fixed in the landscape are detached ktenic stones that have been installed in shrines as *goshintai*. At the Ōagata Shrine an interesting collection of natural stone ktenic symbols sits

25 A photograph appears at http://bikky.at.webry.info/200911/article_1.html (Accessed 30 November 2013).

26 From a personal observation made on 22 April 2012. See also Satō 1995, pp. 166–167.

FIGURE 119 *At the Myōtogi Hime no Miya near Kōfu (Yamanashi Prefecture) a light-coloured ktenic boulder is known as the Myōto Seki. It is a good example of a ktenic image provided by a detached boulder brought to the shrine.*

in a small open shrine at the rear of the main building. They are called the Hime Seki 姫石 and are associated with Tamahime no Mikoto 玉姫尊 who is a patron of women's needs and the focus of attention at the famous phallic festival at the nearby Tagata Shrine.[27] Hime Seki-sama 姫石様 is a ktenic rock at Chino (Nagano Prefecture) that is kept within a locked wooden shrine.[28] Others include the curiously titled Onnagata Stone 女形石 (the stone of the female impersonator) that stands beside a road to the east of Fukushima City in a small wooden shrine where it receives prayers for relief from female illnesses. A number of phallic symbols lie behind it.[29] Another ktenic rock about 50 cm in diameter is enshrined within the grounds of the Yokose Hachiman Shrine 横瀬八幡宮 at Shūzenji (Shizuoka Prefecture). This site is associated

27 From personal observations made on 9 April 1992 and 9 March 2008.

28 From a personal observation made on 14 November 2012.

29 From a personal observation made on 1 November 2012.

with Hōjō Masako, the widow of Minamoto Yoritomo, and the *kami* responds to prayers about female ailments and child rearing.[30]

The importance of a ktenic image compared to some phalluses is best illustrated at Kawaji Onsen (Tochigi Prefecture), where a wayside shrine houses a rock known as the Onade Ishi おなで石. This is a small ktenic stone bearing a slit which is rubbed to ensure conception, easy delivery and matchmaking. The shrine contains several phallic stones, but this naturally occurring ktenic one possesses the main spiritual power.[31] Solitary ktenic images artificially created from wood or stone are comparatively rare. At the Daihiden 大秘殿 in Gamagori (Aichi Prefecture) a wooden kteis is used to represent the goddess Kishimojin.[32] The Takashiba Deco Yashiki 高柴デコ屋敷, a folk-art village in Fukushima Prefecture has a female sexual shrine called the Michiroku Hime Yashiro 道六姫社. Inside are two crude ktenic wood carvings made by using the natural shape of a bifurcated trunk while two carved stone ktenes stand outside.[33]

In all these examples the ktenic symbolism is not difficult to identify. There are cases, however, where the imagery is more abstract. The Mizutani Shrine 水谷神社 in Nara, a numinous place among dark ancient trees where sacred deer roam, is a sub-shrine of the great Kasuga Shrine, which it resembles with its vermilion woodwork. The visitor's eye is first drawn to the main shrine building with its enormous tree, and in front of the protective fence there is a neatly stacked pile of *ema* bearing the written desire for a child. Yet just in front of the *torii* (and at the mercy of trampling feet were it not fenced off) lie the Ko Sazuke Seki 子授石 (child-begetting stones), a small arrangement that together make up a recognisable yet stylised kteis. No phallic element is present.[34]

Paired Arrangements Representing Sexual Harmony

The majority of ktenic images found in shrines today make up one half of paired arrangements of natural stones or carvings from wood or stone that are often placed together in a coital position. In some cases they are identified with Izanagi and Izanami, but most receive devotion as symbols of the abstract

30 Kokonoe 1976, p. 104 and from a personal observation made on 10 November 2012.

31 From a personal observation made on 7 July 2013.

32 From a personal observation made on 13 June 2013.

33 From a personal observation made on 2 July 2013.

34 From a personal observation made on 2 May 2012.

FIGURE 120 *At Kawaji Onsen a wayside shrine houses a natural rock known as the Onade Ishi. This is a small stone bearing a slit which is rubbed to ensure conception, easy delivery and matchmaking.*

FIGURE 121 *Deep beneath the Daihiden at Gamagori (Aichi Prefecture) is this carved wooden kteis that represents the goddess Kishimojin.*

FIGURE 122 *The Mizutani Shrine in Nara is a sub-shrine of the great Kasuga Shrine, which it resembles with its vermilion woodwork.*

FIGURE 123 *In front of the* torii *of the Mizutani Shrine lie the Ko Sazuke Seki (child-begetting stones), a small arrangement that together make up a recognisable yet stylised kteis.*

ideal of *in'yōwagō* 陰陽和合, the harmonious union of the yin and yang duality expressed through sexual congress. Yin is the principle of darkness, cold and femininity. Yang is the principle of brightness, heat and masculinity and their interaction produces the five elements of wood, earth, metal, fire and water. Reverence for the concept of the harmony of the two principles has a long history in Japan, but the ideas lying behind its expression as paired sexual stones must be distinguished from notions of divination found in Onmyōdō 陰陽道 (The Way of Yin and Yang). That is the system of religious Daoism involving geomancy, notions of lucky directions and lucky days together with a wide range of complex taboos relating to the calendar, all of which have been incorporated into the wider Japanese religious world.[35]

No divination was involved when the concept of *in'yōwagō* was embraced by the emerging philosophy of *kokugaku*. Hirata Atsutane's follower Miyao Sadao (1797–1858) a village headman who once described himself modestly as a 'potato-digging village official' used it as a way of re-affirming and even re-creating the stable life of the village that was under threat from the increased

35 Hayashi, Makoto and Hayek, Matthias 2013. 'Editors' Introduction: Onmyōdō in Japanese History' *Japanese Journal of Religious Studies* 40, p. 3.

urbanisation of Edo and the castle towns.[36] The harmony that was vital to the stability of a village community was seen as analogous to the harmony between the male and female principles in the natural world and, by extension, to sexual relations between couples. Miyao Sadao wrote that as a man was born with a penis it was his divine commission to procreate and that it was also not in accordance with the will of the *kami* that the feminine instrument of procreation should go unused.[37] Through work and through their own life-giving sexual relationships men and women returned to the creator *kami* the blessings they had received.[38] Ninomiya Sontoku (1787–1856), the reformer known affectionately as the 'peasant sage of Japan', also wrote:

> The presence of male and female, of necessity, gives birth to harmony, just as the Yin and Yang are different yet one. In the same way, male and female become one when united; where there is harmony there is progeny.[39]

Hirata Atsutane's enthusiasm for sexual beliefs included a deep appreciation of the significance of naturally occurring *in'yōseki*, and in 1832 Miyao Sadao published *In'yō Shinseki-zu*, an illustrated study of them based on comments by Hirata dating from about 1812. Sadao regarded these stones as particularly efficacious for prayer because they were all natural rocks, 'not artificially manufactured by human hands but were begotten from the womb of great nature', so that when prayers were offered before them:

> A lover will be favoured with the blessing of getting his sweetheart, a young man and woman will be favoured with securing a fine match, while married women will never remain barren and sorrowful.[40]

Sadao's central drawing is supposed to depict the mythical island of Onogoro created by Izanagi and Izanami using the jewel spear of heaven. He writes:

---

36 Jansen, Marius B (ed.) 1989. *The Cambridge History of Japan Volume 5: The Nineteenth Century* (Cambridge), p. 209.

37 Miyata, Noboru 1996. 'The Cult of Genitalia and the Return of the Land in Late Edo Culture' in Jones, Sumie (ed.) *Imaging/Reading Eros: Proceedings for the conference, Sexuality and Edo Culture, 1750–1850 Indiana University, Bloomington August 17–20, 1995* (Bloomington), p. 79.

38 Jansen 1989, p. 207.

39 Miyata 1996, p. 79. Statues of Ninomiya Sontoku abound. He is shown as a wanderer totally absorbed in the book he is reading as he walks along.

40 Katō 1924, pp. 8–9.

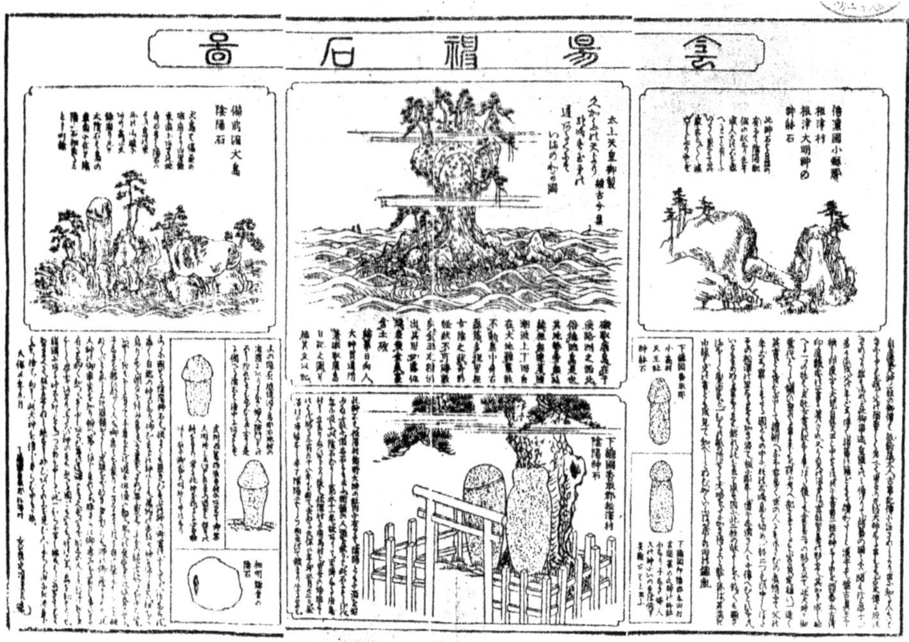

FIGURE 124 *The drawings of naturally occurring or mythical* in'yōseki *published by Miyao Sadao in* Inyō Shinseki-zu *in 1832.*

> It is solitary and has no connection with its roots. It stands in the midst of waves and never moves in spite of great earthquakes. On the island are many curious stones, many of them being shaped like male and female generative organs. The stones produce a dew-like liquid and have a mineral taste on the outside, while within are earths and sands.[41]

Another of Sadao's drawings is of a phallic and a ktenic rock in a position of copulation, of which he writes admiringly (in Buckley's translation) that, 'Someone did injury to the rock, and was destroyed, and all his house'.[42] A similar awe attends the handful of massive sexual stone groupings that now make up the largest naturally occurring *in'yōseki*. They are much revered because if small polished bars of stone could be regarded as either a 'landing stage' for a sexual *kami* or even the body of the *kami* itself, how much more might such attributes have been placed upon huge outcrops of rock of a distinctive phallic and ktenic form?

41 Buckley 1895, p. 24.

42 Buckley 1895, p. 14.

FIGURE 125 *The* In'yōseki *at Kobayashi (Miyazaki Prefecture) is a huge phallic rock 17.5 metres in height. It appears to have completely phallic characteristics but on the reverse side it slopes down towards the water and takes the shape of a kteis.*

The first is to be found in a narrow river valley near Kobayashi in Miyazaki Prefecture. Known simply as the In'yōseki and approached through the red *torii* of the In'yōseki Shrine, its huge phallic rock, 17.5 metres in height, towers above the gorge, an effect heightened by the frail-looking straw rope tied around it. At first sight this object appears to have completely phallic characteristics, but on inspection from the reverse side the rock formation that slopes down towards the water may be seen to have the form of a kteis. Away from the river stands a shrine building that resembles a crude gallery. In front of it a large phallus carved from a tree trunk complements the notion of harmony by being positioned in a coital position in front of a kteis made from the cross section of a hollow tree.[43]

That *in'yōseki* lies in a remote location accessible only by car, but its rival for size in Nakatsugawa (Gifu Prefecture) stands within the city in an area that is now a public park. The large phallic and ktenic rocks are roped off from the footpaths, presumably so that the children playing on the nearby swings and slides are not tempted to see them as an extension of their playground. They

43 From a personal observation made on 4 August 2009.

FIGURE 126 *The Myōto Iwa (husband and wife rocks) at Nakatsugawa (Gifu Prefecture) make up an* in'yōseki *of which the phallus stands 7 metres high and is 22 meters in overall circumference, while the ktenic rock is 3 metres high and 30 metres round.*

are known as the Myōto Iwa 夫婦岩 (husband and wife rocks). The male gives the impression of being a huge phallus that is almost completely buried in the ground below the glans. It stands 7 metres high and is 22 meters in overall circumference, while the ktenic rock is 3 metres high and 30 metres round. The noticeboard says that they enshrine Izanagi and Izanami, who will answer prayers for easy delivery.[44]

Both these sites are however outclassed by the set of rocks that cover a wooded hillside high above the river valley in rural Kurogi (Fukuoka Prefecture). Only one pinnacle can be seen easily from the road, but a strenuous climb that begins within the precincts of the temple of Reiganji and continues up a steep mountain path reveals a dozen or so other rocks ranging in height from 4 to 60 metres. They are best appreciated from the highest point of the climb which is reached on its final ascent with help of chains, where a statue of Kōbō Daishi looks out across the valley towards neat terraces of tea bushes. One's eyes are soon drawn to the large rock pinnacles that protrude from the surrounding foliage. All have been given names and are identified on the notice board beside the road. Three stand out in particular from the high vantage point. To the left

44 From a personal observation made on 1 March 2011.

FIGURE 127 *In Kurogi (Fukuoka Prefecture) a series of phallic rocks tower over the road above the temple of Reiganji.*

is a phallic rock of a very distinctive shape. Further up the slope to its right is the matchmaker rock. Above that is the ktenic rock with a wide cleft in its side. Behind the ktenic rock is a small 'child rock'. Behind them is a squat phallic rock called the Jizō rock, while others bear the name of the '*tanuki* (badger) rock' and the 'monkey rock' from their appearance. Various spots along the way provide a focus for prayers for conception and safe delivery.[45]

At Senmaya to the east of Ichinoseki in Iwate Prefecture there is another well-proportioned example. The phallic rock in front protrudes from its small hill with a *shimenawa* round its hammer-shaped head. Together with the ktenic rock behind they make up a pair known as the Meoto Seki 夫婦石 (wedded rocks).[46] Somewhat smaller are the phallic and ktenic impressions to be seen protruding from a cliff not far from the sea at Shirahama (Wakayama Prefecture). The cliff face provides the focal point for the Kanki Shrine 歓喜神社 to Izanagi and Izanami, whose sexual symbols are no more than one metre high overall. The phallus is somewhat indistinct, but the extraordinary detail of the kteis (reminiscent of the one at Okutama) suggests that nature may have received something of a helping hand. To compensate for the

45 From a personal observation made on 11 April 2012.

46 From a personal observation made on 20 April 2012.

FIGURE 128 *At Senmaya (Iwate Prefecture) an* in'yōseki *pair protrudes from a small hill.*

inaccessibility of the natural features, which are fenced off, an additional phallus and a very explicit kteis have been carved in wood. A separate shrine building houses another large phallus and several votive offerings. There is also an excellent museum displaying a fine collection of sexual statuettes from the Indian sub-continent and a very amusing souvenir shop.[47]

The other natural features used to symbolise sexual harmony are pairs of tree trunks or ones that have grown together, and in places where the shrine has not been built around a natural feature the principle of *in'yōwagō* may be expressed by combining two objects brought to the site from elsewhere. A spectacular *in'yōseki* was added about twenty years ago to the Ōmiya Shrine 大宮神社 in Oguni (Yamagata Prefecture). This beautiful place founded in 712 has long been renowned for matchmaking and safe delivery, but the installation of these two very large stones during the mid-1990s represented a remarkable addition to its sexual ambience. Both stones were found within a few kilometres of the shrine and are very realistic in their phallic and ktenic shapes. They are housed in the hexagonal Wagō Miya 和合宮 (the hall of harmony). At the rear of the display stands a vaguely ktenic tree trunk, but all one's attention is drawn to the phallus (named Kanemaru Tarō after the village where it was

47 Kokonoe 1981, p. 231 and from a personal observation made on 1 May 2012.

FIGURE 129 *At Shirahama (Wakayama Prefecture) a cliff face provides the* goshintai *for the Kanki Shrine as an* in'yōseki *about 1 metre high. The phallus is somewhat indistinct, but the extraordinary detail of the kteis suggests that nature may have received something of a helping hand.*

found) and the kteis (Tanezawa Hanako) with which it is paired in a situation of impending coition. Both are completely as they were found. The phallus has a pronounced glans and the kteis a prominent clitoris.[48]

A more modestly proportioned pair stands within the grounds of the Ichijōji Asama Shrine 一乗寺浅間神社 in Kōfu (Yamanashi Prefecture). The tall phallic rock is more prominent than the kteis and has two spherical rocks as its testicles.[49] Arrangements of *in'yōseki* are also included among the numerous rocks in Japan's most celebrated stroll gardens. They are recognisably phallic or ktenic when one's attention is drawn to them, although most visitors are probably unaware of their existence or significance. The group within the Kenrokuen 兼六園 at Kanazawa (Ishikawa Prefecture) lies on a small island

48 From a personal observation made on 29 June 2013.

49 From a personal observation made on 13 November 2012.

FIGURE 130 *The phallic and ktenic tree trunks at the Chiwaki Shrine in Morioka City (Iwate Prefecture). The 'male' on the right has a pronounced bole in its trunk, the 'female' a simple hole.*

FIGURE 131 *This 'wedded tree' at the Futaarasan Shrine is one of a number to be found within the general area of the Nikkō Tōshogū (Tochigi Prefecture).*

FIGURE 132 *One of the most attractive pairs of* in'yōseki *in all Japan is framed here by a bifurcated tree at the Yasaka Shrine to the east of Matsumoto. The phallic stone was discovered in a river bed and installed at the base of a cryptomeria tree outside the shrine, where it served for a time as the focus for prayers for easy delivery. The ktenic stone, found later in the same river, was brought to join it.*

FIGURE 133 *The natural stone phallus and kteis of Oguni's Ōmiya Shrine (Yamagata Prefecture) are arranged in a coital position to symbolise sexual harmony between the male and female principles.*

FIGURE 134 *A close-up of the* in'yōseki *of the Ōmiya Shrine.*

across a stream. It is marked by a *torii* but the whole ensemble is quite muted. The phallus is small but may be distinguished from the others by its lighter colour. The kteis is much larger but indistinct, and both are overshadowed by a third rock that stands behind them.[50] Several pairs of *in'yōseki* may also be found at the Ritsurin 栗林 in Takamatsu (Kagawa Prefecture), one of which involves a kteis that appears to have been artificially shaped, although an unusually symmetrical natural formation cannot be ruled out.[51] Otherwise a certain degree of imagination is required, as in the case of the very abstract stones on the central hill of the Korakuen 後楽園 in Okayama City.[52]

Other *in'yōseki* may be realistic in their shape but very small indeed, as exemplified by the entwined pair of stones placed within the precincts of the Mishima Shrine near Tōfukuji Station in Kyoto.[53] Much larger but often more abstract are arrangements where the visual emphasis is on vertical lines such as the unmistakeable pairing of a phallus and a ktenic bowl at the Imi Betsugu 伊美別宮社 at Kunimi (Ōita Prefecture).[54]

An unusual example of an *in'yōseki* made from carved stone rather than naturally occurring rocks is at the Okitsu Shrine 澳津神社 at Togura Onsen near Ueda (Nagano Prefecture). Judging from a photograph from the 1970s this site has suffered more than most from modern road developments and speculative building. The shrine that once stood on a bend in the road now looks as though it has been compressed into the decaying concrete wall of a rusty and abandoned spa complex. The *kami* enshrined here is the goddess of the hearth Okitsu Hime.[55] The kteis is carved from stone with a degree of detail that would be only suggested by an unmodified natural boulder.[56] Wood is an alternative medium, and reference was made earlier to the use of small carved figures from branches in the Yama no kami tradition in Shiga Prefecture. They represent sexual harmony, but when that principle is expressed through the medium of wood it usually takes the form of two large tree trunks shaped and arranged in a coital position, as seen at the Shichirōjin, the In'yōseki Shrine and many other places.

---

50 From a personal observation made on 16 April 2012. See also Kokonoe 1981, p. 207.

51 From a personal observation made on 10 June 2013.

52 From a personal observation made on 23 October 2012.

53 From a personal observation made on 3 April 2012.

54 Kokonoe 1981, p. 271. For photographs see http://daizukan9.blog63.fc2.com/blog-entry-985.html.

55 Herbert, Jean 1967. *Shintō: At the Fountainhead of Japan* (Oxford), p. 443.

56 Kokonoe 1976, p. 108 and from a personal observation made on 18 April 2012.

FIGURE 135 *Within the grounds of the Ichijōji Asama Shrine in Kōfu is an* in'yōseki *of a tall phallic rock complete with testicles and a much smaller ktenic rock.*

FIGURE 136 *One of the pairs of* in'yōseki *at the Ritsurin garden in Takamatsu. Unusually, the duo stand some distance apart from each other at opposite ends of a bridge.*

FIGURE 137 *Matchmaking is the speciality of the* in'yōseki *at the Tokuunji to the east of Matsumoto in Nagano Prefecture. Its ktenic stone has an inclusion that could almost be a baby's head beginning to emerge in the act of birth.*

FIGURE 138 *With some* in'yōseki *the emphasis is on vertical lines, as in this pairing in the courtyard of the Shōkakuji in Nagasaki, where the ktenic element is like a large stone bowl. The temple is adjacent to Nagasaki's former pleasure quarter of Maruyama.*

FIGURE 139 *An unusual carved stone kteis is paired with a carved phallus at the Okitsu Shrine at Togura Onsen near Ueda (Nagano Prefecture). It possesses a degree of frank sexual detail that would be absent from an unmodified ktenic boulder.*

In all the above examples the symbolism is fairly obvious, but some very obscure *in'yōseki* are built into the fabric of the Suwa Shrine 諏訪神社 in Nagasaki. No attempt is made to disguise them. They are even described in the shrine's English language pamphlet as places where a couple may enact a very private votive ritual. The three images lie in the ground on the way up to the shrine along a flight of steps. The phallic stone is encountered beneath the second *torii* and consists of nothing more than a flat disc set into the paving. The kteis lies beneath the fourth *torii* and is ktenic by virtue of three stones set within two others shaped like labia. The ritual is to step on both sets with one's right foot on entering the shrine and with one's left foot when leaving. At the top of the steps just outside the main worship hall is the combined couple stone: a simple circle inside a square, an arrangement that can be regarded as an abstract *in'yōseki*. If a couple complete their visit by stepping on this stone and uttering appropriate prayers they will be rewarded with a happy marriage and safe childbirth.[57]

Finally, varied and subtle symbols of sexual harmony may be seen at the Kamigamo Shrine 上賀茂神社 in Kyoto. This venerable institution derives from the myth of Tamayori Hime finding an arrow in a stream, taking it home and placing it under her pillow. She then gave birth to a boy who became

57 From a personal observation made on 7 April 2012.

FIGURE 140 *This is the third and final sexual symbol set into the approach to the* honden *of the Suwa Shrine in Nagasaki, the combined stone of a simple circle inside a square. When a couple complete their visit by stepping on this stone and uttering appropriate prayers they will be rewarded with a happy marriage and safe childbirth.*

Wake-Ikazuchi, the *kami* of thunder, lightning and rain who is now enshrined at Kamigamo. Symbolic arrows are found there, but the key designs on the hanging curtains are of the *aoi* or hollyhock. Nelson identifies two forms according to their locations. The ktenic variety with a strong erect flower is encountered where there is a female *kami* enshrined. These are the buildings through which one passes that are dedicated to Tamayori Hime. Towards the centre of the shrine where her son is deified the symbolism changes, but not to an overtly aggressive phallic form. Instead the leaves take a gently phallic shape. Nelson sees this as indicating not male dominance but a recognition of its protective and procreative roles in cooperation with the female principle. The area in front of the Kamigamo Shrine contains the most delicate sexual symbolism in the whole of Japan. Here are two beautiful symmetrical white cones made by piling and shaping the coarse gravelly sand. They represent Mount Kōyama, the sacred mountain where Kamigamo's deity was worshipped before the present shrine was built, but there is more to them than meets the eye because on the tip of the left hand cone are two pine needles

FIGURE 141 *The two cones at the Kamigamo Shrine in Kyoto stand for the peaks of Mount Kōyama but they also act as Japan's most subtle representation of the harmony between the yin and the yang because each cone has pine needles in its tip: two for the male and three for the female.*

and on the right three. The cones are therefore respectively phallic and ktenic, yang and yin, united in harmony.[58]

In conclusion, a wealth of ktenic imagery exists within Japan's sexual shrines to act as representations of the enshrined *kami* and to provide an appropriate focus for prayers for women's health needs. At these places naturally occurring ktenic objects and items carved from wood or stone provide an important category of sexual imagery in Japanese religion that calls into question the easy attribution of the words 'phallic shrine' to their locations. Some play a vital role as one half of a harmonious pair. In others a kteis is sufficient for the achievement of female goals without the addition of the seemingly ubiquitous phallus other than as a votive offering to it. In Japanese religious belief a female *kami* can quite clearly stand on her own within a distinct and relevant symbolic environment.

58 Nelson 1993, pp. 2–14 and from a personal observation made on 3 April 2012.

CHAPTER 8

The Phallus as *Kami*: The Cult of Konsei Daimyōjin

One of the themes of this book is that the word phallicism, with its conventional concentration on the male element, is an expression that should be employed only with care in the context of Japan's sexual shrines. There are certain places, however, where phallicism would appear to be the only appropriate term to use. This is partly owing to the lack of ktenic imagery at these shrines but also because their central and very prominent phalluses act neither as offerings nor as protective symbols. Instead they provide the *goshintai* for a very individual and mysterious *kami* known as Konsei Daimyōjin, whose name is usually written as 金勢大明神 or 金精大明神 ('Konsei the great shining god').[1] Konsei Daimyōjin may be encountered in a wide variety of shrines located primarily in northern Japan. The Matsunoki Konsei Shrine in Kazuno (Akita Prefecture) is one of the largest in the country.[2] Others include the Dōso Konsei Daimyōjin 道祖金勢大明神 in Atsuta (Nagoya City), where Jizō's protective role is complemented by Konsei Daimyōjin's procreative symbolism.[3]

A dominant phallus is not however entirely sufficient as a means of distinguishing these shrines from other places that display a single phallic symbol. All Konsei Daimyōjin are phalluses, but not all phalluses are Konsei Daimyōjin. Many will be protective *sai no kami* and there are some other named phallic *goshintai* with procreative specialities, although these are quite rare. Named phalluses known as Raseki Daimyōjin 裸石 大明神 are to be found in Hyōgo and Niigata Prefectures, and some phalluses may simply be referred to using the word *mara* in some combination such as *kanamara*.[4] If Konsei Daimyōjin is the enshrined *kami* his name will be found on an accompanying notice or on the phallus itself with the choice of characters for 'Konsei' being split about equally between 金勢 or 金精, although three Konsei Daimyōjin shrines in

1 The name may also be expressed as Konsei-sama and is subject to various dialect interpretations. Masuta identifies the use of Kōsen, Kōhen, Kone and Kōsei-sama within Aomori Prefecture alone. Another in Aomori is called Konsei Ōkami (2012, p. 37).

2 From a personal observation made on 23 April 2012.

3 Ashida 1963, p. 35 and from a personal observation made on 22 October 2012.

4 In Mukabaki (Hiroshima Prefecture) a stone that bears the name Omara-sama オマラサマ is the *goshintai* of a simple rural shrine. A notice board informs visitors that the stone was found by a village headman whose daughter was suffering from gonorrhoea. He prayed to Omara-sama and she was cured, since when it has received great devotion and has phalluses offered to it. (From a personal observation made on 6 March 2014).

 | DOI 10.1163/9789004293786_009

FIGURE 142 *The Konsei Daimyōjin at the Ōwashi Shrine in Ajiki is erroneously claimed to be the largest in Japan. Its height is 2.47 metres and it is 2.3 metres in circumference. Behind it stands a shelf on which are rows of votive phalluses.*

Chiba, Ibaraki and Gifu Prefectures use the characters 魂生. In addition the names of both Konsei Daimyōjin shrines at Komaki Onsen in Misawa (Aomori Prefecture) are expressed using the characters 根精, as is the Konsei Ōkami in Sannohe in the same prefecture.

In only one Konsei Daimyōjin shrine studied in the course of this research does a female symbol appear to enjoy equal status with a phallus. Yet this apparent exception within the precincts of the Hiraide Shrine 平出神社 in Utsunomiya (Tochigi Prefecture) is in fact half of an *in'yōseki* standing outside the inner shrine that holds the unseen *goshintai*.[5] In a similar manner the Konsei Daimyōjin in the village of Kobansawa (Saitama Prefecture) is surrounded by phallic votive offerings and has three female companions at its side. Even the three phalluses and one kteis at the Konsei Shrine at Ashinomaki Onsen (Fukushima Prefecture) are simply explained. The largest phallus is for Konsei Daimyōjin. The kteis is for Ame no Uzume, while the other phalluses stand for Sarutahiko and their offspring Ōta no Mikoto who are also enshrined there.[6]

5 From a personal observation made on 21 October 2012.

6 From a personal observation made on 1 July 2013.

FIGURE 143 *This small pair of* in'yōseki *put together from naturally occurring stones is inside the Konsei Daimyōjin shrine within the Hiraide Shrine in Utsunomiya.*

FIGURE 144 *The Kobansawa Konsei Daimyōjin shrine stands in the middle of the small mountain village in Saitama Prefecture. The central* goshintai *is surrounded by other phalluses and some female companions.*

The geographical distribution of Konsei Daimyōjin shrines may explain why they are less well-known than other shrines involving phallic imagery, because nearly all the surviving examples lie within the Tōhoku and Kantō areas. There are isolated ones in Aichi and Gifu Prefectures and a particularly striking example in Okayama, but none at all on Hokkaidō, Shikoku or Kyūshū. In the course of the present study about one hundred Konsei Daimyōjin shrines have so far been clearly identified, but there were probably many more prior to 1868 because some popular sexual shrines that now have other names bore the title of Konsei Daimyōjin until they suffered from the modernising and moralising tendencies of the Meiji Restoration. They were then required to change their names and in some cases the identity of the deity they enshrined.

The Identity of Konsei Daimyōjin

A brief reference was made earlier to the creation of a divine nature for a *goshintai* as a result of the descent, entry and sacred indwelling by a *kami*. The study of Konsei Daimyōjin now requires a further assessment of this relationship, because whatever additional phallic votive offerings may be found inside the typical Konsei Daimyōjin shrine there will be this focal point in the form of one large phallus, and in terms of its associated behaviour the *kami* and the object will be treated as equal and interchangeable. What may be expected from the god may also be expected from the image because it shares in its very essence, a situation analogous to what would be found if the object were an icon, which is generally understood to be:

> …a specific sort of religious image that is believed to partake or participate in the substance of that which it represents. In other words, an icon does not merely bear the likeness of the divine, but shares in its very nature.[7]

Although derived from a Western religious and artistic tradition, the notion of an icon has received considerable application in discussions of Japanese religious belief. The above quotation is from an article by Robert Sharf and was made in the context of Buddhist images, the same field of inquiry explored by Fabio Rambelli, who also makes extensive use of the word icon, noting that:

7 Sharf, Robert H 1999. 'On the Allure of Buddhist Relics' *Representations* 66, p. 81.

FIGURE 145 *This small Konsei Daimyōjin stands beside a Buddhist graveyard in Kakunodate (Akita Prefecture). It is a* sekibō *and is in a small wooden shrine with a metal tiled roof and a faded purple curtain. The stone bar itself is about 30 cm tall, has no neck and tapers slightly towards each end. The name 'Konsei Daimyōjin' is carved into it from top to bottom.*

> Premodern Buddhist texts do, in fact, frequently discuss symbolism, iconography, and style, but they take up these issues as something bearing on the worship of icons that were considered real presences of deities—not mere doctrinal symbols, ritual supports, copies, or representations of them.[8]

Also, although specifically discussing Buddhist paintings Wu Hung reckons that an icon's significance 'relies on the presence of a viewer or worshipper outside it... the assumption that there is a worshipper who is engaged, in direct relationship with the icon.[9]

This notion could be applied to any Shintō *goshintai* as much as to a Buddhist image, even though the graphical representation to be found within a Shintō shrine is rarely that of a human being. In Konsei Daimyōjin shrines, of course, the image is of *part* of a human being, the penis, yet all the factors that suggest an icon: the creation of an image, a belief in the real presence of a deity and its crucial relationship with the worshipper can be identified in these enshrined phalluses. They may not be icons in a sense that would be generally understood in terms of the Western analogy used by Sharf and Rambelli, but could it be that that they have acquired iconic status because they are regarded as possessing completely the likeness of the divine? In other words, does the Konsei Daimyōjin tradition indicate the worship of the male sexual organ? If so Konsei-sama would effectively provide what the rationale of the Tagata Shrine is popularly but erroneously thought to be: a religious tradition where the expression *dankon sūhai* might be translated literally as penis worship. The answer to this question lies in teasing out the identity of this most phallic of all Japan's phallic gods, and one possibility can be ruled out almost immediately. Konsei Daimyōjin is not derived from Japanese mythology like Sarutahiko. His name never appears in the *Kojiki* or the *Nihongi*. He seems instead to occupy a unique niche in the Shintō pantheon as the *kami* of the penis, and as Japan has several deities concerned with parts of the body and even a deity of coughing it should not really be too surprising to find a god of the male sexual organ.[10]

A cursory glance at the written sources strengthens this impression. Katō refers to Konsei Daimyōjin quite simply as 'the phallic deity' in a brief and very

---

8 Rambelli, Fabio 2002. 'Secret Buddhas: The Limits of Buddhist Representation' *Monumenta Nipponica* 57, p. 282.

9 Hung, Wu 1992. 'What is Bianxiang? On the Relationship between Dunhuang Art and Dunhuang Literature.' *Harvard Journal of Asiatic Studies* 52, p. 130.

10 Ohnuki-Tierney 1984, p. 50.

FIGURE 146 *Within the precincts of the Kumano Shrine at Karibasawa (Hachinohe City, Aomori Prefecture) a Konsei Daimyōjin shrine about 1.5 metres tall is almost filled by its cedar phallus. The white cloth has been lifted for the photograph.*

matter-of-fact discussion.[11] Saitō mentions Konsei Daimyōjin shrines as a separate type, as does Nishioka, but there they are confined to his gazetteer with little in the way of further explanation.[12] Czaja sees Konsei Daimyōjin as being the origin of *sai no kami*, and Casal likens him to Pan.[13] Selected examples of the shrines are discussed in detail by Kokonoe and are very well illustrated while Miura and colleagues provide localised examples in their study of the folk customs of Tōhoku, but the best analysis of them is provided by Satō for Akita and Masuta for Aomori, both of whom recognise Konsei Daimyōjin as a unique phallic *kami*.[14]

It must be noted however that the expressions *konsei* is sometimes used more loosely to mean phallic or sexual in situations where other *kami* are enshrined. The Konsei Wagō Inari Shrine 金勢和合稲荷神社 at the Eikenji 永見寺 in Tokyo, where a pair of *in'yōseki* mark the grave-site of a celebrated Edo courtesan, probably indicates that a shrine to Inari promotes sexual harmony.[15] Satō refers to the three rocks located behind the Karamatsu Shrine in Sakai (Akita Prefecture) as being 'worshipped as *konseijin* (金勢神), which must have the more general meaning of sexual gods because two of the rocks are of female form and there is no reference to any of the three being Konsei Daimyōjin.[16] Kokonoe too uses the term quite freely when describing the deity of any sexual shrine where a phallus is displayed, even if his written account identifies the *kami* as being other than Konsei Daimyōjin. Thus the Kinmara Yakushi きんまら薬師, a relief carving of Yakushi Nyōrai framed by two phalluses in Maebashi (Gunma Prefecture) is referred to by him as a *konseijin*.[17] *Konsei* can also be used in a colloquial sense to describe any naturally phallic topographical feature such as a rock or a mountain.

The Origins and Development of the Konsei Daimyōjin Tradition

A Japanese religious dictionary defines Konsei Daimyōjin as, 'a *kami* that is an amalgam of various beliefs originating from prayers relating to the

11 Katō 1924, p. 10.

12 Saitō 1927, p. 40; Nishioka 1961.

13 Czaja 1974, p. 46; Casal, U.A. 1965. 'Der Phalluskult im Alten Japan' reprinted in Casal, U.A. *Articles on Japanese Folklore 1956–65*, p. 90.

14 Miura et al. 1973; Satō 1995; Masuta 2012.

15 From a personal observation made on 20 April 2012.

16 Satō 1995, p. 135.

17 Kokonoe 1981, p. 89.

FIGURE 147 *This polished wooden Konsei Daimyōjin stands next to an Inari Shrine which was installed centuries ago within the courtyard of the Toyagasaki Shrine in Hanamaki (Iwate Prefecture).*

lower half of the human body, a sexual deity that is usually represented by a phallus'.[18] Katō would no doubt have accepted this working definition, and in his article he discusses the possibility that the source of the *kami* and his name could be the heavenly spear of the *Kojiki* 'otherwise called the Heavenly

18 Ōshima, Tatehiko et al. 2001. *Nihon shinbutsu no jiten* (Tokyo), p. 537.

FIGURE 148 *This small* sekibō *almost fills a tiny Konsei Daimyōjin shrine within the grounds of a Shirohige Shrine in Saitama Prefecture.*

Root or *coelestis penis*'.[19] Satō has explored an alternative theory that the origin of Konsei Daimyōjin lies in the *sekibō* that provide the *goshintai* at some Konsei Daimyōjin shrines. The unearthing of *sekibō* was often regarded as the discovery of a phallus of heavenly origin and the name Konsei Daimyōjin was ascribed to them. Once the tradition was established other phalluses were carved from stone and wood or cast from metal to join those of divine origin as

19 Katō 1924, pp. 8–10.

the cult spread.[20] Examples of *sekibō* acting as Konsei Daimyōjin are the ones at Kakunodate and the Ennyoji in Chiba. To set against Satō's theory is the fact that many other shrines that employ *sekibō* do not make the same association with Konsei Daimyōjin and instead take on a number of different forms and identities.

Satō also explores a possible link between Konsei Daimyōjin and Kanayama Hiko no kami, the male deity born along with his sister from the vomit of Izanami.[21] As early as 852 the Kimpu Shrine 金峯神社 on Mount Kimpu in Nara Prefecture is noted as enshrining Kanayama Hiko. Mount Kimpu was known as the mountain of gold with this deity as its protector, and Satō quotes from a document of 859 that, 'In ancient times the Kimpu Shrine of Yoshino that was known by the name of Kanemitake was also known as Konsei Daimyōjin'.[22] It is interesting to note that when the worship of Konsei Daimyōjin was repressed in 1868 Kanayama Hiko was a popular choice for an alternative *kami* with an impeccable imperial connection. The Konsei Daimyōjin that had been worshipped since the Early Tokugawa Period within the precincts of the Aoe Shrine 青江神社 in Okayama was forced to change its *kami* to Kanayama Hiko and Kanayama Hime. This is the status it still enjoys today. Several wooden phallic symbols stand there as offerings, reflecting Kanayama Hiko's role as a sexual god analogous to Konsei Daimyōjin but falling short of a total identification between the two.[23]

A very different mythological explanation for the origins of Konsei Daimyōjin is suggested at the important Makibori Shrine in Iwate Prefecture, an ancient establishment that was known as the Nambu Konsei Daimyōjin until 1868, Nambu being the name of the *daimyō* of Tsugaru. In this interpretation the *kana mara* (iron phallus) within the shrine is said to be the first ever Konsei Daimyōjin. It was originally known as Konsei no Sukune 金勢のスクネ and was left at the shrine by the semi-legendary Prince Yamato Takeru when he departed from Tōhoku. The title Sukune would appear to be derived from Prince Yamato Takeru's imperial consort Oto Tachibana-hime, the daughter of Oshiyama no Sukune, who sacrificed her life to appease the deity of the sea-crossing.[24] The founding legend continues by telling us that many years

20 Satō 1995, p. 135.

21 Philippi 1969, pp. 57 & 489.

22 Satō 1995, pp 63–64.

23 Kokonoe 1981, p. 243.

24 Aston 1972, p. 212; Philippi 1969, p. 241.

FIGURE 149 *Votive phalluses presented to the* kami *Kanayama Hiko no kami at the Aoe Shrine in Kurashiki (Okayama Prefecture), a place that once enshrined Konsei Daimyōjin.*

FIGURE 150 *This iron phallus stands within the* honden *of the historic Makibori Shrine in Iwate Prefecture. Its accessibility suggests that it may be a replica of the shrine's ancient* goshintai.

later the female ruler who reigned twice as Kōgyoku (642–644) and as Saimei (655–661) ordered that the shrine now known as Makibori should be built.[25]

Prince Yamato Takeru is also associated with the Konsei Daimyōjin that is located within the precincts of the Ōwashi Shrine in Ajiki. According to local legend, when Yamato Takeru travelled through on his expedition to Tōhoku he planted his flag on this very hill. An ancient phallic tradition was subsequently associated with the place with several phallic symbols being enshrined there. The main noticeboard informs the visitor that its main *kami* is associated with the cultivation of flax, and there is no mention at this point of the existence of Konsei Daimyōjin in a subsidiary shrine on the eastern side of the hill. The casual visitor might therefore miss the sight of what is claimed on a noticeboard to be Japan's largest phallus. It is a comparatively new creation, because in 1975 the shrine association in conjunction with local council erected the present shrine building and placed within it this specially commissioned sexual object. Kokonoe puts its height at precisely 2.47 metres and a label states that it is 2.3 metres in circumference.[26]

Japan's most dramatically situated Konsei Daimyōjin lies on the 2,024 metres-high Konsei Pass that spans modern Tochigi and Gunma Prefectures below the peak of Mount Konsei. An account of it appears in Chamberlain's *Handbook for Travellers in Japan* in 1893:

> The way up the Konsei-Tōge is a continued gentle ascent through a forest with an undergrowth of bamboo grass, terminating in a steep climb. Half a *ri* below the summit is a small shrine dedicated to the phallic worship of the god Konsei.
>
> Tradition says that the original object of reverence was made of gold, but that, having been stolen; it was afterwards replaced by one of stone. Ex-votos, chiefly wood and stone emblems, are often presented at the shrine.[27]

Since the building of the Konsei tunnel in 1956 the shrine has been most readily accessed by a short but steep climb on to the ridge from the car park beside the tunnel entrance. The modern concrete shrine building has heavy iron doors and replaces the simple wooden structure shown in Nishioka's book.[28]

---

25 Nishioka 1961, p. 217 and from a personal observation made on 3 November 2012.

26 Kokonoe 1981, p. 106 and from a personal observation made on 19 April 2012.

27 Chamberlain, Basil Hall 1893. *A Handbook for Travellers in Japan* Third Edition (London), p. 170.

28 Nishioka 1961, Plate XXXVIII.

FIGURE 151 *The most dramatically situated Konsei Daimyōjin in Japan sits astride the Konsei Pass that divides Gunma from Tochigi Prefecture.*

Inside is an old carved stone phallus 56 cm in height, and local tradition links it to the exile of the well-endowed priest who became the sexual *kami* Dōkyō-sama. It is a very different story from the one that identifies Dōkyō with the nailed phalluses of the Yuge shrines of Kumamoto. His journey of exile took him over this pass from Kōzuke Province (modern Gunma Prefecture) where he died from his hardships and was enshrined by the local people who then received sexual-related benefits. A more sensational version adds that Dōkyō's large penis was cut off (perhaps even by Dōkyō himself in his despair) and enshrined as Konsei Daimyōjin, thereby providing the name for the shrine and the Konsei Pass. Other authorities however point out that the name predates the Dōkyō legend and probably derives from the supposedly phallic topography of the surrounding mountains.[29]

All these tales speak of Konsei Daimyōjin as a very ancient tradition within which the Makibori Shrine phallus stakes a claim to being the first Konsei-sama in Japan, but the oldest one that can be dated with any accuracy is kept locked away within the temple of Bannaji 鑁阿寺 in Ashikaga City (Tochigi Prefecture). Unlike most of the others this unique 900 year-old Konsei

29 Kokonoe 1981, p. 72; Masuta 2006, pp. 148–149 and from a personal observation made on 20 October 2012.

FIGURE 152 *The interior of the shrine on the Konsei Pass showing the enshrined phallus that is associated with the priest Dōkyō. It is 56 cm in height.*

FIGURE 153 *On the Gunma Prefecture side of the Konsei Pass stands this beautiful Konsei Daimyōjin shrine. It is now within the modern premises of the Shirane Fish Farm. The main building, reminiscent of the Tōshōgū in Nikkō, dates from the early Tokugawa Period and was founded by Abe Tadaaki of Oshi in Musashi province (modern Saitama Prefecture). The* goshintai *is a stone phallus similar to the one on the pass.*

Daimyōjin was never installed in a shrine for public worship and prayers. Instead it became the private property of the Ashikaga family when Ashikaga Yoshikane (1147–96), the brother-in-law of Minamoto Yoritomo, was only able to produce female children. Being in need of a male heir, he summoned the priest Risshin from Izu to offer prayers for a male child. Risshin presented to Yoshikane this small squat natural stone phallus that was found in a river. The result was the conception and safe delivery of Ashikaga Yoshiuji (1189–1254) who went on to become a distinguished warrior. The 35 cm-long object was placed on rare public display during a special exhibition entitled 'Treasures of the Bannaji' in 2004.[30] Although the phallus itself was rarely seen over the centuries its benefits could be extended to others through the purchase of a paper *ofuda* on which was printed a picture of the object. Nishioka includes an illustration of one dating from the Meiji Period and in 1851 one of these prints provided the design for the only stone Konsei Daimyōjin that is carved in relief rather than in the round.[31]

Throughout its history the worship of Konsei Daimyōjin has flourished in remote locations in northern Japan that were occasionally recorded by visitors. In 1804 Sugae Masumi called in at the Sotsuda Konsei Shrine near Lake Tazawa (Akita Prefecture).[32] In 1786 Kudō Hakuryū from Hirosaki noted in his *Tsugaru Zokusetsu sen* that, 'There is a small shrine to Konsei Daimyōjin at the rear of a private house in Ikarigaseki. It is commonly known as Kanamara Daimyōjin'.[33] This is probably the same place mentioned in *Mimibukuro*, a collection of tales put together by the Edo magistrate Negishi Yasumori (1737–1815), where we read:

> Concerning Konseijin
>
> According to a report by a retainer of the Tsugaru there is upon the Tsugaru road a place known as Kanamara Daimyōjin, where is enshrined a male member of black copper that is worshipped.[34]

There is still a shrine in Ikarigaseki called the Atago-gū 愛宕宮 that claims continuity with this place. It has recently been rebuilt and contains a large modern wooden phallus referred to as Konsei-sama. It stands beside the locked

30 Ōtaku, Shinsei et al. 2004. *Bannaji no Takaramono* (Ashikaga), p. 83.

31 Nishioka 1961, p. 225.

32 Satō 1995, pp. 145–147.

33 Nishioka 1961a, pp. 224–225; Masuta 2012, p. 41.

34 Satō 1995, p. 71.

FIGURE 154 *The Konsei Daimyōjin at the Okagami Shrine near Tsurukawa Station in Kanagawa Prefecture is the only one to be carved as a relief rather than in the round. The design was taken from an* ofuda *of the Bannaji in Ashikaga.*

inner shrine containing a *goshintai* that is never revealed, so it is impossible to ascertain whether or not it contains the original *kana mara*.[35]

Konsei Daimyōjin's shrines were fully included in the process of suppression by the Meiji government from 1872 onwards. The official announcement relating

35 Masuta 2012, p. 41 and from a personal observation made on 5 November 2012. The wooden phallus is illustrated in Masuta 2006, p. 135.

to Akita Prefecture begins with a specific reference to Konsei Daimyōjin when it states:

> In villages in every district are the so-called Konsei Myōjin, set up by the side of the road in the shape of large penises (*inkei* 陰茎) made of wood or carved into the side of stones, in a few places they are famous but in common with all the others they must be promptly demolished… and where they have been ignorantly placed on the *kamidana* at the entrance to an ordinary store or home they must similarly be removed in accordance with the above decree.[36]

An example of the possible outcome if the prohibition was ignored appears in Katō's article as a very revealing story about an undated incident at a Konsei Daimyōjin shrine in Izumo Province (modern Shimane Prefecture):

> Those who suffer from diseases of the sexual organs worship there and by virtue of faith in the phallic deity Konsei they often recover. Once a village policeman, it is reported, came to inspect the site and commanded the guardian priest in charge of the phallic deity to abolish such a licentious cult, as injurious to public morality. It was not a long time, however, before the policeman was seized by a violent attack of fever, and his illness compelled him to resign his post at his own request and at last he succumbed. Simple minded village believers took it for a divine penalty inflicted on the infidel policeman because of his iconoclasm, and as a matter of course they doubly fostered their good old faith in Konsei, the phallic deity, quite in contrast to the expectation of the poor intelligent policeman.[37]

Atsuta's Dōso Konsei Daimyōjin was also suppressed at this time and the distribution of its amulets forbidden by law.[38] Other shrines were forced to change their names and even the identity of their enshrined *kami*, so the Nambu Konsei Daimyōjin became the Makibori Shrine and its deities were changed to Izanagi and Sarutahiko.[39] The Chiwaki Shrine 智和伎神社 in Morioka had enshrined a Konsei Daimyōjin in the form of an iron phallus since 1307, but

---

36 Satō 1995, p. 204.

37 Katō 1924, p. 10.

38 Katō 1924, p. 11.

39 Satō 1995, p. 72.

FIGURE 155 *The Konsei Daimyōjin at Nakayamasuku near Naruko Onsen stands next to a shrine that links the place to the wanderings of Minamoto Yoshitsune. The wife of a villager was having a difficult birth, so the monk Benkei fashioned a chestnut tree branch into the shape of a monk's staff and prayed to Kannon. When the woman was safely delivered the villagers built the shrine and dedicated it to Benkei's staff. The shrine still receives prayers for safe delivery.*

with the reforms it now officially enshrined Sarutahiko.[40] Only shrines located deep in the mountains were able to continue undisturbed and the Konsei Daimyōjin at Nakayamasuku in Miyagi Prefecture is probably a case in point.[41] Akita Prefecture also preserves several Konsei Daimyōjin that must once have been known only to local people. One lies just next to the roadside in a village to the north of Kakunodate. Inside are six stone phalluses and one wooden one.[42] Even more remote are the Konsei Daimyōjin at the Yakushi Shrine deep in a forest near Omagari and the Isedō no Konsei-sama near Yokote, which stands amid isolated rice fields beside a stream.[43]

40 Kokonoe 1981, p. 39 and from a personal observation made on 3 November 2012.

41 From a personal observation made on 18 June 2013.

42 From a personal observation made on 23 April 2012.

43 From a personal observation made on 21 April 2012.

Konsei Daimyōjin Shrines Today

During the twentieth century some Konsei Daimyōjin shrines reverted to their pre-Meiji status. The Chiwaki Shrine in Morioka is now referred to as the Konsei Shrine as much as by its other name and has a considerable sexual ambience. In the precincts is one large carved stone phallus surrounded by a large number of naturally occurring ones of stone placed there as votive items.[44] Modern roads have also made some once remote Konsei shrines accessible to the casual visitor. In Sannohe the Konsei Ōkami Shrine below the hill on which the remains of Sannohe castle stands is no longer surrounded by woods as it was when Kokonoe described it, but it still contains twenty-three neatly arranged votive phalluses around a central image.[45] At Kasamatsu in Gifu Prefecture a small but very interesting Konsei Daimyōjin shrine may be found beside the levee of the Kiso River. A line of banners leads the visitor along the path where there is also a *dōsojin* of an embracing couple.[46] Another very fine example sits within a wooded hillside in the Kuwagasaki district of Miyako (Iwate Prefecture). This Konsei Daimyōjin, established in 1842, escaped by only a few metres from the devastation caused to Miyako by the tragic *tsunami* of March 2011. A large wooden phallus dressed somewhat comically in a headband provides the main image inside the well-maintained shrine along with several smaller votive phalluses, many less than the 2,000 counted when the shrine was rebuilt in 1946. With one wooden phallus there is a healing tradition of rubbing it upon an affected area of one's body.[47]

Elsewhere in Iwate Prefecture several very active Konsei Daimyōjin shrines have benefited from the publicity Tōno has received from Yanagita Kunio's *Tōno Monogatari*, although the following account is the only mention of the tradition in the famous collection of stories published in 1910:

---

44 Kokonoe 1981, p. 39 and from a personal observation made on 3 November 2012.

45 Masuta 2012, p. 46; Kokonoe 1981, p. 35 and from a personal observation made on 8 November 2012.

46 From a personal observation made on 3 May 2012. A large wooden phallus stands outside the locked shrine, but photographs of the central image appear in Nishioka (1961, Plate XXXV) and Kokonoe (1981, p. 202).

47 From personal observation and notes of a conversation held with shrine officials at the shrine on 20 June 2013 that was kindly arranged by Mr Kariya Yuichiro of the Miyako Board of Education.

FIGURE 156 *The Konsei Daimyōjin within the grounds of the Suwa Shrine in Hachinohe (Aomori Prefecture) was once in a rural location but has recently been swallowed by urban development.*

FIGURE 157 *The interior of the Konsei Daimyōjin Shrine in the Kuwagasaki district of Miyako City. It was established in 1842 and narrowly escaped total destruction during the tragic* tsunami *of March 2011.*

> Not a few households worship Konsei-sama. The *shintai* of this *kami* resembles Okuma-sama. There are many shrines to Okuma-sama in the village. The object of worship is a phallus made from stone or wood. Nowadays this is practised less and less.[48]

This brief passage indicates the impression Yanagita had that the practice was dying out, yet today six Konsei Daimyōjin are well-signposted on forested hillsides around the area. The Hodobora no Konsei-sama 程洞のコンセイサマ dates from 1765 and shares a small area of forested hillside with an Inari shrine. There are a number of phallic symbols within its crude wooden shrine building where a notice invites one to pray for the gift of children. There is another Konsei-sama within the grounds of the ancient Hayachine Shrine 早地峰神社. It contains a large heavy wooden phallus carved from a tree trunk where the natural curves have been utilised to dramatic effect. Not far away is the Tsukimōshi Komagata Shrine 附馬牛駒形神社 where there is also a Konsei sub-shrine. Finally, Tōno contains the much more accessible Yamazaki no Konsei-sama 山崎 のコンセイサマ. A plastic baby doll in

48 Morse states that this is the name of a *kami* who protects horses (2008, p. 20).

FIGURE 158 *This enormous two metre high phallic rock to which additional carving has been applied stands next to the sacred water basin at the Yamazaki Konsei Daimyōjin Shrine in Tōno (Iwate Prefecture).*

FIGURE 159 *Inside the Yamazaki Konsei Daimyōjin Shrine in Tōno a plastic baby doll reminds worshippers that the achievement of conception is Konsei Daimyōjin's speciality.*

front of the phallus reminds worshippers of Konsei-sama's primary function as the achiever of conception.[49]

The Yamazaki Konsei Shrine owns a phallic *mikoshi* that may be a recent addition to the worship tradition, because specific festivals to celebrate Konsei Daimyōjin appear to be few and far between. Nishioka provides a photograph of one that once took place at Hachimantai (Akita Prefecture), where local women are seen carrying wooden phalluses of about 60 cm in length in a procession, but he gives no further details about it.[50] Kokonoe indicates that the ritual was still going in 1981 and that the annual date was 13 June, but it has since been abandoned.[51] One that is still performed nowadays occurs at the Konsei Shrine in Miyako, although it would appear to consist more of a quiet gathering than a raucous celebration.[52] Elsewhere, as part of the revival of interest in phallic matters, phallic festivals have simply been invented to boost local tourism. Examples involving Konsei Daimyōjin include the Ōwashi Shrine *matsuri* which is no older than 1975, the year of the giant phallus's installation. Another takes place at Ōsawa Onsen in Iwate Prefecture. It has been held every May since 1965 and culminates when women enter one of the open-air baths and try to climb on to a floating wooden phallus, an activity that has probably been inspired by other 'phallus-riding' events.[53]

The Votive Powers of Konsei Daimyōjin

Konsei Daimyōjin responds to his worshippers by providing a wide range of benefits, not all of which are sexual. The Sotsuda Konsei Shrine in Akita Prefecture includes traffic safety and business prosperity. At the Ōwashi Shrine the benefits of prayer are listed as 'abundant crops, marriage, fertility, smooth delivery and marital harmony' while a notice at the Konsei Daimyōjin inside the Hiraide Shrine informs worshippers that this is a place to pray for 'child-begetting and child-rearing'.[54]

49 From personal observations made at Tōno on 2 November 2012.

50 Nishioka 1961a, p. 227.

51 Kokonoe 1981, p. 49 and from a personal communication with Masuta Kimiyasu of the Aomori Prefectural Folk Museum.

52 From notes of a conversation held at the shrine on 20 June 2013 kindly arranged by Mr Kariya Yuichiro of the Miyako Board of Education.

53 Masuta 2012, p. 53. A collection of photographs of the event may be found at http://www.youtube.com/watch?v=nUb67L6LpVU.

54 From personal observations made on 19 April 2012 and 21 October 2012.

FIGURE 160 *At the Yuki Ryokan in Kawatabi Onsen (Miyagi Prefecture) Konsei Daimyōjin shares a shrine with the seven gods of good luck.*

The achievement of conception is the speciality of this most phallic deity, and websites exist to direct childless couples towards *onsen* 温泉 (hot spring resorts) where a combination of a luxury hotel and the spiritual power of enshrined sexual gods such as the great procreative Konsei Daimyōjin will help achieve their desire for a family.[55] Two *onsen*-related Konsei-sama shrines stand beside the lake within the extensive area of Komaki Onsen in Misawa (Aomori Prefecture). One contains a wonderfully eclectic mix of wooden phalluses and straw figures of humans. The other has one large heavy stone phallus secured in its position by a chain and padlock, although this is not for modern reasons of security because a notice adds the amusing legend that it was believed that in its original location the phallus would leave the shrine during the night to play tricks on the local girls![56] Even more striking is the Konsei Daimyōjin kept within a large reception room inside the Fujimi Hotel in Goshokawabara (Aomori Prefecture). It is without question Japan's largest man-made phallus and stands behind a table on which lie offerings of *sake*, a bell and a collection box. This enormous phallic symbol easily outstrips the object at the Ōwashi Shrine because it is a full five metres tall and is set firmly

55 For an example see http://wrd2425.ciao.jp/2jinja.html (accessed 4 June 2012).

56 Masuta 2012, p. 40 and from a personal observation made on 21 June 2013.

FIGURE 161 *The chained-up Konsei Daimyōjin at Komaki Onsen in Misawa (Aomori Prefecture). It was transferred to Misawa from its original site near Shichinohe Castle and the tradition has been maintaining of keeping it locked up so that it does not go round causing mischief.*

in concrete with two supportive boulders that act as its testicles. The head is securely roped to the ceiling and the whole ensemble stands within a frame of four surrounding curtains. It was installed there in the mid-1990s. I was shown round by the Assistant Manager of the hotel Mr Itō, who explained that the phallus was carved from the trunk of a Katsura tree (*Cercidiphyllum japonica*) 'for the good of mankind'. His understanding of Konsei Daimyōjin was that he was the god of the penis.[57]

Wherever his shrines may be located nowadays, in busy hotels or along remote mountain paths, it is most unusual to find a Konsei Daimyōjin without any evidence of recent activity. The shrines are maintained and supported for reasons that go far beyond their importance as local cultural artefacts, and the names and dates added to votive phalluses, on *ema* and in visitors' books speak not of nostalgia but of a living tradition. The remote Konsei Daimyōjin in Akaiwa is isolated on a narrow mountain road and separated from its more numerous counterparts in northern Japan, yet this sole example of a Konsei Daimyōjin shrine for several hundred miles around is well used. One double-page opening of its visitors' book contains the names and addresses of those who chose to record their visits during the summer of 2012, the numbers being eight for May, eighteen for June, eight for July and nine for August.

At the Ōwashi Shrine several stone phalluses that may be very old stand beside row upon row of many more wooden ones, each looking very new and each bearing the donor's name.[58] An expression of gratitude for a life granted through prayers to Konsei Daimyōjin is the probable explanation for an interesting offering observed at a shrine in Ōmori (Akita Prefecture) in 2012. An ornate paper envelope of the sort used to present monetary gifts was attached to the *goshintai* and bore the name of someone who had died in 2010 and had been born, presumably with the help of Konsei Daimyōjin, in 1923.[59] The Akaiwa Konsei Daimyōjin appears to be the only Konsei Daimyōjin shrine that makes use of traditional *ema* alongside donated phalluses.[60] Four were on display in 2012. They were several years old and somewhat weather-beaten, indicating that it may be a minor tradition. Nevertheless, a translation of the petitions written on them provides a unique insight into recorded prayers to Konsei Daimyōjin. They involve both petitions and thanks and read as follows:

---

57 Masuta 2012, p. 40 and from a personal observation made on 5 November 2012.

58 From a personal observation made on 19 April 2012.

59 From a personal observation made on 21 April 2012.

60 A visitor to the Kobunoki Shrine in 2011 saw phallic *ema*. See http://blog.goo.ne.jp/sakusaku29_szk/e/e94606f8374768o1d061cdb01d739e05.

FIGURE 162 *The power of Konsei Daimyōjin to assure fertility is expressed at Goshokawabara (Aomori Prefecture) by Japan's largest phallus, a 5 metre tall giant.*

FIGURE 163 *A shrine to Konsei Daimyōjin in Ōmori (Akita Prefecture) has twelve large stone phalluses outside it, six on one side of the* torii *and six on the other. Each is of carved stone and as they are partly buried they look as though they are sprouting from the ground.*

Example A
Name of petitioner
I pray that I may give birth to a healthy child
29 April 2004

Example B
Thank you for my pregnancy. My expected date of confinement is 23 November 2001. I pray for a safe delivery.
Name of petitioner
Date [obscured]

Example C
Please may I have a child?
Address of petitioner
Name of petitioner.[61]

61 From a personal observation made on 23 October 2012.

Erotic souvenirs are available at several Konsei Daimyōjin shrines. At the Ōwashi Shrine one may purchase phallic-shaped candles and a variety of cups and ashtrays where phalluses or ktenes have been built into the design,[62] At the Konsei Daimyōjin Shrine in Hanamaki there is on sale a small golden phallus and kteis mounted in plastic within a gold ring hung from a chain.[63] The Ōwashi Shrine also has its own version of the erotic folding paper *ofuda* that becomes a penis and vulva, but more conventional types of *ofuda* are available elsewhere. Over a century ago Buckley noted in his collection one Konsei Daimyōjin *ofuda* for easy delivery and another that was probably from the Makibori Shrine. It was stained from being dumped into the river when beliefs in Konsei Daimyōjin were suppressed. He translated it as follows:

> *Shō ichi: Konsei Daimyōjin tai hatsu*: 'true first rank root life great shining deity'. Right and left of this central text stand the words, 'Good for all illnesses below the belt. Life will be long. Good for woman when rearing child. Mother and child will be healthy'.[64]

The Sotsuda Konsei Daimyōjin as a Case Study

One of Japan's most interesting Konsei Daimyōjin foundations is the Sotsuda Konsei Shrine 卒田金勢神社, which stands close to Jindai Station on the main road between Kakunodate and Lake Tazawa (Akita Prefecture). It was described by Sugae Masumi in 1804.[65] The shrine lies on a small patch of land behind a private house next to the driveway of a large stone-built rice warehouse owned and run by the same family since 1892. The current proprietor Mr Fujimura Ryōhei kindly agreed to be interviewed about the shrine and its history to provide a detailed case study. He also supplied a newspaper article dating from 1982 when an interview was conducted with his late father.[66]

The Sotsuda Konsei Shrine has no shrine association, no committee and no priest. Instead it is maintained on a voluntary basis by the local community out

62 From a personal observation made on 19 April 2012.

63 From a personal observation made on 19 June 2013.

64 Buckley 1895, pp. 17–18.

65 Satō 1995, pp. 145–147.

66 Two interviews were conducted. The first was on 22 April 2012 with the assistance of Mark Williams and Darren Ashmore. A longer one was conducted on 31 October 2012 with the assistance of Miss Ellen Usui. Their help is gratefully acknowledged. The anonymous article is 'Konsei-sama' *Akita-ken Doku Shinpō* (13 July 1982), p. 8.

FIGURE 164 *Two worshippers inside the Sotsuda Konsei Daimyōjin near Lake Tazawa in Akita Prefecture. At the rear may be seen one of the large stone phalluses that are threatening the shrine with collapse.*

of whom the Fujimura family have felt a certain responsibility simply because of their proximity to the site. The shrine consists of a *honden* and a conjoined *haiden* to its right, the latter providing floor space for about twenty people. There is no lively annual *matsuri*, merely a simple gathering every 16 August, although some people meet there on New Year's Eve. Otherwise the only time the shrine hosts groups of people is when families who have benefited from Konsei Daimyōjin's blessings meet there for a reunion with the god. The members of one family from Yokote come regularly.

At the Sotsuda Shrine Konsei Daimyōjin grants petitions for business prosperity, traffic safety and peace within families as well as his most visible role of the achievement of conception. In former times, Mr. Fujimura said, this was a very serious matter, because if a marriage was still childless after three years the wife could not refuse the husband's request to divorce her. The internal ambience of the shrine is therefore highly phallic with a massive stone phallus on either side of the main display. These were carved from material that was left over when the first rice storehouse was built and are very heavy, as a glance at the exterior of the shrine will confirm because the floor beneath them appears

FIGURE 165 *A box of donated phalluses at the Sotsuda Konsei Daimyōjin Shrine.*

to be in imminent danger of collapse. The two images are flanked by numerous votive phalluses of different shapes and sizes. The practice is the usual one. A phallus is borrowed and when a birth occurs it is returned along with a newly created one, or, in the case of twins, two new ones! The appearance of the new phalluses depends entirely on the artistic skills of the donor. Phalluses can be bought, explained Mr Fujimura, but he prefers the more natural look of ones carved personally by the donor from wood. He was also able to provide a unique insight into what is actually done with the phallus that is borrowed. On being taken back to the petitioner's home it is placed beside the pillow on the marital bed until conception occurs. It is then kept in a safe place (usually the *kamidana*) until the baby is safely delivered. The borrowed phallus is then returned along with the new one. Mr Fujimura was also able to supply some crude statistics relating to Konsei Daimyōjin's efficacy. Out of eleven couples personally known to him who had visited the shrine to pray for conception ten had been blessed with a child, a figure that suggests a 90% success rate. With reference to an earlier generation his aunt had visited the shrine in 1975 and gave birth to twin girls. He also informed me, with something of smile, that he was part of the evidence because his mother had prayed at the shrine and he was the happy result.

Mr Fujimura felt that there was a genuine and continuing trust in the value of prayer to the unique *kami*, yet not even Konsei Daimyōjin is immune from decline, and at other places serious changes may be noted when a lack of local involvement with the shrines leaves them open to neglect and damage. The Kobunoki Shrine 枋ノ木神社 in Ninohe (Iwate Prefecture) also enshrines Konsei Daimyōjin, but instead of displaying the phalluses shown in Kokonoe's book of 1981 the shrine is now empty and all its contents are stacked up inside a locked and secure modern storehouse with a glass window, presumably on the grounds of security.[67] That such concerns are not unfounded is shown by the experience of the Konsei Inari Shrine in Hachiōji (Tokyo) where the *sekibō* illustrated by Kokonoe in 1981 was reported as stolen in 2006.[68] Another sadly neglected Konsei shrine consists of a simple wooden *hokora* at Ishinadamachi on the old Nikkō Road. Although almost hidden among the ancient avenue of cedar trees it still enjoys a close proximity to the ancient highway and may have been among those seen by W.G. Aston, but its fabric is crumbling and the two phalluses in front of it illustrated by Kokonoe have disappeared. In a conversation with a local man it was reported that the two phalluses had been stolen.[69]

This could well become the fate of other shrines if the older people who have voluntarily maintained and protected them are not replaced by younger believers. In spite of the good use still made of the Sotsuda Konsei Daimyōjin Shrine even Mr. Fujimura's impression was that devotion was under threat, and he summed up his fears in the words, 'Not enough people believe in it'. He also related the shrine to the question of Japan's declining birthrate, a concern expressed in many quarters. The birthrate is going down in the area around the Sotsuda Shrine with one local school closing because of falling intake, but Mr Fujimura believed that Konsei Daimyōjin could possibly help to arrest the slide in some way. The sexual gods and their shrines have always been primarily concerned with the achievement of conception, and in the past they have largely responded to individual concerns prompted by a lack of fertility and the desire for a wanted child. The new situation could provide them with an additional role whereby they would move from the personal to the political to

67 Kokonoe 1981, p. 44 and from a personal observation made on 3 November 2012.

68 Kokonoe 1981, p. 44. A report of the theft appears at http://members3.jcom.home.ne.jp/seihaku/data/seishin/tokyo_07.html (Accessed 22 March 2013).

69 From a personal observation made on 7 July 2013. For a photograph of what the shrine once looked like see Kokonoe 1981, p. 70. Exact copies of the phalluses were made in fibre glass a number of years ago are were on show at the Kinugawa Hihōden until that establishment closed down in December 2014.

encourage people to produce more babies, although Mr Fujimura added his impression that most young people, 'want to stay single anyway'. One practical problem for the Sotsuda Shrine in achieving greater influence is the fact that it is hardly visible from the main road. It therefore attracts visits only from people deliberately seeking it out, and Mr Fujimura felt that if the shrine could be relocated to a new and more prominent location its blessings might become better known. Yet there is no funding available to renew the collapsing building, so it is to be hoped that the Sotsuda Konsei Daimyōjin will not go the way of the Konsei Tenma Shrine 金勢天魔神社 in Kamitaya (Aomori Prefecture). This place was once visited by Sugae Masumi, but has disappeared completely in recent years. Masuta includes a photograph of its remains after it was badly damaged by severe weather in 2006. It has since been completely abandoned.[70]

The Konsei Daimyōjin Tradition as Genital Worship

Mr Fujimura was considerably vague in his understanding of or interest in the actual identity of Konsei Daimyōjin. He made no reference to Konsei-sama being the god of the penis. It was just the name of the *kami* who was worshipped there for whom a phallus was a symbol, which suggests that such precision is more of an obsession for Western researchers than Japanese believers. My own observation of many shrines confirms this point. The naming of the *kami* as Konsei Daimyōjin and the use of a prominent phallus as his *goshintai* is usually quite clear, but few clues are provided that would allow him to be identified unequivocally as the unique *kami* of the penis derived solely from an abstraction of the male sexual organ.

That association is made much more clearly by two unusual additions to the Japanese religious landscape. The first is to be found at the Akaiwa Konsei Daimyōjin, where a large modern stone statue greets the visitor half-way up the wooded path from the car park. A photograph inside the shrine of the statue before it was moved to its present location suggests that it was added within the past decade or so. The naked male figure, carved with heavy exaggerated features in a deliberately abstract style, clutches in his right hand his large erect penis.[71] An identical message is conveyed inside the interesting and otherwise underplayed sex museum housed within the Izu Gokurakuen 伊豆極楽苑 ('Paradise Park'), a sincere religious tourist facility in Shizuoka Prefecture.

70 Masuta 2012, p. 49 and from personal correspondence with Masuta Kimiyasu of 2 May 2013. A sketch of what it once looked like appears in Kokonoe 1981, p. 37.

71 From a personal observation made on 23 October 2012 and from personal correspondence with Takahata Tomiko of the Akaiwa City Sanyō Kyōdo Shiryōkan.

The main building, created and lovingly maintained by a committed Buddhist evangelist, exhibits in vivid and gruesome details the horrors of Hell and the joys of the Pure Land by means of tableaux depicting demons torturing sinners and angels comforting the blessed. The sex museum is entirely separate and is reached by an outside staircase. Inside is a life-sized plastic human figure who is dressed as a *yamabushi* 山伏, a follower of the religious tradition of Shugendō. He is identified as Konsei Daimyōjin and clearly receives devotional attention. His erect penis is covered by a brocade bag, and by means of a notice the visitor is invited to intone *Namu Konsei Daimyōjin* (Hail, Konsei Daimyōjin) and ring the bell that dangles from his member to obtain 'financial gain and matchless sexual powers'.[72]

These two concrete interpretations of Konsei Daimyōjin may appear flippant at first sight, yet they reinforce very strongly the impression given in the academic literature that he is the *kami* of the penis. The various theories listed above have attempted to explain how this may have come about, but a simpler explanation may be suggested by examining the process whereby *kami* acquire names and forms. Historically the idea that the *kami* have a true and permanent form is a later development influenced by Buddhist iconography. 'In the early cult', writes Carmen Blacker, 'a *kami* had no shape of his own, his occasional visionary appearances being temporary disguises only'.[73] Through the subsequent development of naming a *kami* the deity entered more readily into the human sphere so that it could be addressed and petitioned, and with the granting of a name an abstract power became somehow more knowable.

This is probably what happened when the abstract power of the male sexual organ gave rise to the concept of a *kami* called Konsei Daimyōjin, perhaps under the inspiration of the ancient symbol of the jewel spear of heaven and strengthened by the discovery of ancient *sekibō*. In these ways the penis was granted its own *kami* in the familiar process that has been applied over the centuries to, 'everything that is strange, fearful, mysterious, marvellous, uncontrolled, full of power or beyond human comprehension', expressions that those who first established the concept of Konsei Daimyōjin would have recognised in the tremendous power of human sexuality.[74] If thunder and lightning could indicate a divine presence, how much more would the process of child-begetting, so miraculous in its succession of stages and so hazardous in its completion?

---

72 According to the facility's owner the *yamabushi* costume once belonged to his father, the founder of the institution and does not indicate any connection between Konsei Daimyōjin and En no Gyōja. (From a personal observation made on 10 November 2012 and from personal correspondence with Satō Kōshi of the Izu Gokurakuen).

73 Blacker 1975, p. 38.

74 Holtom 1993, p. 79.

FIGURE 166 *Beside the steps leading up to the Konsei Daimyōjin Shrine at Akaiwa stands this statue. The human figure is a vehicle for displaying the defining sexual organ.*

Konsei Daimyōjin was therefore the name given to the *kami* who simply had to be present somewhere within that tremendous process. By being named he transcended the anonymity of other sexual *kami* such as the god of the pine tree at the Kinone Shrine in Tottori. The Kinone *kami* is also able to respond to petitions of a sexual nature, but the Kinone *kami* is the *kami* of that one tree. Konsei Daimyōjin is the *kami* of all penises, and is therefore the sole occupant of the fifth category of sexual *kami* that has been employed in this book: the one god of sex derived solely from an abstraction of the male sexual organ.

Yet can the further step be taken to identify the cult of Konsei Daimyōjin as being the actual worship of the organ? This impression is certainly hinted

FIGURE 167 *Another attempt to represent Konsei Daimyōjin in human guise where all the attention is drawn to his member can be found at the Izu Gokurakuen in Shizuoka Prefecture. Dressed in a* yamabushi *costume Konsei Daimyōjin's erect penis is hidden by a brocade bag.*

FIGURE 168 *This Konsei Daimyōjin stands in a corner of the men's bath house at the Sekitei Ryokan in Atami. It is said to have been carved by a man who found it as a piece of driftwood. Creating the Konsei Daimyōjin cured his impotence.*

at by the statues at Akaiwa and Itō where all one's attention is drawn towards the penis. It is also suggested by the iconic status of any Konsei Daimyōjin phallus, for which two further examples are instructive. The first is the story that lies behind the heavy wooden Konsei Daimyōjin that stands in a corner of the men's bath house at the exclusive Sekitei Ryokan in Atami (Shizuoka Prefecture). Many years ago a local woodcutter was married to a beautiful wife and they were unable to have children. The blame fell on the husband who, having tried every remedy, decided to commit suicide by throwing himself into the sea. It happened that, when near to death and losing consciousness, his hands seized upon a piece of floating driftwood, at which point he received a divine message. If he carved the wood into a large Konsei Daimyōjin and prayed to it his impotence would be cured. The woodcutter did as he was bid and put all his heart into creating the image, in front of which he then prayed for one hundred nights. His wife conceived and they both lived happily ever after. The phallus he had carved showed a total iconic correspondence with the *kami* because the power they possessed was the same. The phallus did not merely represent Konsei Daimyōjin, the phallus *was* Konsei Daimyōjin.[75]

The second example concerns the similar iconic status that may be shared by the phalluses that can be borrowed from Konsei shrines. This correspondence is particularly acknowledged at the Konsei Daimyōjin in Ōhata (Aomori Prefecture) where the noticeboard states that *goshintai* are borrowed.[76] This cannot possibly refer to the huge central stone phallus and must mean the small loan phalluses that share fully in Konsei-sama's powers. A Konsei-sama phallus does not therefore merely denote, represent or even symbolise the indwelling *kami*, it shares its very nature as an icon. Its status is 'presence'; there is no practical or doctrinal distinction between the object and the *kami* of the penis in terms of how they may be approached or petitioned.

So do these observations lead to the conclusion that the cult of Konsei Daimyōjin is the worship of the male genital organ? That concept is certainly widespread in the more general literature on phallicism. For example, in 1927 Stone stated that the phallus was, 'an object of ancient adoration and worship', and a similar assumption lay behind Jennings' 1889 book.[77] Neither author linked the idea to Japan in any way, but there is a popular understanding among Western commentators that all Japanese sexual beliefs involve the worship *of* genitalia rather than worship *using* (images of) genitalia. Henry D. Smith II referred to 'the long-standing rural practices of the display and worship of both male and female genitals, practices intimately concerned with prayers for both agricultural and human fertility'.[78] Ian Buruma wrote in his

---

75 This legend has echoes of Buddhist tales whereby a statue carved from driftwood is regarded as possessing miraculous powers because of its unknown or mysterious origins. In the *Nihongi* we read, 'This month Unate no Atahe went upon the sea, and the result was that he discovered a log of camphor-wood shining brightly as it floated on the surface. At length he took it, and presented it to the Emperor, who gave orders to an artist to make of it two images of Buddha (Aston 1972, p. 68). Camphor trees found in this way were regarded as particularly sacred, and in the sixteenth century a monk sculpted a Daikokuten from a piece of camphor trunk that was already hallowed from supposedly been used for two famous Kannon statues. See Grapard, Allan G. 1992. *The Protocol of the Gods: a study of the Kasuga cult in Japanese history* (Berkeley), pp. 153 & 155.

76 From a photograph of the sign displayed at http://www11.atpages.jp/ruisho/myweb3_04444.htm.

77 Hargrave Jennings subtitled his 1899 book *A Description of the Worship of Lingam-Yoni in Various Parts of the World*, and in 1927 Stone defined phallic worship as 'the high respect and adoration paid to the generative organs' (1927, p. 4).

78 Smith 1996, p. 28.

review of the British Museum exhibition that, 'Japanese religion sometimes took the form of worshipping genitals', and even the exhibition's organisers refer to, 'Veneration of both male and female sex organs, in the form of models or appropriately shaped features of the natural landscape, to encourage fertility or ward off evil'.[79]

In answering the question much hinges on the difference in meaning between *sūhai* 崇拝 (worship) which implies adoration or veneration and the more general expression *shinkō* 信仰 (beliefs), a distinction that Byron Earhart makes between *sangaku shinkō* 山嶽信仰 'mountain beliefs' and *sangaku sūhai* 山嶽崇拝 'mountain worship'. The latter term, he argues, derives from a misleading Western notion that, 'falsely implies that a mountain is deified and worshipped'.[80] Japanese scholars, however, use *sūhai* in broader terms. Thus Ōta's book *Sei Sūhai* and Nishioka's chapters on *dankon sūhai* and *join sūhai* encompass matters that are not restricted to acts of veneration.[81] More specifically, Suzuki Kenkō recognises that protective deities 'took the form of female and male sex organs' and that 'statues of deities represented by male and female sex organs were worshipped at the side of roads'.[82]

It could be that the cult of Konsei Daimyōjin differs from this general rule, but that possibility is much diminished when one compares the worship of Konsei Daimyōjin to that of other *kami* who are devoted to different parts of the body. Ashite Kōjin 足手荒神 is the *kami* of the limbs, and in two of his shrines in Kumamoto Prefecture replicas of hands and legs are employed in a similar way to the phalluses of Konsei Daimyōjin. At a shrine in Nagomi roughly carved wooden limbs are used as *ema* and petitioners write their prayers on one side of the crude objects. In Kumamoto City's Kai Shrine 甲斐神社 carved stone hands and lower limbs are offered to Ashite Kōjin in an identical manner to Konsei Daimyōjin's votive phalluses, while a few designated wooden specimens that clearly possess great powers are rubbed on to the affected part of one's body by the petitioner. By these means the power of Ashite Kōjin is brought to bear on the illnesses associated with the parts of the body of which he is the *kami*.[83]

---

79 Buruma, Ian 2013. 'The joy of art' *The Guardian Saturday Review* 28 September p. 18; Clark, Timothy; Gerstle, C. Andrew 2013. 'What Was Shunga?' in Clark, Timothy; Gerstle, C. Andrew; Ishigami, Aki and Yano, Akiko (eds.) *Shunga: Sex and Pleasure in Japanese Art* (London), p. 19.

80 Earhart 1970, p. 7 and 169.

81 Ōta 1986.

82 Miyata 1996, p. 79; Suzuki 2013, pp. 364–365.

83 From personal observations made on 2 June 2010 and 11 February 2011.

FIGURE 169 *At the Kai Shrine in Kumamoto City replicas of hands and feet are offered to Ashite Kōjin,* kami *of the limbs, in much the same way that phalluses are offered to Konsei Daimyōjin,* kami *of the penis.*

Yet even though Ashite Kōjin has this complete correspondence with limbs the activities associated with the shrines involve the worship of the *kami* of the limbs and not the worship of limbs as such. The conclusion must therefore be that even though the associated and indwelling *kami* called Konsei Daimyōjin may have similar powers and a total iconic correspondence with the enshrined phallus, his worship does not represent *dankon sūhai* in the literal sense of penis worship any more than the similar devotion to Ashite Kōjin indicates the worship of feet. The reason for this distinction lies in the concept of *kami*, because although Japanese religion may allow for vagueness over a *kami*'s identity, the whole notion of the existence of *kami* and the nature of their indwelling places one step between the god and its icon, no matter how all-consuming that icon may be.[84] Following this argument, the difference between worship

84 A similar distinction may be noted within Buddhism. In his article cited earlier Sharf claims that the vast majority of Buddhists in East Asia make no distinction between the consecrated visible image of the deity and the deity itself, but Rambelli warns that 'we should be careful not to overemphasize this point, however: doctrinally there is an important distinction between the Buddha and its image; whereas the former is unconditioned, the latter is conditioned by its place, shape, and materiality'. (Sharf 1999, p. 83; Rambelli 2002, p. 283).

of the god of the penis and worship of the penis may be very slight, poorly understood and doctrinally unchallenged but it is nonetheless there, so that through the tradition of Konsei Daimyōjin we are taken as near as is possible towards phallicism in this most acute sense, but no further.[85]

In conclusion, the study of Konsei Daimyōjin reveals that the topic of Japanese sexual beliefs is a more complex phenomenon than is popularly understood. Although his name is sometimes extrapolated to indicate anything that is of phallic appearance, the shrines to Konsei Daimyōjin represent a significant sub-category of sexual-related religious establishments and enshrine a very special *kami* with specific powers of procreation that are still valued in this modern age. In his unique nature Konsei Daimyōjin, the greatest among all of Japan's gods of sex, differs from other sexual *kami* because his origin is not to be found in a human being or a mythological tale, wondrous and sexual though that tale may be. Konsei Daimyōjin's origin lies instead in human wonder at the tremendous power of the male reproductive organ. Within the pantheon of Japan's sexual gods Konsei Daimyōjin stands alone as a phenomenon that clearly deserves more recognition and attention than is paid to the Tagata Shrine where the prominent phallus is merely an offering to a *kami*, not the *kami* itself. With no other enshrined *kami* and with a total concentration on the iconic phallus, the shrines to Konsei Daimyōjin represent phallicism *par excellence*, and as the god of the penis we come as close as is possible to encountering phallic worship in a literal sense.

---

85 By extension the expression *join sūhai* expression used by Nishioka and others does not imply the worship of the vulva.

CHAPTER 9

Hidden Buddhas and Sexual Gods

The Ryōsenji 了仙寺 in Shimoda (Shizuoka Prefecture) is a place steeped in history. Founded in 1635 by the third Tokugawa Shōgun Iemitsu, its premises were used as an official guesthouse by the Tokugawa and in 1854 it received Commodore Perry, who arrived there to sign the Treaty of Amity between Japan and the United States. A fine purpose-built modern museum beside the temple now commemorates this historic event, and although most of the displays are concerned with the 'Black Ships' and the opening-up of Japan, a separate gallery to the rear houses a very different type of artefact referred to as the temple's collection of *hibutsu* 秘仏 (hidden Buddhas). In one of the most interesting and best displayed collections of this type in Japan are a large number of erotic statuettes from India, China, Nepal and Tibet. Some of the latter are in the position of copulation or *yab-yum*, literally 'mother and father'. Typically the multi-armed (and sometimes multi-headed) male god stands firmly on two feet with the smaller female deity straddled across him in sexual congress to symbolise the union of the masculine principle of wisdom and the feminine principle of benevolence. Thus united in creative bliss, the figures trample evil underfoot to show their powers of exorcism and the bestowal of blessings. Several of these deities were to make the journey from continental East Asia to Japan where they continue play a role in Japanese religion alongside native *kami*. Some are still worshipped as sexual gods, even though they have experienced many changes in name, form and function including the adoption of a secret identity as *hibutsu*. Certain examples also enhance the scope of Japanese sexual beliefs by bringing in the dimension of the sacralising of human sexual pleasure.

The element of secrecy implied by the term *hibutsu* may be expressed by keeping the image out of sight except on special occasions, the partial concealment of the figure or the inclusion of an esoteric sexual hand gesture. As far as the casual visitor to Ryōsenji is concerned the unmistakeable sexual nature of the objects would fully justify concealment, although this was only one factor behind the practice. The full reasoning is explained very well by Fabio Rambelli in his detailed study of the wider Buddhist phenomenon of *hibutsu*, which are generally defined as images regarded as so sacred that they are only displayed on rare occasions.[1] The rationale lay in shifting the emphasis

1 Rambelli 2002, p. 271.

 | DOI 10.1163/9789004293786_010

FIGURE 170 *Two anonymous deities in the position of copulation or* yab-yum, *literally 'mother and father'. The male god stands firmly on two feet with the smaller female deity straddled across him in sexual congress to symbolise the union of the masculine and feminine principles. (Private Collection).*

of understanding and appreciation from the visible image towards the transcendence that lay behind it and through which the total transcendence of the Buddha himself was expressed. The worshipper was thereby taken to a higher level of consciousness than the one that could be supplied by what was seen. The concealment of these images and their secret nature would therefore evoke in worshippers a greater feeling for their power and potential, and 'with their invisibility, display the very concept of Buddhahood—omnipresent but out of sight'.[2] Various types of hidden images continue to be worshipped to this day as *hibutsu* at certain temples. They will stand inside a small closed shrine called a *zushi* 厨子. Sometimes a replica of what is inside may be on display, but the image itself will be shown only at rare intervals or only to those of a certain status. Some are periodically revealed to the public with great fanfare and an even greater reverence while some are never seen at all, their exact appearance remaining unknown even to those who have inherited the care of them over hundreds of years.

The sexual *hibutsu* present a special case of this general principle. The inclusion of nudity or sexuality in the design of the image could easily be seen as a form of desecration provoking unsuitably heretical thoughts among their viewers, but because Buddhist belief maintains that everything is imbued with Buddhahood these images were seen as possessed of a greater sacredness, even though that higher spiritual power had to be controlled by concealment.[3]

In October 2012 I was privileged to have shown to me the sexual-related *hibutsu* that is preserved and venerated at the Ontokuji 恩徳寺, a Shingon temple located on the outskirts of Okayama City. The Shingon sect provides the Japanese version of esoteric Vajrayāna or Tantric Buddhism and was founded by the monk Kūkai (Kōbō Daishi) after a period of study in China. Shingon Buddhism is characterised by the use of mandalas and its esoteric ritual, some of which is secret, as was the hidden image that I was shown after the offering of incense and a short ceremony of prayer. The Chief Priest of Ontokuji, the Reverend Tai Kōhei, carefully moved to one side a number of objects that stood in front of the *zushi* and then opened it to reveal the image, which was of two elephant-headed human figures embracing each other in almost perfect symmetry. The female was standing on the toes of the male, and the conjoined pair stood on top of a lotus. Two tiny phallic symbols had been placed in front of the statue.[4]

---

2 Rambelli 2002, p. 302.

3 Rambelli 2002, p. 294.

4 From a personal observation made on 23 October 2012. A smaller Dual-body Kangiten kept in the *zushi* next to it is illustrated in Kokonoe 1976, p. 140.

FIGURE 171 *The motif of the Sōshin Kangiten or 'Dual-body Kangiten' shows Vināyaka, the Buddhist version of Gaṇeśa embracing the Bodhissatva Avalokiteśvara, identified in a female form with the goddess Kannon. They take the form of two elephant-headed people. This example is in the Ontokuji in Okayama City.*

The image at the Ontokuji was an example of a Sōshin Kangiten 双身歓喜天 or 'Dual-body Kangiten', an interpretation of Vināyaka, the Buddhist version of the elephant-headed Hindu god Gaṇeśa (Ganesh) and one of the most important sexual deities to have come to Japan from India. In Japan he is called either Kangiten 歓喜天 (the Deva of Bliss) or Shōten 聖天 (The Saintly Deva) and sometimes Daishō Kangiten 大聖歓喜天 (Great Holy Deva of Bliss). 'Deva' is a Sanskrit word that means celestial being or demi-god who is neither a Buddha nor a *bodhisattva*, one who delays their enlightenment for the good of others. It is indicated in Japan by the suffix *-ten* 天, which indicates that the deity originated in Hindu mythology but was incorporated into the Buddhist pantheon as a protective deity.

The Dual-body Kangiten, as a god of happiness locked in an embrace from which bliss flows, is a version that evolved only in China and Japan, although images of the original Gaṇeśa in erotic *yab-yum* poses are to be found in Tibet and Nepal.[5] As Yuvraj Krishan points out, the notion of Vināyaka being represented as the Dual-body Kangiten received some opposition in China, particularly from Confucian scholars, but was fully accepted by Kōbō Daishi.[6] The image at Ontokuji is gilded and quite plain, but other versions exist in forms described in an article by James Sanford. In some of these the male has a white coloration and the female red to represent the union of semen and menstrual blood, the key procreative essences in Tantric thought. The female may have shorter tusks than the male and may wear a crown. In another variation the figures are gazing into each other's eyes.[7]

The goddess whom Kangiten is embracing is the *bodhisattva* Avalokiteśvara, who is identified with Japan's popular deity Kannon 観音. Her presence with Kangiten is explained by myths that begin with the story of how Gaṇeśa acquired his elephant head. Śiva leaves his wife Pārvatī for a long period while he goes to meditate. She longs for company and rubs unguents on to her limbs. Out of their secretions she creates a boy whom she places at the doorway of her bathroom, ordering him to let no one pass. When Śiva returns he finds his way blocked by this stranger, and after a fight cuts off his head. Overcome by grief, Pārvatī tells Śiva that unless he restores her son to life she will destroy the universe. Śiva's servants are sent away with orders to cut off the head from the first creature they meet, which is an elephant. The elephant's head is placed

5 Nishioka 1961, Plates XIX and XX; Sanford, James H. 1991. 'Literary Aspects of Japan's Dual-Gaṇeśa Cult' in Brown, Robert L. *Ganesh: Studies of an Asian God* (New York), p. 313. One is on show at the Ryōsenji.

6 Krishan, Yuvraj 1999. *Gaṇeśa: Unravelling an Enigma* (Delhi), p. 164.

7 Sanford 1991, p. 289. For photographs see Itō and Richie 1967, pp. 146–151.

on the boy's body, at which Śiva restores him to life and names him Gaṇeśa. He then adopts him as his own son and gives him charge of Śiva's devotees. Gaṇeśa thus becomes the 'Lord of Obstacles' who places barriers against those who fail to honour him but smooths the path of those who follow him. He is therefore the guardian of entrances, the deity to be worshipped first before all other religious observances begin.[8]

The Buddhist Vināyaka is very different in temperament from the jovial little creature now encountered in popular Hindu iconography, and paintings at the Ryōsenji show this demonic side to his personality when the newly revived and now elephant-headed Gaṇeśa reacts with violence against the populace. His unpleasant behaviour reveals him as the creator of obstacles rather than their remover, a fierce and frightening god who will have to be pacified, and this happy outcome comes about through the good offices of Avalokiteśvara. She assumes the same elephant-headed shape as Vināyaka and tames him by having sexual intercourse. However, although thereby ritually and mythologically pacified, Vināyaka remains an ambivalent character in Japanese religion because his violence has not been completely extinguished. He has to be regularly propitiated by prayers and libations, and his dark powers can even be employed as a weapon through which one's enemies might be overcome.[9]

The taming of Vināyaka/Kangiten by the seduction of Avalokiteśvara/Kannon is the act depicted in the motif of the Dual-body Kangiten, although the theme has sometimes been regarded as showing only Kangiten but in both a male and female form.[10] It has also been viewed in a different way because a South Indian variation on the myth of Gaṇeśa's creation involves no act of beheading by Śiva. Instead he and Pārvatī produce Gaṇeśa through their own sexual intercourse after they have changed themselves into the form of elephants in order to increase their sexual pleasure, a decision based on the notion of elephants as powerful sexual beings.[11] Seen in this light, the Japanese Dual-body Kangiten image has sometimes been interpreted as depicting not Gaṇeśa but Śiva and Pārvatī locked in their creative embrace.[12] Different sexual imagery may also be provided for Kangiten when he is shown brandishing

8 As summarised in Courtright, Paul B. 1985. *Ganesa: Lord of Obstacles, Lord of Beginnings* (Oxford) pp. 5–6.

9 Faure, Bernard 2006. 'The elephant in the room: The cult of secrecy in Japanese Tantrism' in Scheid, Bernard and Teeuwen, Mark (eds.) *The Culture of Secrecy in Japanese Religion* (London), pp. 255–257.

10 Yato 2005, pp. 72–73.

11 Courtright 1985, p. 31.

12 This is the interpretation implied in Itō and Richie 1967, p. 136.

a *daikon* 大根 (giant radish) as a phallic symbol, but depictions of Kangiten in the conventional pose of Gaṇeśa as a single figure are very rare in Japan.[13]

According to Krishan in 1979, Kangiten was being worshipped in Japan at 243 places.[14] Both Itō and Kokonoe include photographs of the hidden Dual-body Kangiten image at the Gumyōji 弘明寺 in Yokohama (Kanagawa Prefecture), but the most important worship centre is probably the Ikoma Hōzanji, founded by the monk Tankai (1629–1716) who was a devotee of Kangiten.[15] Kangiten's hidden image lies inside an impressive worship hall as the focus of prayerful attention so that the temple is often referred to as the Ikoma Shōten.[16] The only phallic imagery on display anywhere on site is the symbol of a *daikon*, which appears as the motif of two radishes crossed over each other. They are superimposed upon the design of a draw-string bag or depicted alone on lanterns and cups.[17] A more extensive use is made of the same image at the Gumyōji and at the Asakusa Matsuchiyama Shōten 浅草 待乳山聖天 in Tokyo. At the former an *ema* with the design of two crossed bifurcated radishes on top of a yellow draw-string bag indicates a desire to find a partner.[18] At the latter the radishes are deeply bifurcated and intertwined.[19] Small bells in the shape of bags with the crossed radish motif are on sale at Asakusa.

Through his role as 'The Deva of Bliss' Kangiten adds a further dimension to Japanese sexual beliefs by the sacralising of sexual pleasure. A Dual-body Kangiten is therefore also an erotic statue that celebrates sex itself rather than just procreation and may even echo something that once existed in Japan in a much livelier form, because during the medieval period a minor offshoot of Shingon once flourished under the name of the Tachikawa-ryū 立川流. The cult was so thoroughly suppressed that almost all we know of it comes from the writings of its denouncers, but it would appear to have begun with the notion of the unity of the male and female elements. By extension that harmonious unity was most completely expressed through the act of sexual intercourse, and if its critics are to be believed the Tachikawa School went beyond symbolism to maintain that sexual intercourse was the most important thing in Shingon teaching and the highest means of practice for attaining

13 Yato 2005, p. 65. One image is in the shrine outside the Izu Gokurakuen in Shizuoka Prefecture.

14 Krishan 1999, p. 163.

15 Itō and Richie 1967, pp. 148–149; Kokonoe 1976, pp. 62–63.

16 Sanford 1991, pp. 302–309 and from a personal observation made on 25 October 2012.

17 From a personal observation made on 25 October 2012.

18 From a personal observation made on 29 April 2012.

19 From a personal observation made on 20 April 2012.

FIGURE 172 *At the Gumyōji in Yokohama two crossed* daikon *on a bag indicate a desire to find a partner.*

FIGURE 173 *A lantern showing the sexual motif of two crossed and bifurcated* daikon *at the Asakusa Matsuchiyama Shōten in Tokyo.*

Buddhahood. When this was put into practice by its adherents the sect was suppressed.[20]

Sanford provides a detailed description of their most notorious practice, the so-called 'Skull Ritual',[21] although Iyanaga points out that nowhere in the textual source for this infamous rite is any direct connection made to link it to the Tachikawa-ryū.[22] Briefly put, its devotees are supposed to have made small spheres from crushed up human skulls mixed with the bodily fluids of their acts of intercourse. The alleged process whereby these items were completed is lurid and highly unlikely to have been successfully attained, but other 'proof' of the Tachikawa-ryū's sexual obsessions is provided by written and pictorial accounts of their supposed beliefs. These date from the 1660s, centuries after the Tachikawa-ryū was excommunicated and repressed and are therefore of doubtful authenticity. One is on show at the Ryōsenji and depicts two sets of bodies about to engage in intercourse, while a different illustration in the form of a mandala is depicted both by Itō and in Sanford. Here the two bodies are shown overlapping.[23]

There is however little need to dwell on what may or may not have been alleged about sexual practices among members of the heretical Tachikawa-ryū, because sexual elements may be identified elsewhere in Shingon which conform more to what would be expected from an esoteric religion because they are implied or suggested through symbols and by mystical and poetic language. So, in addition to the explicit visual depiction of the sexual embraces of the Dual-body Kangiten, the language used in certain written scriptures may be interpreted as referring to the conjugal union of certain deities. One example concerns Fudō Myōō 不動明王 and a female incarnation of Aizen Myōō 愛染明王. Although his visual depiction is that of a Hindu deity, Aizen is the product of Chinese and Japanese esotericism. His body is red, symbolising the power he possesses to purify sexual desire and to convert lust into a spiritual awakening. In the materials discussed by Sanford, Aizen and Fudō are described as being coupled in a sexual manner. The source is an initiatory text (a means typical of the transmission within Shingon) dating from 1310 and received by the priest Gonraku from the Yoga Sūtra. In some interpretations the 'roar of a lion' mentioned in the sutra is an encrypted reference to

20 Iyanaga, Nobumi 2006. 'Secrecy, sex and apocrypha: Remarks on some paradoxical phenomena' in Scheid, Bernard and Teeuwen, Mark (eds.) *The Culture of Secrecy in Japanese Religion* (London), p. 224.

21 Sanford, James H. 1991. 'The Abominable Tachikawa Skull Ritual' *Monumenta Nipponica* 46, pp. 1–20.

22 Iyanaga 2006, p. 207.

23 Itō and Richie 1967, pp. 156–157; Sanford 1991, p. 13.

their cries at orgasm and their sexual ecstasy is a 'revelational state in which all differentiations of self and other have been lost'. Also involved in the priest Gonraku's initiatory learning was the symbolism of the *kongō* 金剛 (the *vajra*, diamond or thunderbolt), which is an important ritual instrument of phallic origin. Its normal shape is that of a metal stick with five points at each end. When it has a bell at one end the bell represents the womb. The 'human-shape' *vajra*, made from two united halves, represents the 'heads, limbs and generative organs of a sexually united man and woman'.[24] The phallic nature of the *vajra* is also attested in a discussion by Ananda Coomaraswamy.[25]

Another apparently phallic object from India that may be found in certain Japanese temples is Śiva's lingam, although the exact nature and meaning of this item has been a controversial topic in Hinduism for many centuries. To some scholars it is a phallic symbol representing Śiva's sexual organ; to others it is a completely abstract and profound indicator of divine energy.[26] The use of the lingam in devotional terms is explained by a Hindu myth that finds Brahmā and Viṣṇu arguing about which of them is the greatest, when a gigantic lingam, wreathed in flames, suddenly appears before them. Out of it steps Śiva, who proclaims that he is henceforth to be worshipped in the form of a lingam.[27]

The Ryōsenji collection owns two examples. The first resembles a stupa and is of very slight phallic appearance, the other is a symbol that combines a yoni with a lingam to symbolise sexual and spiritual unity. Here the stupa of the lingam stands on the flat surface of a rounded yoni.[28] A similar one may be found at the Sōtō Zen Tōganji 桃巌寺 in Nagoya, where there is a considerable eclectic element derived from Indian religion because one of its priests completed his training in India during the 1960s. The lingam stands outside a building dedicated to Sarasvatī (Benzaiten) in a small garden courtyard which contains much that is visibly sexual. A large bronze censer occupies a central position, and cast into the stand beneath its bowl are eight curious male figures, each with an enormous penis, that are very similar to some statues from Bali illustrated by Nishioka.[29] The combined lingam and yoni takes the form of a large

---

24 Sanford, James H. 1997. 'Wind, Waters, Stupas, Mandalas': Fetal Buddhahood in Shingon' *Japanese Journal of Religious Studies* 24, pp. 5–7.

25 Coomaraswamy, Ananda K. 1935. 'Angel and Titan: An Essay in Vedic Ontology' *Journal of the American Oriental Society* 55, pp. 373–419.

26 I am indebted to Dr. James McHugh for sharing his insights into this debatable topic.

27 As summarised by Yato (2005, p. 84).

28 Nishioka 1961, Plate IX.

29 Nishioka 1961, Plate VIII.

FIGURE 174 *The* vajra, *an important Shingon ritual instrument identified by scholars as having a phallic origin.*

bronze water fountain sitting on top of a rock. Water enters the shallow yoni from the mouth of a coiled snake. The words *seimei no kongen* (the source of life) are inscribed upon the side of the yoni in characters of gold. Worshippers pour water from the yoni over the central lingam, and the temple's pamphlet encourages this practice as an annual memorial act for *mizuko* (aborted or still-born babies).[30]

30 From a personal observation made on 22 October 2012 and from the temple's pamphlet.

FIGURE 175 *A lingam and yoni at a temple in Hita (Ōita Prefecture).*

FIGURE 176 *This combination of a lingam and a yoni is used to make a water fountain at the Tōganji in Nagoya. Water enters the shallow yoni from the mouth of a coiled snake.*

Sex and the Seven Gods of Good Luck

Of all the deities who made the journey from the continent to Japan none entered more fully into Japanese religious life than the *shichifukujin* 七福神, the popular and ubiquitous 'Seven Gods of Good Luck'. Six out of the group came to Japan from overseas. All were transformed along the way as profoundly as was Gaṇeśa, but they exist today as approachable manifestations of Japanese religious belief with an iconography ranging from priceless medieval statues to comic key rings. Nevertheless, certain elements of secrecy may be noted for them, particularly when they take on a sexual nature.

The one who changed most radically on his journey from India was Daikokuten 大黒天 (The Great Black Deva), who is often referred to as Daikoku-sama or simply Daikoku. In his original Hindu form he is the god Mahākāla, a terrifying, demon-suppressing divinity, and Yato includes a photograph of a statuette of him in the *yab-yum* pose.[31] By the time Daikoku reaches Japan the sexual element has disappeared and only his face is still in any way terrifying, but as shown by an old statue at a temple in Fukuoka Prefecture it is more anger or

31 Yato 2005, p. 85.

annoyance that is now being displayed.[32] It was not long before he merged with the *kami* Ōkuninushi no Mikoto 大国主命 and assumed the appearance by which he is usually known, which is of a stout and kindly fellow with a smile and a goatee beard and wearing a cap. In his hand is a mallet, over his shoulder is a sack, and he is standing on two bales of rice. A variation on the theme shows him as three-headed.

Daikoku has a strong connection to the notion of fertility, and his iconography sometimes reflects the notion of the mystical transference to the fields of the power symbolised by an image associated with human sexuality. In this role he is pictured carrying on his back a huge bifurcated phallic *daikon*, an object called in some places 'the bride of Daikoku'. It is offered as a symbolic betrothal to ensure an abundant harvest.[33] Both Nishioka and Itō include photographs of statues of Daikoku that project a different erotic element. Nishioka shows him effectively absorbed into a ceramic phallus.[34] Itō shows a similarly envisaged figure of him in wood seen as Daikoku from one side and a phallus from the other together with another variation whereby he strokes a phallus with his right hand and holds a ktenic ball with his left.[35] At the Tarō Shrine 太郎神社 in Godo (Gunma Prefecture) a wooden Daikoku has an erect penis that is normally covered by a white cloth.[36]

In a few rare examples Daikoku presents an instance of the third category of secrecy noted at the beginning of this chapter because he makes with his right hand the ancient sexual gesture of the thumb held between the index and middle fingers.[37] The first example shown in Nishioka's book is of an old type of image of a bare-headed Daikoku. It is kept in a separate room at the Sangatsu-dō in Nara and is locked away from view, as is Nishioka's other example from Shiga Prefecture.[38] One however can be seen on a modern and more conventional bronze statue of Daikoku installed in a recently constructed building high up under the cliff behind the Ikoma Hōzanji.[39]

The partial concealment of an image by clothing is displayed most commonly by the otherwise naked statues of Benzaiten 弁財天 or Benten 弁天. She is the only female deity among the *shichifukujin* and originates from Hindu

32 Yato 2005, p. 94.

33 Nishioka 1961, Plate XVI; Hori 1963, p. 84.

34 Nishioka 1961, Plate XV.

35 Itō and Richie 1967, pp. 188–189 & 192.

36 From a personal observation made on 10 March 2014.

37 Nishioka 1961, pp. 128–132 and Plates XIII and XIV.

38 From personal observations made on 1 April 2012 and 2 May 2012.

39 From a personal observation made on 25 October 2012.

FIGURE 177 *Daikoku carrying a bifurcated* daikon *'the bride of Daikoku', offered as a symbolic betrothal to ensure an abundant harvest. (Private Collection).*

FIGURE 178
A statuette of Daikoku in the Tarō Shrine at Godo (Gunma Prefecture) that involves phallic display. His erect organ is normally concealed under a white cloth.

FIGURE 179 *Daikoku making the ancient sexual gesture of the thumb held between the index and middle fingers at the Ikoma Hōzanji.*

mythology as Sarasvatī, the wife of Brahmā, whose name is also that of a mythical river. She became a goddess of water and indeed of anything that flows, such as music. This aspect of her was lost for a time when she entered Japan as Happi (eight-armed) Benzaiten 八臂弁財天, a martial goddess who also represented a link to the rice-god Inari through the image of a key that she carried in one hand. Further development took place when she merged with the snake *kami* Ugajin 宇賀神, a deity of food, to produce the syncretic Uga Benzaiten 宇賀弁財天 where an image of a snake was included in her iconography.[40] It

40 Hardacre, Helen 2002. *Religion and society in nineteenth-century Japan: a study of the southern Kantō region, using late Edo and early Meiji gazetteers* (Ann Arbor), pp. 119–120.

FIGURE 180 *This statue of Nemuri Benten (Sleeping Benten) at the Tōganji shows the beloved goddess lying peacefully in repose with her* biwa *at her side.*

is esoteric Buddhism that we have to thank for rescuing her aesthetic side, to the extent that these early Japanese depictions of her are now almost eclipsed by her popular style as a beautiful and very feminine player of the *biwa* (the Japanese lute).

There is a particularly strong tradition relating to Benten at the Tōganji, and the main sanctuary, referred to in the temple's pamphlet as the Sarasvatī Hall, contains a rich iconography relating to the goddess. Its main image is of a large Happi Benzaiten, in front of which stands a smaller wooden statue of a bare-breasted Benzaiten playing her *biwa*. They are flanked by a wide collection of phallic and ktenic imagery from Japan and other countries that continues into two locked glass-fronted cabinets to each side, both of which are filled with votive phalluses and other Benzaiten statues.[41] An additional focus of devotion is presented in an adjacent room along the corridor, because here lies the temple's greatest treasure: the Nemuri Benten ねむり弁財天 or 'Sleeping Benten'. The goddess lies peacefully in repose with her *biwa* behind her, and underneath the robes she is naked.[42] This is theme is known as the Hadaka Benzaiten 裸弁才天 (Naked Benzaiten). The most famous example of the

41 From a personal observation made on 22 October 2012.

42 Kokonoe 1981, p. 193.

style is her completely unclothed statue within the Hōan-den 奉安殿 on the island of Enoshima (Kanagawa Prefecture). It is one of two Benten images on Enoshima. The other is a Happi Benten, and until comparatively recently both were kept as *hibutsu* and only displayed once every six years. Both images have also undergone many vicissitudes, from being visited by pilgrims in their thousands to being unceremoniously dumped when Shintō and Buddhism were forcibly separated under the Meiji government. The Naked Benten as it is seen today was extensively restored after World War II, having lost its left hand, left leg and right ankle.[43]

The other Hindu deity found within the *shichifukujin* is Bishamonten 毘沙門天 (Vaiśravaṇa). He is a fierce protective warrior god, one of the four guardian kings of heaven, and the only remotely sexual role to be projected on to him is to be regarded as Benten's husband. Bishamonten's physical appearance also makes it difficult for any artist to twist his features or bodily appearance into a phallic symbol, unlike Fukurokuju 福禄寿, a god of wisdom and longevity and one of three *shichifukujin* derived from Daoism. Fukurokuju's most visible physical characteristic is his elongated head that is almost a gift for phallic caricature. The Daoist Jurōjin 寿老人 also has a similarly shaped head although it is by no means elongated. He is often seen with a deer and is said to be fond of female company. The third Daoist is Hotei 布袋, the corpulent deity popularly and inaccurately known as the 'Laughing Buddha'. Finally we have Ebisu 恵比須, the only native Japanese god among the seven. He is a jolly fisherman with his catch of a sea bream dangling from his line. Ebisu is said in some accounts to be Hiruko 蛭子 the deformed 'leech child' who was the first offspring of Izanagi and Izanami and was cast off into the sea; in other traditions he is the son of Daikoku.

Taken as a whole the seven gods of good luck do not have strong links to sexual beliefs, although they have recently acquired some in a newly created variation on the notion of a *shichifukujin* pilgrimage. In common with other examples of the great Japanese pilgrimage tradition, temples that house images of the seven are linked together to create the opportunity for a physical and spiritual journey. Ian Reader describes joining in one such pilgrimage around a series of places where the seven were enshrined and writes of the 'benevolent and happy nature' of the seven gods and the 'relaxed, touristic approach' of his travelling companions, who purchased little models of the gods and placed them in a toy boat as they went round.[44]

---

43 From a personal observation made on 30 March 2008.

44 Reader 1991, pp. 164–167.

FIGURE 181 *The Naked Benten on the Island of Enoshima (Kanagawa Prefecture).*

This notion has been given an interesting twist on the Bosō peninsula of Chiba Prefecture. Known as the Kazusa Shichifukujin Meguri 上総七福神めぐり (the pilgrimage of the Seven Lucky Gods round Kazusa, the old provincial name for central Chiba) it can be done comfortably in one day by car using a very helpful pamphlet that includes the telephone numbers of all seven locations for one's satellite navigation system. What the pamphlet does not make clear is that sexual imagery is included in most of the seven statues to be visited. Each statue has its niche in the temples, and their presence is prominently advertised from the roadside. Six of the statues date from the early 1990s when they were added to an existing image of Bishamonten, who alone has escaped the consequences of the decision to relate prayers for abundant harvests and business prosperity to the theme of sex. The stated intention was to represent the gods with sexual features so subtle that they appeared innocuous to the casual eye, a goal that has met with only limited success.

The pilgrimage begins at the Narita-san Fudō-dō in Kisarazu City, where one finds Benzaiten in her conventional naked form playing the *biwa* but with a white cloth that modestly conceals her charms. A short drive then takes one to a temple displaying a stone statue of Fukurokuju that stands in the middle of a pond. Even though Fukurokuju's elongated head is an easy target for phallic representation, the sculptor did not stop at this obvious feature but has built several other phallic and ktenic motifs into his depiction. Jurōjin is next to be encountered. The lucky god's sexual appearance is limited to ktenic designs of his robe and sleeves. After the innocuous Bishamonten at another temple one meets Daikoku, whose bent right knee is somewhat phallic. The opening of his sack is also made to look ktenic, although this feature is obscured by a large flower vase. At a further site Hotei simply rests his hand upon the top of a phallus, but the most extraordinary assemblage is provided for Ebisu. His own statue is somewhat restrained as it possesses only a ktenic sleeve, but standing next to him and carved out of similar stone are a huge phallus and kteis and a life-sized naked woman. The inscription on the rear of the plinth states that she is modelled on the wife of a former chief priest.

Apart from Ebisu's companions the 'secret' sexual imagery along the pilgrimage route is so restrained as to make one question why it was felt necessary to include it at all. Yet even Ebisu's sexual display is very modest compared with the *ema* on sale at the Kanayama Shrine in Kawasaki. This is a larger version of the usual *ema* that are made to be left behind at shrines. It is meant to be taken home and a stand is provided into which it may be slotted for display. The design shows the *shichifukujin* entering harbour in their treasure ship to bring prosperity. Children are traditionally urged to put a picture of the seven gods and the ship under their pillows at New Year, but certainly not this depiction of them because the heads of all the male gods have been transformed into large phalluses, as has the figurehead of the boat that ploughs through suggestive white foam. An embarrassed-looking Benten alone remains untransformed; instead the sail behind her is painted to represent a kteis.

FIGURE 182 *Fukurokuju is given a multiple sexual makeover at the Enmyō-In on the Seven Lucky Gods' Pilgrimage route on the Bosō peninsula in Chiba Prefecture.*

The Traditions of Kishimojin, Kannon and Jizō

Two other goddesses with links to conception and childbirth came to Japan from the East Asian continent. The first is Kishimojin 鬼子母神 (sometimes romanised as Kishibojin), who was originally the Iranic deity Hārītī.[45] She may

45 The standard work on Kishimojin is Miyazaki, Eishū 1985. *Kishimojin no shinkō* (Tokyo).

FIGURE 183 *Hotei's sexual distortion is limited to giving his exposed right knee a phallic appearance in his shrine at the Fudō-In.*

FIGURE 184 *The extraordinary sexual ambience that accompanies a statue of Ebisu at the Enkyōji on the Chiba pilgrimage route.*

FIGURE 185 *This* ema *from the Kanayama Shrine in Kawasaki provides a sexual take on the motif of the Seven Gods of Good Luck travelling on their treasure ship.*

be approached for help with conception, and is mentioned in the descriptions of Japanese village life during the 1930s in the book *The Women of Suye-mura*. 'Mrs Fujita says that the woman who has ninety-eight children, and then had them taken away from her and returned, and was changed into a goddess is exceptionally good'.[46] This is a reference to the myth of Kishimojin, which relates that she was originally a monstrous figure who devoured other people's babies despite having hundreds of children of her own. In response to the entreaties of the bereaved mothers the Buddha removed Kishimojin's youngest son. She searched frantically for him until, utterly distraught, she appealed to the Buddha for help. The Buddha made her realise how her anguish at losing one child might be compared with the agony of the hundreds of mothers whom she had harmed. Kishimojin received the mercy of the Buddha and had her child restored to her, so that she is now a guardian goddess of fertility and childbirth. The Buddha also gave her pomegranates to eat, whose red flesh and sharp taste resembled raw meat and thus compensated for the human flesh she had been used to. Pomegranates appear on the *ema* of the Zoshigaya Kishimojindō 雑司が谷鬼子母神堂 in Tokyo.[47]

Far more widespread than the cult of Kishimojin is the devotion given in Japan to Kannon. She derives from Avalokiteśvara, Kangiten's mate in the dual-body images, who was originally male, changing gender on the way from India to China where she emerged as Guan Yin and then became a popular deity in Japan. Kannon's great role in Japanese religion is as the benevolent and beloved goddess of mercy who embodies compassion. She has therefore acquired many roles including, quite recently, the prevention and treatment of senile dementia.[48] She is also a goddess of childbirth with the title Koyasu Kannon 子安観音 (Kannon of safe or easy childbirth). Statues of Kannon in this role often depict her nursing a baby, but her identity is a little complicated because she has merged with the *kami* Koyasu-sama, otherwise Konohana Sakuya Hime. Otherwise she may be known as Jibo (Loving Mother) Kannon, and in this guise she appears in several giant statues erected around Japan in recent years. Kannon is rarely concealed from view, but easy delivery is one of several prayer intentions that may be made to a nominally secret image of her at the Daihiden in Gamagori, a place that proclaims itself as Japan's

46 Smith, Robert and Wiswell, Ella Lury 1982. *The Women of Suye Mura* (Chicago), p. 93.

47 From a personal observation made on 19 April 2012.

48 Mullins, Mark 2008. 'The Many Forms and Functions of Kannon in Japanese Religion and Culture' *Dharma World* April-June. http://www.rk-world.org/dharmaworld/dw_2008ajmanyforms.aspx (Accessed 8 June 2014).

FIGURE 186 *The pomegranate motif appears on the* ema *to Kishimojin at the Zoshigaya Kishimojin-dō in Tokyo.*

FIGURE 187 *The statue of a naked Tibetan-style Avalokiteśvara/Kannon at the Daihiden in Gamagori.*

'number one *hibutsu* temple'.[49] Beneath the hill on which the temple stands a series of twisting passages have been created to provide the worshipper with a 320 metre-long symbolic pilgrimage through the ten worlds of existence. Numerous statues and paintings, many of them involving sexual imagery, provide visual illustration for the journey that culminates in the main temple hall where a naked statue of Avalokiteśvara/Kannon sits within the open doors of a *zushi*.[50] A different naked interpretation of Kannon is her strange identification with Okichi, the Japanese girl who became the mistress of the first US Consul-General to Japan, Townsend Harris. Okichi's life has been romanticised in novels and films, and at the Chōrakuji in Shimoda (Shizuoka Prefecture), her delicate effigy stands in a small museum under the name of Okichi Kannon.[51]

Kannon is clearly a highly adaptable deity, and her name is associated with several sexual shrines. The natural ktenic outcrop at Okutama is called the Hime Seki Kannon, but the most explicit sexual imagery to be associated with her is found at places that go under the name of Mara Kannon 魔羅観音, an expression that combines *mara* (penis) with the goddess's name. At the Onitsuka Kannon 鬼塚観音 in Fukutsu (Fukuoka Prefecture) phalluses are offered to her and there is a seated statue that is reminiscent of the one at the Daihiden, although this is more suggestively sexual because she is depicted in a kneeling position and one phallus has been placed beneath her vulva.[52] Also in Fukuoka Prefecture is the small Mara Kannon near Dazaifu. It lies next to the ancient earthwork known as the Mizuki that was created to provide a defence line against an anticipated attack from Tang China. The *goshintai* is a small phallic stone that may be a *sekibō*. An old wooden votive phallus illustrated by Kokonoe is still there with names written on it of families who have benefitted from its powers.[53]

Japan's most famous Mara Kannon is the place near Tawarayama Onsen that was mentioned earlier because of its accumulation of thousands of ceramic phallic offerings. These phalluses are mass-produced and are available in the three colours of white, tan and black. The shrine is much patronised and has its origins in the sad story of how in 1551 Ōuchi Yoshitaka was overthrown in a coup and committed suicide. His sons were killed including the youngest who

49 From the pamphlet supplied by the temple.

50 From a personal observation made on 13 June 2013. For a brief video of the labyrinth see my posting at http://youtu.be/Nll4bwl9gvM.

51 From a personal observation made on 11 November 2012.

52 I have not visited this place and draw my conclusions only from the photographs at http://spotto.web.fc2.com/fukuoka-1.html (Accessed 8 June 2014).

53 Kokonoe 1976, p. 99 and from a personal observation made on 16 November 2006.

FIGURE 188 *At the Chōrakuji in Shimoda a delicate naked effigy of Okichi, the mistress of Townshend Harris, stands in a small museum under the name of Okichi Kannon.*

FIGURE 189 *The Mara Kannon shrine next to the earthwork known as the Mizuki (Fukuoka Prefecture) contains a sexual Okame and a large phallus that is borrowed.*

had been discovered disguised as a girl. The boy's penis was cut off in revenge, hence the phallic association with the shrine that was raised in the victim's memory, and the Mara Kannon provides one of Japan's most visually spectacular phallic establishments. It is built on the side of a hill and around it is a veritable garden of large phalluses made from stone, concrete and metal that seem to be growing out of the ground among the trees. Inside the main building are a large number of the ceramic phalluses donated as votive offerings beside the *goshintai* of a stone phallus that may be a *sekibō*, but next to it is a small seated statue of Koyasu Kannon who appears to be the main focus of devotion. The visitors' book is full of prayers and thanks for easy delivery and healthy children, and sometimes the comments are accompanied by crude drawings.[54]

Kannon may also be linked to deities that attract similar devotional intentions. In Kamikawa (Saitama Prefecture) she shares a shrine with Kodakara Yakushi 子宝薬師, a manifestation of Yakushi Nyōrai 薬師如来, the 'Buddha of healing' or 'the medicine Buddha', who sometimes appears in a sexual guise as Kinmara Yakushi framed by two phalluses. Perhaps uniquely Kannon appears here not as Koyasu Kannon but as Batō Kannon (Horse-headed Kannon) who is normally the protector of animals. In 2013 there were nine

54 From a personal observation made on 4 March 2014.

FIGURE 190 *A late afternoon view of the Mara Kannon shrine at Tawarayama Onsen showing the collection of large phalluses arranged around it.*

wooden votive phalluses lying in front of her statue with babies' bibs hanging from the lattice.[55]

Koyasu Kannon's most interesting shared shrine lies down the hill from Tawarayama Onsen's Mara Kannon. Beside a stream is a newly rebuilt shrine that shelters her in company with Jizō 地蔵 (the *bodhisattva* Kṣitigarbha), a deity as popular as Kannon. He normally appears as a standing figure and is often childlike, kitted out with a bib and a woolly hat. Jizō may also take on a visual appearance that is phallic when his robe and hood are viewed from behind. Some of those Jizō statues are protectors of the wayside and may even be disguised phallic *sai no kami*, a matter that will be discussed in a later chapter. At Tawarayama Onsen his appearance is more conventional, although the setting is not because a phallus is included in what is otherwise a shrine for *mizuko*. Jizō occupies the central position and in front of him are offerings of toys that characterise such places. A small Koyasu Kannon stands next to him. She has acquired one of Jizō's bibs and in front of her is a stone phallus in a neat little jacket. Her inclusion reflects a recent trend whereby Kannon has joined Jizō in this role, her compassion making her ideal as the recipient of prayers for the babies in the other world and for those who have to cope with

55 From a personal observation made on 5 July 2013.

FIGURE 191 *A copy of the Kinmara Yakushi at the Saizenji in Maebashi appears here in the garden of the Tōganji in Nagoya. The healing Buddha is flanked by two phalluses.*

FIGURE 192 *The Kodakara Yakushi-dō at Kamikawa (Saitama Prefecture) where Kodakara Yakushi shares a shrine with Bato Kannon. Both receive phallic offerings.*

guilt and remorse.[56] The presence of a phallus probably signifies an intention to have babies at some time in the future when the mother's circumstances might be different, a conclusion I base on comments by William LaFleur in relation to Jizō's manifestation as Koyasu Jizō and Mizuko Jizō. Noting that Jizō seems to be performing contradictory roles in abortion and conception he concludes that, '"Not now", for many such people, obviously would not have meant "never"'.[57]

At Tawarayama Onsen Koyasu Kannon is the recipient of the phallic offerings. Elsewhere phalluses are presented to Jizō. For example, inside the Saifukuji 西福寺, a Buddhist temple in a tranquil rural area near Kikugawa (Shizuoka Prefecture), an ancient *sekibō* has become a representation of him. Until very recently it was housed in a wooden shrine that stood at the side of the temple's car park together with some smaller phallic symbols. It has now been moved inside the main building where it occupies a newly refurbished recess in a corner. Judging from old illustrations the *sekibō* could once hardly be seen beneath the lengths of coarse ropes holding *ema* that worshippers formerly tied round it, because this Jizō is a Shibarare Jizō 縛られ地蔵 (Bound Jizō) in addition to its other names of Mara Jizō and Ko Sazuke Jizō (Jizō who grants children). The *sekibō* was stripped of these ropes a few years ago when the outside shrine was replaced. Its new location has involved a modified restoration of this votive practice, and a new design of *ema* bearing a three-dimensional soft-toy baby has been created. The walls of the recess are already covered with them, as is much of the body of the *sekibō* apart from its head. With this transformation the phallic element in the offerings has been much reduced.[58]

Another *sekibō* has found a place within a Buddhist temple to the west of Tokyo as a representation of Jizō. This is the Kenseki Jizō 剣石地蔵 'the stone sword Jizō' that stands on a side altar in the Matsudake-In 松岳院, a temple that lies within walking distance of Kodomonokuni Station (Kanagawa Prefecture). It is of a more oval cross section than most *sekibō*, hence the attribution as a *sekken* (stone sword). It is mounted within a gilt wooden holder shaped like a lotus.[59] The Kubodera, the Buddhist temple in Komaki that once

56 Mullins 2008.

57 LaFleur, William 1992. *Liquid Life: Abortion and Buddhism in Japan* (Princeton), p. 127.

58 From a personal observation made on 26 October 2012 and from the temple's official pamphlet. See also Kokonoe 1976, p. 190. The process of adding the ropes is illustrated on the temple's now outdated website http://saifuku.jp/sanpai/index.htm (accessed 30 November 2012).

59 From a personal observation made on 27 October 2012.

FIGURE 193 *The phallic offering to Koyasu Kannon in the shrine she shares with Jizō at Tawarayama Onsen.*

FIGURE 194
At the Dōso Konsei Daimyōjin in Atsuta (Nagoya City) Jizō shares a shrine with the great phallic god.

FIGURE 195 *Inside the Saifukuji, a Buddhist temple near Kikugawa, an ancient* sekibō *has become a representation of the popular deity Jizō. The walls of the recess are covered with* ema *with the design of a baby, as is much of the body of the* sekibō *apart from its head.*

had jurisdiction over the Tagata Shrine, the home of the famous phallic festival, houses a statue of Shōgun Jizō that receives phallic offerings.[60] There is also a variety known as the Hadaka (naked) Jizō. In the examples discussed by Glassman his nakedness is concealed by robes that are renewed in special ceremonies. The one illustrated in his article is seen to have vaguely suggested genitalia suggested only by a spiral pattern, which has led to the suggestion that it represents a retractable penis, one of the thirty-two marks of an extraordinary being in ancient India. Otherwise it may show the dual male and female origin of the deity.[61]

The Cult of Kōshin-sama

There are also sexual elements within the imported cult of Kōshin-sama. The word *kōshin* 庚申 refers to position fifty-seven on the sexagesimal system, whereby the familiar twelve animals of the Chinese zodiac that give, for example, 'The Year of the Dragon' are combined with a decimal cycle that arises from the five elements of wood, fire, earth, metal and water expressed either as *e* (senior brothers) or *to* (junior brothers). The fifty-seventh year or day on the resulting calendar is known in Japanese as *ka no e saru* 'the elder brother of metal, the day (or year) of the monkey', otherwise read as *kōshin*.[62]

Because of its close proximity to the point at which the sexagesimal cycle changes, the day of *kōshin* was regarded as a boundary, and just as in the case of beliefs about placing guardian *sai no kami* at physical boundaries there was seen to be a need for protection against evil. Yet the *kōshin* day posed an additional threat, because according to an ancient Chinese belief something very strange and frightening could happen that night. It states that three worms dwell in the human body. Their natures are described in a Japanese work on Chinese folk medicine as early as 982. They cause disease in the parts of the body where they reside by stimulating life-shortening gluttony and sensuality. The superior worm is black and lives in the head, where it stimulates a love of luxuries such as horses, carriages and luxurious clothes. The green worm, located in the back, encourages gluttony for food, while the white worm in

60 From a personal observation made on 15 March 2014.

61 Glassman, Hank 2002. 'The Nude Jizō at Denkōji: Notes on Women's Salvation in Kamakura Buddhism.' in Ruch, Barbara (ed.) *Engendering Faith: Women and Buddhism in Premodern Japan.* (Ann Arbor), pp. 385 & 396.

62 Papinot, Edmond 1972. *Historical and Geographical Dictionary of Japan* New Edition with an introduction by Terence Barrow) (Rutland Vt) pp. 836–837.

FIGURE 196 *There is a completely naked Jizō in Chichibu (Saitama Prefecture). His sub-shrine stands just inside the gate of the Tokuunji. He holds a staff in his right hand and a jewel in his left and is clearly male because of the carefully delineated penis and scrotum.*

the stomach stimulates sexual licence. On the night of *kōshin* these worms temporarily leave the human body for heaven, where they report on their host's behaviour during the previous cycle and judgement is handed down. Depending upon the number of transgressions the life of the host is either lengthened or shortened.[63]

So influential was this belief that a tradition developed in Japan of deliberately staying awake throughout the whole of *kōshin* night so that the worms could not escape, and the oldest written record of such a practice among the Japanese aristocracy dates from 838, by which time it had developed into something of a ritual within the imperial court with the provision of games and entertainment to pass away the hours before dawn. By the fifteenth century the practice had spread to the lower classes, and towards the end of the sixteenth century we have the first evidence of specifically religious rituals being performed to protect worshippers against the dangers.

Stone monuments known as *kōshin-tō* 庚申塔 were created as part of the practice and hundreds still exist. Some bear only the characters *kō* and *shin*, while others include an effigy of a god named as Kōshin-sama. His identity was originally very vague, but over time he became identified with the terrifying Shōmen Kongō 青面金剛 (blue-face diamond, thunderbolt or *vajra*) who protects the eastern direction against diseases caused by demons. Shōmen Kongō is derived from the Hindu group of protective deities called the Raksasa and is usually shown as either four-armed or six-armed.[64] There are two six-armed reliefs of him at the Gumyōji. In one of them two of his hands are set in an attitude of prayer. In the other he holds a club-like instrument in his extra right hand, while from his left a subjugated demon dangles, held by the hair.[65]

In many examples Shōmen Kongō has additional animal companions carved into a lower cartouche. These are the famous three wise monkeys, who 'hear no evil, see no evil and speak no evil'. They are familiar characters, although their origins are surprisingly obscure, and sometimes they appear on *kōshin-tō* without Shōmen Kongō. To some extent the presence of the monkey images on the *kōshin-tō* derives from the fact that it was 'monkey night', but the monkey was not responsible for the machinations of the three worms. Instead it was seen as acting in a protective or even mediatory capacity on behalf of the human race. One way in which the monkey could help developed from a belief in Tokugawa Japan that a child conceived on the night of *kōshin* would grow up to be a thief. Sexual intercourse was therefore best avoided at this time, hence

63 Blacker 1975, p. 329.

64 Fukuta, Ajio et al. 2012. *Nihon no Minzoku* (Tokyo), p. 242.

65 From a personal observation made on 29 April 2012.

FIGURE 197 *Near Yokote (Akita Prefecture) at a place called Kashima Ōkami a* kōshin-tō *shares its roadside shrine with several phallic symbols.*

a further need for the provision of alternative entertainment or the protection of a sexual animal.[66]

On some *kōshin-tō* the monkeys are given sexual characteristics, as at the Hōōji in Kumamoto City where one wise monkey is cradling something phallic in one hand.[67] At the Tomioka Hachiman Shrine in Tokyo there is an example

66 Nishioka 1961, pp. 190–191.

67 From personal observations made on 10 and 11 April 2012.

FIGURE 198 *A six-armed Shōmen Kongō within the grounds of the Gojōten Shrine in Tokyo. At the top of the stone are the partially eclipsed sun and the full moon, while the god holds in his two right hands a trident and an arrow, and in his two left hands the wheel of the law and a bow. Below are three very stylised 'wise monkeys'.*

FIGURE 199 *The three wise monkeys at the Aito Shrine in Jūmonji (Akita Prefecture).*

of subtle female imagery on the central character of its three wise monkeys who has carefully delineated female genitalia. There is also a disguised phallic emblem beneath them in the shape of a flower.[68] In the Yasaka Kōshin-dō, which is located just down the hill from the Yasaka pagoda in Kyoto, the sexual element is represented by small 6 cm-long pottery amulets labelled 'monkey's penis', which are believed to assist conception. The most striking items to greet the visitor to the shrine are hanging strands of small soft toys called *kukurizaru* くくり猿 that represent a faceless monkey. There are hundreds of them, and the belief is that they take away the evil desires that prevent human beings from attaining goals that are both moral and worthy. The tradition is that they should be returned to the shrine when they have been finished with, so donated *kukurizaru* are hung all around the building. The English language pamphlet issued by the shrine says:

> The Kukurizaru is a monkey which has its hands and feet tied together and cannot move. It is said that the monkey is an animal very like man, but after all it is an animal that simply acts upon its will or desire. If you go to a zoo you can see that a monkey just plays about as it likes. That figure is compared to the desire in man, and in order that 'desire' cannot come out it is tied by Kōshin. In order to have one of your wishes granted by the monkey, you should get rid of one of your desires.

68 From a personal observation made on 19 April 2012.

FIGURE 200 *A 'monkey's penis' purchased from the Yasaka Kōshin-dō in Kyoto.*

There is another Kōshindō in Nara where several monkeys are perched upon the roof tiles and many local establishments have strands of *kukurizaru* hanging from them, but here they are called *migawari-zaru* 身代わり猿 or 'substitution monkeys' who will take away one's bad luck.[69] Another important Kōshin shrine is attached to the Hida Kokubunji in Takayama City (Gifu Prefecture). Once again the image of the faceless monkey is to be found, but

69 From a personal observation made on 2 May 2012.

FIGURE 201 *These three wise monkeys stand in front of a frame of* kukurizaru *at the Yasaka Kōshin-dō in Kyoto.*

with a variation. Strings of *kukurizaru* are present but much is also made of the faceless monkey in an unfettered state, which is then known as a *sarubobo* さるぼぼ. *Sarubobo* are more closely associated with good luck and making wishes than are the *kukurizaru*, but again there is a local tradition of returning a used *sarubobo* to a shrine, so outside the Hida Kokubunji hang hundreds of these colourful characters. There is also a large sculpted stone *sarubobo* that is popular with worshippers and is rubbed for good fortune. Not surprisingly, several shops in Takayama, which is a popular cultural and tourist resort, specialise in selling *sarubobo* that are depicted in a wide range of sizes, colours and attributions including popular cartoon figures.[70]

In summary, the contribution to Japanese sexual beliefs made by the deities who have their origins on the East Asian continent is a very mixed one. Their introduction to Japan clearly shows that innovation is not just a modern phenomenon in Japanese religion. Some left their sexual identities behind as *yab-yum* statues while others took their erotic natures with them in varying degrees of secrecy under the influence of esoteric Buddhism. The seven gods of

70 From a personal observation made on 15 April 2012.

FIGURE 202 Sarubobo *both large and small are hung on a frame outside the Hida Kokubunji in Takayama.*

good luck, Kannon and Jizō are firmly established and important figures, and have acquired a sexual nature on some occasions. Kangiten adds the further dimension of the sacralising of sexual pleasure, yet in some cases the impression is given that images of the gods have been exploited in a manner akin to the erotic depiction of certain deities in *shunga*.

CHAPTER 10

The Phallus at the Crossroads: Wayside Gods of Protection and Fertility

This chapter will shift the focus of sexual imagery away from the shrine to the wider world outside it and the wayside gods (*michi no kami* 道の神 or *robō no kami* 路傍の神) who stand alone or in small groups beside roads or rice fields. They may be made from stone, wood, clay or straw. Many are fully exposed to the open air or have only a simple roofed shelter to provide protection from the elements. Some are prominent phalluses; others display a human couple chastely holding hands. Many are less than one year old; others have stood there for centuries.

The wayside gods exercise two roles. Some act protectively as guardians against disasters, plagues and the unwanted entry of outsiders. Others receive devotion as providers of fertility, although the two functions often overlap because protection from danger is of course an essential item in ensuring any form of fertility. Nowadays the sexually innocuous variety may possess additional value as symbols of their local communities, in whose economic regeneration they help by being adopted as a logo for the promotion of commerce and tourism.[1]

A number of different permanent and temporary objects are currently used to represent wayside gods, and because of a considerable overlap in their names and roles they will be described here in terms of their overall appearance rather than primarily through the titles given to them or the functions they perform. Apart from a few large wooden phalluses the permanent images are made from stone and may be classified as relief carvings depicting a human or mythological couple, relief carvings of phalluses, three-dimensional phalluses or some combination of phallus and human figure. The temporary figures are created on an annual basis and left to decay naturally. A combination of straw strengthened with wood is the usual medium for this, and in one area alone there is a tradition of making temporary wayside figures out of clay.

Two names are commonly used for the gods represented by wayside images: *dōsojin* 道祖神 (road ancestor deities) and *sai* (or *sae*) *no kami* 塞の神 (blocking deities, written also as 賽の神 and 才の神). *Sai no kami* can also appear

1 Kubota, Masayuki 2006. 'Dōsojin to machi okoshi: Nagano-ken chūshin chihō no jirei o chūshin ni' *Zasshi 'Shinshū'* 58, 1 (Nagano), pp. 25–36.

 | DOI 10.1163/9789004293786_011

FIGURE 203 *The large phallic* sai no kami *that protects the crossroads in Hadano (Kanagawa Prefecture). It dates from 1711.*

FIGURE 204 *A modern example of the sexually innocuous version of the* dōsojin *that involves a couple holding hands. In this wayside relief carving the husband and wife are gazing into each other's eyes.*

FIGURE 205 Dōsojin, *otherwise known as* sai no kami, *the protective god (or gods) of the highways, realised here at the entrance to Kabuto Onsen (Kanagawa Prefecture) by a stele bearing the name and the characteristic phallus.*

under the characters 幸の神 which means gods of good fortune, happiness or harvest yield. In those cases the stress is on fertility rather than protection.[2] In the literature on the subject it sometimes appears that the names refer to individual gods; on other occasions they clearly indicate types of gods. Sometimes the names appear to be interchangeable. In other contexts a strict distinction is made between them, and to add to the confusion the characters *dōso* can also be read as *sai*. Much depends upon the local tradition.[3]

The notion of interchangeability between the two names is first encountered in the earliest written mention of *dōsojin* as the name of a god. It occurs

2 Yato 2004.

3 The pamphlet supplied by the Gochū Shrine 御柱神社 in Jūmonji (Akita Prefecture) describes its prominent phallic *sai no kami* 塞の神 as a guardian deity who defends against evil spirits of the highway but who 'may also be called *dōsojin*' Takahashi, Yūfūko 1979. *Sai no kami (Gochū Jinja) kenritsu no yurai* (Jūmonji). For an interesting list of regional variations see Satō 1995, p. 207.

FIGURE 206 *This* sōtei dōsojin *on the Kunisaki peninsula (Oita Prefecture) follows the traditional design regarding the positioning of a couple who are standing side by side and gazing forwards.*

in the *Wamyō ruiju-shō* of 934, Japan's first dictionary, where the Sino-Japanese term *dōsojin* is stated as being identical to the Japanese god *sae no kami*.[4] Some scholars argue to the contrary that there is a functional difference between the two names that derives from equally ancient local traditions. For example, while accepting some overlap between the two categories Kubota Masayuki, the Director of the Matsumoto City Museum, draws a general distinction between 'the fertility symbols called *dōsojin* and the protective symbols called *sai no kami*', stating that within Nagano Prefecture at least the *dō* in *dōsojin* denotes not merely a physical road or path. It can be a person's 'way' in term of proper conduct and it can also be the 'way' of male and female, thus enabling the *dōsojin* to become procreative gods. Nagano Prefecture's *dōsojin* are therefore concerned with fertility, matchmaking, sexual relations, families and children. They stand beside rice fields, while the protective *sai no kami* guard against disasters or undesirables and tend to be found at crossroads or at

4 Naumann 2000, p. 80. For the text see Satō 1995, p. 19.

FIGURE 207 *Saya no Gozen, a small phallic shrine on a hill on what was once a detached island in Ōmura Bay at Matsubara (Nagasaki Prefecture).*

entrances to villages.[5] There are however considerable variations in other prefectures. Tottori's wayside gods are called *sai no kami-san*, regardless of which function they perform. In northern Kyūshū a dialect version of *sai* appears as *saya* or *sayan*.[6] In Kagoshima they are called *ta no kami* (gods of the rice fields) and always appear as single figures, while in Miyagi the word *dōsojin* is used quite loosely to describe all shrines and images of a sexual nature.

Whatever the actual expression used, when 'blocking deity' is intended the word makes a direct reference to the represented god's primary function of protecting a locality against evil spirits, disaster or pestilence by blocking their entry. A strong phallic appearance (no single ktenic image is ever encountered in this role) is particularly effective in frightening away the unwanted entity and reassuring those whom it guards, because, in Itō's well-chosen words, 'The erect penis both frightens and protects, both warms and consoles; it affirms life and denies death'.[7] A phallus is therefore reassuring to friends and intimidating to foes. The original blocking deities are introduced in the *Kojiki* and *Nihongi*

5 Kubota, Masayuki 2011. 'Matsumoto chihō no dōsojin shinkō ni tsuite kangaeru' (Slides to lecture with this title given at Matsumoto City Museum, 10 October 2011), pp. 1 & 4.

6 Kokonoe also suggests a possible link between the name and the legend of Sayo-hime who watched her lover sail off to war and turned to stone (1981, p. 275).

7 Itō and Richie 1967, p. 51.

as the objects that Izanagi drops when he tries to escape from the underworld. His staff becomes Funado 岐神 or Kunado no Ōkami 久那斗の大神, the god who protects the path between this world and the next and the first blocking deity to be given a name. The peaches further hinder Izanagi's pursuers, and then he drags into place the great boulder that closes off the passageway.[8] None of these items is a phallus or a kteis, although a phallic or ktenic nature may be implied. Other blocking deities appeared subsequent to the compilation of the *Kojiki* and *Nihongi*. Chimata no kami 衢の神 the god of the crossroads may be the same as Kunado, and by the year 735 the male and female 'deities of the eight crossroads' Yachimata Hiko 八衢比古 and Yachimata Hime 八衢比売 are being evoked in prayers during an epidemic, as translated by Aston:

> I humbly declare in the presence of the Sovran gods, whose functions first began in the Plain of High Heaven, when they fulfilled the praises of the Sovran grandchild by guarding the great eight-road-fork like a multitudinous assemblage of rocks.
>
> Naming your honoured names, to wit, Yachimata-hiko, Yachimata-hime, and Kunado, I fulfil your praises. Whenever from the Root-country the Bottom-country there may come savage and unfriendly beings, consort not and parley not with them, but if they go below, keep watch below, if they go above, keep watch above, protecting us against pollution with a night guarding and with a day guarding.
>
> ... Peacefully partaking of these plenteous offerings, which I lay before you in full measure like a cross range of hills, hold guard on the highways like a multitudinous assemblage of rocks, preserving from pollution the Sovran Grandchild firmly and enduringly, and bless his reign to be a prosperous reign.[9]

The trio of Kunado, Yachimata Hiko and Yachimata Hime are enshrined at several sites. At the Matsumori Tenmangu 松森天満宮 in Nagasaki their names cut deeply into a large boulder are regarded as sufficient to intimidate baleful influences.[10] The other *kami* hindering progress in the *Kojiki* is of course Sarutahiko, who defies the gods when they wish to descend and possess the earth. His protective powers are then put to good use along with those of his wife, as was described earlier. Within the culture of ancient Izumo Province (modern Shimane Prefecture) Sarutahiko is said to be the child of Kunado

---

8 Aston 1972, pp. 25 & 30; Philippi 1969, p. 65.

9 Aston 1972, pp. 306–307.

10 From a personal observation made on 3 June 2013.

no Ōkami and Sai Hime Mikoto. In this area of Japan he and his parents are regarded as making up a crucial trio of blocking gods equivalent to the threesome noted above.[11]

Relief Carvings of Human or Mythological Couples

An early reference to the devotion given to the wayside gods is an account in the *Fusō Ryakki* 扶桑略記. This work was compiled by the monk Kōen and dates from the mid-twelfth century. It describes paired male and female figures of wood, each with its sex organs carved below the belly.[12] Nowadays stone is the usual medium of choice rather than wood, and the most common type of permanent stone images concerned with fertility usually go under the name of *sōtei dōsojin* 双体道祖神 (paired *dōsojin*). They consist of a human or mythological couple carved into a stone about one metre in height that often stands unprotected in the open air. Some are still to be found in their original locations beside roads and fields, although many now stand in municipal public areas or inside the grounds of shrines. These images enhance the agricultural fertility of the nearby fields.

A modern visitor to a *sōtei dōsojin* is highly unlikely to encounter anything overtly sexual in appearance. This is particularly true of popular tourist areas where they are enthusiastically embraced as part of a colourful local culture, and whole books have been devoted to the subject to produce page after page of very similar-looking photographs of these archetypal and usually innocuous 'happy couples'.[13] Czaja includes a table that lists 2,069 'deities showing affection to each other' and 1,149 'deities standing side by side'.[14] A pair in Matsumoto (Nagano Prefecture) date from 1505 and are probably the oldest surviving examples in Japan.[15] Until recently *dōsojin* was the attribution given to a paired male and female carving excavated in 1902 in Asuka (Nara Prefecture) and dated to the seventh century.[16] The dwarf-like couple carved in the round are embracing, but there is no evidence that the image was used to enhance the fertility of the fields. Indeed, current opinion now favours its identification as a mildly erotic garden ornament, because it was designed so

11 Yato 2004, p. 25.
12 Ashida 1963, p. 11.
13 The best photographic collections are to be found in Ashida 1963.
14 Czaja 1974, p. 35.
15 Kubota 2011, p. 2.
16 Czaja 1974, p. 45; Kokonoe 1981, p. 111.

that water could rise up inside it and be discharged from the female's mouth and from a cup held by the male.[17]

The greatest concentration of *sōtei dōsojin* is to be found within the modern administrative area known as Azumino City that is located to the north of Matsumoto, with most interest being focussed on the town of Hotaka. When Azumino was created by the amalgamation of existing local authorities in 2005 its *dōsojin* were seen as a visible means of bringing the new community together. Old ones were restored and new ones created, and pictures of *dōsojin* were adopted as logos and advertising motifs.[18] In almost all cases the figures are completely devoid of sexual content, a feature that has helped to make them into a safe tourist attraction, and the interested visitor may spend many a happy hour touring the surroundings armed with maps and guides in search of these pleasant little artefacts.[19] One booklet sets out nine walking courses where prominent or interesting *dōsojin* are drawn to the visitor's attention.[20] There is also a map that gives an identifying number to 131 different examples within the area. The latter publication has a more devotional purpose than the booklet and includes six different walking courses arranged in the manner of short pilgrimages related to the votive intentions of marriage, successful harvest, child prosperity, marital harmony, protection from pestilence and the guardianship of highways. It identifies all the *dōsojin* along the routes by their dates of creation, the oldest being 1759 and the newest 1897, and gives brief descriptions of them and photographs of ninety-one.[21]

Even though these walking courses are themed according to certain prayer intentions the *dōsojin* represented along the routes are all very similar in design, as a glance at the photographs on the map will reveal. None suggests any of the stated votive intentions in particular, because all depict an almost identical pairing of a man and a woman dressed in ancient court costume including headgear. They are standing side by side with the male on the couple's left. They all gaze forward and touch each other in some way. This can be done by holding hands while in some there is the implication of an embrace made by the other hand slipped behind their backs. In many examples this suggested embrace provides the only physical contact between them because the female

---

17 http://www.asukanet.gr.jp/asukahome/ASUKA2/ASUKAISI/sekizinzou.html (Accessed 15 October 2014).

18 Kubota, Masayuki 2006. 'Dōsojin to machi okoshi: Nagano-ken chūshin chihō no jirei o chūshin ni' *Zasshi 'Shinshū'* 58, 1 (Nagano), pp. 25–36.

19 From a personal observation made on 5 August 2008.

20 Azumino Tourist Association (no date) *Dōsojin ga michi-annai* (Azumino).

21 Hotaka Town Tourist Association (no date) *Dōsojin no meguri* (Azumino).

FIGURE 208 *A* sai no kami-san *in Tottori Prefecture showing the arrangement of two figures typical of the area. Unlike the practice in Nagano,* sai no kami-san *are usually named. This example is in the village of Taikyuji.*

is holding a flask of *sake* made from a gourd in her right hand and the male has a cup in his left. In some the wife is kneeling submissively; in others they are posed as if for a wedding photograph. Some have their hands folded in prayer and they may be standing under a *torii* or a temple entrance gate. The Nagano couples are always anonymous, but in Tottori Prefecture the *sai no kami-san* are usually identified by names carved down each side. These are usually Sarutahiko and Ame no Uzume but on some examples Izanagi and Izanami are indicated. The male usually carries a spear. The couple are rarely touching and usually gaze forwards.[22]

The respectable appearance of most existing *dōsojin* disguises their ancient sexual origins, but enough older versions have survived to show how they once looked when they were doing far more than just holding hands. On these *dōsojin* the couples are making a profound symbolic statement about the link between human sexual harmony and agricultural fertility by being carved in the act of kissing, embracing or even engaging in coitus.[23] A couple

22 It is possible to get a rapid impression of the range of Tottori's *sai no kami-san* from DVDs playing in the folklore section of Tottori Prefectural Museum.

23 For examples see Itō 1965, pp. 16–17.

FIGURE 209
This dōsojin *dating from 1757 shows a couple kissing. It is located beside a rice field in Nakamuroda (Gunma Prefecture).*

FIGURE 210
On the Kamisawa dōsojin *which dates from 1795 the male is using both hands to tease open his partner's kimono. It is located to the north of Matsumoto.*

FIGURE 211 *In the village of Ishizumi stands this* dōsojin *dated 1766 that shows a couple embracing sexually in a standing position. The female appears to be guiding the man's penis into her with her hand.*

kissing tenderly in a gentle embrace are shown on a *dōsojin* dating from 1757 at Nakamuroda (Gunma Prefecture).[24] A more erotic embrace appears on a *dōsojin* of 1795 beside a road at Kamisawa to the north of Matsumoto. The sexual gesture is provided by the man who is using both hands to tease open his partner's kimono.[25] At a crossroads in the village of Ishizumi (Yamanashi Prefecture) stands a *dōsojin* that shows a couple embracing sexually in a

24 From a personal observation made on 11 March 2014.

25 Czaja 1974, Figs. 9 & 46 and p. 130 and from a personal observation made on 15 November 2012.

FIGURE 212 *The 'night and day* dōsojin*' at Miyahara shows one couple in a chaste pose and this pair having intercourse.*

standing position. The female appears to be guiding the man's penis into her with her hand. This *dōsojin* dates from 1766 and proved very difficult to locate, being apparently unknown even to some local inhabitants.[26]

Two *dōsojin* depicting sexual intercourse in an unmistakeable way have been widely illustrated in books. One is located at the village of Miyahara to the east of Matsumoto. Known popularly as the 'night and day *dōsojin*' it is protected by a metal grill and shows two couples. The more prominent pair at the top are standing side by side in a chaste embrace. Below them in a separate cartouche a naked couple are having intercourse with the male on top of the

26 From a personal observation made on 14 November 2012 and Itō 1965, p. 24.

FIGURE 213 *The so-called 'dancing* dōsojin' *at Natsugari shows side-by-side sexual intercourse as viewed from above.*

female.[27] The other is in Natsugari (Yamanashi Prefecture) and shows side-by-side sexual intercourse as viewed from above on a wayside carving euphemistically known as the 'dancing *dōsojin*'.[28] A less well known example is at Ochiai (Gunma Prefecture). The couple are clothed but the woman's left leg shows the passion of the embrace.[29]

27 Kokonoe 1976, p. 45; Czaja 1974, Plate 11 and from a personal observation made on 15 November 2012.

28 Kokonoe 1976, p. 48; Czaja 1974, Plate 4.

29 From a personal observation made on 11 March 2014. Excellent photographs are in Itō 1965, pp. 32–33.

FIGURE 214 *A* dōsojin *at Ochiai shows sexual intercourse by a fully clothed couple viewed from the side.*

These frank carvings may represent the replacement of supposed acts of ritual human copulation in rice fields by unmistakeable illustrations of them, but subtle signs of sexual behaviour can be included even on the apparently innocuous examples. This is a topic discussed very well by Czaja, who provides a wealth of fascinating detail about how the things held in the hands and the design of the clothes may indicate erotic elements. Hands may be enlarged as they approach the other's body. The sleeves of the woman's overlapping garments may imply the shape of the kteis. The gourd *sake* flask in the woman's hand may easily be taken for the penis and scrotum with the identification being heightened by its closeness to the man's body, while the cup held by the

FIGURE 215 *The couple on this* dōsojin *from 1867 stand within a circular depression on the front of the stone and are picked out in applied colour. There may be a ktenic shape in the mouth of the cup held by the man, and the proximity of the serving gourd to the man's legs suggests very strongly that it is meant to be his genitalia.*

man to receive the drink may have a ktenic shape.[30] Only one of the Azumino City *dōsojin* appears to display such sexual connotations. It dates from 1867 and is within walking distance of Azumi Oiwake station as No. 117 on the Hotaka map. The couple stand within a circular depression on the front of the stone and are picked out in applied colour. The woman has a pink kimono and the man a brown robe. Kokonoe identifies a ktenic shape in the mouth of the cup held by the man, and the proximity of the serving gourd to the man's legs suggests very strongly that it is meant to be his genitalia.[31]

Elements like these led Satō Tetsurō to compare *sōtei dōsojin* to the passionate embraces of the Dual-body Kangiten images,[32] and indeed the *dōsojin* showing sexual intercourse could be taken as expressing a similar delight in sexual pleasure, but that is highly unlikely to be their primary aim.

30 Czaja 1974, p. 38.
31 From a personal observation made on 14 November 2012.
32 Satō 1995, pp. 95–99.

Broadly speaking the venerated images represent human sexual union, and their simulated copulation, however abstractly it may be portrayed, is somehow transferred to the fertility of the fields. When the figures are named as either Izanagi and Izanami or Sarutahiko and Ame no Uzume two great mythological acts of marital union are brought to bear on the problems of fertility.

Relief Carvings of Phalluses

The second type of relief carving is that of a phallus rather than a human couple. This motif is nowadays quite rare and will tend to be found only in remote locations, although most of the carvings are now grouped within shrines or public areas. Some may have been moved there during periods of reaction against their sexual explicitness, but the majority have acquired their new locations more recently because of modern road building or changes in the shape and boundaries of rice fields due to mechanised farming. Community Centres are popular alternative choices for their new settings, but even though the images may now be protected from damage they have been stripped of their original significance. A phallus carved into a stone on a narrow path between rice fields conveys a blunt message of protection. Much is lost when it is grouped with three others beside a council car park. Among the few in its original position is one that stands beside a road in a rural area of Annaka City (Gunma Prefecture). In front of a round boulder bearing the characters *dōsojin* and a date of 1792 a second stone bears a lightly incised phallus.[33]

Only one phallic relief carving is to be found among the *dōsojin* of Matsumoto and it is not immediately noticeable. It is at Suwamura just to the north of Matsumoto Castle and consists of a large boulder with the characters *dō-so-jin* carved on the front, while on its rear surface is the date of installation (1859) and a deeply incised phallus. Unlike all the other phalluses depicted throughout Japan this one is not shown in a state of erection but as a flaccid organ, although this may simply be explained by the shape and surface layout of the stone, because the tip is projecting towards a naturally occurring ktenic hole in the lower half of the rock.[34]

In Miyagi Prefecture there is an almost total absence of human couple *dōsojin*. Instead there is a strong tradition of phalluses carved in relief, although unfortunately very few are now to be seen in their original positions. One is at

33 From a personal observation made on 11 March 2014. See also Kokonoe 1976, p. 43.

34 From a personal observation made on 15 November 2012. See also Ashida 1963, pp. 30–31 and Itō 1965, p. 20.

FIGURE 216
The Annaka dōsojin *that bears a lightly carved phallus beneath the characters for* dōsojin. *It dates from 1792 and is in Annaka City (Gunma Prefecture).*

FIGURE 217
As a wayside god of protection and procreation the Suwamura dōsojin *of 1859 is probably unique in its depiction of the phallus as a flaccid organ.*

FIGURE 218
This small phallus carved in relief is at the Hachiman Shrine in Shikano (Sendai City) and is a classic example of an incised phallus used at a field boundary.

FIGURE 219 *A number of old phallic relief carvings have been assembled and preserved at a sub-shrine of the Hitsuzaki Shrine in Ishinomaki (Miyagi Prefecture).*

FIGURE 220 *Another carving preserved at the Hitzuzaki Shrine dates from 1893 and has two carved phalluses standing side by side.*

the Shikano Hachiman Shrine 鹿野八幡神社 in Sendai City where it still stands near a field boundary.[35] Ishinomaki City has several examples including a large group transferred from elsewhere to the protection of the Hitsuzaki Shrine 零羊崎神社 on Makiyama. The phallic stones are arranged on either side of a small shrine at the side of a path leading down the dark forested mountain to the rear of the main shrine. All are very realistic in their depictions of the male sexual organ and two have testicles. One from 1863 has a large carved phallus and another from 1893 has two carved phalluses standing side by side.[36] A nearby group are very likely to be in their original positions because they stand at a crossroads near rice fields. On the corner is a simple monument bearing the word *dōsojin* and the date of 1795. The three phallic reliefs are obscured by grass around their bases and lichen on their details, but can be identified as single phalluses.[37] At Tajiri (Ōzaki City) a very vivid relief carving of a single phallus stood beside a field boundary until 2010. It was then moved

35 From a personal observation made on 17 June 2013.

36 From a personal observation made on 19 June 2013.

37 From a personal observation made on 18 June 2013.

FIGURE 221 *Even though it has been newly relocated next to a Community Centre this small phallic carving still stands by a rice field in the village of Sakura (Miyagi Prefecture).*

along with other stones to the Community Centre in nearby Sakura village, where it has been placed on the edge of a different rice field to continue its protective function.[38]

One small phallic carving that has survived serious urban encroachment within a city is the tiny phallic relief opposite the entrance to the Tochigi Prefectural Hospital in Utsunomiya. It is easily missed; I walked up and down the road three times before a helpful passer-by drew my attention to the fact that I was almost standing on top of it. The image consists of a bas-relief of a phallus only 27 cm in height carved deeply into the upright of a stone *hokora* that is itself only 59 cm tall. Its probable role was once to guard the highway. Now a small surrounding wall of concrete blocks on three sides protects the protector.[39]

Another way in which a sexual object can be represented is by changing components of the ideographs for *dōsojin* into phallic or ktenic symbols. On three different stones the right-hand section of the second character 祖 is carved so that the upper third is made circular, thus giving it a phallic appearance.[40]

38 From a personal observation made on 18 June 2013.

39 From a personal observation made on 28 April 2012.

40 Ashida 1963, p. 31 and Plates 93–94.

FIGURE 222 *The Nakatomatsuri-chō* dōsojin *is a tiny phallic relief carving that stands at a roadside opposite the entrance to the Tochigi Prefectural Hospital and is one of very few to have survived urban encroachment without being relocated.*

On the stone outside the Yasaka Shrine in Aoyama (Kanagawa Prefecture) the characters have recently been picked out using red paint in case anyone should miss the allusion.[41] Kokonoe includes a photograph of a stone from 1788 that uses the character *ku* (*chimata*) 衢 (crossroads) in place of the *dō* of *dōsojin*. *So* is carved as a phallus as in the example above, while *ku* is twisted into a ktenic shape.[42]

41 From a personal observation made on 12 March 2014.

42 Kokonoe 1981, p. 90.

FIGURE 223 *On this* dōsojin *in Aoyama (Kanagawa Prefecture) half of the second ideograph has been given a phallic appearance.*

Three-Dimensional Phalluses

Innocent and respectable versions of the 'happy couple' *sōtei dōsojin* now appear on numerous roadsigns, publicity fliers and websites around the Matsumoto area as symbols of their communities, but it is highly unlikely that any would have become a logo for urban regeneration if they had displayed the considerable sexual appearance enjoyed by the variety that assume the shape of three-dimensional phalluses.[43] A small rural example may be found at a peaceful spot in Aomori Prefecture. Here there is a Tenjin shrine by a minor

43 Kubota 2006, pp. 25–36.

FIGURE 224 *An excellent example of a protecting phallus still guarding a crossroads is found to the north of Tajiri (Miyagi Prefecture).*

FIGURE 225 *In a rural area of Aomori Prefecture a small* sai no kami *with a few little phalluses stands guard over a quiet crossroads.*

FIGURE 226 *This small wayside phallic shrine stands behind the Noguchi Yakushi-dō beside the old road to Nikkō and may well have been one of those seen by W. G. Aston.*

crossroads and beside its *torii* stands a simple *sai no kami* of unadorned natural rock that has three small stone phalluses leaning against it to help protect the ancient and undeveloped wayside.[44] Another fine collection of larger protective phalluses sits within a small shrine to the rear of the Noguchi Yakushi-dō about 2 km from Nikkō on the quiet avenue of cedars that forms the old Nikkō road.[45]

Some of the three-dimensional phalluses are quite difficult to find because the feature they are supposed to be guarding has been relocated as a result of modern town planning. A good example is provided by the Gochū Shrine 御柱神社 in Jūmonji. This is the place that does not appear on the list of religious establishments compiled by the local town office, suggesting that it may now be seen as something of an embarrassment. As a protective god its *sai no kami* was set up at a commanding position beside a crossroads, but modern road developments have altered the arrangements of the traditional intersection so that its guardian now lies some distance away. The shrine has become

44 Masuta 2012, p. 43 and from a personal observation made on 7 November 2012.

45 From a personal observation made on 19 October 2012.

FIGURE 227 *The Gochū Shrine in Jūmonji (Akita Prefecture) houses a protective* sai no kami *but is now hidden from the crossroads it once protected.*

hemmed in behind a new housing development and a garage and is almost hidden from view, being accessible only on foot along a narrow path or across someone's back yard. Inside the small building stands a fine 1.5 metre tall stone phallus with a pile of printed leaflets giving a history of the shrine.[46]

At the other extreme of visibility stands the prominent *sai no kami* at the entrance to the Nemunodake roadside services in Kisakata (Akita Prefecture) mentioned in the preface to this book. A noticeboard explains that it and its smaller companion inside a conventional shrine are the modern version of an ancient foundation put there to protect travellers against evil spirits and

46 Takahashi 1979; Satō 1995, p. 196 and from a personal observation made on 26 April 2012.

FIGURE 228 *The wayside guardian phallus at the Nemunodake roadside service centre in Kisakata (Akita Prefecture).*

pestilence, but that it will also answer prayers for conception, marital harmony and a good match. Three similar examples in Kanagawa Prefecture also have an enduring visible presence. The first is the *sekibō* mentioned earlier that stands within a metal cage. Not far away on a small hillock called Kokagezan is a much larger example, also caged.[47] The finest of the three is however the one at Hadano illustrated earlier.[48]

Finally, mention must be made of an unusual Korean import of protective deities at Koma (Saitama Prefecture). Koma takes its name from the ancient Korean kingdom of Goguryeo, because it was this place that provided sanctuary for a distinguished refugee afterwards known as Kokishi Jakko. The Koma Shrine 高麗神社 was founded to enshrine him on his death and for centuries it has acted as a link between Japanese and Korean culture. Among the visible items that may be encountered are *jangseung* (protective male and female figures). They stand like gateposts and resemble totem poles, with their gender indicated only by their headgear. Just like Azumino's *dōsojin* Koma's *jangseung* have been enlisted as symbols of the local community, and in addition to being

47 From a personal observation made on 12 March 2014 and Kokonoe 1976, p. 36.

48 From a personal observation made on 13 March 2014 and Kokonoe 1976, p. 37.

FIGURE 229 *The guardian phallus on the hill of Kokagezan in Sagamihara City (Kanagawa Prefecture).*

displayed on *ema* in the Koma Shrine they support the noticeboard outside Koma Station and are found around the area as direction markers. The large stone pair in front of the Koma Shrine with their huge teeth and goggle eyes are quite comical in appearance and must surely rank as Japan's least terrifying guardian figures.[49]

---

49 Kokonoe 1981, p. 102 and the booklet produced by the Koma Shrine Office entitled Koma-jinja and the Home of the Koma People. Details of the artefacts are from a personal observation made on 4 June 2013.

FIGURE 230 *Japan's most comical guardian figures are the Korean-style protective deities at Koma (Saitama Prefecture).*

Human Figures Combined with Phalluses

In Kagoshima Prefecture the custom has long been to create *ta no kami* 田の神 (gods of the rice fields) as single human figures and to depict them in the round with hats and robes that suggest a phallus when they are viewed from the rear.[50] Some examples are more noticeably phallic than others, such as a very old example dating from 1726 at Iriki. In the figure's hands are a rice scoop and a pestle, and even though either item might be taken as a phallic symbol it is his hat, shaped as a hood-like *shiki* (rice steamer) on top of the robe, that brings out the phallic shape. All these points of detail are noted on the accompanying sign, yet without any reference being made to the overall impression of phallicism that they provide.

50 Many of them may be found complete with photographs and map references on the excellent and extensive website http://5.travel-way.net/~niemon/kagosima/tanokami/tanokami.html. For a more localised study of the former Ōsumi Province see Noda Chihiro 1979. *Ōsumi michi no ta no kami* (Tokyo).

FIGURE 231 *A typical Kagoshima* ta no kami *still guarding the rice fields as he has done for centuries.*

FIGURE 232 *The* ta no kami *in Iriki (Kagoshima City) dating from 1726 has a pronounced phallic appearance from behind owing to the design of his robes and his hat.*

When the *ta no kami* is broad shouldered or his hat is very wide the phallic shape is much less apparent. In these cases additional forms of sexual expression may be added. The *ta no kami* at Nozato and Shugi-En have large hats but the former is portrayed in a raised kneeling position and his knees make an apparent scrotum to add to his overall phallic ambience. The Shugi-En *ta no*

FIGURE 233 *The Magai* ta no kami *showing the typical rice spoon and hat based on a rice-steamer. This figure has the appearance of a distorted phallus when viewed from behind.*

FIGURE 234 *The Nozato* ta no kami *has two thighs that look like a scrotum.*

FIGURE 235 *The Shugi-En* ta no kami *is of less pronounced phallic appearance overall. Instead his right knee is extended as a phallic exaggeration.*

kami is resting on his heels and his right knee protrudes upwards.[51] Other *ta no kami* can be found beyond Kagoshima; there is a group of four next to Ikebukuro Station in Tokyo.[52]

In other prefectures examples may be found where a *dōsojin*-like couple have been carved not into a plain boulder but into a large free-standing three-dimensional stone phallus that completely envelops them. Although sometimes presented as an ancient tradition this is in fact a modern development which is quite revealing about present-day attitudes towards sexual display.

---

51 From a personal observation made on 1 June 2013.

52 From a personal observation made on 19 April 2012.

FIGURE 236 *The Ikebukuro (Tokyo)* ta no kami *as seen from behind, showing their distinctive phallic shapes.*

The popular explanation for the style is that it is a disguised phallic symbol, and an accompanying text may well relate how subterfuge became necessary when phallicism was suppressed under the Tokugawa and Meiji regimes, but most are too modern for that ever to have been necessary. Instead they provide a further example of the care that has to be exercised when drawing conclusions about earlier practices from observations of modern phenomena.

It is nevertheless true that free-standing sexual carvings suffered as much as their companions inside shrines during periodic outbursts against sexual display. In the Tokugawa Period Neo-Confucians such as the lord of Hirado, Matsuura Seizan (1760–1841) were enraged by the frank sexual motifs employed as wayside gods and even claimed to have seen people reject what they stood for. Seizan wrote, 'Two phallic emblems of stone on the roadside, each representing a male or a female, stand face to face while people when passing

FIGURE 237 *A couple carved into the face of a vaguely phallic stone at the Kagami Shrine next to the Shin-Yakushiji in Nara.*

by scornfully laugh at them'.[53] In pursuit of its twin goals of modesty and modernity the Meiji regime then tried to abolish all sexually explicit *dōsojin*. Some were destroyed or taken away, an unpopular move that led to public protests and in Ōtsu, reported one newspaper, 'many farmers and crowds of women and children followed ... with lamentations and violent protestations, imploring [the police] not to deal with the stones too roughly, nor to hurt them'.[54] Others were replaced by the innocent images seen today of couples holding hands.

The alternative to change could be to attempt a disguise, and it would not have taken a stone carver much trouble to transform a standing phallus into a statue of Jizō with an enveloping hood. From the front it had become the acceptable *bodhissatva*; from the rear the figure still retained its ancient meaning. One genuine, if somewhat ambiguous, example goes regularly unno-

53 Katō 1924, p. 20.

54 Itō and Richie 1967, pp. 53–54.

FIGURE 238 *The phallus in Ueno Park (Tokyo) as seen from the rear, where its sexual shape persists.*

ticed by thousands of visitors who are probably unaware of its existence or significance even though it lies in the middle of Ueno Park in Tokyo. The precise location is next to the island of Bentenjima in Shinobazu Pond, which can be reached by walking along a causeway. To one side of the main island lies another tiny island crossed by a bridge and protected by a locked metal gate. On this island is a shrine to Kangiten and a carved stone that has the appearance of a phallus when viewed from the gate side. When viewed from the other side the shape of a human figure is revealed, although it is amusing to note that the object's phallic side is now the only practical view obtainable because the tiny island is securely fenced off. Unless one is willing to risk life and limb and climb round the outside of the fence the sanitised image is only visible from a considerable distance using a path within the grounds of Ueno Park Zoo. The image is popularly known as Hige Jizō 髭地蔵 (Bearded Jizō) but a close inspection of the carved figure reveals that it is nothing like Jizō in appearance, an observation that prompted an article by Shizume Tōsen in 1922. He identified the figure as En no Gyōja 役行者 the traditional founder of Shugendō, whose image was added at the time of the Meiji Restoration to what was once a

FIGURE 239 *The old phallus in Ueno Park, known as the 'Bearded Jizō', as seen from the front.*

very old and plain phallus.[55] Shizume compares it to other examples of phallic statuary of a similar nature depicting En no Gyōja, and both Nishioka and Satō agree with his conclusions, although Yato believes the depiction to be that of Kunado, the blocking deity created from Izanagi's discarded staff.[56]

55 Shizume, Tōsen 1922. 'Seitekijin toshite no En no Gyōja' *Kyōdo Shumi* 3, p. 16.
56 Nishioka 1961, p. 236; Satō 1995, p. 64; Yato 2004, pp. 79–80.

FIGURE 240 *A modern carving of a phallus enveloping a couple at the In'yōseki Shrine in Miyazaki. There is no attempt to disguise the phallus, quite the reverse.*

This figure would therefore appear to be the result of a genuine attempt to add respectability to an old phallic symbol, but the more modern enveloping phallic *dōsojin* have been created to enhance their sexual nature, not to disguise it. One may be seen at the In'yōseki Shrine in Miyazaki Prefecture, where a human couple are found holding hands on the front of a large modern phallus. This place, of course, enshrines one of Japan's largest natural sexual stone groupings, so it is not surprising to find the addition to it of items that enhance its sexual ambience.[57] Another modern example dating only from 1961 is the

57 From a personal observation made on 4 August 2009.

FIGURE 241 *The enveloping phallic* dōsojin *at Kowada (Kanagawa Prefecture) that dates from 1961.*

dōsojin at Kowada (Kanagawa Prefecture). It consists of an embracing human couple holding hands within an all-enveloping phallus. The image replaced a previous one damaged by a fire.[58] In Chino (Nagano Prefecture) a large, squat phallus into which a kneeling couple are carved was set up in 1999 next to the ktenic stone known as Hime Seki-sama. As in so many other examples,

58 Kokonoe 1976, p. 38.

FIGURE 242 *A modern phallus at Chino with a couple carved into it. This style is supposedly a disguise but most are too modern for that ever to have been necessary.*

the highway they once guarded has now moved some distance away and the pair now stand sentinel in the far corner of the car park of a 100 Yen Store.[59] These new styles of wayside gods represent the introduction to the genre of less-inhibited modern views of sexual display. The figures may still reflect ancient beliefs in protection and procreation, but their design involves no attempt at disguise, quite the reverse.

Temporary Wayside Gods of Wood and Straw

Throughout Japan a wide range of symbolic creations are made using the perishable elements of wood and straw as part of annual rituals associated with the seasons. A simple example is described by Nishioka in his book of 1961. Following the rice-planting in May at the Mifune Shrine 御船神社 in Ibaraki Prefecture the farmers would weave from straw what was known as a *nawabanagashi* ナハバナガシ. Two bamboo poles were erected about four

59 From a personal observation made on 14 November 2012.

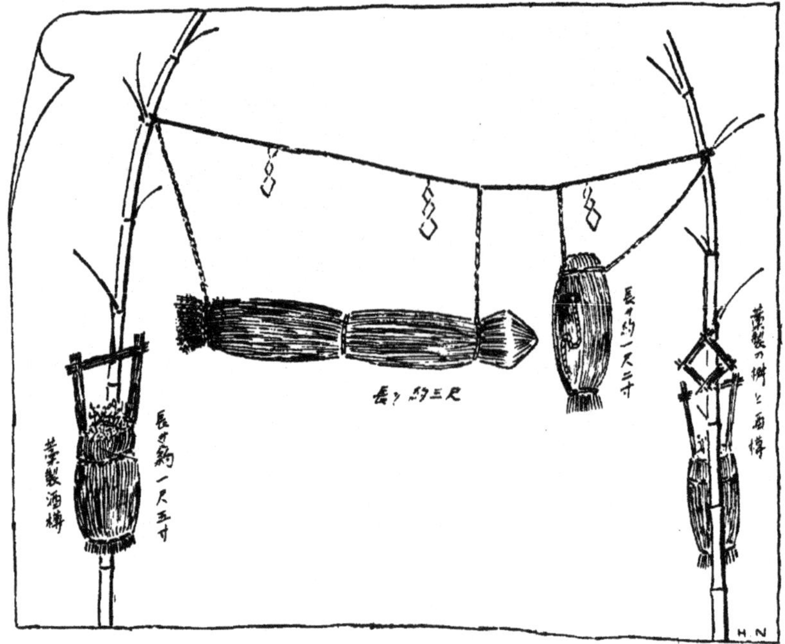

FIGURE 243 *The* nawabanagashi *represents phallic and ktenic objects and are brought into contact with each other by the action of the wind, thus assuring an abundant rice crop. (Drawing supplied by courtesy of the Nishioka Research Archive).*

metres apart and on each was hung a straw-plaited *sake* barrel in which were placed branches of cedar or *sakaki*. On the right-hand one was hung a straw-plaited measure and between the two poles a straw rope was stretched. From the rope a straw phallus and a kteis were suspended. In the phallus were placed uprooted rice plants which represented pubic hair. The two male and female objects would be brought into contact with each other by the action of the wind, thus assuring an abundant rice crop.[60] A similar idea lies behind the construction of an object called a *kandekko* カンデッコ which forms the centrepiece of the festival of the same name still held every January at the Sai no kami Shrine that guards the road through the village of Ugo-Nakazato in Akita Prefecture. A *kandekko* is a small plough made from magnolia wood that is attached by a short length of cord to a phallus carved from walnut. The combination is tossed up into the branches of an ancient tree along with prayers for a good harvest, successful marriage and household prosperity. The *kandekko*

60 Nishioka 1961, pp. 196–197.

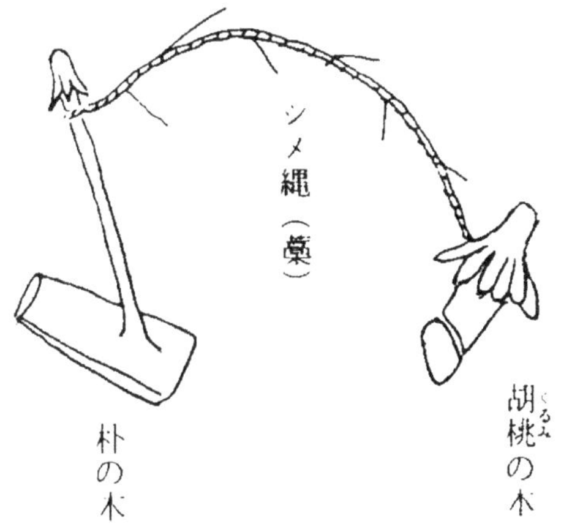

FIGURE 244
A kandekko *is a small plough made from magnolia wood that is attached by a short length of cord to a phallus carved from walnut. (Drawing supplied by courtesy of the Nishioka Research Archive).*

is later removed and hung in the branches of fruit trees to encourage their fertility.[61]

In the Mochizuki area of Higashi-Matsuyama City (Saitama Prefecture) there is the ritual of making *fusegi* (written usually as フセギ and more rarely as 防ぎ). A *fusegi* is a phallus made from straw with clearly defined testicles and a stream of straw issuing from it to symbolise the fertilising of the fields that it will bring about. They are made as part of a local celebration every July and are hung from trees or poles at various locations throughout the area.[62] More elaborate creations made from straw are found in Tottori Prefecture. All are temporary images, but an excellent permanent display is on show at Tottori Prefectural Museum in Tottori City, together with DVDs showing the rituals associated with their making and the benefits they provide. Pride of place goes to the very large straw phalluses set in a stance of coition with straw ktenes. Straw horses well-endowed with male genitalia are also included. The normal practice is for the objects to decay naturally except in the case of the horses which are ritually burned.[63]

The smallest of all roadside images employing straw are the ones where a permanent stone is given a hat and apron of straw in a manner akin to the

61 Satō, 1995, p. 150.

62 From a personal observation made on 4 July 2013. A detailed article about *fusegi* may be accessed at http://www.city.higashimatsuyama.lg.jp/ikkrwebBrowse/material/files/group/37/23_8.pdf.

63 From a personal observation made on 9 June 2013.

FIGURE 245
A fusegi *is a phallus made from straw with clearly defined testicles and a stream of straw issuing from it to symbolise the fertilising of the fields. They are hung from trees or poles in the Mochizuki area of Saitama Prefecture.*

addition of bibs and hats to statues of Jizō.[64] At the other end of the scale the largest straw creations of all make up some of Japan's most striking religious images. These are enormous figures standing up to four metres high with fierce carved wooden faces, weaponry and genitalia, and one area that still maintains the tradition of making them lies in Niigata Prefecture along the banks of the Aganogawa. Here the local villagers recreate on an annual basis their own protective Shōki Daimyōjin 鍾馗大明神 or Shōki-sama, named after Shōki (Zhong Kui) the Tang dynasty queller of demons. Shōki, who protects against plague, is encountered in Japanese art as a black-clad, bearded fellow who is often frustrated by the demon that is trying to elude him. In Niigata this protective role has been enlisted as a spectacular version of a *michi no kami* with distinctive sexual characteristics.[65] Two Shōki-sama of approximately human proportions stand in separate shrines along the mountain road that follows the contours of the river between the railway stations of Kanose and Hideya. Their bodies are cylindrical and their tiny arms project upwards on either side

64 From a personal observation made on 21 April 2012.

65 Kokonoe 1976, p. 61.

FIGURE 246
One of the two Shōki-sama that stand along the mountain road beside the Aganogawa in Niigata Prefecture. This one has female sexual characteristics.

FIGURE 247 *Like a fallen warrior, the discarded Shōki-sama from the shrine containing the image shown above lies decaying in the forest behind the shrine. This one has male characteristics including a large phallus and protected the village in 2012.*

FIGURE 248 *The most elaborate Shōki-sama in Niigata is this huge figure at the Taga Shrine. He is recreated every year.*

of scowling faces painted on to white cloths. The sexual element is provided by either a straw phallus or kteis, and it is the tradition to alternate the genders of the two figures on an annual basis, as is revealed by the discarded figure from the previous year that is left to decay in the woods behind the shrine.[66]

The larger varieties are more elaborate in their style of weaving and are almost twice the size of a human being. The most magnificent Shōki Daimyōjin of all is the one who occupies the Taga Shrine 多賀神社 in the village of Ōmaki. This Shōki-sama is as wide as he is tall and a photograph in Kokonoe's book of 1976 shows how his overall appearance has not changed much over the years.[67] The 2013 and 2014 versions were practically identical. Each wore a conical hat and was well-armed against evil with two spears, a bow and arrows and two swords. His male genitalia were large and very prominent. The shrine lies on the edge of a steep slope, where traces of straw from the previous figure could be discerned on both visits.[68]

In 2014 I observed the making of a new Shōki-sama in the village of Kumawatari. In this case the very large figure stands under a roofed enclosure

66 From personal observations made on 2 July 2013 and 8 March 2014.

67 Kokonoe 1976, p. 61.

68 From personal observations made on 2 July 2013 and 8 March 2014.

FIGURE 249 *The new Shōki-sama for 2014 is carried to the Shōki Shrine in Kumawatari by the team who have spent all morning weaving him from straw.*

behind his shrine rather than inside it. Here there is a sturdy old tree that provides support for the protective deity who has a spear in his left hand, a dagger in his right and a large bulbous sexual organ. The process of replacing him represents a division of labour between the priests of the Shōki Shrine and the village community. On the previous evening the villagers visited the shrine to pay their respects and on the morning they gathered at the Community Centre for the long and complex business of weaving and assembling the figure. The different parts of his body were woven separately and where necessary, such as with his arms and feet, they were formed around a central supportive wooden core made from a stout branch. After about four hours the figure had reached the stage when he could be transferred to the shrine on the shoulders of eight men, a walk of about 500 metres. He was then placed carefully against the wall of the shrine while the tricky operation began of removing his predecessor, who was discarded reverently in the snow-covered woods behind the shrine on top of the much decayed remains of the 2012 Shōki-sama. The new figure was then lifted into place and tied securely and safely to his supporting

FIGURE 250
In this picture the author is standing next to Kumawatari's new 2014 Shōki-sama to show the scale of the figure who will protect the village for the coming year.

frame and to the tree. The finishing touches were provided by giving him his feet, gaiters, hat and weapons. Their strenuous tasks completed, the villagers withdrew for well-earned refreshment and were joined later by the priests after they had completed the short ritual process of converting a giant of straw into a protective deity.[69]

Although the name Shōki-sama is also used in Akita Prefecture, the more common name for guardian straw figures there is Kashima-sama 鹿島様. A rather comical pair called Shōki-sama protect the village of Kogake near Futatsui against evil spirits and plague. Kogake is accessed via a narrow bridge and the male stands quite near to it. The female guards the opposite end of the village, although in 2012 this approach was temporarily undefended as she was undergoing a makeover in the Community Centre. Each is of a simple design with a bright red carved face, staring eyes, clenched teeth and the incongruous addition of a cigarette held in a cigarette holder. Both have bodies that are heavy and round and wear swords at their belts, and the only thing that distinguishes the female from the male is the wearing of a modest straw apron, although Kokonoe's sketch of a previous version of the female Shōki Daimyōjin

69 From a personal observation made on 8 March 2014. For my video of part of the ceremony see https://www.youtube.com/watch?v=7vo6D49ofU8.

FIGURE 251 *One of two protective figures at opposite ends of the village of Kogake in Akita Prefecture.*

shows her with breasts.[70] Another male and female pair of straw figures guard Yamada village in Odate City, but these two stand side-by-side at the central crossroads within a protective enclosure. They are known locally as Jinju-sama but each bears a personal nameplate that is a variation on the names of the blocking deities Sai no kami and Funado. The male has a red face and a black beard, with a straw headband. He wears a sword and has a large straw phallus. The cute-faced female has equally recognisable genitalia but in both cases the actual organs are covered by modesty aprons of paper on which appear an image of a radish for the male and a turnip for the female.[71]

Three other sites in Akita Prefecture display large and splendid single-figure protective Kashima-sama that resemble Niigata's giants in terms of their size. Two very similar examples appear near Yuzawa as huge straw figures with intricately woven straw heads and faces. At Mitsumura the inclusion of breasts and the absence of a phallus show that she is female. She has a sword at her side and wears a bright red scarf. A detailed noticeboard explains that she is

70 Satō 1995, p. 164; Kokonoe 1981, p. 48 and from a personal observation made on 24 April 2012.

71 From a personal observation made on 24 April 2012.

FIGURE 252 *The protective couple who guard the crossroads at Yamada (Akita Prefecture).*

the product of an ancient local tradition of making *dōsojin* from straw to protect against plague and disaster that dates back to a time when one of these figures was credited with warding off a plague of typhus. The almost identical male a few miles away has a small phallus and a sword.[72] The two most impressive examples stand at the rear of the Iwasaki Hachiman Shrine in Yuzawa City. Judging by the absence of a phallus and apparent breasts both of these colossal figures are female. Each has a wooden face and the one that looks quite new is supported by a tree. The other stands within a protective enclosure, where a noticeboard informs us that she was once exhibited in the Smithsonian Museum in Washington D.C.[73] Finally, Onyosama is the name given to a figure labelled *dōsojin* in a remote rural area of Daisen City. This one is unmistakably male with carefully delineated yet modestly concealed straw genitals. Once again he is armed with a sword and has a newly painted bright red face.[74]

In only one place in Japan is a temporary figure made out of clay. Its creation is the culmination of the Chombo Jizō festival in Niigata Prefecture. Chombo

72 From a personal observation made on 21 April 2012.

73 From a personal observation made on 21 April 2012.

74 From a personal observation made on 22 April 2012.

FIGURE 253
The Mitsumura Kashima-sama looks like a giant straw rabbit but is the successor to a figure that was once credited with averting a plague of typhus.

FIGURE 254 *The finest of all the Akita Kashima-sama is this huge creation at the Hachiman Shrine in Yuzawa. Its twin, preserved nearby, was exhibited in Washington* D.C.

FIGURE 255 *The red-faced figure of the protective god called Onyosama in Akita Prefecture.*

FIGURE 256 *The Chombo Jizō, the only protective figure made out of clay. It has an enormous phallus.*

Jizō ちょんぼ地蔵 is a seated figure reminiscent of Jizō in all but his enormous phallus that is equivalent in length to his entire body. He also has huge testicles. The figure is created anew on 26 August every year on the side of the road just outside the Otoko Shrine 音子神社 in a village to the east of Nagaoka City. Natural clay is scooped up from the soil and moulded by hand to make this unique fertility figure who is then allowed slowly to decay. Almost a year had passed when I observed the 2012 creation, out of whose crumbling body weeds were growing.[75]

In conclusion, some of the most important representations of Japan's sexual gods to be found today stand beside fields and roadsides. Known variously as *dōsojin* and *sai no kami* and written using a choice of characters they provide protection and ensure fertility. In some cases a named deity is intended. In others some anonymous expression of male and female harmony or a depiction of the act of copulation is regarded as sufficient for the sympathetic magic to work on the fields. When protection is the intention a single three-dimensional phallus or an elaborate figure woven from straw with strong sexual characteristics provides both intimidation and reassurance.

75 From a personal observation made on 1 July 2013.

CHAPTER 11

Continuity and Change in Japan's Phallic Festivals

Most of the descriptions and discussions presented so far have linked the religious display of sexual imagery to human and agricultural fertility within the dimension of space. This chapter will add the dimension of time, because much activity takes place within the context of a sexual shrine's annual *matsuri* 祭り, a word usually translated into English as 'festival', although the Spanish word *fiesta* conjures up more readily the exuberance and gaiety that is commonly involved. If such events are publicised in English the expression 'phallic festival' is likely to be used, and this is not entirely inappropriate because very little ktenic imagery is to be seen at these lively gatherings.

The study of phallic festivals adds greatly to our knowledge of the sexual gods, because no other aspect of Japan's sexual beliefs reveals more about the balance between continuity and change and the relationship between human and agricultural fertility. Both concerns are reflected in recent changes to the *matsuri* calendar, which was once firmly tied to the cycle of seedtime and harvest. In many cases it still is, but far more numerous are the occasions when the link with agriculture has been broken. Also broken may be its historical continuity, with some festivals being discontinued and then revived long afterwards. Some can even be shown to have been invented recently for commercial purposes.

During the course of any shrine's *matsuri*, sexual or not and regardless of whether it is a small-scale local event or a highly publicised celebration attracting thousands of onlookers, the establishment and its associated beliefs are placed firmly on public show. A building that may seem empty and almost abandoned for much of the year becomes for a short interval of time a riot of colour and activity where sacred and secular combine in a communal celebration. This archetypal *matsuri* is a communion between the human and the divine where the enshrined *kami* joins its worshippers in a celebration that combines the two elements of religious ritual and social rejoicing. Both these factors, each of them vital to the success of a *matsuri*, are expressed reverently, freely, joyously and sometimes very noisily. In a ritual akin to the offering of hospitality to an honoured guest in one's home the *kami* is invited to attend, received into a prepared space, entertained, petitioned and then seen off again with thanks, and at almost every *matsuri* a key element in the activities is the carrying in procession of an ornate *mikoshi* 御輿, the sacred palanquin in which the *kami* is conveyed in a symbolic journey around a set route.

 | DOI 10.1163/9789004293786_012

That, at any rate, is the ideal view of a *matsuri* as set out by scholars of the subject such as Ashkenazi, and at first sight most of the phallic *matsuri* conform to these expectations.[1] All involve a considerable element of phallic symbolism, and it is almost inevitable that if there is a parade a large phallus will be included along with the *mikoshi*. This one large phallus can perform two roles. It may be the quintessence of the devotional function whereby it acts as a representation of the enshrined deity and is paraded to receive adoration. The phallus that is used for this purpose may even be the shrine's *goshintai*, although a large and heavy one is difficult to manipulate, as shown by my observation of the Hodare *matsuri* ほだれ祭り in Tochio (Niigata Prefecture) in 2014. A block and tackle were needed to take the huge phallus from the shrine. It was fastened on to the carrying framework not by traditional ropes but using modern webbing and locking devices, and then carried with some difficulty over the slippery hard-packed snow.[2]

FIGURE 257 *The heavy wooden phallus of the Hodare Shrine is returned to its normal location with great difficulty.*

1 Ashkenazi, Michael 1993. *Festivals of a Japanese* Town (Honolulu).

2 From a personal observation made on 9 March 2014.

FIGURE 258
This print by Hiroshige III illustrates a lively scene at the year-end market of the Asakusa Kannon in Tokyo during the early Meiji Period. Two men are carrying a crude wooden dummy involving a mask of Otafuku and a large phallus.

The other role of a giant phallus carried in a parade is to be a votive offering presented to the *kami* on behalf of the whole community to ensure a good harvest. In this way it parallels and complements the numerous smaller individual offerings for human fertility presented at other times during the year. Solemnity may attend the large phallus's departure and arrival at the shrine. In between those points the procession will be a lively event with people shouting, chanting, dancing and even riding on the processional phallus in a scene of uninhibited sexual display that would not have been unfamiliar to W.G. Aston, who described an encounter with a phallic festival in the early 1870s in the following words:

> I once witnessed a phallic celebration in a town some miles north of Tokio. A phallus several feet high, and painted a bright vermilion colour, was being carried on a sort of bier by a crowd of shouting, laughing coolies with flushed faces, who zig-zagged along with sudden rushes from

> one side of the street to the other. It was a veritable Bacchic rout. The Dionysia, as will be mentioned, had their phalli. A procession of this kind invaded the quiet thoroughfares of the Kobe foreign settlement in 1868, much to the amazement of the European residents.[3]

Aston would have been similarly impressed by the noise and vigour of the numerous phallic festivals that have proliferated during the past half-century, which begs the question as to how authentic or traditional some of them are. This matter will be considered in the light of Hobsbawm and Ranger's classic and useful notion of an 'invented tradition':

> ... a set of practices, normally governed by overtly or tacitly accepted rules and of a ritual or symbolic nature, which seeks to inculcate certain values and norms of behaviour by repetition, which automatically implies continuity with the past.[4]

The invention of tradition is not necessarily a pejorative term. None of the examples noted in Hobsbawm and Ranger's book have been dreamt up from nothing and Hobsbawm adds that, 'there is probably no time and place with which historians are concerned that has not seen the 'invention' of tradition in this sense'. He also identifies 'the use of ancient materials to construct invented traditions of a novel type for quite novel purposes' that, 'extends the old symbolic vocabulary beyond its established limits'.[5] All these points can be applied to the Japanese situation.[6] For example, in Robert Smith's study of imperial Japanese weddings and funerals in the twentieth century he concluded that the rituals associated with them were not ancient rites but new ones, which prompted him to pose the question of how many times something had to be performed to become a tradition.[7] 'Is it possible simply to make them up out of real cloth?' he asks, and who could fail to love the deliciously dry answer

3 Aston 1972, pp. 11–12.

4 Hobsbawm, Eric and Ranger, Terence (eds.) 1983. *The Invention of Tradition* (Cambridge), p. 1.

5 Hobsbawm and Ranger 1983, pp. 4 & 7.

6 An interesting collection of Japanese examples, some of which involved religious beliefs, was published in 1998. See Vlastos, Stephen (ed.) 1998 *Mirror of Modernity: Invented Traditions of Modern Japan*. (Berkeley).

7 Smith, Robert J. 1995. 'Wedding and funeral ritual: analysing a moving target' in Van Bremen, Jan and Martinez, D.P. (eds.) *Ceremony and Ritual in Japan: Religious practices in an industrialized society*. (London), p. 26.

provided in the introduction to the volume in which Smith's paper appears. 'For something to be called a tradition it has to be performed at least once'.[8]

Large-scale phallic festivals are now part of the local scene in many towns and cities of modern Japan. Some have ancient origins but almost all have experienced considerable change in their contents and performance. This dynamism is something that the events have in common with other shrines' *matsuri* because very few festivals have ever remained static, and the most common development concerns the links between a *matsuri* and the calendar. The festival may still occur at seedtime or harvest, but in past years the precise date was usually chosen according to the lunar calendar. This has largely changed to the solar calendar, and a further trend has been to make festivals weekend events on the 'nth' Saturday or Sunday of the appropriate month because of the demands of modern life.[9]

Also much weakened is the link with agriculture. Over the past century Japan has moved from being an agricultural society to an industrialised one, and many rituals that were designed to enhance agricultural fertility are now performed in situations where the needs of farming are very slight. One instance is to be found at Yokohama's Tsurumi Shrine, where an elaborate *matsuri* to ensure the fertility of the rice fields involving dance, drama and music has been painstakingly and lovingly re-created in the most minute detail even though there is a distinct lack of rice fields in Yokohama. Nevertheless, the accompanying booklets proudly relate how local enthusiasts studied old records and restored the performance exactly with authentic costumes, props, music and dialogue including an amusing phallic set-piece drama.[10] It has been revived in this way not because of any effect it will produce upon a non-existent crop but simply because the activities themselves are regarded as intangible cultural properties that are worth preserving. One might add (perhaps cynically) that any increased yield from the fields has been replaced by an increased financial yield from the tourists who are expected to flock into the area to watch the spectacle.

On the face of it the preservation or restoration of local folklore and tradition is to be applauded, but when taken to extremes a commercially driven festival re-creation may result in a traditional *matsuri* being completely

8 Van Bremen, Jan 1995. 'Introduction: The myth of the secularisation of industrial societies' in Van Bremen, Jan and Martinez, D.P. (eds.) *Ceremony and Ritual in Japan: Religious practices in an industrialized society*. (London), p. 14.

9 This can cause particular problems for a researcher who may easily find two or three important annual festivals happening on the same day!

10 From a personal observation made on 29 April 2012. See Tsurumi ta matsuri hōzon kai 2007. *Tsurumi no ta matsuri fukattsu shiryō* (Yokohama).

replaced by a secular *ibento* (イベント event). This expression derived from the English language has been defined by Irit Averbuch as 'a standard referent to describe a staged and choreographed public event involving shows, processions, food and fairs'.[11] In some cases this relates to the requirements of the 1946 Constitution that separated church and state, so that when a local government funds an event it has to be non-religious.[12] This consideration lies behind the situation described movingly and well by Averbuch in her article on the *Nunohashi kanjōe* (the cloth bridge consecration rite) in Tateyama (Toyama Prefecture), a ritual for women's salvation that had not been performed for 130 years until it was revived in 1996. The motivation behind restoring it was the revitalisation of the town, and one matter that was insisted upon was that it should not be religious in any way. The process, however, involved the re-creation of the words and gestures of what had indeed once been a religious ritual, and the remarkable discovery was made that the majority of the participants enjoyed a profound and unexpected spiritual experience as a result of it.[13]

Japan's Festival Law of 1992 approached the matter from a different direction when it called for the use of folk performing arts in the promotion of tourism, commerce and industry, and some excellent large scale events without any prior links to shrines were one positive result of this.[14] Yet some *ibento* are neither new productions nor replacements for long abandoned religious festivals but are instead clumsy re-creations of them tipped awkwardly into the secular sphere. Stripped of their religious content they become '*matsuri* without *kami*' where there has been a shift from catering for the needs of *kami* as honoured guests to catering for the needs of tourists as paying guests.[15] Lying behind these changes, of course, is a movement away from deeply held religious beliefs that once regarded performances like these as essential to the achievement of a good harvest, although most modern-day phallic *matsuri* still seem to be anchored around a religious core, no matter how tenuous the belief supporting it may be. Religion has therefore not been totally abandoned among all the sexual jollity, yet some searching questions arise when phallic festivals are examined in detail.

---

11 Averbuch, Irit 2011. 'Discourses of the Reappearing: The Re-enactment of the "Cloth-Bridge Consecration Rite" at Mt. Tateyama' *Japanese Journal of Religious Studies* 38, pp. 3–4.

12 Reader 1991, p. 72.

13 Averbuch 2011, pp. 1–54.

14 Hashimoto Hiroyuki 2003. 'Between Preservation and Tourism: Folk Performing Arts in Contemporary Japan' *Asian Folklore Studies* 62, pp. 225–236.

15 Averbuch 2011, pp. 3–4.

FIGURE 259 *The giant votive phallus of the Tagata Shrine Festival has become the means by which Japanese sexual beliefs have become widely known. In this picture the 2008 phallus leaves the Shinmei Shrine at the start of the procession.*

The Evolution of the Tagata Festival

Reference was made earlier to the discovery in 2002 of a phallic *sekibō* in Fuchū and the subsequent creation of a *sekibō* festival that would bring benefits to the local economy. The centrepiece of the festivities was be the carrying of a large wooden replica of the *sekibō*, so a delegation from the town went on a fact-finding visit.[16] Their choice of which festival to study was not a difficult one, because no event is better known or better supported than the famous Hōnen-sai 豊年祭 of Aichi Prefecture's Tagata Shrine 田縣神社 with its well-known tradition of carrying in procession a giant wooden phallus. It is held in March to pray for a bumper harvest in the autumn.

This event will now be examined in detail, partly because it provides a classic illustration of a phallic festival in action but also because there is considerable evidence to suggest that Fuchū's festival is not the only one to have used Tagata as the standard reference for how a phallic festival should be conducted and what it should contain. Any enthusiasm to copy the Tagata ritual, however,

16 http://www.toyama.hokkoku.co.jp/subpage/T20100209203.htm (Accessed 12 October 2012).

conveniently ignores the fact that the Tagata Festival has itself experienced important changes during its recent history. Instead the presence of a votive phallus and the related activity is simply taken as read, an attitude that has ensured that the festival's influence has been spread widely to become the most important means through which the existence of Japanese sexual shrines has become disseminated to a wider world. Indeed, the image of Tagata's processional phallus (and little else) is what most people understand by the term 'Japanese phallicism'.

The Tagata Festival is best understood when it is studied in relation to the annual *matsuri* performed a week earlier by its near neighbour: the female-orientated Ōagata Shrine 大縣神社. The Ōagata Shrine enshrines the same *kami* and, until recently, involved a display of ktenic symbolism in its *matsuri* every bit as frank as the phallic element still seen at Tagata. Commenting on both festivals in 1996 P.G. O'Neill stated bluntly that, 'The removal of government funding after the Pacific War, however, led to the purely sexual aspects of the gods being emphasised above all else, in order to attract bigger audiences and more income'.[17] Whether or not the shrines' authorities made such a cynical decision his concluding phrase does indeed describe the economic result, but as for emphasising a sexual theme the ensuing years have demonstrated that the display at Tagata has become more exuberant while the Ōagata Festival has if anything gone into reverse.

The Tagata Festival has been so well documented that it is possible not only to appreciate its significance as it is understood today but also to see how it has developed over a period of about 150 years. Katō Genchi refers to it as it was in the early 1920s.[18] Okawara Masakatsu's article of 1932 describes it in the late 1920s.[19] Numazawa Kiichi's two descriptions take us forward into the 1950s while also looking back to the 1890s.[20] Deguchi Yonekichi mentions the Tagata Festival and compares it to the fertility cults of Ancient Rome.[21] More recent contributions may be found in the books by Nishioka, Saitō, Satō and Kokonoe. In the course of my own research I was able to discuss the details of the festival with the Chief Priest in 1992 and then witnessed the entire festival for myself in 2008 and again in 2014 with the help of a very detailed pamphlet

17 Plutschow and O'Neill 1996, p. 262.

18 Katō 1924, p. 6.

19 Ōkawara Masakatsu 1932. 'Agata no mori no Hōnen-sai' *Kaibō* (Aichi-ken Shinshoku-kai, January), pp. 20–30.

20 Numazawa, Kiichi. 1957. 'Tagata Jinja no Hōnen-sai' *Minzokugaku kenkyū* 21, pp. 24–32; Numazawa 1959, pp. 193–217.

21 Quoted in Nishioka 1961, p. 201.

that explains the route of the procession and the relevance of the huge phallus, a sight repeated a dozen times every year on *YouTube* and recorded in the astonished words of many a traveller's blog.[22]

The festival takes place in and around the Tagata Shrine in what was once a forested area known as Agata no Mori (the Agata woods) to the north of Komaki City. The discovery in 1935 of a sword and some potsherds indicate that the place is an ancient religious establishment dating back about 1,500 years. According to one theory the name Agata is derived from the surname of the local lord whose daughter Tamahime became the *kami* of the Tagata Shrine that marks the location of her dwelling. Alternatively the *kami* of the Tagata Shrine is listed as Mitoshi no Kami, the recipient of a votive phallus to appease his wrath in the *Kogoshūi*, although this conclusion was reached by the simplistic deduction that because a phallus was involved in the festival its *kami* had to be Mitoshi no Kami.[23] The recipient of the giant phallus nowadays is certainly a female *kami*, although the naming of her as Tamahime is a fairly recent development. In an 1893 account of the festival no name for her is given. The official version now states that Tamahime was married to a chieftain called Takeinadane. It was the ancient custom for a husband to visit his wife in her ancestral home rather than taking her away from it. She continued to live there following his untimely death, and the present-day Tagata Festival is in some way a recreation of a visit by Takeinadane to his bride that is symbolic of the achievement of harmony between the male and female principles.[24]

Both Okawara and Numazawa draw attention to the fact that a separate identity for the Tagata Shrine as a Shintō shrine dates only from the Meiji Restoration. Before that time it fell under the jurisdiction of the local Buddhist temple called the Kubodera, of which the most prized image is a statue of the deity Shōgun Jizō, a variation on the better known versions of Jizō in that he is dressed as an armoured general. Phalluses are still offered to the figure.[25] In 1918 Katō was told by a local resident aged 72 that the divine emblem of the shrine was a female figure of Tamahime dressed in armour, an interesting local interpretation of the image.[26]

---

22 From personal observations made on 9 April 1992, 8 March 2008, 15 March 2008 and 15 March 2014.

23 Numazawa 1959, p. 196.

24 Ōkawara 1932, p. 23; Numazawa 1959, pp. 193–194.

25 From a personal observation made on 15 March 2014 and Ōkawara 1932, p. 29.

26 Numazawa 1959, p. 197.

FIGURE 260 *The Shōgun Jizō in the Kubodera is the most prized image in a temple that once included the Tagata Shrine within its jurisdiction. Phalluses are still offered to the figure.*

The Tagata Shrine lies about 500 metres away from the Kubodera and its atmosphere is appropriately phallic. There are sexual symbols placed around the grounds to add to the ambience including a shrine built on the site of a pine tree described by Numazawa. A natural phallic stone was once placed across its double trunk, and it was believed that a woman who wanted a child had to step over it.[27] On approaching the large sub-shrine at the rear of the premises where votive phalluses are stored one's eye is immediately drawn to the phallic-shaped bell with which the *kami* are ritually summoned. A large wooden phallus set at 45 degrees is brought forward to stand just behind the offertory

27 Numazawa 1959, p. 210.

FIGURE 261 *The procession at the Tagata Shrine Festival is re-enacted by crowds of* tanuki *in an amusing votive painting at the Tagata Shrine.*

box at festival times and produces many a smile from visitors. Another very large phallus lies at the rear of the shrine with two amusing paintings that show the phallic procession being re-enacted by hundreds of *tanuki*.[28] A comparison of photographs taken by the author in 1992, 2008 and 2014 indicates that the ritual of borrowing and presenting votive phalluses is an active one as there had been many changes and apparently many additions. Numazawa notes that during the periodic stirrings of moral outrage during the Tagata Shrine's existence these phalluses were sometimes thrown into a nearby pond, but that always the perpetrators were struck down by mysterious illnesses until the emblems were restored.[29]

Like all large-scale Japanese *matsuri* the Tagata Festival attracts vendors supplying food, drink and souvenirs, and it is not surprising also to find numerous stalls that sell a vast range of erotica. The merchandise begins at the railway station and continues into the shrine's extensive car park where one may purchase an imaginatively carved tree trunk, or for a much smaller outlay a plastic clockwork phallus that jumps up and down. There are also reproductions of *shunga* and mass-produced erotic statuettes. One's hunger may then

28 From a personal observation made on 08 March 2008.

29 Numazawa 1959, p. 211.

FIGURE 262 *A few of the votive phalluses presented to the* kami *of the Tagata Shrine as of March 2008.*

be satisfied by a range of festival food deliberately shaped for the occasion. Hot dogs, minus the customary bread roll and with a stick inserted at one end, provide an easy challenge for the artistically inclined caterer, while phallic toffee apples are created by placing the original apple in a rotating slicer to cut the fruit into an extended helix. Phallic lollipops complete the bill of fare. Yet all this stops at a notional dividing line that passes invisibly along the line of the *torii*. Inside this boundary many more phallic objects may be bought, but no matter how imaginatively they may be designed (and some do not differ greatly in appearance from those on sale outside) they are regarded as sacred objects.

That this dividing line also covers visitors' behaviour was brought home by an incident witnessed during the afternoon in 2008. There are tens of thousands of people in attendance throughout the festival day. They are well-behaved and good-humoured as they make the customary obeisance at the main shrine and wait in long, quiet and patient queues to pray at the small shrine at the rear which holds the votive offerings. During the afternoon the queue was joined by a man who sat down on a portable chair. He took from his rucksack a phallus in the shape of a glove puppet and another of red-painted wood that he held at his crotch. He then proceeded to make gestures with them towards females standing in the line. Within minutes he was approached by two policemen who had a short word with him, at which his gestures ceased and the phallic symbols were put away. The offender, of course, was sitting in a phallic shrine courtyard surrounded by phallic symbols and engaging with a crowd who were waiting to see even more phallic symbols, but somehow he had crossed the line of acceptability.

The main event of the Tagata Festival has always been the parade of the famous giant phallus, a communal votive offering to Tamahime whose divine benevolence is the key to the achievement of a bumper harvest, yet this crucial object has experienced more changes over the past century and a half than any other aspect of the festival. Numazawa states that the original phallus was small enough to be carried by one person.[30] A custom then developed of attaching the phallus to a figure of a man of straw that represented Takeinadane. Nowadays he appears in the procession separately from the giant phallus as a modern lifelike statue carried in a *mikoshi*, but in 1924 he was 'a wooden figure rudely carved with a large male sexual organ protruding'.[31] The figure is mentioned in *Owari-shi* (A History of Owari Province) in 1893 as follows:

> The local people believe that this deity is a female *kami* who protects their crops. At the start of every year as part of a religious ceremony they construct a human figure with a phallus (*dankei*) and laugh a lot. When the festival finishes they place a paper amulet in every rice field in the village to ensure a bumper harvest.[32]

Descriptions from 1921 and 1923 mention a straw man seated on a phallus in a palanquin.[33] That contrivance could be carried easily by four or five bearers, but sometime around the 1930s the combination of man and exposed phallus was considered vulgar, so the man was withdrawn and the solitary phallus restored.[34] It now lay partly concealed in the palanquin, hence O'Neill's description of the Tagata and Ōagata festivals in the 1930s as being modest affairs compared to today.[35] By the 1960s the phallus had grown in size as if to compensate for its partial concealment and effectively burst out of its

30 Numazawa 1959, p. 199.

31 Ōkawara 1932, p. 24; Katō 1924, p. 25.

32 Nakao, Yoshiine and Okada, Kei 1893. Owari-shi Volume 10 (Nagoya), p. 25.

33 Numazawa 1959, p. 206.

34 Numazawa 1959, p. 198.

35 Plutschow and O'Neill 1996, p. 262.

carriage. In 1976 Kokonoe described it as being two metres in length.[36] By 2008, according to the leaflet handed out that year by the shrine, the phallus was 2.5 metres long and weighed 280 kg. Together with its new and strengthened *mikoshi* the whole assembly now tops 400 kg, requiring it to be carried by teams of twelve men. There may be scope for it to grow still further because of the ritual requirement for a new phallus to be created every year. Each year's phallus looks slightly different because it is 'carved from life' as the Chief Priest put it so enigmatically in 1992.[37]

Prior to the separation of Shintō and Buddhism the procession would start at the Kubodera and make its way downhill to the Tagata Shrine.[38] Nowadays the starting point alternates between the Kumano Shrine (adjacent to the Kubodera) and the Shinmei Shrine. The latter place was used in 2008 and 2014. It becomes very crowded on the festival morning because this is the best place during the entire event to have one's photograph taken with the spectacular devotional items. Thousands of people line the route back to the Tagata Shrine with the densest crowds waiting in its courtyard for the parade to arrive, and as is the case with all large scale Japanese festivals the organisation is most impressive. Attendants unwind ropes to make temporary barriers while the procession proceeds, but crowd safety never compromises the need to see and touch the smaller devotional items that accompany the massive centrepiece.

Following the recitation of prayers by the priests the parade departs with two men leading the way and scattering salt for purification. Behind them comes Sarutahiko in his *tengu* mask and a priest carrying a large banner on which is painted a colourful image of a phallus. Following the flag are local government representatives and musicians with ancient instruments, all of them dressed in ceremonial attire, and then come a number of women, each of whom carries a wooden phallus 60 cm in length which the crowd are invited to rub for good luck. The choice of who takes part in the carrying is a privilege extended to those women who are of the ritually unlucky age of thirty-six. Behind them is carried the effigy of Tamahime. This is a recent development which rather spoils the symbolism of her husband journeying to meet her at the shrine.

Two sacred trees come after that, their branches festooned with hundreds of the paper amulets that will be taken to the rice fields after the festival is over. Both trees are very large and have to be mounted on wheeled carts, one of which has to be dragged along with ropes by a noisy team of men, but here

36 Kokonoe 1976, p. 8.

37 As can be appreciated by comparing Figures 1 and 259. The highly ritualised process may be seen on a video shown in the museum of the nearby Komaki Castle.

38 Numazawa 1959, p. 201.

FIGURE 263
The large banner bearing an image of a phallus is carried in procession during the Tagata Festival in 2014.

FIGURE 264
Small wooden phalluses are carried during the Tagata Festival procession. People in the crowd are invited to rub them for good fortune.

FIGURE 265 *Nowadays an effigy of Tamahime is carried in a* mikoshi *during the Tagata Festival, which somewhat spoils the symbolism of her husband journeying to meet her at the shrine.*

there has been a major change in the festival proceedings. These paper amulets are regarded as possessing great ritual power and until the 1930s the trees were situated at the rear of the procession. As soon as they had passed under the *torii* there was a free-for-all as hundreds of people pounced on them and ripped them apart to get at the amulets and also the wooden phallic symbols that were attached to the branches in those days.[39] Knives were employed to cut them off and many people were hurt in the scrambles. This ritual of fighting has now been abandoned, but it is interesting to note that a similar rite involving imitation paper trees has been retained at the much smaller annual

39 For a picture see Numazawa 1959, p. 205.

festival of the Ōagata Shrine.[40] Another detail described by Numazawa is also now absent; this is the wearing of phallic symbols at the belt by those pulling the carts.[41]

The next object to pass by is a barrel of *sake* hung from a pole and a cart from which drink is dispensed to the crowd, and then, almost unnoticed by the crowds because the enormous phallus is so close behind it, comes a wooden chest in which are offerings of food and a natural stone phallus that constitutes the *goshintai* of the Shinmei Shrine. Now appears the *mikoshi* carrying Takeinadane while close behind him is the giant phallus. It protrudes at each end from its white curtained enclosure and its bearers takes many a rest, partly to change crews and also so that they can entertain the crowds by swinging the phallus backwards and forwards and rotating it at speed.[42] These men are also of an unlucky age, in their case forty-two. Bringing up the rear of the procession is another phallus borne by a further group of men. This one is much smaller and stands erect as its bearers sing traditional songs and perform rhythmic movements. Some carry smaller phalluses.[43] Eventually they all reach the Tagata Shrine to be greeted with much rejoicing and prayers for thanks.[44] The *matsuri* ends with the tradition of hurling *mochi* (pounded rice cakes) into the crowd from a raised dais. To catch one is considered very lucky. After the festival is over the newly carved giant phallus will be installed in the place in the shrine where its predecessor has lain for the past year and the old phallus is sold off, usually to a private house, an inn or a restaurant. However, I was reliably informed by the Chief Priest in 1992 that the 1991 phallus had been given to an old peoples' home![45]

So the festival ends with the happy reunion of Tamahime and Takeinadake, and among the souvenirs that visitors can take away from the event is a small ceramic bell. On one side is a representation of the happy couple holding hands in the style of a *dōsojin*, while the overall shape of the bell that envelopes them is a phallus. It is through this phallic symbolism that the Tagata Shrine's *matsuri* makes a vital link between the generative power of male sexuality and

---

40 From a personal observation made on 9 March 2008.

41 Numazawa 1959, p. 206.

42 For my video of this stage of the parade in 2014 see https://www.youtube.com/watch?v=YFxRIBTjI3Q.

43 This group was absent in 2014 and the order of the procession was also slightly different from the 2008 festival.

44 As shown in my video at http://youtu.be/DENsM1ogsNg.

45 One former Tagata phallus is on display at the Utsunomiya Seishin no Yakata.

FIGURE 266 *Preceded by the* mikoshi *carrying the effigy of Takeinadane, the giant phallus arrives at its final destination at the conclusion of the Tagata Festival in 2014.*

Tamahime, the receptive *gokoku hōjō no kami* (the *kami* of the 'fertility of the five cereals' or of an abundant harvest). She is always the focal point of the festival, so the festival is indeed not about worshipping the phallus, it is about worshipping the *kami* of a bountiful harvest and the achievement of harmony through the union of male and the female. The symbolic votive phallus anthropomorphises the sexual power without which nothing can be produced.

The Ōagata Shrine's Hime no Miya *matsuri*

The Hime no Miya *matsuri* of the Ōagata Shrine is effectively the ktenic counterpart to the Tagata Shrine's phallic event, and like the Tagata Shrine's Hōnensai it is held to pray for an abundant harvest. Tamahime again takes centre stage, but this time her role and the symbolism employed in the performance are entirely different. The Ōagata Shrine's chief *kami* is Tamahime's father Ōagata who is regarded as a patron *kami* of business prosperity among a range of other benefits that include traffic safety. The overall area of the shrine is large and includes two important sub-shrines to Daikoku and Ebisu but also the Hime no Miya, a striking vermilion-coloured building for Tamahime, who

FIGURE 267 *At the Ōagata Shrine an interesting collection of natural stone ktenic symbols are in a small open shrine at the rear of the main building. They are called the Hime Seki and have been presented to its female* kami.

is enshrined here not only as the *kami* of abundant harvest but also as the guardian *kami* of women. This role is emphasised by the tiny building near to her shrine where may be found six ktenic stones, and there is also a small stone *torii* under which a woman may crawl in a popular ritual to ensure a lucky marriage, pregnancy and safe delivery.

Whereas the Tagata Festival involves a procession to her shrine, at Ōagata the procession ends at the main shrine building where her father is enshrined rather than the Hime no Miya itself even though the event is called the Hime no Miya *matsuri* and it is her image that appears everywhere. This choice of destination would appear to have been made for purely practical reasons because the Hime no Miya is too small to house the offering of a giant *kagami mochi* 鏡餅 that replaces the large phallus. This is a festive variant on the usual form of a traditional New Year's decoration consisting of two *mochi*, the smaller placed on top of the larger and sometimes with an orange on top of both. The Ōagata Shrine's remarkable piece of confectionery is white in colour and adorned with red and white ropes, but with an interesting addition at its

FIGURE 268 *The huge ktenic* kagami-mochi *that acts as a communal votive offering at the Ōagata Festival.*

front where an excrescence is added picked out in brown that gives the *kagami mochi* the appearance of a kteis when viewed from that angle. It is carried on its wooden supporting frame to the main shrine in a separate parade that leaves its resting place while the main procession is being made ready.

I was unable to witness this parade in 2008 as I was watching the other being assembled, but a posting on *YouTube* for 2011 shows the earlier procession from start to finish. It begins with a Shintō priest accompanied by a number of decoratively dressed children and their parents. At a short distance behind the children's procession come nine priests and five female shrine attendants. Noise begins with the encouraging chants of the team carrying the *kagami-mochi*, its great weight indicated by fact that forty-two men are required to carry it. Behind them come two smaller *kagami-mochi* and a *sake* barrel. All three *kagami-mochi* are preceded by a man carrying a notice board with the name of that year's sponsor.[46] When the second parade begins Sarutahiko marches at its head followed by brocade banners and a group of women of an unlucky age, all dressed in long white veils. There is an ornate *mikoshi* and at the rear a

46 http://www.youtube.com/watch?v=FtUBtAti6xY&feature=related (Accessed 25 June 2012).

collection of very colourful artificial tree branches made of paper for which the crowd at the Ōagata Shrine wait in eager anticipation. Once everyone else is safely inside the *torii* the watchful police drop the rope barriers they have been holding and a good-natured scrum ensues as people compete in a distinctly non-aggressive manner to obtain a favour. With a session of *mochi* throwing the festival concludes.[47]

If Kokonoe's account and his illustrations from 1976 are anything to go by this festival has experienced as many changes as the Tagata Festival over the past half century. The first concerns the display of sexual items, because until comparatively recently the phallic imagery of the Tagata Festival was mirrored by the ktenic imagery on show at the Ōagata Shrine. It was during the second parade that a banner was carried that depicted female genitalia. This is not seen nowadays, and instead Tamahime herself appears in two alternative guises on two different banners and on the shrine's *ema*, where Tamahime is shown bare-breasted and playing the *biwa* reminiscent of images of Benten. The other flags show her face in the guise of Otafuku but without the characteristic distended ktenic shape. This survives, however, in the pottery souvenir bells on sale, the only overtly sexual item now present at the shrine other than the ktenic stones.

Two other aspects of the event illustrated by Kokonoe also seem to have been abandoned. One was the carrying in an open *mikoshi* of a natural stone kteis adorned with pubic hair made from horse hair that Kokonoe identifies as Tamahime's *goshintai*. It is possible that this may still be carried inside the processional *mikoshi*, but if so it cannot now be seen. The other feature from earlier festivals and now abandoned was a strange opening ktenic clam shell from which a woman emerged from time to time to distribute *mochi* to the crowd.[48] O'Neill mentions this and also a 'treasure boat' with a wooden phallus ejaculating ears of corn, but I have found no illustrations or other descriptions of this for recent years.[49]

Today's procession has therefore been toned down a great deal, making it look very innocuous compared to its brash neighbour, but the two festivals at Tagata and Ōagata are still complementary in their symbolism. Both are explicitly intended to ensure an abundant harvest and both festivals honour

---

47 From a personal observation made on 9 March 2008. My videos of the event may be seen at https://www.youtube.com/watch?v=-NT-lzS_C_I and https://www.youtube.com/watch?v=PaLQYCQW-QE.

48 Kokonoe 1976, pp. 10–11.

49 Plutschow and O'Neill 1996, p. 263.

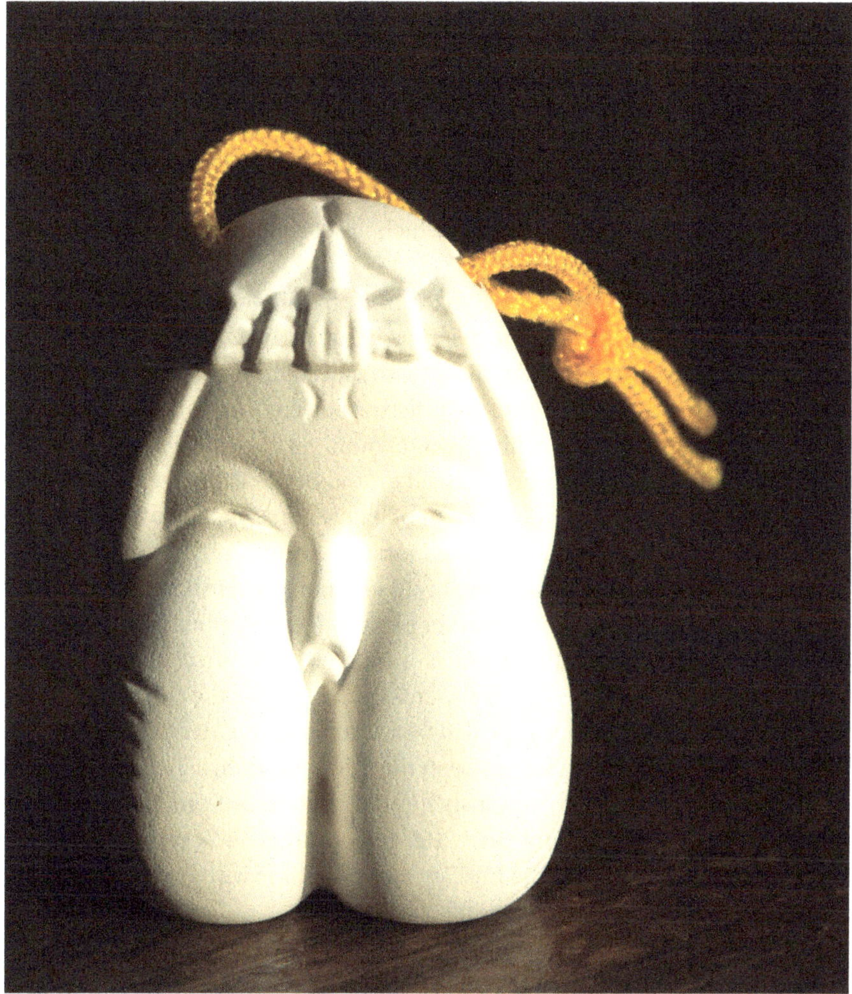

FIGURE 269 *A pottery bell from the Hime no Miya at the Ōagata Shrine uses a sexual distortion of the face of Otafuku to represent its* kami *Tamehime.*

and supplicate the same female *kami*. At the Tagata Shrine the visual images are almost exclusively phallic. At festival time the emphasis is on her receiving her husband and the sexual power of fertility that only the male element can provide. At Ōagata, where she is the guardian of women and the patron of their unique needs, the imagery is ktenic and has also moved on in time. No longer does it involve a symbol of impregnation. Instead we see the receptive and womb-like *kagami-mochi*, where the seed will be nurtured by the woman.

Phallic Festivals and the Invention of Tradition

The Tagata and Ōagata Festivals are but two among many sexual-related *matsuri* currently being performed in Japan. Some possess a similar antiquity and display their own distinctive and time-honoured rituals. Others are revivals of festivals lost for over a century, while certain ones appear to be prime examples of invented traditions upon which the Tagata Festival is likely to have exerted a considerable influence.

The Tenteko *matsuri* of the Hachiman Shrine in Niike (Aichi Prefecture) provides an excellent example of the first type because there is a well-established continuity to a simple ancient ritual with no commercial overtones. It is claimed that this restrained and dignified event can be traced back to the shrine's foundation in 859 which commemorated the auspicious occasion when the nearby rice fields were selected for the Daijōsai, the great thanksgiving service held after the enthronement of a new emperor. The festival, which takes its onomatopoeic name from the sound of the drums used, has never lost its connections with agricultural fertility. The activity is akin to the hanging up of the *nawabanagashi* described earlier to provide the symbolism of the male and female elements coming together in sexual intercourse. At the Mifune Shrine the wind blows the objects towards each other. At the Niike Hachiman Shrine the female element is provided by the surrounding rice fields while the male element is a phallus that has been newly carved from a giant radish. It is worn at the waist, although curiously not at the groin but on the back above the buttocks. This is no doubt the better to accentuate an overtly sexual up-and-down movement when the hips are moved in time with the drum and the phallus symbolically impregnates the fields.

Six men who are almost completely masked and dressed in red wear the phalluses. They represent farmers who have become *kami* and all are of a ritually unlucky age. The first of each trio carries a drum to provide the crucial beat that is the only sound heard in the entire proceedings. The second carries a rice chest, the third the sort of food that the farmers would have eaten at their lunch break from rice-planting. As they make their way slowly past the silent crowds their hips are jerked upwards and downwards in a simulation of sexual intercourse. Walking with them are three men with bamboo brooms who scatter ash like compost on fields over the silent crowds whose restraint alone expresses a powerful sense of belief in the sympathetic transference of the power of fertility.[50]

50 I am greatly indebted to Michael Gakuran for supplying a complete photographic record of the 2013 performance together with useful notes. These have provided the basis for the

FIGURE 270 *The phallus carved from a* daikon *at the Tenteko Festival and worn at the back. Rhythmical movements simulate sexual intercourse and are symbolic of the impregnation of the ricefields (Picture kindly supplied by Michael Gakuran).*

The second type of phallic festival is one that was once abandoned and then revived. The Tsurumi Shrine in Yokohama and the Asuka Niimasu Shrine were cited earlier as examples of revived traditions relating to agricultural fertility that involve drama. A very different style of revived festival in Uonuma (Niigata Prefecture) is concerned instead with human fertility. It was discontinued in

description given here together with Kokonoe 1976, pp. 18–19 and a local website http://kikuko-nagoya.com/html/tenteko-matsuri.html (Accessed 16 March 2013).

1874 and restored in 1977. The *matsuri* is performed in the depths of winter and involves a brave volunteer in the person of a recently married man who pays his respects to a phallus and is then doused with water as he kneels upon the snow. The ordeal is regarded as helping his future fertility and the harmony of his marital relationship.[51]

Other performances are of the third type in that they have a completely modern origin and are therefore prime examples of invented traditions. A start date of sometime during the 1980s or 1990s is likely for the somewhat restrained sexual simulation seen in Morioka when a team from the Chiwaki Konsei Shrine bring a large straw phallus into sexual contact with a straw kteis from the Awashima Shrine. The ritual is not mentioned by Kokonoe in his 1981 account of the Chiwaki Shrine but now takes place on the third Saturday of every July. The two images are symbolically married and then consummate their union in a half-hearted performance to ensure the prosperity of the city of Morioka as well as family harmony, the health of children and abundant crops.[52] A much livelier form of simulated sexual intercourse may be seen at Koide (Niigata Prefecture) where a large wooden phallus mounted on wheels penetrates a ktenic straw circle fastened to a shrine's *torii*. This noisy and quite hazardous operation is the climax of the Shineri Benten Tataki Jizō *matsuri* しねり弁天たたき地蔵祭り. Couples who have been married during the previous year ride on a huge wheeled wooden phallus, and the culmination of the evening's festivities is this symbolic act of sexual intercourse. Using ropes tied to the front and rear of the carriage the phallus is dragged towards a large straw circle suspended within the *torii* of the Benten Shrine. The circle's ktenic symbolism is obvious, but the phallus is not simply pulled through in one go. To add to the reality of sexual intercourse the two sets of ropes are pulled alternately at an ever-increasing speed to make the phallus move forwards and then back. Great hilarity attends the process, with the phallus almost reaching its goal on several occasions. Finally with a huge surge forward the symbolic marriage is consummated.[53]

51 Masuta 2012, p. 53. For an excellent video of the 2012 performance see http://www.youtube.com/watch?v=6Hpo_P8owKU.

52 For the 2012 performance see http://www.youtube.com/watch?v=Ucx7w3laXAg (accessed 20 September 2012). A similar-looking event is enacted every year by art students in Tokyo. See Shui 2009, p. 198.

53 From a personal observation made on 30 June 2013. For my video of the 'consummation' see http://youtu.be/hA8xtwN8Axo.

FIGURE 271 *The climax of the Shineri Benten Tataki* matsuri *at Koide is the symbolic consummation of the marriage of a phallus with a ktenic straw circle at the shrine gateway.*

Fuchū Town's debt to the Tagata Shrine for inspiring its newly invented Sekibō Festival has been publicly acknowledged, but something similar is very likely to have happened at Morioka, Koide and at least four other phallic festivals that are known to be less than fifty years old. The practice of carrying a large phallus in procession, sometimes with people sitting on it, is included in all these recently introduced events, and it is not unreasonable to conclude that their creation has been influenced in some way by the publicity surrounding the Tagata Shrine's working blueprint of what might profitably be done with a very large phallus. Yet none is a complete invention. In each case the *matsuri* has been grafted on to the religious life of an existing sexual shrine with the intention of cashing-in on the religious, let alone the financial benefits displayed annually at the Tagata Shrine. As in Hobsbawn and Ranger's notion of an invented tradition they strive to provide continuity with a notional historical past using 'ancient materials' that 'extend the old symbolic vocabulary beyond its established limits'.[54]

54 Hobsbawm and Ranger 1983, pp. 4 & 7.

FIGURE 272 *The Hodare Festival in Niigata Prefecture features phallus riding by three women who are carried on the very heavy phallus over a short distance in the snow.*

It was noted earlier that the ancient phallic presence at the Ōwashi Shrine in Ajiki was greatly enhanced by the introduction to its Konsei Daimyōjin shrine of one of Japan's largest phallic symbols. Since 1965 there has been a festival that involves the parading of a separate large wooden phallus on a cart.[55] Konsei Daimyōjin is also the enshrined deity at Ōsawa Onsen in Iwate Prefecture where the Konsci *matsuri*, also begun in 1965, features an interesting variation on phallus riding because a number of young women dressed in festive attire ride a large wooden phallus while it is floating in an open-air hot spring bath.[56] At Utsukushigahara Onsen near Matsumoto City one may enjoy the phallic parade of the Dōsojin Festival that takes place late in September. It involves the carrying of a wooden phallus 160 cm long and 90 kg in weight, making it light enough to allow a man to ride it as it moves along. Although the event where it is paraded appears to be ancient it only dates from 1968.[57]

55 Kokonoe 1981, p. 106.

56 Masuta 2012, p. 53.

57 From a personal observation made on 15 November 2012 and Kubota 2006, p. 29. For a simple account of the festival and good photographs see Kokonoe 1976, pp. 20–21.

Finally, the Hodare Festival in the snows of Niigata has all the trappings of an ancient fertility ritual including phallus riding but dates only from 1979.[58] This event too is seamlessly integrated into the worship life of the ancient shrine which is built around a sacred tree, just as one would expect in any of Hobsbawm's 'inventions'.[59]

All these events are sexual-related examples of what Ashida Tetsurō once called the festival boom, while Ian Reader believes that nostalgia and a desire for renewal play their part in the decision to create something from virtually nothing.[60] Yet the invention of a 'traditional' local phallic festival is not an automatic guarantor of economic success. One in Shizuoka Prefecture that was set up by the local council rather than a shrine for purely commercial reasons has since been abandoned, presumably from lack of interest by the tourists it was hoping to attract. It took place at Izu-Nagaoka and was inspired by the presence on nearby Mount Katsuragi of a pair of *in'yōseki* and a local tradition associating the place with En no Gyōja. Every May, according to Kokonoe who provides the only account of the now redundant event and includes a photograph, an overtly phallic ceremony was held that involved a procession led by two large banners on which were painted brash representations of male and female genitalia. They were followed by a man dressed in *yamabushi* costume as En no Gyōja. The sexual element was completed by the wooden phallus he held with his left hand at his groin. He was followed by 150 other participants each carrying smaller bamboo ladles and phallic symbols of a more modest design. As they marched along they chanted to expel evil through the power of male sexuality.[61]

Phallic Festivals and Changes in Modern Attitudes

Commercialisation and public safety are responsible for most of the changes noted earlier in the Tagata and Ōagata Festivals, but elsewhere different changes have been made to established or revived festivals because the events have conflicted with modern shifts in attitude towards various aspects of sexual behaviour. If old records are to be believed some of these longer-term

58 Masuta 2012, p. 53.

59 From a personal observation made on 9 March 2014.

60 Ashida, Tetsurō 1994. 'The Festival and Religion Boom: Irony of the "Age of the Heart"' in Inoue, Nobutaka (ed.) and Havens, Norman (trans.) *Folk Beliefs in Modern Japan* (Tokyo), pp. 175–197; Reader, Ian 1987. 'Back to the Future': Images of Nostalgia and Renewal in a Japanese Religious Context' *Japanese Journal of Religious Studies* 14, pp. 287–303.

61 Kokonoe 1981, p. 182.

developments are quite profound, because certain ancient *matsuri* allegedly provided cover for uncontrolled night-time sexual orgies. In their book Itō and Richie devote a number of paragraphs to festivals 'that included dancing and concluded with copulation'. When the lights in the shrine precincts had been doused and after drinking copious amounts of *sake* the men and maidens of the town would disappear into the undergrowth. At one shrine near Tokyo in the early 1950s:

> ... the main power switch was pulled and the town plunged into darkness. The deity... was fond of darkness and encouraged all kinds of excess. Eventually the streets were filled with screaming girls and boys more possessed than drunk, all making for the temple grounds. These, although ordinarily large enough, soon became packed as the youth of the entire city forced their way in and milled about singing, dancing, and pleasing the god in other ways until dawn.[62]

Orgies have long since disappeared, and nowadays different shifts in attitude have brought about other changes. The first involves the tradition of using phallic objects in mock assaults on women to ensure their fertility. In 1951 Nishioka described rituals of touching that used the vaguely phallic wooden batons employed to stir rice porridge. They were often carved with various designs and bore a kind of tuft made by slivers hewn from but still adhering to the shaft in a manner not unlike the Ainu *inau* (worship sticks).[63] It was believed that a barren woman struck on the buttocks with one of these sticks would conceive and bear children. Nishioka provides a large number of examples of similar practices drawn from Japanese literature, and notes that women were pleased when it happened and did not regard it in any way as an assault.[64]

That comment was made in 1951, so it is interesting to note that some modern festivals still involve similar rituals. For example, even though the event finishes with phallus-riding, the Shineri Benten Tataki Jizō *matsuri* at Koide retains some elements of touching for fertility. Traditionally, men shouting 'Shineri Benten' would pinch women in the grounds of the Benten Shrine and the women would later retaliate by slapping men to cries of 'Tataki Jizō!' in front of the image of Jizō in the Kannonji temple. Yet during the 2013 festival the only remnant of molestation that I observed was a token pinch on a

62 Itō and Richie 1967, pp. 101–104.

63 Kitahara 2014, pp. 204–205.

64 Nishioka 1961, pp. 146–147.

woman's shoulder after permission had been sought from her by the assailant.[65] Elsewhere the Dontsuku Festival どんつく祭り that takes place at Inatori Onsen (Shizuoka Prefecture) still includes the prodding of women using a wooden phallus. Short video clips on *YouTube* show it being done by two men dressed in traditional costume wearing *tengu* masks. Each is accompanied by a 'minder' who holds the *tengu* by his belt to help guide him round. In one sequence from 2010 the *tengu* rushes towards any unsuspecting female in the crowd with a one metre long wooden phallus in his hands. Very little actual contact appears to be made and the assault appears to be taken with an air of good humour.[66] During the Hassaku Festival 八朔祭 of the Hiyoshi Shrine in Mihama (Fukui Prefecture) similar *tengu* run around on their own to prod women with wooden phalluses concealed within the breasts of their jackets.[67]

Touching for fertility was also once a feature of the *matsuri* celebrated at the Otonashi Shrine 音無神社 in Itō (Shizuoka Prefecture) every 10 November. It is still known by the suggestive title of the Shiritsumi *matsuri* 尻摘み祭り or 'bottom pinching festival' but has changed out of all recognition. The shrine lies within a small grove of trees which are all that remains of an ancient forest that once provided a degree of privacy for two famous clandestine lovers. The man was the young Minamoto Yoritomo, later to become Japan's first *shōgun*, who was exiled to the Izu peninsula following the abortive Heiji Rebellion of 1160. He was then fourteen years old and developed a relationship with Yaehime, the daughter of the local Itō lord. Under the cover of darkness the pair would sneak off into the woods. Their dalliance is recalled at the Otonashi Shrine, although only two aspects of the present shrine directly link the place to the lovers. The first are the pictures of them on the *ema* that hang in the shrine as petitions for love. The 'bottom-pinching' festival is the other, and Kokonoe described in 1981 how the lights in the shrine were extinguished and a man would pinch the bottom of the girl standing next to him to enhance her fertility. He includes a photograph of a smiling woman dressed in traditional costume receiving that attention from her companion.[68]

Much has changed. The festival still uses the words *shiri tsumi* but pinching bottoms is no longer acceptable. Instead a different form of buttock contact is

---

65 From a personal observation made on 30 June 2013.

66 http://www.flickr.com/photos/only1tanuki/4663382002/ (Accessed 20 February 2013). See also Kokonoe, Kyōji *Seishin* (Tokyo, 1976), pp. 6–7.

67 From a leaflet describing the event produced by Mihama city and available as a PDF at http://www1.kepco.co.jp/wakasa/shintanbou/images/mihama.pdf (Accessed 27 September 2013).

68 Kokonoe 1981, p. 173.

FIGURE 273 *The Shiritsumi Festival at Itō has changed dramatically over the years from a ritual of touching a woman to enhance her fertility to a strange contest of 'bottom sumo'.*

made. The lights are not extinguished, nor is there any opportunity for the participants to slip away like Yoritomo and Yaehime. Instead the courtyard is brilliantly illuminated with floodlights shining on to a small raised stage just large enough to hold two people standing back to back. A man dressed like a sumo referee controls the proceedings. A musical countdown is played and when it ceases the competitors attempt to knock each other off the dais using their buttocks. The evening begins with a children's competition and proceeds to a noisy adult knock-out tournament. In 2012 there was a team event between two of Tokyo's universities that attracted lively support. Some people were in fancy dress, but the wearing of national costume as illustrated by Kokonoe appears to have gone the way of actual bottom-pinching, and an event that may once have resulted in unsupervised sexual coupling has been replaced by a session of 'boomps-a-daisy' contested between students dressed as Donald Duck and Winnie the Pooh.[69]

The other shift in attitude that has affected phallic festivals concerns the effect that participation in or observation of them may have on children. An

69 From a personal observation made on 10 November 2012. See also Plutschow and O'Neill 1996, p. 45. See my video from 2012 at http://youtu.be/1YvBCL2qt1I.

old custom in Matsumoto has long been for groups of children to tour the city holding by a cord a wooden phallus called *onmara-sama* オンマラ様. They visit houses in order to obtain an offering in a Japanese version of 'trick or treat'. If gifts are refused the phallus may be thrown into the house, sometimes causing damage to the flooring or the paper screens. The ritual is still performed virtually intact but in recent years the age of the participants has been restricted to those over the age of fifteen.[70] Similar concerns may also have had some influence on an ancient event at the Chikuma Shrine 筑摩神社 in Maibara (Shiga Prefecture) where there is a festival called the Nabe kamuri *matsuri* 鍋冠り祭. The centrepiece is a colourful procession to the shrine along the lakeside by eight girls aged between seven and eight years of age dressed in green kimonos and wearing on their heads imitation cooking-pots (*nabe*) made from papier-mâché. They are the children for whom prayers will be offered, and according to the shrine's notice board the hats recall a time when the local women once placed cooking pots on their heads as makeshift helmets. The procession is led by Sarutahiko, but his extended *tengu* nose is the only object on view that could in any way be called phallic.[71]

There would appear to be no restraint on children taking part in the highly localised Yama no kami festivals still held in Nara, Shiga and Mie Prefectures, even though sexual symbolism is involved.[72] There also seems to be little concern about them being involved indirectly at festivals. At the Kanamara Festival in Kawasaki young girls are still placed astride a large wooden phallus as a prayer for their fertility as future brides, a ritual that surprises Western observers but is clearly acceptable to the girls' parents. If privacy is sought the girls can also be brought to the shrine at any time to sit on top of one of several large stone phallic symbols within the courtyard.[73] Children are also present in the audience to see some very frank sexual dances such as the *tsuburosashi* at

70 Kinoshita 2012, p. 99. Examples of the wooden phallus and photographs of the event are on show in the folklore section of Matsumoto City Museum.

71 From a personal observation made on 3 May 2012 and Kokonoe 1981, p. 212.

72 Child involvement at the Yama no kami rituals of the Rokujizō area shrines is illustrated in Rittō City 2001, p. 32. Photographs at the temporary exhibition at Nara Prefectural Museum in 2015 showed children present at local Yama no kami festivals. (From a personal observation made on 17 February 2015). Mie Prefectural Museum also has a display with videos showing children participating in rituals involving phallic and ktenic objects made from *daikon*. (From a personal observation made on 30 January 2015.)

73 From a personal observation made on 6 April 2008. For an earlier picture of such a ritual see Bornoff, Nicholas 1991. *Pink Samurai: An Erotic Exploration of Japanese Society* (London) Plate 4.

FIGURE 274 *The male and the beautiful female characters in the* tsuburosashi *dance at Hamochi on Sado Island (Niigata Prefecture).*

Hamochi on Sado Island (Niigata Prefecture). This is part of the annual festival that provides some of Japan's richest displays of folk-dancing together with performances by Sado's famous drummers. The dance is performed several times along the main street of the town and to large crowds in the main square. There are three characters: the male, the beautiful female and the ugly female. The male holds between his legs a long wooden phallus which he caresses as the two women try to persuade him to marry them. The beautiful one argues for her looks, while the ugly one promises him money. The dance is watched by many young people.[74]

In October 2012 children made up about a third of the audience for the Sanbiki Shishimai 三匹獅子舞 (three animals lion dance) performed at the Koroku Shrine 胡録神社 in Matsudo (Chiba Prefecture). According to the shrine's website the dance can only be traced back about a century and a half and probably had its origins in prayers for a successful harvest following

74 Kokonoe 1976, pp. 12–13 and a personal observation made during the performance on 15 June 2008. For a photograph of it dating from 1953 see Nishioka 1961, Plate XXIX.

a crop failure. The three animals are masked drummers who perform a stately and rhythmical dance that contrasts with the behaviour of the fourth animal who prances round them and interacts with the audience. This is the clown-like monkey whose unrestrained movements act as a charm for easy delivery and successful matchmaking. He is dressed in red and sports a vivid red monkey mask. The sexual element is provided by the long red padded sash he wears around his waist, which terminates in the shape of a phallus. At times the sash simply keeps his costume in place; at others the phallic end is employed to make sexual gestures including ejaculation. The monkey will also embrace young women in the audience. At the time of the 2012 performance it was raining heavily so the dance was moved indoors, thus allowing the thirty or so spectators a closer physical access to the performance than may have been the case in the shrine courtyard. The monkey's embrace was therefore much facilitated and the sexual gestures made with his belt were that much more noticeable. The children in the audience however, some of whom were invited to stroke the prominent end of his sash, were far more concerned with the traditional practice of the monkey distributing sweets and tangerines at intervals during the performance. It is therefore most unlikely that any of the youngsters appreciated the sexual overtones in the monkey's antics, and the close proximity of

FIGURE 275 *The monkey character at the Koroku Shrine dances while brandishing a bright red phallus made from his belt.*

the monkey to the audience at one point allowed three small boys to grab hold of the other end of the monkey's padded sash and almost cause havoc.[75]

Modern Social Concerns and the Kanamara Festival

The above examples have shown how changes in attitude can influence the contents and activity of well-established or recently revived phallic festivals, although these factors have had much less influence overall on the status of such events than commercialisation or the desire to preserve local culture. Other festivals have been affected by different modern concerns. One is the fear about Japan's declining population, and at least one recently established *matsuri* appears to have risen to the challenge. In 2014 the master of ceremonies at the Hodare Festival provided a constant commentary on the proceedings, and I was assured by local people that his exhortations included a frequent repetition of a phrase translatable as, 'Have more babies! Keep popping them out!'[76]

There is one festival, however, where certain modern concerns have had a unique impact. This chapter will therefore conclude with an examination of the annual Kanamara Festival of the Kanayama Shrine in Kawasaki. A *matsuri* that involved carrying a *mikoshi* through the streets was noted by Nishioka in 1950, but the festival in its present form dates back only to 1977, hence the absence of any reference to it in Itō and Richie's book.[77] The modern Kanamara *matsuri* is therefore an invented tradition with an extraordinary phallic nature. It is also one that has experienced considerable change within its own very short history.

The Kanamara Festival takes place a few weeks after the Tagata Festival and has become almost as well-known. This is partly because of similar internet and guidebook publicity, but its easy accessibility for the population of Tokyo and Yokohama has ensured that huge crowds attend, including a growing preponderance of foreign visitors.[78] The Kanayama Shrine lies within the courtyard of a Hachiman shrine located about one kilometre away from a very

75 From a personal observation made on 28 October 2012. See my video at http://youtu.be/mwQRwMr7nFw. The very informative shrine website is http://japanfestival.web.fc2.com/16-shishi/oohashi/oohashi.html.

76 From a personal observation made on 9 March 2014.

77 Nishioka 1961, p. 238; Masuta 2012, p. 53.

78 A friend who had considered a trip reported in June 2013 that he had been told, 'It's not worth going any more. It has been ruined by foreigners.'

FIGURE 276 *Worshippers bow before the phallus of the Hodare Shrine at its annual festival in 2014.*

important Shingon temple called the Kawasaki Daishi. The shrine is dedicated to Kanayama Hiko and his sister Kanayama Hime, but the festival bears the name Kanamara because of its concentration on the shrine's *goshintai* which is precisely that: a phallus made from iron. In an area once noted for the blacksmithing industry, the story grew that a priest from the shrine had a wife who was unable to conceive. He prayed to the *kami*, who told him to have an iron phallus forged by a local blacksmith. This was done and their prayers were answered. There is another version of the story involving a *vagina dentata*,

FIGURE 277 *A modern votive painting from the Kanayama Shrine in Kawasaki showing a woman cradling a large phallus also appears in other shrines. Here it provides a centrepiece for the phallic offerings at the Danseki Shrine in Ueda (Nagano Prefecture).*

whereby a toothed demon lurked in the vagina of a prostitute until one of her customers substituted an iron phallus for his own member.[79]

The entire shrine complex was rebuilt following its destruction in World War II, and a prominent large iron phallus is now to be found in the courtyard beneath a roofed enclosure. It stands on an anvil and women step over it to ensure conception. All around hang *ema* of a rich feminine imagery that express the desire for a child. The infant Momotarō is shown leaping out of a peach or as a baby snuggled into a shawl within the protective walls of a trunk of green bamboo, while all around are much larger phallic symbols and paintings.[80] These elements have been a feature of the Kanayama Shrine since

79 The story has gained wide currency since being mentioned by Nicholas Bornoff as a 'recently adopted tale' in *Pink Samurai* (1991, p. 150) and is now quoted on every internet blog written by Western visitors to the festival.

80 From personal observations made on 4 November 1993, 1 April 2008, 27 October 2012 and during the festival on 8 April 2008.

FIGURE 278 *Phallic radish-whittling followed by a mock auction of the creations is a feature of the Kanamara Festival.*

its rebuilding and include an erotic picture showing a woman cradling a phallus that has been copied and displayed in many other shrines.

These fine details are best observed at times other than the *matsuri*, when it is the behaviour of the crowd rather than the objects themselves that attract one's attention. Like most *matsuri* the performance transforms its surroundings, and on returning on the festival day in 2008 I found the shrine totally changed from how I had remembered it. The main shrine building was now open. It is octagonal and is built around a blacksmith's forge, where a priest was making an iron phallus in accordance with the foundation legend. To the rear inside the forge was a more conventional Shintō shrine where offerings could be made, and here was a collection of votive phalluses carved out of wood. Because of the confined space and the immense numbers that are attracted to it the event feels far more crowded and restricted than the one at the Tagata Shrine, and the stalls and the levity associated with them fill the courtyard almost to the steps of the shrine. People suck phallic lollipops and in 2008 one man was wearing a huge rubber phallic costume. In the morning one may take part in the carving of giant radishes into phalluses that are sold in a mock auction at the end of the day. Prior to the procession a strong focus of attention is provided by two large wooden phalluses set on frames at an angle

FIGURE 279 *It has long been the custom for young girls to be seated astride a large phallus at the Kanayama Shrine to ensure their future fertility. Nowadays one is more likely to see a Western tourist posing for a photograph.*

of 45 degrees. Young girls may still be placed astride them to pray for their future fertility if their parents are able to get through the crush and are willing to suffer the indignity of a hundred cameras, but most of the people who clamber on to them now are foreign visitors seeking a unique photo opportunity.

Almost needless to say the festival procession is a noisy affair that finds difficulty in threading its way through the tightly packed crowd. Unlike the Tagata Festival the Kanamara procession does not make its way from another shrine back to the host shrine. Instead the *kami* is taken on a circular tour of the neighbourhood. The main emblem for the parade is a large wooden phallus on a wooden boat, but the phallus that attracts all the attention from the crowds and also from the media is a much larger one made from expanded polystyrene and painted a lurid pink. No reference is made to it in Kokonoe's book, so it can be no older that the 1980s. It is carried by a dozen members of a cross-dressing club called the Elizabeth Club who are clearly welcome guests.

FIGURE 280 *During the past few decades a large pink phallus has been carried in procession at the Kanamara Festival by the members of a cross-dressing club. This object inevitably attracts most attention.*

They are dressed in matching pink and display both supreme self-confidence in their proud sexual identity and a tireless enthusiasm.[81]

So what is the Kanamara Festival actually for? Agricultural fertility has become irrelevant in an urban location like Kawasaki where farmers are now even rarer than blacksmiths, and the overall impression is that a sexual-related *ibento* has taken over a traditional *matsuri*. This is certainly how it is understood by foreign visitors, and this impression is greatly strengthened because of the media domination by the Elizabeth Club's pink phallus. The leaflet produced by the shrine at festival time may mention the usual list of benefits such as business prosperity, marriage, marital harmony and conception, but it is now its nature as a sex festival that defines the proceedings. It is as if the erotica within a sexual shrine have displaced the votive phalluses so that sexual pleasure has become the main goal of the celebration. However, in what can only be described as a moment of inspiration the Chief Priest realised that

81 For my videos of the 2008 performance see https://www.youtube.com/watch?v=aOQyMSLRVqE and https://www.youtube.com/watch?v=IbiRE9kNQuk and https://www.youtube.com/watch?v=-gbsgBIntEw and https://www.youtube.com/watch?v=RIg_lDQvyF4.

FIGURE 281 *The* AIDS*-prevention* ema *of the Kanayama Shrine showing five wise monkeys rather than the usual three.*

the popularity of what was rapidly becoming a sex festival might be put to positive use, so the opportunity was taken to spread the message of safer sex and HIV prevention. By 1993 the shrine was handing out souvenirs in the form of a plastic baseball cap on a key ring. Inside the cap was a condom. This was complemented by an *ema* bearing the familiar figure of the three wise monkeys, here joined by two more whose hands cover their genital areas, advising the worshipper to 'transmit no evil' and 'receive no evil' in a sexual sense.[82] The shrine's hand-out from 2008 put it very simply. The *matsuri* is now 'a festival of AIDS prevention' in addition to any previous significance it may have had.

The Kanamara Festival therefore has a unique identity among Japan's sexual *matsuri*, but in spite of all the invented elements there is still a firm link to the shrine and the beliefs that sustain it. In this way the Kanamara Festival shows a very positive example of dynamism within Shintō. It may be argued that Shintō has always been ready to transform itself in response to changing needs in society, but the changes wrought by the Kanamara Festival are

82 Reader, Ian and Tanabe, George J. 1998. *Practically Religious: Worldly Benefits and the Common Religion of Japan* (Honolulu), p. 57 and from a personal observation made on 4 November 1993.

quite profound. First, through its transformation into a largely secular *ibento* the Kanamara Festival has become what Tagata is popularly thought to be: a celebration not of agricultural or even human fertility but of human sexuality. This is best demonstrated by Kanamara's new role in HIV prevention, because the traditional emphasis on human fertility has been turned completely on its head. Patient queues of worshippers still pay their traditional respects at the shrine during the festival, but otherwise the focus is very much on non-procreative sex, not conception.

The Kanamara festival has also moved with the times in a very different sense, because the festival's alternative aim of safer sex and avoiding HIV. is not presented as the result of petitioning a *kami*. Instead the responsibility has been placed in human hands. One might therefore reasonably conclude that this aspect of the event is directed more at those who do not believe that at those who do. The final observation concerns the Elizabeth Club, whose pink phallus takes all the attention away from the shrine's *mikoshi*. As its bearers dance and chant in honour of the phallus their audience might be forgiven for perceiving the existence of what was earlier ruled out for the cult of Konsei Daimyōjin: the worship of the male sexual organ in a literal sense.

FIGURE 282 *As the day ends at the Kanayama Shrine's Kanamara Festival a rubber phallus costume is taken away.*

In conclusion, the phallic *matsuri* is a very important element in contemporary Japanese sexual beliefs. It provides a vehicle whereby the shrine may be accessed by a large audience who receive ritual benefits through their attendance while the shrine receives from them their support and donations. Yet few festivals have remained static. All have had to cope in their own ways with the pressures of commercialisation, changing social attitudes and modern worries, and to maintain a precise continuity when the surrounding environment is now so different is an option available to very few. Seen like this, the revival or even the invention of phallic festivals is fully understandable as a valid response to questions regarding the status of the shrines in the modern age. Just as in Hobsbawn and Ranger's theoretical model, all of Japan's invented phallic festivals have some genuine link to their surrounding religious environment, and by appropriating that history they have added to it in a very positive way. The Hodare *matsuri* may be only thirty-five years old, but the daily devotion offered for centuries to the Hodare Shrine is greatly enhanced on the second Sunday of every March. It does not matter whether or not the idea of employing a large wooden phallus was derived from ancient practice or through a copy of the Tagata Shrine Festival, it can still be a valid means of expression. So phalluses are carried, ridden or stroked throughout Japan for a wide range of possible motivations both sacred and secular. Yet some form of balance is always necessary lest the vital social aspect of a festival overwhelms the equally crucial religious element to become, in Averbuch's well-chosen words, 'a *matsuri* without *kami*'.

There is one further observation to be made concerning the balance between human and agricultural fertility. The well-established phallic festivals such as the Tenteko *matsuri* and the Tagata Hōnen-sai still retain their links with agriculture through an emphasis on the fertility of the fields. Revived festivals such as the one at the Tsurumi Shrine go through the motions of praying for a good harvest even when the fields have disappeared, but in the case of the invented festivals the emphasis seems to have shifted towards human fertility. This suggests very strongly that their origins lie in the imagination of people who have long been separated from the land. So the Shineri Benten Tataki Jizō *matsuri* celebrates the fertility of the young couples of the town rather than the fertility of the fields. Their giant wheeled phallus penetrates the straw kteis as a symbol of human sexual intercourse, but the phallus is not a gift to a benevolent *kami* of the harvest, nor is its symbolism intended to impregnate the fields through sympathetic magic. Both the symbolism and its intentions stop at human procreation.

The Kanamara Festival is different again. A shrine destroyed by fire-bombing in 1945 has been rebuilt, restoring an ancient phallic tradition and adding a sex festival that extends the remit of the enshrined gods in a contemporary way. Not only has agricultural fertility been abandoned at the Kanayama Shrine, so (almost) has human fertility through the festival's emphasis on protected and non-procreative recreational sex, a break in continuity that the huge pink phallus of the Elizabeth Club symbolises so perfectly. The Tagata Festival may have changed because of concerns over crowd safety, but its goals are still what they have always been. The inspired invented tradition currently being enjoyed at the Kanayama Shrine shows that Japanese religion has come to terms with a new reality and a new challenge, and once again the vivid symbolism of the phallus has been enlisted to help, just as it has in so many ways over so many years.

FIGURE 283 *A discarded phallic lollipop lies among the litter at the conclusion of the Kanamara Festival at the Kanayama Shrine in Kawasaki.*

CHAPTER 12

Sexual Beliefs in Contemporary Japan

In 1895 W.E. Griffis commented on Japanese phallic shrines in the words, 'some are already matters of memory or archaeology, and their very existence even in former days is nearly or wholly incredible to the generation born since 1868 … [who have] scarcely suspected the universality of phallic worship'.[1] The preceding pages have shown how wrong that statement was and how wrong it still is. Far from being matters of memory, the sexual gods and their shrines are an extensive if poorly recognised phenomenon within contemporary Japanese religious belief, and their phalluses are still powerful religious symbols explained by foundation myths and dramatised in votive rituals. They provide a mystic explanation for life's most fundamental activity and supply a means of influencing it. Through the sexual objects the enshrined gods that they represent and satisfy become knowable and open to manipulation through the processes of service and prayer. By these means sexual beliefs are integrated into a coherent system of understanding and behaviour.

Many other aspects of Japan's sexual gods remain to be investigated at a social, political and psychological level, so I trust that this research will prove useful to future researchers skilled in those fields. These pages have nevertheless led to a number of preliminary conclusions which I have grouped together according to the useful comments by Clifford Geertz in his 1973 collection of essays *The Interpretation of Cultures*:

Religious symbols, dramatized in rituals or related in myths, are felt somehow to sum up, for those for whom they are resonant, what is known about the way the world is, the quality of the emotional life it supports, and the way one ought to behave when in it.[2]

Following his notion of 'what is known about the way the world is', my first four conclusions are these:

1. Within Japanese religion there are a number of deities who may with complete justification be referred to as sexual gods.

This study has shown that among the thousands of deities enshrined and worshipped in Japan today there are certain ones who specialise in procreation

1 Griffis 1895, pp. 27–28.

2 Geertz, Clifford 1973. *The Interpretation of Cultures* (New York), p. 127.

 | DOI 10.1163/9789004293786_013

FIGURE 284 *A phallus adds to the sexual ambience of the garden of the Ohana Daigongen.*

and protection. Their shrines and temples are characterised by the presence of phallic and ktenic symbols, some of which may be of a highly abstract design. Although they exist primarily in the pantheon of Shintō the *seishin* are also to be found within Yin-Yang beliefs and in Buddhism, and several of them came to Japan from continental East Asia. Some of the most notable sexual *kami* are named in ancient Shintō mythology. Others were once human beings, while some take their identities from a naturally occurring feature such as a phallic-shaped rock. The sexual gods can influence the fertility of rice fields and of humans, and may also exercise a powerful protective presence. Those who specialise in conception and sexual health form an important sub-set of the *kami* who have traditional roles in healing and medical matters.

2. The number of sexual shrines is much greater than was previously believed.

This is one of the most interesting findings of the present study. The popular perception of the Tagata Shrine is that it is almost the sole survivor of an ancient tradition, but there are in fact many other places like it. Nishioka had already identified 642 locations before the year 1950 by using old written records. The

2006 website started by a group of enthusiasts doubled Nishioka's number by adding the names of sites that had never been recorded outside their immediate vicinity, and in 2012 the website of Miyagi Prefectural Museum demonstrated that the number of shrines within that one prefecture was ten times the 2006 number. Masuta Kimiyasu is also currently identifying many previously unknown shrines in Aomori, so that as of the beginning of 2015 about 2,000 sites are known to have been recorded somewhere. There appears to be a greater concentration in northern Japan compared with southern Japan, but this may simply be due to under-reporting in areas where little research has been done and further investigation is clearly needed. The true figure is therefore likely to be much higher than 2,000, but one thing that can be said for certain is that the vast majority of sexual shrines are still little known beyond their immediate locality, leaving the more sensational variety at the Tagata and Kanayama Shrines to divert all the attention away from them. So successful has this been that their existence is popularly regarded as proof that almost everything else has disappeared, which of course has had the advantage of leaving vulnerable sites undisturbed.

FIGURE 285 *Phalluses are offered to the trio of Kunado and the two crossroads gods at the Sai no kami Shrine in Ugo-Nakazato (Akita Prefecture).*

3. The cult of Konsei Daimyōjin represents the nearest thing to phallic or genital worship that exists in Japan.

The expression 'phallic worship' is often found in the general literature on sexual beliefs around the world, and there is a popular perception that Japanese religion involves the worship of male and female genitalia. The present study has shown that the reality of the situation is that worship activity is directed towards gods who are represented by these objects rather than the physical organs themselves, and only the cult of Konsei Daimyōjin comes close to phallic worship in a literal sense. This is because as the *kami* of the penis Konsei Daimyōjin enjoys a unique iconic status. Konsei Daimyōjin is therefore the most sexual of all the sexual gods, yet there is still a distinction to be made between the worship of the phallus and the worship of the divine entity it represents. Indeed, the apparent worship of the penis as symbolised by the Elizabeth Club's phallus at the Kanamara Festival demonstrates how far that event has strayed from traditional religious beliefs.

4. The inclusion of ktenic imagery alongside the phallic is an important feature in Japanese sexual beliefs.

The role of ktenic imagery in sexual beliefs has long been a neglected topic that is usually subsumed under the general heading of Japanese phallicism, and the present study has shown that there are a large number of important ktenic images in shrines and temples. They may represent individual female *kami* or be included as one half of an *in'yōseki*. In shrines that use ktenic imagery as their central feature phallic symbols play a subservient role to the ktenic *goshintai*, while shrines employing *in'yōseki* give the ktenic element equal billing through their symbolism of sexual harmony. There is also a difference in the protective role exercised by ktenic images because they never stand alone. The vast majority of ktenic images are of natural occurrence, although a few are carved from wood and one or two from stone. The female sexual *kami* whom they represent form a distinct and significant group with powers that are the equivalent of those of any male deity, so that the devotion they receive and the number of their ktenic images fully justify the employment of the term 'sexual beliefs' instead of phallicism. The only occasions where the word phallicism is to be preferred are the highly phallic cult of Konsei Daimyōjin and certain festivals.

Three further conclusions arise from a consideration of Geertz's 'quality of the emotional life it supports':

FIGURE 286 *The Takatsu Shrine in Ōsaka has this complex stone arrangement. On the two sides may be seen a ktenic and phallic stone, each marked by a small* torii.

5. The phallic and ktenic objects found within the shrines have clearly defined functions.

Apart from the items of popular erotica left as mementoes by visitors, the phallic and ktenic objects found within shrines or at the roadside are never purely decorative. They have specific functions that may be classified as either devotional, votive or protective. The devotional role is one of providing a symbolic representation for the enshrined gods. This can take the form of a *goshintai* within a shrine or a prominent symbol standing outside it. Alternatively the act of devotion may be directed towards the abstract principle of *in'yōwagō* as indicated by a paired phallus and kteis or a carving of a human couple. The gods thus represented respond to prayers and votive offerings and exercise a mystical effect on fertility. In the case of agricultural fertility a carved image of human copulation acts on the fields through the process of sympathetic magic, but because of the imagery thereby employed some of these sites have become associated with human fertility and sexual needs as well. Otherwise human fertility is normally dealt with inside a shrine where the sexual god responds to the erotic gift of a phallus.

The sexual gods' protective role enlists the reassuring and intimidatory powers of the phallus against unwanted entities. A village may place a simple phallus at a crossroads or by the wayside. Alternatively, an elaborate symbol of the god may be woven from straw on an annual basis to stand guard against disasters. In such ways a balance is achieved between the three functions because the protection provided by the represented god indirectly brings about an increase in fertility. As to the balance between human and agricultural fertility expressed by these devotions, neither excludes the other but there is some observable degree of specialisation. The primary focus of the *dōsojin* and *ta no kami* is the fertility of the adjacent fields, even though they use images of human fertility to do so. The traditional phallic festival is of similar intent because a large phallus, the ultimate human sexual image, is used as a symbolic offering to a *kami* to ensure a good harvest. Inside the shrines, however, the emphasis is different. Votive phalluses are not offered to the *kami* for the needs of farmers. The intention there is human fertility or sexual-related human health issues, so a certain division of labour may be identified for Japan's sexual gods.

6. It is difficult to establish continuity between modern practices and ancient ones beyond the Tokugawa Period, although some aspects of sexual beliefs may represent the survival of very old religious practices.

This study has added a note of caution to any rush to draw conclusions about past practices based only on observations of today's shrines, and the further one goes back in time the more difficult it becomes to establish continuity. Beliefs in gods of procreation and protection may well reveal the survival of ancient beliefs that the arrival of the new gods written about in the *Kojiki* did not entirely supplant, but there are two difficulties involved in drawing that conclusion. The first is the obvious lack of written records to indicate the intentions that lay behind the creation of ancient objects that are unquestionably phallic to uncritical modern eyes. The *sekibō* may invite speculation about their use during the Jōmon Period, yet all that can be said for certain is that when they were rediscovered many centuries later some were taken to be a gift from, if not the actual organ of a very special sexual god. They were enshrined as *goshintai* and received identical treatment to that given to stones of a naturally occurring phallic or ktenic shape. Inferences of a similar kind are involved if modern hunters' initiation rites of sexual exposure to Yama no kami are cited as proof that their ancestors carried out similar rituals.

The second difficulty is provided by the huge gaps in the phallic 'fossil record'. The making of *sekibō* ceases with the end of the Jōmon Period, and

FIGURE 287 *The tiny Omara-sama Shrine in Mukabaki (Hiroshima Prefecture) has these unusual phallic endings to its roof beams.*

even though the Kofun Period provides one example of a phallic *haniwa*, once again the intention behind it can only be inferred. The *Kojiki* and *Nihongi* may tantalise their readers with the tempting phallic imagery of the jewelled spear of heaven, scarcely disguised acts of sexual intercourse and the creation of the blocking deities, but none of the symbolism is ever overt. At some later stage Sarutahiko and Ame no Uzume become guardian gods, but their roles in human and agricultural fertility only develop when they are transformed into male and female archetypes.

By the time of the *Kogoshūi* in 807 the use of an unambiguous phallic symbol in a votive role has become an established practice, and from then onwards various sexual gods are identified, enshrined and celebrated. The Niike Hachiman Shrine was founded in 859, although it is not known for certain if the phallic *daikon* now used in its festival were involved as early as that date. *Sai no kami* and *dōsojin* are accepted as established phenomena in a dictionary of 934. The *Fusō Ryakki* of the mid-twelfth century describes wooden wayside gods with sexual organs, and the Konsei Daimyōjin in the Bannaji at Ashikaga may be reliably linked to events occurring around the year 1200. The foundation legend of 1551 for the Mara Kannon at Tawarayama Onsen is fully believable, and by 1776 Konsei Daimyōjin is sufficiently well-known for his symbolic phallus to be included in an erotic book. Yet because of the rural obscurity of most sexual shrines it is only with the repression of the Tokugawa Period and a few travellers' tales that anything is known of their existence until comparatively modern times. Some changes of names and contents certainly took place during the Meiji Period, and the exuberant sexual displays seen in some places today may indicate a return to a time before this repression. Otherwise they may simply reflect modern attitudes towards sexual depiction. This applies to restored shrines, new wayside images and the choreography of some festivals. For example, wayside images showing a phallus enveloping a human couple owe nothing to notions of disguise because they emphasise the phallus rather than concealing it. Such manifestations of sexual beliefs must therefore be regarded as contemporary phenomena, although some link to a long tradition can usually be inferred.

7. The phallic festival is an active tradition but one that has been subject to considerable change. Some festivals are revivals of old ones while others are recent inventions.

Sexual beliefs exist in an atmosphere of change within Japanese society, and nowhere is their dynamic nature demonstrated more clearly that in the development and revival of the phallic *matsuri*. The revelation that some apparently ancient fertility rituals are in fact modern 'inventions of tradition' has been a surprising discovery. Other changes have arisen out of modern social concerns and shifting public attitudes regarding public safety, respect for female privacy and the effect on children, but the most important developments have come about either from a desire to preserve local culture or as a result of blatant commercialisation. The Kanamara Festival represents the most extreme example of the trend towards an *ibento* in the context of Japan's sexual gods. The message of its festival stresses human rather than divine endeavour and celebrates non-procreative sex, but it is still expressed in the environment of a Shintō shrine. The Sekibō *matsuri* of Fuchū is revealing in a different way, showing how the discovery of a *sekibō* in the twenty-first century may fail to provoke religious awe, but that it is through a quasi-religious event that it is celebrated. Just as is the case with the new wayside images, a modern phenomenon still has links to traditional practices.

Finally, in terms of 'the way one ought to behave':

8. The sexual shrines confirm that in Japan there is a traditional acceptance of the display of sexual symbolism that is historically absent from Western society.

The study supports this popular view, but with some qualifications. As for Western attitudes, the British Museum's *shunga* exhibition may have broken

FIGURE 288
The proprietor of the shop located next to the Usu-sama Myōō-dō near Shūzenji (Shizuoka Prefecture) not only sells votive phalluses and ktenes, he carves them too, and is shown here with two of his unambiguous creations.

new ground in terms of what people in the United Kingdom are allowed to see, but it is still hard to imagine the Tagata Festival being re-enacted on the streets of London! Similarly, the Brading exhibition revealed to the public that sexual imagery was present in a religious context in the ancient world, but it also illustrated how completely the practices then disappeared. As for Japan, apart from sporadic periods of repression a long tradition of the acceptability of sexual display can be traced, with many similarities and sometimes even links between the sacred and secular spheres. In spite of official condemnation in the Tokugawa and Meiji Periods the sacred phalluses and the secular *shunga* both survived, although various strategies had to be adopted if their traditions were to continue. The censorship of *shunga* was paralleled by the censorship of wayside phalluses that were turned into images of Jizō, but in distant rural areas the prohibitions on sexual shrines were simply ignored. At the same time those in sympathy with the phallic tradition saw it as a positive trait in Japanese society that reflected well on supposedly indigenous beliefs and badly on dull, alien Buddhism. To people of that persuasion the preservation of something ancient was far more important than any need to appear modern to satisfy Western entrepreneurs.

A different train of thought during the Tokugawa Period regarded religious figures and sacred themes as fair game for erotica, but even then there were taboos involving location and behaviour, and similar concerns may still be identified today. Changing tastes too, as shown by the decline in *hihōkan* and the rise in internet pornography, have also had an effect on how sexual imagery is perceived in contemporary Japanese society. The situation today is that in the West museum displays of Japanese *shunga* are now acceptable, although works by Western artists depicting phalluses or ktenes might still be taboo under certain circumstances. In Japan, where large phalluses protect roadside service areas, the situation is largely reversed because the Japanese problem

FIGURE 289 *The interior of the small sex museum at the Takashiba Deco Yashiki, an art and craft village near Kōriyama (Fukushima Prefecture). Like a mini-hihōkan, it packs into a small space two animated illustrations (one of which is of Marilyn Monroe), museum displays of sexual objects, a huge kteis made from a tree trunk, large carved phalluses and a souvenir dispenser.*

has long been concerned with what can be displayed behind the closed doors of public institutions. The *shunga* exhibition planned for Autumn 2015 at the Eisei Bunko Museum in Tokyo will be an interesting event to observe.[3]

Yet even within the wider religious context a certain reticence still remains about about including some well-established sexual shrines in publicity materials. The large phallus of the Yaegaki Shrine in Matsue is the first thing a visitor sees on passing through the *torii*, yet it is not mentioned in the Japanese-language leaflets encouraging people to come and pray for sexual-related needs. That situation echoes the prejudices of the Meiji reformers against any folk religious element that would distract from the worship of a shrine's official *kami*. The omission of the sexual shrine of Jūmonji from the town's map may reflect the other great Meiji obsession. This was the desire to be seen as rational, modern and in tune with Western sensibilities rather than supporting traditional Japanese feelings about sexual display. Such a viewpoint clearly persists in some areas.

9. Most sexual shrines are regarded as valuable local cultural assets and are carefully maintained even if the beliefs lying behind them may be in decline. At some places the tradition still has considerable vigour.

Japan's sexual shrines appear to be well cared-for and appreciated. Very few places visited in this study could be described as neglected, although a refurbished sexual shrine with a gleaming new roof may indicate no more than the preservation of an important local cultural property. There have been a few reports of vandalism and theft, but on the whole maintenance has continued as long as there is a local community to carry it out. As for the sincerity of the beliefs that lie behind them, the larger shrines such as the Mara Kannon in Tawarayama Onsen appear to be thriving as indicated by the sheer number of donated phalluses that continue to be presented and the comments written on *ema* and in the visitors' books. This may indicate an absence of the trend seen elsewhere of the growing secularisation of Japanese society, although other factors make it difficult to draw firm conclusions. The liveliness of a phallic festival must also not be taken as proof that its participants are necessarily expressing deep-seated religious feelings. Nevertheless the continued devotion

3 The enormous ktenic sculpture that stands outside the Tübingen University Institute of Microbiology seems to have attracted little publicity over a period of thirteen years until a student got stuck inside it! See http://jezebel.com/american-student-gets-stuck-in-13-foot-marble-vagina-1594718294 (Accessed 18 October 2014).

FIGURE 290 *The Anaba Shrine on the island of Ōmishima includes this open-sided shrine for the offering of votive phalluses. It is carefully maintained and free from vandalism.*

FIGURE 291 *Raseki Daimyōjin, the phallus in the courtyard of the Suwa Shrine in Kashiwazaki (Niigata Prefecture).*

to Konsei Daimyōjin, the comments on *ema* to find a mate, the entries in visitors' books and the piles of recently donated phalluses in many shrines indicate that belief in the powers of Japan's sexual gods is a living tradition.

10. Sexual beliefs show the breadth and dynamic nature of Shintō.

This final conclusion is an important one, because the worship activity associated with Japan's sexual gods confirms that the embrace of Shintō is far wider than the narrow focus once envisaged by the Meiji reformers who strove to eliminate folk religious elements along with Buddhism. As John Breen and Mark Teeuwen write in *Shintō in History: Ways of the Kami*, a multiplicity of 'Ways of the Kami' is an approach that promises 'to open our eyes to aspects of kami cults and Shintō traditions that have previously been ignored'. I believe that the 'kami cult' of the sexual gods and their shrines provides an excellent example that supports this point of view, because they have 'grown out of different historical circumstances, and each with its own ritual and theological agenda'.[4]

The ancient beliefs that first associated phallic objects with the goal of fertility must have arisen from the making of some mystical connection that transcended the physical world. The precise link was between what was required for agricultural fertility and the image of the organ that was known to be essential for the similar process within the human sphere. In the specific case of the development of the Konsei Daimyōjin cult a *kami* simply had to be involved in that wondrous process, and the discovery of strange phallic stones seemed to confirm his mystical presence. Even the *Kojiki* and the *Nihongi* hint at an ancient origin for their stories of copulation and fruitfulness, because the new gods who descend from heaven do not completely supplant the old ones. Instead heaven and earth are joined in the persons of Sarutahiko and his wife, who go on to become powerful gods of fertility and protection. The traditions of Japan's sexual gods therefore demonstrate that Shintō has a dynamic nature that is not always appreciated, and this dynamism is by no means a modern phenomenon. It can be observed in the ancient transformation of Sarutahiko and Ame no Uzume and the introduction and absorption of new gods from the East Asian continent. Sexual beliefs are therefore not just pre-modern cults that entered a period of change only with the onset of modernity, but a dynamic system that has always been open to change.

4 Breen, John and Teeuwen, Mark 2000. *Shintō in History: Ways of the Kami* (Richmond), p. 8.

FIGURE 292 *A small wayside arrangement of phalluses called Oshanguri-sama at the village of Kuroya in Saitama Prefecture, typical of the continued care devoted to such places.*

In his 1907 study of Japanese sexual behaviour the idealistic Krauss identified a primitive innocence about it all, and this attitude was embraced by those Japanese who liked to contrast exuberant Shintō with the dourness of imported Buddhism. Yet the expression of sexual beliefs has never been simply one of unbridled primitive sexual joy. As the preceding pages have shown, the rituals surrounding the sexual gods reveal a considerable element of anxiety about the hazardous processes of growing food and producing children. The gods are enlisted to help, but the *kami* to whom phalluses are offered are not completely benevolent by nature. They can behave capriciously and may have to be placated. If they are offended they will punish in return so, far from simply affirming a plain and happy love of life, a votive phallus reveals a fear that goes far beyond pre-modern concerns about the physical processes of conception and childbirth. In a similar manner a seemingly joyous phallic festival is not merely a time when, in the words of Ian Reader, 'the troubles of the everyday are set aside'.[5] It is also an opportunity for the worries of the day to be addressed by

5 Reader 1991, p. 70.

FIGURE 293 *A solitary phallic stone marks the path up towards the Yakushi-dō at Utsukushigahara Onsen (Nagano Prefecture).*

the community as a whole through the invocation and if necessary the placation of the divine entity.

The situation in which the sexual shrines find themselves today involves a lessening of that anxiety. Just as modern medical and agricultural science reduces fears over the processes of human and agricultural fertility, so too does the modern age lose its fear of the gods through a growing secularisation. In a recent article Reader presents evidence of this development through the decline in pilgrimages and the lack of use of *butsudan* 仏壇 (Buddhist altars) and *kamidana* (Shintō god-shelves) in the home.[6] Other scholars regard Japan as bucking the trend, and the vigour apparent in the field of sexual beliefs seems to support that point of view.[7] This topic is of course closely linked to the effects of the shift from an agricultural to an industrial society, and there was once a time when the maintenance of a shrine and the performance of its *matsuri* would have been regarded as essential to the fertility of the adjacent rice crop. Nowadays rituals to increase the fertility of the fields are performed where there are no longer any fields and no longer any fear.

---

6 Reader, Ian 2012. "Secularisation, R.I.P.? Nonsense! The 'Rush Hour Away from the Gods' and the Decline of Religion in Contemporary Japan" *Journal of Religion in Japan* 1, pp. 7–36.

7 E.g. Stark, Rodney 1999. 'Secularization, R.I.P.' *Sociology of Religion* Vol. 60, pp. 249–273.

The sexual gods also suggest a wider remit for Shintō in human life than is commonly accepted. There is a popular saying that the Japanese are born Shintō and die Buddhist, and in their procreative role the sexual gods stand most splendidly for the creation and continuity of life. Yet they also have a very important protective role, and on occasions this extends even to protection from death, or at the very least from its effects on those still living. This is illustrated by the story about the farmer in Tōno who was annoyed at the presence of a *sekibō* on his land and decided to remove it. Human bones were discovered and, fearing that he would be cursed, the farmer left the *sekibō* undisturbed. All of Geertz's points are illustrated there. The *sekibō* is resonant with meaning for the local people because its phallic shape helps explain the world around them and supports their quality of life by being a unique source of divine healing. No one knows about the presence of the grave until the farmer tries to remove the *sekibō*. This exposes a further layer of meaning, and the farmer's reaction of ceasing the desecration exposes unwritten rules about how one ought to behave towards such a powerful manifestation of divine power. The farmer feared a curse if he disturbed the ritual tranquillity of the site, just as his neighbours would have feared the consequences if the *sekibō*'s healing properties had ceased.

Satō concluded from different sources that during the Jōmon Period *sekibō* were placed as guardians on the boundary between the worlds of the living and the dead.[8] The Tōno *sekibō* therefore had a protective function that was even more tremendous than the role performed by an image guarding a crossroads against evil spirits. The graveside phallus was standing guard against death itself, just as Izanagi's boulder had blocked the exit from the underworld. As Itō writes, 'The erect penis ... affirms life and denies death'.[9] It represents the continual creation of life over successive generations, showing that death may have claimed the victims whose bones lay all around, but life in its uninterrupted and unconquerable flow goes on. Along with the equally important but often neglected kteis, the phallus provides the most potent symbol for Japan's sexual gods by representing them in a form that expresses the eternally regenerative power of life itself.

8 Satō 1995, pp. 11 & 79.

9 Itō and Richie 1967, p. 51.

FIGURE 294 *It may be a complete coincidence, but a stone that has the shape of a phallus, the ultimate symbol of life, marks the entrance to the graveyard which lies below Yokote Castle in Akita Prefecture. The graves are of the men killed defending Yokote during the Boshin War of 1868.*

Glossary of Technical Terms

butsudan	仏壇	Buddhist altars found in the home.
daikon	大根	The giant radish, often carved into a phallic symbol.
dankei	男茎	The word for phallus in its first mention in the *Kogoshūi.*
dankon	男根	A penis or phallus.
dogū	土偶	Ceramic figurines from the Jōmon Period.
dōsojin	道祖神	Guardian gods placed at the wayside or by rice fields.
ema	絵馬	Small painted wooden prayer boards left at shrines.
engidana	縁起棚	A smaller version of the *kamidana.*
engimono	縁起物	Objects placed on an *engidana.*
gohei	御幣	The ritual 'wand' used by Shintō priests.
gongen	権現	An avatar.
goshintai	御神体	The 'body of the god' that is the central focus of a shrine.
haiden	拝殿	The worship hall of a shrine that accommodates believers.
haniwa	はにわ	Clay images from burial mounds.
hibutsu	秘仏	'Hidden Buddhas': concealed religious images.
hihōkan	秘宝館	An elaborate and commercialised version of a sex museum.
hokora	祠	A small Shintō shrine, often a sub-shrine of another.
honden	本殿	The main building of a Shintō shrine.
inau	イナウ	The worship sticks of the Ainu akin to a *gohei.*
inkei	陰茎	The penis.
in'yōseki	陰陽石	Paired male and female sexual stones of yin and yang.
in'yōwagō	陰陽和合	The harmonious union of yin and yang.
ishigami	石神	A general term for a god represented in stone.
jingu	神宮	A prestigious shrine, often with imperial connections.
jinja	神社	A Shintō shrine.
join	女陰	Female genitalia.
kami	神	The deities of Shintō.
kamidana	神棚	A household god-shelf.
kofun	古墳	Burial mounds c. 300–500.
kongō	金剛	The *vajra*, a hand-held ritual implement.
kōshin	庚申	The 57th position on the Chinese calendar.
kōshin-tō	庚申塔	A monument erected as result of *kōshin* beliefs.
kyokon	巨根	An abnormally large penis.
mara	魔羅	The penis.
matagi	マタギ	The traditional hunting communities of Tōhoku.
matsuri	祭り	A shrine festival.

 | DOI 10.1163/9789004293786_014

michi no kami 道の神 Gods of the wayside.

mikoshi 御輿 The palanquin in which the *kami* is conveyed at a *matsuri*.

mitama 御霊 The spirit of a *kami*.

miya 宮 A Shintō shrine.

mizuko 水子 Aborted foetuses.

ofuda お札 A talismanic souvenir traditionally of printed paper.

okina 翁 A masked figure representing an old man.

omamori お守り Small brocade bags acting as talismanic souvenirs.

onsen 温泉 Hot spring resort.

robō no kami 路傍の神 Gods of the wayside.

sai no kami 塞の神 Blocking or guardian deities.

sai no kami 幸の神 Gods of good fortune, happiness or harvest yield.

seishin 性神 Sexual gods.

sekibō 石棒 Stone rods or bars from the Jōmon Period of a phallic shape.

sekitō 石刀 Single-edged stone sword-like versions of *sekibō*.

sekkan 石冠 Stone 'crowns', prehistoric phallic and ktenic carvings.

sekken 石剣 Stone sword-like versions of *sekibō*.

shinbutsu bunri 神仏分離 The separation of *kami* and Buddhas.

shinbutsu shūgō 神仏習合 The cooperation between kami and Buddhas.

shintai 神体 See *goshintai*.

Shintō 神道 'The way of the gods', regarded as Japan's indigenous religion.

shunga 春画 Erotic pictures and books.

sōtei dōsojin 双体道祖神 Human couple *dōsojin*, the most common variety.

tanuki 狸 The symbolic badger, actually a raccoon dog.

tengu 天狗 A goblin of the forest.

torii 鳥居 A Shintō shrine gateway.

warai-e 笑い絵 Laughter pictures, another word for *shunga*.

yashiro 社 A Shintō shrine.

yorishiro 依代 A residence for a *kami*.

zushi 厨子 A small shrine made to contain a *hibutsu*.

FIGURE 295 *One of the phalluses referred to as Omara-sama at the small roadside Akiyama Mitake Shrine in Saitama Prefecture.*

FIGURE 296 *An example of the 'mated' phallic and ktenic sticks made as part of the Yama no kami rituals in Shiga prefecture. This display with typical offerings is in the Rittō City History and Folk Museum.*

Bibliography

Abe, Michiyoshi 1963. *Kyūshū sei sūhai shiryō* (Ōita).

Anonymous 1965. 'Kagerō ni kudaru sei no kamigami' *Rekishi Dokuhon* (May 1965) pp. 184–189.

——— 1982. 'Konsei-sama' *Akita-ken Doku Shinpō* (13 July 1982) p. 8.

Ashida, Eiichi 1963. *Dōso no kamigami* (Tokyo).

Ashida, Tetsurō 1994. 'The Festival and Religion Boom: Irony of the "Age of the Heart"' in Inoue, Nobutaka (ed.) and Havens, Norman (trans.) *Folk Beliefs in Modern Japan* (Tokyo) pp. 175–197.

Ashkenazi, Michael 1993. *Festivals of a Japanese Town* (Honolulu).

Aston, W.G. 1972. *Nihongi: Chronicles of Japan from the Earliest Times to AD 697* (Volume I and II) (Reprint) (Vermont).

——— 1974. *Shintō the Way of the Gods* (Reprint) (New York).

Averbuch, Irit 2011 'Discourses of the Reappearing: The Re-enactment of the "Cloth-Bridge Consecration Rite" at Mt. Tateyama' *Japanese Journal of Religious Studies* 38, pp. 1–54.

Azumino Tourist Association (no date) *Dōsojin ga michi-annai* (Azumino).

Bender, Ross 1979. 'The Hachiman Cult and the Dōkyō Incident' *Monumenta Nipponica* 34, pp. 125–153.

Blacker, Carmen 1975. *The Catalpa Bow: A Study of Shamanistic Practices in Japan* (London).

——— 1996. 'The Mistress of Animals in Japan: Yamanokami' in Billington, Sandra and Green, Miranda (eds.) *The Concept of the Goddess* (London) pp. 178–185.

Bornoff, Nicholas 2001. *Pink Samurai: An Erotic Exploration of Japanese Society* (London).

Breen, John and Teeuwen, Mark 2000. *Shintō in History: Ways of the Kami* (Richmond).

Britton, Dorothy 1980 *A Haiku Journey: Bashō's Narrow Road to a Far Province* (Tokyo).

Buchanan D.C. 1935. 'Inari, its Origins, Development and Nature' *Transactions of the Asiatic Society of Japan* 2nd Series XII, pp. 1–191.

Buckley, Edmund 1895. *Phallicism in Japan* (Chicago).

Buruma, Ian 2013. 'The joy of art' *The Guardian Saturday Review* 28 September 2013 p. 18.

Casal, U.A. 1950. 'Ramblings in Chinese and Japanese Lore: O-Tafuku' *Ethnos* 1–12 (1950) pp. 33–45.

——— 1965. 'Der Phalluskult im Alten Japan' reprinted in Casal, U.A. *Articles on Japanese Folklore 1956–65* pp. 72–94.

Chamberlain, Basil Hall 1893. *A Handbook for Travellers in Japan* Third Edition (London).

Clark, Timothy; Gerstle, C. Andrew; Ishigami, Aki and Yano, Akiko (eds.) 2013. *Shunga: Sex and Pleasure in Japanese Art* (London).

Clark, Timothy; Gerstle, C. Andrew 2013. 'What Was Shunga?' in Clark, Timothy; Gerstle, C. Andrew; Ishigami, Aki and Yano, Akiko (eds.) *Shunga: Sex and Pleasure in Japanese Art* (London, 2013) pp. 18–33.

Clarke, John R. 2014. 'Sexuality and Visual Representation' in Hubbard, Thomas K. (ed.) *A Companion to Greek and Roman Sexualities* (Oxford) pp. 509–532.

Cocks, Richard 1883. *Diary of Richard Cocks; Cape Merchant in the English Factory in Japan 1615–1622 with correspondence* (London).

——— 1979. *Diary of Richard Cocks 1615–1622 Volume II January 1, 1617–January 14, 1619* (Tokyo).

Collcutt, Martin 1986. 'Buddhism: The Threat of Eradication' in Jansen, Marius B. and Rozman, Gilbert *Japan in Transition: From Tokugawa to Meiji* (Princeton NJ, 1986) pp. 143–167.

Coomaraswamy, Ananda K. 1935. 'Angel and Titan: An Essay in Vedic Ontology' *Journal of the American Oriental Society* 55, pp. 373–419.

Courtright, Paul B. 1985. *Ganesa: Lord of Obstacles, Lord of Beginnings* (Oxford).

Czaja, Michael 1974. *Gods of Myth and Stone: Phallicism in Japanese folk religion* (New York).

Deguchi, Yonekichi 1919. *Nihon ni okeru seishokki sūhai* (Tokyo).

——— 1920. *Nihon seishokki sūhai ryakusetsu* (Tokyo).

Earhart, H. Byron 1970. *A Religious Study of the Mount Hagurō Sect of Shugendō: An Example of Japanese Mountain Religion* (Tokyo).

——— 1974. *Japanese Religion: Unity and Diversity* (Encino Ca.).

Famin, Stanislas Marie César 1871. *The Royal Museum at Naples, being some account of the erotic paintings, bronzes and statues contained in that famous 'Cabinet Secret' by Colonel Fanin* (London). http://www.sacred-texts.com/sex/rmn/rmn00.htm (accessed 11 February 2013).

Faure, Bernard 2006. 'The elephant in the room: The cult of secrecy in Japanese Tantrism' in Scheid, Bernard and Teeuwen, Mark (eds.) *The Culture of Secrecy in Japanese Religion* (London) pp. 255–268.

Freitag, Barbara A. 2004. *Sheela-na-gigs: Unravelling an Enigma* (London).

Fukuta, Ajio et al. 2012. *Nihon no Minzoku* (Tokyo).

Funahashi, Kurando 2006. *Ganso Kokusai Hihōkan: Kōshiki Gaidobukku* (Nagoya).

Geertz, Clifford 1973. *The Interpretation of Cultures* (New York).

Gerstle, C. Andrew and Clark, Timothy (eds.) 2013. *Shunga: Sex and Humor in Japanese Art and Literature (Japan Review Special Issue) Volume 26* (Kyoto).

Glassman, Hank 2002. 'The Nude Jizō at Denkōji: Notes on Women's Salvation in Kamakura Buddhism.' in Ruch, Barbara (Ed.) *Engendering Faith: Women and Buddhism in Premodern Japan* (Ann Arbor) pp. 382–413.

Gōrai, Shigeru 2007. *Ishi no shūkyō* (Tokyo).

Grapard, Allan G. 1982. 'Flying mountains and walkers of emptiness: toward a definition of sacred space in Japanese religions' *History of Religions* 21, pp. 195–221.

——— 1992. *The Protocol of the Gods: a study of the Kasuga cult in Japanese history* (Berkeley).

Griffis, W.E. 1895. *The Religions of Japan: From the dawn of history to the era of Meiji* (New York).

Groemer, Gerald 1999. 'The Arts of the Gannin' *Asian Folklore Studies* 58, pp. 275–320.

Habu, Junko 2004. *Ancient Jomon of Japan* (Cambridge).

Hardacre, Helen 1989. *Shintō and the State 1868–1988* (Princeton).

——— 2002. *Religion and society in nineteenth-century Japan: a study of the southern Kantō region, using late Edo and early Meiji gazetteers* (Ann Arbor).

Hashimoto, Mineo 1976. *Sei no kami* (Tokyo).

Hayakawa, Monta 1996. 'Shunga and Mitate: Suzuki Harunobu's *Eight Modern Views of the Interior* (Fūryū Zashiki Hakkei)' in Jones, Sumie (ed.) *Imaging/Reading Eros: Proceedings for the conference, Sexuality and Edo Culture, 1750–1850 Indiana University, Bloomington August 17–20, 1995* (Bloomington) pp. 122–128.

Hayashi, Makoto and Hayek, Matthias 2013. 'Editors' Introduction: Onmyōdō in Japanese History' *Japanese Journal of Religious Studies* 40, pp. 1–18.

Hearn, Lafcadio 1894. *Glimpses of Unfamiliar Japan Volume I* (London).

——— 1894a. *Glimpses of Unfamiliar Japan Volume II* (London).

Hegel, Georg Wilhelm Friedrich 1987. *Lectures on the Philosophy of Religion. Vol 2 Determinate Religion* (edited by Hodgson, Peter C.; translated by Brown, R.F.; Hodgson, P.C. and Stewart T.M. (Berkeley).

Herbert, Jean 1967. *Shintō: At the Fountainhead of Japan* (Oxford).

Hobsbawm, Eric and Ranger, Terence (eds.) 1983. *The Invention of Tradition* (Cambridge).

Holtom, Daniel C. 1938. 'Japanese Votive Pictures (The Ikoma ema)' *Monumenta Nipponica* 1, pp. 154–164.

——— 1993. 'The Meaning of Kami' in Reader, Ian; Andreasen, Esben and Stefánsson, Finn *Japanese Religions Past and Present* (Folkestone) pp. 77–79.

Hori, Ichirō 1963. 'Mysterious Visitors from the Harvest to the New Year' in Dorson, Richard M. (ed.) *Studies in Japanese Folklore* (Bloomington) pp. 76–103.

——— 1966. 'Mountains and their importance for the idea of the other world in Japanese folk religion' *History of Religions* 6, pp. 1–23.

Hotaka Town Tourist Association (no date) *Dōsojin no meguri* (Azumino).

Hubbard, Thomas K. 2014. (ed.) *A Companion to Greek and Roman Sexualities* (Oxford).

Hung, Wu 1992. 'What is Bianxiang? On the Relationship between Dunhuang Art and Dunhuang Literature.' *Harvard Journal of Asiatic Studies* 52, pp. 111–192.

Imamura, Keiji 1996. *Prehistoric Japan: New perspectives on insular East Asia* (London).

Inoue, Nobutaka 2002. 'The Formation of Sect Shintō in Modernising Japan' *Japanese Journal of Religious Studies* 29, pp. 405–427.

Ishigami, Aki 2013. 'The Censorship of *Shunga* in the Modern Era' in Clark, Timothy; Gerstle, C. Andrew; Ishigami, Aki and Yano, Akiko (eds.) *Shunga: Sex and Pleasure in Japanese Art* (London).

Ishii, Masumi 2010. *Tōno Monogatari Sekai* (Tokyo).

Itō, Kenkichi 1965. *Robō no Seizō* (Tokyo).

Itō, Kenkichi with Richie, Donald 1967. *The Erotic Gods: Phallicism in Japan* (Tokyo).

Iyanaga, Nobumi 2006. 'Secrecy, sex and apocrypha: Remarks on some paradoxical phenomena' in Scheid, Bernard and Teeuwen, Mark (eds.) *The Culture of Secrecy in Japanese Religion* (London) pp. 204–228.

Jansen, Marius B. 1989. (ed.) *The Cambridge History of Japan Volume 5: The Nineteenth Century* (Cambridge).

Jennings, Hargrave 1889. *Phallism: A description of the worship of lingam-yoni in various parts of the world, and in different ages, with an account of ancient & modern crosses particularly of the Cruz Ansata (or handled cross) and other symbols connected with the mysteries of sex worship* (London).

Jones, Sumie (ed.) 1996. *Imaging/Reading Eros: Proceedings for the conference, Sexuality and Edo Culture, 1750–1850 Indiana University, Bloomington August 17–20, 1995* (Bloomington).

Jun, Aika. 2005 'T-bakku nama hōnō' *Tokyo Sport (Tōpo)* 21 June 2005, p. 15.

Kalland, Arne 1995. 'A Japanese Shintō Parade: Does it 'say' anything', and if so, what?' in Van Bremen, Jan and Martinez, D.P. (eds.) *Ceremony and Ritual in Japan: Religious practices in an industrialized society* (London) pp. 162–182.

Kaner, Simon (ed.) 2009. *The Power of Dogū: Ceramic Figures from Ancient Japan* (London).

Karlgren, Bernhard 1930. 'Some fecundity symbols in Ancient China' *Bulletin of the Museum of Far-Eastern Antiquities, Stockholm* 3, pp. 1–67.

Katō, Genchi 1924. 'A Study of the Development of Religious Ideas Among the Japanese People as Illustrated by Japanese Phallicism' *Transactions of the Asiatic Society of Japan* Supplement to the Second Series, Volume 1, pp. 5–70.

Katō, Genchi and Hoshino, Hikoshirō (trans.) 1926. *The Kogoshūi: Gleanings from Ancient Stories* (Tokyo).

Kidder, J.E. 1966. *Japan Before Buddhism* (Revised Edition) (London).

Kinoshita, Naoyuki 2012. 'Kaettekita kokan wakashū' *Geijutsu Shinchō* 63, 11, pp. 88–101.

Kitagawa, Joseph M. 1987. *On Understanding Japanese Religion* (Princeton).

Kitahara, Jirōta 2014. *Ainu no saigu inau no kenkyū* (Sapporo).

Knight, Richard Payne 1786. *A Discourse on the Worship of Priapus and its Connection with the Mystic Theology of the Ancients* (London).

Kokonoe, Kyōji 1976. *Seishin* (Tokyo).

——— 1976a. *Furusato no Seishin* (Tokyo).

——— 1981. *Nippon no Seishin* (Tokyo).

Kovner, Sarah 2012. *Occupying Power: Sex Workers and Servicemen in Postwar Japan* (Stanford).

Krauss, Friedrich S. 1907. *Japanisches Geschlechtsleben. Abhandlungen und Erhebungen über das Geschlechtsleben des Japanischen Volkes. Folkloristische Studien von Friedrich S. Krauss und Tamio Satow. Bearbeitet von Hermann Ihm. Neu hrg. von G. Prunner* (New edition 1931).

Krishan, Yuvraj 1999. *Gaṇeśa: Unravelling an Enigma* (Delhi).

Kubota, Masayuki 2006. 'Dōsojin to machi okoshi: Nagano-ken chūshin chihō no jirei o chūshin ni' *Zasshi 'Shinshū'* 58, 1, pp. 25–36.

——— 2011. 'Matsumoto chihō no dōsojin shinkō ni tsuite kangaeru' (Slides to lecture with this title given at Matsumoto City Museum, 10 October 2011).

——— 2012. 'Jōkamachi no dōsojin shinkō—dōsojin mokuzō o chūshin' (Slides to lecture with this title given at Matsumoto City Museum, 19 May 2012).

LaFleur, William 1992. *Liquid Life: Abortion and Buddhism in Japan* (Princeton).

Lindsey, William 2007. *Fertility and Pleasure: Ritual and Sexual Values in Tokugawa Japan* (Honolulu).

Macaulay, G.C. (translated). 1904. *The* History *of Herodotus* (London).

Masuta, Hideko (ed.) 1993. *Onmyōdō no hon* (Tokyo).

Masuta, Kimiyasu (ed.) 2006. *Tsugaru no shinkō: fushiki fushiki* (Aomori).

——— 2012. 'Aomori-ken ni okeru seishokuki sūhai shiryō' *Aomori Kenritsu Kyōdokan Kenkyū Kiyō* 36, pp. 37–54.

——— 2013. 'Tenjin-sama to Tenma-sama—Tenmangū dankon-gata' *Aomori Kenritsu Kyōdokan Kenkyū Kiyō* 37, pp. 63–72.

McClelland, Mark 2012. *Love, Sex and Democracy in Japan during the American Occupation* (New York).

Meshida, Taitei 1962. *Ishigami sekibutsu shinkō no kenkyū* (Tokyo).

Miura Teiji, Ishii Takeshi, Igari Bunji, Eguchi Bunshirō, Misaki Kazuo, Igarashi Yūsaku 1973. *Tōhoku no minkan Shinkō* (Tokyo).

Miyata, Noboru 1980. 'Sei shinkō oboegaki' in Chiba, Tokuji (ed.) *Nihon Minzoku Fūdoron* (Tokyo) pp. 307–319.

——— 1983. *Onna no reiryoku to ie no kami* (Tokyo).

——— 1996. 'The Cult of Genitalia and the Return of the Land in Late Edo Culture' in Jones, Sumie (ed.) *Imaging/Reading Eros: Proceedings for the conference, Sexuality and Edo Culture, 1750–1850 Indiana University, Bloomington August 17–20, 1995* (Bloomington) pp. 79–80.

Miyazaki, Eishū 1985. *Kishimojin no shinkō* (Tokyo).

Morse, Ronald A. (trans.) 2008. *The Legends of Tono (100th Anniversary Edition) by Yanagita Kunio* (Plymouth).

Mullins, Mark 2008. 'The Many Forms and Functions of Kannon in Japanese Religion and Culture' *Dharma World* April–June, 2008. http://www.rk-world.org/dharmaworld/dw_2008ajmanyforms.aspx (Accessed 8 June 2014).

Murakami, Kenji and Mizuki, Shigeru 2005. *Nihon Yōkai Daijiten* (Tokyo).

Myōki, Shinobu 2014. *Hihōkan to iu Bunka Sōchi* (Tokyo).

Nakao, Yoshiine and Okada, Kei 1893. *Owari-shi* Volume 10 (Nagoya).

Naumann, Nelly 1963. '"Yama no Kami": die japanische Berggottheit (Teil I: Grundvorstellungen)' *Asian Folklore Studies* 22, pp. 133–366.

——— 1964. '"Yama no Kami": die japanische Berggottheit (Teil II: Zusätzliche Vorstellungen)' *Asian Folklore Studies* 23, pp. 48–199.

——— 2000. *Japanese Prehistory: The Material and Spiritual Culture of the Jomon Period* (Wiesbaden).

Nelson, John 1993. 'Of flowers and Phalli: Sexual Symbolism at Kamigamo Shrine' *Japanese Religions* 18 (1993) pp. 2–14.

——— 2000. *Enduring Identities: the guise of Shintō in contemporary Japan* (Honolulu).

Nishioka, Hideo 1950. *Nihon ni okeru seishin no shiteki kenkyū* (Tokyo).

——— 1956. *Seishin Taisei* (Tokyo).

——— 1961. *Nihon Seishin shi* (History of Phallicism in Japan) (Tokyo).

——— 1961a. *Zusetsu Sei no kamigami* (Tokyo).

Noda, Chihiro 1979. *Ōsumi michi no ta no kami* (Tokyo).

Numazawa, Kiichi 1957. 'Tagata Jinja no Hōnen-sai' *Minzokugaku kenkyū* 21, pp. 24–32.

——— 1959. 'The Fertility Festival at Tagata Shintō Shrine' *Acta Tropica* XVI, pp. 193–217.

Ogura, Manabu 1963. 'Drifted Deities in the Noto Peninsula' in Dorson, Richard M. (ed.) *Studies in Japanese Folklore* (Bloomington, 1963) pp. 133–144.

Ohnuki-Tierney, Emiko 1984. *Illness and Culture in Contemporary Japan* (Cambridge).

Ōkawara Masakatsu 1932. 'Agata no mori no Hōnen-sai' *Kaibō* (Aichi-ken Shinshokukai, January 1932) pp. 20–30.

Ōshima, Tatehiko et al. 2001. *Nihon shinbutsu no jiten* (Tokyo).

Ōta, Saburō 1986. *Sei Sūhai* (Tokyo).

Ōtaku, Shinsei et al. 2004. *Bannaji no Takaramono* (Ashikaga).

Page, T.E. et al. (translated and edited). 1927. *Plutarch's* Moralia (London).

Papinot, Edmond 1972. *Historical and Geographical Dictionary of Japan* New Edition (with an introduction by Terence Barrow) (Rutland Vt.).

Philippi, Donald L. 1969. *Kojiki* (Princeton).

Plutschow, Herbert with O'Neill, P.G. 1996. *Matsuri: The Festivals of Japan* (Richmond).

Preston, Jennifer 2013. '*Shunga* and Censorship in the Edo Period (1600–1868) in Clark, Timothy; Gerstle, C. Andrew; Ishigami, Aki and Yano, Akiko (eds.) *Shunga: Sex and Pleasure in Japanese Art* (London).

Quejada, Ellen 1998. *Phallic Worship in Japan: Celebrating the Phallus* (Unpublished MA Thesis, University of Toronto).

Rambelli, Fabio 2002. 'Secret Buddhas: The Limits of Buddhist Representation' *Monumenta Nipponica* 57, pp. 271–307.

Reader, Ian 1987. 'Back to the Future': Images of Nostalgia and Renewal in a Japanese Religious Context' *Japanese Journal of Religious Studies* 14, pp. 287–303.

——— 1991. *Religion in Contemporary Japan* (London).

Reader, Ian and Tanabe, George J. 1998. *Practically Religious: Worldly Benefits and the Common Religion of Japan* (Honolulu).

Reader, Ian 2012. 'Secularisation, R.I.P.? Nonsense! The 'Rush Hour Away from the Gods' and the Decline of Religion in Contemporary Japan' *Journal of Religion in Japan* 1, pp. 7–36.

Rittō City History and Folk Museum 2001. *Kikaku ten Matsuri, matsuri, sairei,* (Rittō, Shiga Prefecture).

Saitō, Shōzō 1927. *Hentai sūhai shi: (Hentai jūni shi Volume 9)* (Tokyo).

Sanford, James H. 1991a. 'The Abominable Tachikawa Skull Ritual' *Monumenta Nipponica* 46, pp. 1–20.

——— 1991b. 'Literary Aspects of Japan's Dual-Gaṇeśa Cult' in Brown, Robert L. *Ganesh: Studies of an Asian God* (New York) pp. 287–335.

Sanford, James H. 1997. 'Wind, Waters, Stupas, Mandalas': Fetal Buddhahood in Shingon' *Japanese Journal of Religious Studies* 24, pp. 1–38.

Sasaki, Kome 1971. *Inasaku izen* (Tokyo).

Satō, Nobuhiro 1873. *Yōzō kaiku ron* (Tokyo).

Satō, Tetsurō 1995. *Seiki shinkō no keifu* (Tokyo).

Schalow, Paul G. 1996. 'Response to the Panel: "The Rhythm and Play of Flesh and Words" in Jones, Sumie (ed.) *Imaging/Reading Eros: Proceedings for the conference, Sexuality and Edo Culture, 1750–1850 Indiana University, Bloomington August 17–20, 1995* (Bloomington) pp. 139–141.

Sekimori, Gaynor 2005. 'Paper Fowl and Wooden Fish: The Separation of Kami and Buddha Worship in Haguro Shugendō, 1869–1875' Japanese Journal of Religious Studies 32, pp. 197–234.

Sharf, Robert H. 1999. 'On the Allure of Buddhist Relics' *Representations* 66, pp. 75–99.

Shizume, Tōsen 1922. 'Seitekijin toshite no En no Gyōja' *Kyōdo Shumi* 3, 6, pp. 285–291.

Shui, Ryūji (ed.) 2009. *I ♡ Hihōkan* (Tokyo).

Smith, Henry D. II. 1996. 'Overcoming the Modern History of Edo "Shunga"' in Jones, Sumie (ed.) *Imaging/Reading Eros: Proceedings for the conference, Sexuality and Edo Culture, 1750–1850 Indiana University, Bloomington August 17–20, 1995* (Bloomington) pp. 26–34.

Smith, Robert and Wiswell, Ella Lury 1982. *The Women of Suye Mura* (Chicago).

Smith, Robert J. 1995. 'Wedding and funeral ritual: analysing a moving target' in Van Bremen, Jan and Martinez, D.P. (eds.) *Ceremony and Ritual in Japan: Religious practices in an industrialized society* (London) pp. 25–37.

Smyers, Karen A. 1999. *The Fox and the Jewel: Shared and Private Meanings in Contemporary Inari Worship* (Honolulu).

Stanley, Amy 2012. *Selling Women: Prostitution, Markets, and the Household in Early Modern Japan* (Berkeley).

Stark, Rodney 1999. 'Secularization, R.I.P.' *Sociology of Religion* 60, pp. 249–273.

Stein-Frankle, Rebecca L. and Stein, Philip L. 2005. *The Anthropology of Religion, Magic and Witchcraft* (Boston).

Stone, Lee Alexander and Starr, Frederick 1927. *The Story of Phallicism with other essays on related subjects by eminent authorities: Volume 1* (Chicago).

Suzuki, Kenzō 2013. 'Popular Cults of Sex Organs in Japan: Guardian Deities, Auspicious Objects and Votive Paintings' in Clark, Timothy; Gerstle, C. Andrew; Ishigami, Aki and Yano, Akiko (eds.) *Shunga: Sex and Pleasure in Japanese Art* (London) pp. 364–367.

Takahashi, Yūfūko 1979. *Sai no kami (Gochū Jinja) kenritsu no yurai* (Jūmonji).

Thal, Sarah 2002. 'Redefining the Gods: Politics and Survival in the Creation of Modern Kami' *Japanese Journal of Religious Studies* 29, pp. 379–404.

——— 2005. *Rearranging the Landscape of the Gods: The Politics of a Pilgrimage Site in Japan, 1573–1912* (Chicago).

Tsunoda, Ryūsaku; De Bary, Wm. Theodore; Keene, Donald (eds.) 1958. *Sources of Japanese Tradition Volume 1* (New York).

Tsurumi ta matsuri hōzon kai 2007. *Tsurumi no ta matsuri fukattsu shiryō* (Yokohama).

——— 2012. *Tsurumi no ta matsuri* (Yokohama).

Van Bremen, Jan 1995. 'Introduction: The myth of the secularisation of industrial societies' in Van Bremen, Jan and Martinez, D.P. (eds.) *Ceremony and Ritual in Japan: Religious practices in an industrialized society* (London) pp. 1–22.

Vlastos, Stephen (Ed.) 1998 *Mirror of Modernity: Invented Traditions of Modern Japan* (Berkeley).

Wakamori, Tarō 1963. 'Initiation Rites and Young Men's Associations' in Dorson, Richard M. (ed.) *Studies in Japanese Folklore* (Bloomington) pp. 291–304.

Waley, Arthur 1931. 'Magical use of phallic representations, its late survival in China and Japan' *Bulletin of the Museum of Far-Eastern Antiquities, Stockholm* 3, pp. 61–62.

Walthall, Anne 1998. *The Weak Body of a Useless Woman: Matsuo Taseko and the Meiji Restoration* (Chicago).

Weir, Anthony & Jerman, James 1986. *Images of Lust: Sexual Carvings on Medieval Churches* (London).

Williams, Dyfri 2006. *The Warren Cup* (London).

Yamada, Yūji 2014. *Onryō to wa nanki ka* (Tokyo).

Yamamoto Yukari 2013. 'Traditional Uses of *Shunga*' in Clark, Timothy; Gerstle, C. Andrew; Ishigami, Aki and Yano, Akiko (eds.) *Shunga: Sex and Pleasure in Japanese Art* (London) pp. 296–299.

Yanagita, Kunio 1955. *Shinpon Tōno Monogatari fu Tōno Monogatari Shūi* (Tokyo).

Yano, Akiko 2013. 'Shunga Paintings before the 'Floating World' in Clark, Timothy; Gerstle, C. Andrew; Ishigami, Aki and Yano, Akiko (eds.) *Shunga: Sex and Pleasure in Japanese Art* (London) pp. 62–73.

Yato, Sadahiko 2004. *Sai no kami to ryū—kodai ga wakaru ken* (Tokyo).

——— 2005. *Shichi fukujin to Shōtensan: minkan shinkō no rekishi* (Tokyo).

Yoshida, Teigo 1981. 'The Stranger as God: The Place of the Outsider in Japanese Folk Religion' *Ethnology* 20, pp. 87–99.

——— 2007. 'Strangers and pilgrimage in village Japan' in Rodríguez del Alisal, Maria, Ackermann, Peter and Martinez, Dolores P. (eds.) *Pilgrimages and Spiritual Quests in* Japan (London) pp. 49–62.

Zwalf, W. (ed.) 1985. *Buddhism: Art and Faith* (London).

Index